Tele-Healthcare

Scrivener Publishing
100 Cummings Center, Suite 541J
Beverly, MA 01915-6106

Artificial Intelligence and Soft Computing for Industrial Transformation

Series Editor: Dr. S. Balamurugan (sbnbala@gmail.com)

Scope: Artificial Intelligence and Soft Computing Techniques play an impeccable role in industrial transformation. The topics to be covered in this book series include Artificial Intelligence, Machine Learning, Deep Learning, Neural Networks, Fuzzy Logic, Genetic Algorithms, Particle Swarm Optimization, Evolutionary Algorithms, Nature Inspired Algorithms, Simulated Annealing, Metaheuristics, Cuckoo Search, Firefly Optimization, Bio-inspired Algorithms, Ant Colony Optimization, Heuristic Search Techniques, Reinforcement Learning, Inductive Learning, Statistical Learning, Supervised and Unsupervised Learning, Association Learning and Clustering, Reasoning, Support Vector Machine, Differential Evolution Algorithms, Expert Systems, Neuro Fuzzy Hybrid Systems, Genetic Neuro Hybrid Systems, Genetic Fuzzy Hybrid Systems and other Hybridized Soft Computing Techniques and their applications for Industrial Transformation. The book series is aimed to provide comprehensive handbooks and reference books for the benefit of scientists, research scholars, students and industry professional working towards next generation industrial transformation.

Publishers at Scrivener
Martin Scrivener (martin@scrivenerpublishing.com)
Phillip Carmical (pcarmical@scrivenerpublishing.com)

Tele-Healthcare

Applications of Artificial Intelligence and Soft Computing Techniques

Edited by

R. Nidhya
Manish Kumar
and
S. Balamurugan

Scrivener
Publishing

WILEY

This edition first published 2022 by John Wiley & Sons, Inc., 111 River Street, Hoboken, NJ 07030, USA and Scrivener Publishing LLC, 100 Cummings Center, Suite 541J, Beverly, MA 01915, USA
© 2022 Scrivener Publishing LLC
For more information about Scrivener publications please visit www.scrivenerpublishing.com.

Wiley Global Headquarters

111 River Street, Hoboken, NJ 07030, USA

For details of our global editorial offices, customer services, and more information about Wiley products visit us at www.wiley.com.

Limit of Liability/Disclaimer of Warranty

While the publisher and authors have used their best efforts in preparing this work, they make no representations or warranties with respect to the accuracy or completeness of the contents of this work and specifically disclaim all warranties, including without limitation any implied warranties of merchantability or fitness for a particular purpose. No warranty may be created or extended by sales representatives, written sales materials, or promotional statements for this work. The fact that an organization, website, or product is referred to in this work as a citation and/or potential source of further information does not mean that the publisher and authors endorse the information or services the organization, website, or product may provide or recommendations it may make. This work is sold with the understanding that the publisher is not engaged in rendering professional services. The advice and strategies contained herein may not be suitable for your situation. You should consult with a specialist where appropriate. Neither the publisher nor authors shall be liable for any loss of profit or any other commercial damages, including but not limited to special, incidental, consequential, or other damages. Further, readers should be aware that websites listed in this work may have changed or disappeared between when this work was written and when it is read.

Library of Congress Cataloging-in-Publication Data

ISBN 978-1-119-84176-0

Cover image: Pixabay.Com
Cover design by Russell Richardson

Set in size of 11pt and Minion Pro by Manila Typesetting Company, Makati, Philippines

Printed in the USA

10 9 8 7 6 5 4 3 2 1

Contents

Preface

In the current world scenario, public healthcare has become one of the prime importance. Providing a better health service to one and all is the major concern. Scientists around the world working on different Artificial Intelligence and soft computing techniques to provide a better healthcare service. Along with the scientists, Industries also coming forward to transfer the application of soft computing techniques for providing e-health and telehealth service to public. Countries which are densely populated require industrial services like telehealth for day-to-day health issues.

In today's scenario healthcare industry is growing at a greater pace. Telehealth is the application of AI, soft computing, digital information and communication technologies, to provide healthcare services remotely and manage your healthcare. The services may comprise of the technologies which one use in home or those which are suggested or recommended by the doctors to improve or support healthcare services. In general, telehealth or e-health is the industrial transformation of soft computing techniques for the common people. The most basic element of telehealth is telecommunications, which uses a wider range of information and communication technologies (ICTs).

As said earlier, telehealth service is now a day's provided by many industries. Telehealth can also be seen as examples for virtual home healthcare, where patients suffering from chronicle diseases are taken care by the family members with certain procedures and services available at home. Telehealth revolution has made the things easier for those situated at a remote place and is in need of diagnosis, care and referral of patients. Training of proper healthcare or health related issues may sometimes be provided via telehealth schemes or with related technologies such as e-health, which make use of small computers and internet.

Now-a-days soft computing techniques are directly influencing human life in terms of healthcare analysis and management. Soft Computing techniques are currently being used for monitoring and recording patient diseases and their symptoms for proper diagnosis of the same. There are numbers of soft computing techniques which can be used for early detection and prevention of diseases. It may help us in identifying the root cause of the disease and provide a better solution for telehealthcare application. In the era of technology and industrial revolution, many agencies are working to develop a soft computing-based paradigm which can easily identify and monitor the health status of persons situated a distance place within a specified period of time.

There are number of soft computing application that can easily be used in industries to solve telehealthcare problem. These applications include gathering information of patient, medical records and data, intelligent diagnosis and carefulness strategies, detecting disease etc. A Telehealth industry provides an innovative combination of new applications that underlines the advancement in medical fields. Today, the world is in huge humanitarian crises with respect to healthcare workforce shortages, and a growing burden of chronic disease. As a result, telehealth has become one of the fastest-growing service areas in medical sector. Telehealth supports and ensure the availability of proper healthcare services, public health, and health education services at a distance and remote places. It is assumed that telehealth applications has become one of the fastest growing area of research, but to grow at a larger scale it requires the following: 1) the availability of use cases for exact identification of problems that need to be visualized. 2) A well supported market that can promote and adopt the telehealthcare concept. 3) Development of cost-effectiveness applications and technologies for successful implementation of telehealth at a larger scale.

Coverage area of the book, importance and intended audience:

1. The major objective of this book is providing a platform for presenting soft computing-based telehealthcare service. It will cater to the needs of undergraduate and postgraduate students as well as research students. It will also aid academicians, researchers, and industry experts working on healthcare systems backed by soft computing techniques.
2. To enlist the challenges in promoting and implementing telehealth industry.
3. To globalize the agenda of personalized telehealth in integrative medical treatment for disease diagnosis and its industrial transformation.

4. Design of machine learning technique for better implanta-
    tion of telehealthcare system in current scenario.

In chapter 1, Vinutha *et al.* has introduced a ML based remote monitoring of patients with Data Analytics. Monitoring the health condition
post-discharge or post-operation is required to ensure a speedy recovery.
We all know that, healthcare services can be benefited from technological
advancements to ensure better service. In the proposed work the authors
have collected the patient's data using sensors and uploaded them to the
cloud. The collected data is subjected to pre-processing followed by analysis. In the proposed approach, the patient's health is remotely monitored
and machine learning techniques are applied to foretell abnormalities in
patients' health condition. The suggested method can also be effective
during the pandemics like COVID-19 with the scare availability of medical personnel and treatment resources, this prediction may help in taking
appropriate measures at the earliest.

In chapter 2, Priyadarshani and Jagdeesh Kannan did an extensive
survey for an intelligent system which can used for detecting Diabetic
Retinopathy. As we all know that Diabetic retinopathy (DR) is a complication that causes changes in blood vessels present in the retina which leads
to vision loss at later stages and has no or lesser symptoms during the initial stages. In this research, authors have summarized and analyzed all the
recent computer-aided diagnosis (CAD) systems based on the nature of
data, recent approaches taken in classifying DR, performance comparison
using statistical parameters, existing limitations, and challenges.

In current scenario the world is in need of e-health services. In chapter
3, Dipesh *et al.* propsed an e-Health applications based on cloud computing environment that allows healthcare services to monitor the health and
health related information of patients dynamically. The main aim of this
work is to provide a secure infrastructure for e-Health application hosted
in cloud computing environment.

In chapter 4, authors have assessed if tele-dermatology could improve
primary care provider (PCP)-delivered care for cutaneous disease at a
clinic serving uninsured patients. They respectively analysed all consultations and collected patient age, tele-dermatology diagnosis, time to
tele-dermatology reply, time to next dermatology appointment, as well as
PCP and tele-dermatologist proposed care plans. By their investigation,
authors analysed that expanding tele-dermatology for PCPs in underresourced clinics has the potential to improve treatment of cutaneous disease by non-specialists and to mitigate suboptimal care for disadvantaged
patients.

In chapter 5, Shanmugaraja T. *et al.*, a significant issue has been addressed for the ageing population. As there is a lack of medical centres to meet the needs for in-person assessment. Authors suggested remotely distributed evaluations using webcam eye-tracking data, such as visual paired comparison (VPC) tasks, could enhance access to external, intermittent neuropsychological testing for cognitive decline, and can be seen as solution for future e-health application.

In chapter 6, Venkatesh T. *et al.* presented an approach in which smart devices, Computational Intelligence (CI) and Soft Computing Techniques (SCT) may help the doctors to monitor the data of their patients suffering with various healthcare issues and also to diagnose and to provide state-of-the-art treatment. Applying SCT, identification of correlated features, feature ranking or importance and feature selection are performed on UCI Machine learning datasets and also classification and prediction are performed on the datasets to examine the accuracy of the predictions for the classification algorithms.

In chapter 7, COVID-19 has become a global pandemic in such a short period of time that it should be taken seriously and we all need to be precautious about it at all times. In such times, it is difficult to visit hospitals physically and spend a lot of time there for manual tests. The use of CXR images for diagnosis of COVID-19 proves to be of great help. As the traditional methods used for diagnosis are not enough for clinical purposes, there is a need to make use of artificial intelligence to improve the performance of these methods. During the development of the model, authors realized how complicated the architecture was becoming, and hence tried their best to optimize the whole network to diminish erroneous situations and bring out the best result possible. As the traditional methods used for diagnosis are not enough for clinical purposes, they made use of artificial intelligence to improve the performance of these methods.

In chapter 8, authors have proposed an enhanced IoT framework for patient health monitoring and predicting the heart disease based on Machine Learning Algorithms. Proposed method combines both IoT and machine learning concepts and is used to provide efficient and effective remote health monitoring for patient, determine whether a patient is having a particular disease or not as well as to provide a quick solution to the patients in case of some emergency situation which requires immediate doctor attention. As per the experimental result carried out by the authors it is concluded that naïve Bayes is good for handling clinical data.

In chapter 9, authors have addressed the information security and authentication issue using neural network and discrete wavelet transform methods. To provide security and authentication to the data, authors proposed biometric based authentication method. In this method, the brain waves activity is used as a biometric authentication for user recognition. The acquisition of EEG signal is done and compressed using DWT (Discrete Wavelet Transform). The Feed Forward Neural Network (FFNN) is used for pattern matching to provide accurate results than existing methodologies.

Autism Spectrum Disorder (ASD) is the most challenging developmental disorder among the children. In chapter 10, authors were discussed about the various details related to ASD such as how ASD is diagnosed using assessment tools called ASD Screening Tools used by the medical staff with the support of parents/caregiver, improving the accuracy and classification of ASD using computational intelligence, etc. This chapter provides a detailed review of different screening tools and machine learning methods for ASD diagnosis.

The novel drug discovery for most of the complex diseases is based on the drug target proteins. In chapter 11, authors proposed a multi-functional score based co-clustering approach MR-CoC$_{multi}$ which is introduced for drug target module mining with five novel biological scores namely hydrophobic residues density, sequence length, polar residues density, amino acid density, molecular weight scores. Authors suggested the drug target modules based on the biological functionality and drug target proteins in the results. As per their experimental result the proposed method outperforms than the existing methods.

Telehealth has become a necessary technology in this pandemic situation. So, in chapter 12, authors have proposed the telehealth method for predicting and treating breast cancer using machine learning algorithms such as Logistic regression, K-nearest neighbor, Support Vector machines, Kernel SVM, Decision Tree algorithm and Random forest classification. Based on the experimental results the authors concluded that K-SVM method is predicting the malignant cells with more accuracy than other algorithms. However, after the prediction the patient can be given remote treatment based on the severity of the cancer.

In continuation with previous chapter, Chapter 13 also deals about data sharing and prediction using Machine Learning algorithms for remote patient monitoring. The proposed system recommends an instantaneous solution and provides proper assistance during an emergency, by predicting its seriousness using modern algorithms. The data stored in the database is tested by the KNN classifier and linear regression for better performance. Hence the system proposed by the authors has scalability that deals with the online prediction and facilitates patient care remotely.

In chapter 14, authors have discussed about the different Machine learning models to forecast presence of the coronavirus disease in a patient. This proposed work analyses the foreseen of the diseased people from people with minor indications built on 111 impute relating to medical and the clinical examination facts and performed the prediction and severity analyses using various models such as Naïve Bayes, Support Vector Machine, Artificial Neural Network, K-Nearest Neighbour (KNN), Convolutional neural network (CNN), Logistic regression and Decision tree. From the experimentation results it was identified that Artificial Neural Network is the best when compared to other models in terms of Accuracy, Specificity and Precision.

In chapter 15, the authors concentrated about the health informatics. Medical recording is not only an observation or storage it acts as communication medium between physicians and other medical people involve in observing and recoding the patient data. Recorded high standard medical data is a preventive measure of serious disorders from the people in high-risk future. This chapter aims to provide information about current trends, challenges and issues in healthcare informatics and analyzing the performance of various compression techniques in medical image.

The Editors
June 2022

Machine Learning–Assisted Remote Patient Monitoring with Data Analytics

Vinutha D. C.[1*], Kavyashree[2] and G. T. Raju[3]

[1]Dept. of CS &E (AI&ML),Vidyavardhaka College of Engineering, Mysuru, India
[2]Dept. of ISE, Vidyavardhaka College of Engineering, Mysuru, India
[3]Dept. of CSE, The Oxford College of Engineering, Bengaluru, India

Abstract

The health condition of the patients needs to be monitored with immense care. Healthcare promotes good health, helps in monitoring the patient's health status, disease diagnosis, and its management along with recovery. Monitoring the health condition postdischarge or postoperation is required to ensure a speedy recovery. Healthcare services can benefit from technological advancements to ensure better service. Healthcare assisted with machine learning techniques plays a significant role in the effective diagnosis of ailments, monitoring patient's health condition, and extend support in taking suitable measures during abnormality. In the proposed work, we collect the patient's data using sensors and upload them to the cloud. The collected data are subjected to preprocessing followed by analysis. The patient's health is remotely monitored, and machine learning techniques are applied to foretell abnormalities in the patient's health condition. Existing remote monitoring systems are not flexible and, hence, may result in an increased number of false positives. We try to reduce unnecessary alerts via machine learning methods and data analytics. Essential attributes like pulse rate, blood pressure, temperature, gender, and cholesterol levels of the patient are taken into consideration while predicting the results. In the time of pandemics, like COVID-19 with the scarce availability of medical personnel and treatment resources, this prediction may help in taking appropriate measures at the earliest. We train the model with the Kaggle Heart Disease UCI data set and test the model with real-time patient data. We apply our model to k nearest neighbor (KNN) and Naïve Bayes algorithm. The KNN has performed well over the Naïve Bayes algorithm.

Corresponding author: vinuthadc@vvce.ac.in

R. Nidhya, Manish Kumar and S. Balamurugan (eds.) Tele-Healthcare: Applications of Artificial Intelligence and Soft Computing Techniques, (1–26) © 2022 Scrivener Publishing LLC

Keywords: Remote patient monitoring, machine learning, cardiovascular disease, k-nearest neighbor (KNN), Naïve Bayes

1.1   Introduction

Health is the one of the most important factors that has a significant impact in life. In the current era, both internal and external factors contribute to ill health. Heredity aspects, mental status, and lifestyle also have an influence on the health condition. The heart, being a vital organ in the human circulatory system, operates diligently by performing various functions, such as pumping blood, supplying oxygen, and nutrients to all other organs parts of the body. Nowadays, heart-related diseases are observed in individuals of all age groups. Patients undergo diagnosis, treatment, and surgery if necessary. Monitoring the health status of a patient regularly especially postsurgery is crucial. Diagnosing a heart disease is a challenging task that requires expert support and technological assistance. In this regard, remote patient monitoring (RPM) appears as a boon serving distant patients by monitoring their health status continuously.

1.1.1   Traditional Patient Monitoring System

The conventional medical system involves patient consulting a doctor related to a health problem. The doctors suggest necessary medical scans or tests required to diagnose the ailment of the patient whenever essential. Depending on the test results or scans, doctor diagnoses the disease and advices the future course of action, like medicine prescription and surgery, if required. After the course of the medicine or postsurgery, the patient has to undergo check-ups at regular intervals to keep track of the patient's health state. The doctor recommends further action to be taken based on the health condition and observations recorded during the regular checkups.

The abovementioned traditional patient monitoring system has the following limitations:

- The patient's health condition is monitored only during the regular checkups and is not monitored continuously.

- This method requires physical presence of the patient at the hospital, which may cause inconvenience.
- This type of monitoring may not be suitable for diseases, where real-time monitoring abnormality identification is crucial to save lives.
- Emergency situations cannot be predicted in prior.
- Limited hospital resources may not be sufficient to fulfill the needs of the patients.

1.1.2   Remote Monitoring System

Remote patient monitoring systems provide an attractive solution to overcome these limitations. Remote monitoring system (RMS) accompanied with technological advancements monitors the health status of the patients remotely. Unlike the traditional system where telephone calls were used to obtain patient data, telemonitoring systems offer additional benefits. Technological advancements in information and communication systems have enabled the telemonitoring systems to collect and transmit valuable patient health monitoring data, such as blood pressure, blood sugar level, weight, and electrocardiographic signals through wired and wireless networks.

Remote monitoring system provides the following advantages over the traditional patient monitoring system:

- Patient's health status is monitored continuously in real time.
- Patient can be at home without the need to travel to hospital for check-ups.
- RMS can issue an alert at the time of emergency to hospital personnel to make necessary arrangements (e.g., ambulance service, notifying the doctor, setting up ventilators, etc.).
- RMS with continuous analysis can predict the emergency situations in advance.
- These predictions can help the hospital personnel to undertake suitable measures to increase the hospital resources.

With many attractive solutions, RMS has its own issues [25] to be addressed.

1.1.3   Challenges in RPM

Remote patient monitoring systems involve electronic gadgets, and additionally, the Internet to connect patients and their healthcare service providers. The patient monitoring systems include measurements from several devices, such as glucometer, weighing machine, and blood pressure monitor. These measured values are transmitted to a backend service via medical hub.

Some of the challenges faced by RPM systems are as follows:

Information reliability: Healthcare professionals expect the measurements from the registered devices at standard condition to be trusted. Care should be taken to ensure that the measurement is that of the registered patient under monitor and not someone else. Malfunctioning device may affect the measurement.

Without reliable information, the efforts made to monitor, analyze, and predict the health condition will not be fruitful. An authentication method proposed in the study of Petković [1] tries to address the reliability issue by attaching the patient's identity with the device used to obtain measurement. Device authentication and user authentication methods are employed to ensure user and their device appropriately. Here cryptographic keys are derived from information related to user and device authentication.

Information quality: In RPM, measurements are usually taken using user devices, and the quality of the measurement is not always acceptable. Healthcare providers need to rely on the obtained measurement without having knowledge of user device condition. Manual errors while recording measurements can also influence the process.

Two kinds of metadata mentioned in the study of Petković [1] specify the standard of health-related data collected by the patient using a RPM system. The first kind of metadata is regarding the usage of the device by a patient who collected measurements to ensure that the device was used the way it was intended. The second kind of metadata is pertaining to the device.

User privacy: User data collected need to be managed with utmost care with good security practices, policies, and protocols. The information could be taken care of by arbitrators or mediators, which makes hazard for patients possibly having their information taken. The difficulties are no less intense for emergency clinics, who incorporate the mediator frameworks that could be compromised in security putting the patient's well-being and safety in danger.

Real-time access to data: Transferring the gathered information to the RPM system involves multiple hops. Data from the end-user equipment are accumulated and uploaded to a remote site, such as server, for analysis. If an end user is relying on cellular network, then the information has to travel thru the corresponding network service provider's substructure and then out onto the Internet. This involves multiple hops before reaching the destination. Mobile networks are not always available. They can induce delays and may put life of the patient into danger because of network issues.

High power consumption: The RPM monitors and collects the health status continuously. The collected data are transmitted very often. This may cause high power consumption and may drain the battery in a short time for battery-driven devices. An RPM system with low power consumption is proposed in Noman *et al.* [3] tries to lower the power consumption in smart phones.

1.2   Literature Survey

Proposed system in Jeya Priyadharsan *et al.* [2] monitors the patient health remotely using sensor networks. The system consists of hardware components, such as heart rate sensor, temperature sensor, blood pressure sensor, and Raspberry Pi board. The heart rate is measured at every instant. The data gathered from the sensors are stored in the cloud for analytics. These data subjected to analytics help in determining abnormal health condition. k Nearest neighbor (KNN) classifier is employed to classify a patient's health status.

The system in Padmashree *et al.* [4] aims at improving the healthcare systems by analyzing desirable health factors, such as blood pressure, heart rate, and body temperature, to predict heart issues. The systolic and diastolic blood pressures are taken into account. The work efforts to alert the user with an application. The patients who were previously diagnosed with heart diseases were the users. The application enabled the patient to view their health status on their personal device, like mobile phones, and the doctor could view his patient's data and analyze the data using multilayer perceptron (MLP) algorithm.

A system that tracks and monitors the health condition remotely is proposed in Mohammed Baqer *et al.* [5] collects the health status of a patient via medical sensor. Along with the data collected from the sensors, the patient's current location is obtained using GPS coordinates. Confidentiality and authentication is ensured via encryption through AES algorithm. During emergencies where the patient's health condition is abnormal, a rescue alarm is issued to notify the medical team for assistance.

Remote electrocardiogram (ECG) monitoring system proposed in Pagadala *et al.* [6] continuously monitors the health condition, collects the required data using AD8232 sensor, and processes the data using ESP 8266 microcontroller.

A noninvasive framework with spatiotemporal filtering and convolution neural network (CNN) is suggested in Ying *et al.* [7] to remotely monitor heart rate. The MMSE-HR data set is used for the intended research work. Eulerian Video Magnification (EVM) is used with an intent to obtain desirable features that relate to the information on the heart rate. CNN is used to evaluate HR from the feature image.

A pervasive RPM system operating in four modes was proposed in Chao *et al.* [8] triggers the healthcare services based on physical status rather than feelings. The monitoring system sends physical signals to remote medical applications in real time. Various physiological and environmental indicators are considered in the monitoring process.

An Internet of Things (IoT)-based RPM system in Fayoumi and Bin Salman [9], along with the vital signs measurement, considers the posture, physical activity, and heart rate during monitoring, generates the patient heart risk report with five levels indicating the magnitude of the risk.

A smart healthcare system discussed in Catarinucci *et al.* [10] suggests the use of RFID in body-centric systems to collect temperature, humidity, and other information from the patient's existing location. These wireless communication-based RFID systems have the potential to collect and process multichannel data about human behavior in agreement with the power exposure and sanitary guidelines.

The IoT tiered architecture (IoTTA) proposed in Nguyen *et al.* [11] aims at transforming sensor data into real-time clinical feedback. The work proposes a five-tiered architecture comprising sensing layer that involves necessary devices and sensors for recording health parameters, sending layer offers a procedure to connect and share data. Storing and processing layer stores and processes the data, respectively. Mining and machine learning applications are applied for feature extraction, classification, and regression.

Conventional methods do not provide sufficient warning because they involve determining the variation in weight and warning sign monitoring. This has resulted in implantable devices. The implantable devices [12] can be specifically designed sensors or they can be devices, such as permanent pacemakers, cardiac resynchronization therapy devices, and cardioverter defibrillators, whose role is to identify different symptoms.

1.2.1 Machine Learning Approaches in Patient Monitoring

Machine Learning based Health Monitoring System in Gnana and Anu [13] considers five parameters for monitoring system, such as ECG, pulse rate, pressure, temperature, and position detection by using wearable sensors. The data from sensors are subjected to classification using support vector machine (SVM) classifier with the ability to identify emergency conditions.

Work in Wenfeng et al. [14] uses CNN to attain a unified analysis of ECG recordings and radar data. Unlike the traditional system that is based on arrhythmia classification that lacks capability to manage the motion state and low accuracy, work in the study of Chao et al. [8] has improved performance and achieved good accuracy.

The work in Baucas and Spachos [15] proposes a framework to tackle several issues pertaining to remote monitoring system. High power consumption, data security, and privacy concerns are addressed suitably with sound recording, surveillance capture, and speech classification components. With the intension of reducing the power consumption, data are transferred only upon the detection of abnormality instead of transmitting data continuously 24/7.

The intelligent hybrid remote patient-monitoring model proposed in Hassan et al. [16] is context-aware and uses local components along with cloud-based components. The cloud serves the need for storage and processing of big data. The local portion of the system is used at times when the Internet connectivity is lost or at the times of failure in cloud operations. The information discovery procedure is carried out in this structure vertically through changing low-level information into a greater degree of abstraction. High-level feature provider (HLFP) is used to change raw data from low-level to higher level of abstraction, features selection, and classification.

A framework to tag real-time health-related sensor data, HealthSense is developed in Stuntebeck et al. [17]. This framework transmits the sensor data from the patient to a server. Machine learning technique is employed to analyze the sensor data in the server. The system interacts with the user to assist in classification of desired events, like pain, itching, and so on. Weka classifiers were used in training the system. The system is incorporated with a feedback mechanism to increase the accuracy of the machine learning technique.

A noninvasive RPM system proposed in Zhang et al. [18] predicts the risk of heart failure. Variations in levels of N-terminal prohormone in the blood pressures and bodyweight helps in determining whether a patient is at the risk of heart failure or not using SVM. The intended system develops a scoring method that can determine the risk of HF on a long-term basis.

Machine learning–based model for monitoring cardiovascular disease [19] observes trends of vital signs contextualized with data from clinical databases. The data collected from the sensors are analyzed locally and fed to SVM to monitor extracted features and classify the patient as continued risk and no-longer risk.

Patient monitoring system proposed in Siva Priya *et al.* [20] collects data, such as temperature and heartbeat, which are collected using sensors and uses KNN classifier to predict the patient health status. The work has a buzzer that gives a signal to the duty nurse available if any abnormal condition is found. If the condition gets even worse, it also sends an email through SMTP protocol from the registered mail to the current duty doctor mail.

An electronicmedical record-wide (EMR-wide) feature-based selection approach along with machine learning patient readmission probability prediction proposed in Shameer *et al.* [21] considers two classes, namely readmitted and non-readmitted. Significant features that matter the most are united into a model with the help of correlation-based feature selection (CFS) method. The model is trained and tested using the fivefold cross-validation method.

A remote patient multimodular system discussed in Medjahed *et al.* [22] remote monitoring system working with two databases with the help of which distress situations are predicted in elderly people. This telemonitoring system collects data with sensors. Different machine learning algorithms are applied, and their effects are studied.

An e-health traffic flow classifier in Kathuria *et al.* [23] utilizes machine learning concept to identify the important features and classify the traffic data. This work efforts to train and test the data set using the combination of genetic algorithm along with binary decision tree to recognize desirable features and assign appropriate priority to every packet in the traffic.

1.3   Machine Learning in RPM

Machine learning finds application in several domains. Machine learning algorithms are commonly used in regression, classification, and prediction. Machine learning algorithms are applicable to the medical field as well. In this section, we give an overview of some of the commonly used machine learning algorithms in patient monitoring systems.

1.3.1   Support Vector Machine

Support vector machines are supervised learning models that can analyze data and perform classification and regression analysis. Support vector machine works by finding the optimal hyperplane that maximizes the margin between the data points. An optimal hyperplane that separating the two classes is shown in the Figure 1.1.

The equation of a hyperplane is given below.

$$w \cdot x + c = 0$$

where, w is a vector that is normal to the hyperplane and c is an offset.

Multiple possible hyperplanes separating two classes is shown in Figure 1.2.

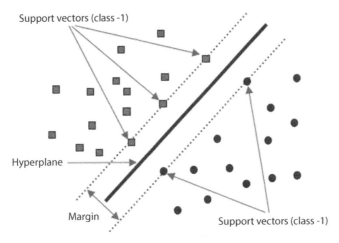

Figure 1.1 Hyperplane that maximizes the distance between the classes.

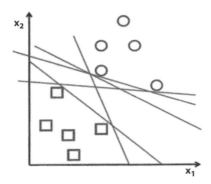

Figure 1.2 Multiple hyperplanes in SVM.

When the data are nonlinearly separable, such data are made nonlinearly separable data using the Kernel Trick.

1.3.2   Decision Tree

Decision tree is a supervised machine learning algorithm. The decision tree makes choices primarily based on the current state of the data. Decision tree can help in creation of a model that can learn from trained data and predict correct class when test data are given. The structure of decision tree is shown in Figure 1.3.

The decision tree algorithm works as follows:

    i.   chooses the finest attribute using attribute selection method to divide the records;

    ii. The chosen attribute or feature is made a decision node and further divides the data set into smaller subgroups;

    iii. Step i and ii are repeated recursively to construct the tree for each child until one of the conditions is met.

Decision trees predict the class label for a given record by the method of comparison. The process is initiated at the root node. The attribute value of the root is compared with the attribute value of the given record. Based on the result of the comparison, the process proceeds with the corresponding tree branch. This process continues till a leaf node is encountered. Decision

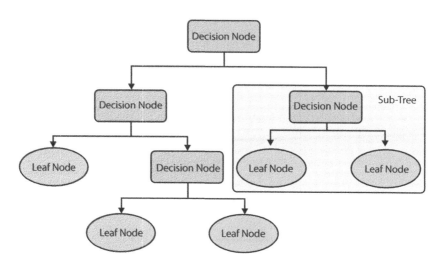

Figure 1.3 Decision tree.

trees predict the label by processing the tree to the point where no more classification is possible on reaching the leaf node.

1.3.3   Random Forest

Random forest is a group of decision trees that operate as a unit. Every tree in the random forest gives out a class prediction. The class with majority vote will be the declared as the final prediction. Low association or correlation among the models is the key. Uncorrelated models can create predictions that are more exact than any of the individual predictions. The working of Random Forest algorithm is shown in Figure 1.4.

1.3.4   Logistic Regression

Logistic regression is a supervised classification algorithm used to predict the probability of a target variable. Logistic regression computes the association between the dependent variable and one or more independent variables by estimating probabilities by means of a logistic function or sigmoid function. The hypothesis of logistic regression tends it to limit the cost function between 0 and 1.

Sigmoid function formula is as follows:

$$f(a) = \frac{1}{1 + e^{-(a)}}$$

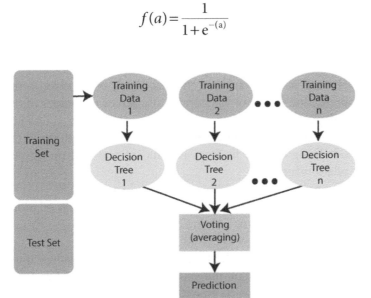

Figure 1.4 Random forest.

1.3.5   Genetic Algorithm

A genetic algorithm is an optimization method that imitates the technique of natural selection. The algorithm begins with an essential or principal population collectively with random chromosomes comprising genes with a collection of zeros (0) or ones (1). Further steps of the algorithm biases people toward the most useful solution through iterative strategies like selection operators, crossover, and mutation.

Genetic Algorithm works as follows:

1. population of individual solution is randomly initialized;
2. choose the individuals from the populations randomly;
3. evaluate the fitness and the individuals are compared according to their fitness;
4. continue the process till the termination condition is met;
5. modify the individuals using the following operations;
6. reproduction, copy an individual lacking change;
7. crossover, exchange sub structure between two individuals;
8. mutation, exchange a single unit in an individual at a random position.

1.3.6   Simple Linear Regression

Simple linear regression model is used to evaluate the relationship between two continuous variables.

This regression model has the subsequent assumptions:

1. Homogeneity of variance: the magnitude of the error in the prediction does not vary drastically across the values of the independent variable.
2. Independence of observations: statistical sampling methods bring out the findings in data set and find no unseen relationships.
3. Normality: the data follow a normal distribution.
4. The dependent and dependent variable have linear relationship between them.

The linear regression model take up a linear relationship among the input variables (x) and the output variable (y). The value of variable y can be determined by the linear combination of input variables (x).

Formula for simple linear regression

$$y = \beta_0 + \beta_1 x + \varepsilon$$

y is the predicted value, β_0 is the y-intercept of the regression line, β_1 is the slope.

Regression with a single input variable x is called a simple linear regression. Regression with multiple input variables is referred to as multiple linear regressions.

1.3.7   KNN Algorithm

The k nearest neighbor (KNN) [24] is supervised learning algorithm suitable for classification and regression problems. The KNN algorithm is simple and easy to understand. The KNN does not require assumptions or parameter tuning. The KNN algorithm depends on labeled information to memorize a work and predict an appropriate label when a new unlabeled information is given. We calculate the distance between the points using Euclidean distance.

$$d(x,y) = \sqrt{\sum_{i=1}^{n}(y_i - x_i)^2}$$

where a and b are two points; a_i and b_i are Euclidean vectors; n is space. Figure 1.5 shows the use of KNN for classifying the data points into one of the 3 classes.

The KNN algorithm assumes that similar things exist in close proximity.

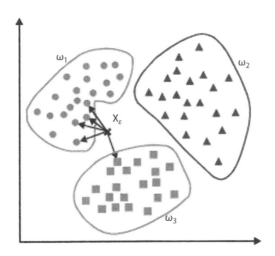

Figure 1.5 KNN classification.

KNN Algorithm

1. load the training data, as well as test data;
2. initialize K to your chosen number of neighbors where K can be only integer;
3. for every point in the test data do the following:
>   compute the distance between test data and training data,
>   sort the distance in ascending order.
4. select the top K entries from the arranged group;
5. simple majority of the category of nearest neighbor return a label as a prediction value.

1.3.8   Naive Bayes Algorithm

Naive Bayes is a statistical classification technique based on Bayes Theorem. It is a probabilistic supervised machine learning algorithm. Bayes theorem relies on the conditional probability to determine the probability of a hypothesis with previous knowledge. Figure 1.6 shows Naive Bayes classification.

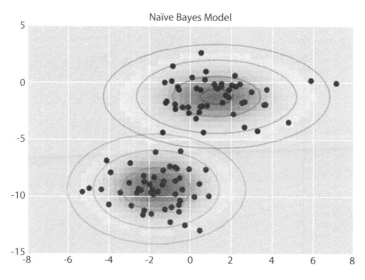

Figure 1.6 Naïve Bayes algorithm.

Bayes theorem is given as:

$$P\left(\frac{X}{Y}\right) = \frac{P\left(\frac{Y}{X}\right) * P(X)}{P(Y)}$$

The probability of hypothesis X on the event Y is called as posterior probability denoted by P(X/Y).

The probability of the evidence given that the probability of a hypothesis is true is called likelihood probability and is denoted by P(Y/X).

The probability of hypothesis prior to the observance of evidence is prior probability denoted by P(X).

The probability of evidence is marginal probability denoted by P(Y).

Naive Bayes classifier calculates the probability of an event as follows:

Step 1: For the given class labels compute the prior probability.

Step 2: For each attribute in each class compute the likelihood probability.

Step 3: Find the posterior probability by substituting these values in the Bayes formula.

Step 4: Observe the class with higher probability, the input given belongs to the class having higher probability.

Contributions of Proposed Work

In the proposed work, we apply machine learning algorithm to classify the health status of the remotely monitored patient as risk and nonrisk. In the traditional threshold-based systems that generate alarm for minor variations in attribute values, we try to reduce the false alarms by monitoring the values and raise an alarm only when repeated major abnormalities are observed. The proposed work not only considers the physiological data but also considers the symptoms experienced by the patient. We apply our model to KNN and Naïve Bayes algorithm and compare their performances.

1.4   System Architecture

We propose a RPM system that collects the patient's health-related data from sensors and medical equipment. The collected data are uploaded to the cloud for analysis. We choose attributes that influence the heart health condition the most and then apply the machine learning algorithm to predict the health condition.

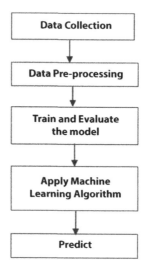

Figure 1.7 Flow diagram of the proposed system.

The proposed system consists of the following modules:

1. Data collection module to collect the patient's sensory data.
2. Data processing module processes the data before analysis.
3. Apply machine learning algorithm to train the model.
4. Prediction.

The flow diagram of the proposed system is given in Figure 1.7.

1.4.1   Data Collection

The proposed system considers clinical data and physiological data of the patient. The clinical data, such as age, sex, BMI, blood group, and previous medical records of the patient, are considered. Healthcare centers register and maintain the consistent detail of the patient throughout the diagnosis of the ailment and its treatment. Clinical data of the patient can be obtained at these healthcare centers. Physiological data are obtained by measurements of sensors and questionnaires. Physiological data include blood pressure values, pulse rate, ECG values, body weight, and sugar levels. These values can be obtained by devices, such as sphygmomanometer, oximeter, mobile ECG device, and mobile sugar-level measuring device.

Some of the common symptoms related to heart disease are as follows:

1. Uneasiness or tightness in arms and neck.
2. Pain in left arm, chest, jaws and abdomen.

3. Heart palpitations are heart beats that feels like pounding or irregular beating.
4. Excessive fatigue or sweating.
5. Experiencing light-headedness or dizziness.
6. Experiencing heartburn or abdominal pain.
7. Difficulty in speaking and lack of hunger.
8. Inability to sleep, depression, or sweaty skin.

In order to know the mental status and the current health condition, the patient is made to answer a few questions when abnormal measurements are observed in the chosen health parameters. These questions are related to the commonly encountered symptoms.

1.4.2   Data Pre-Processing

The collected data are uploaded to the cloud for analysis. Data collected from the devices may not be suitable to be fed into the analysis phase directly, thus data should be subjected to cleaning or noise removal.

The data are processed with the following steps as given below:

i.   Data Cleaning

Missing data: Data collected from the user end devices may be incomplete or lacking in certain behaviors. Unlike the ignore the tuple approach, which ignore the entire tuple, we concentrate on filling the missing values. In the data cleaning process, we focus on validating the data, filling in the missing values with the most probable value, and correcting inconsistent or out of range values.

Noise reduction: Faulty data collection may result in noise and harden the process of proper interpretation. Noise is handled with different methods.

1. Binning Method works by dividing the sorted data into segments of equal size. Segments are handled individually after which different methods are applied on the sorted data with the intent to smooth it.
2. Regression approach uses regression function to smoothen the noise. The regression can be with single or multiple independent variables.
3. Clustering techniqueworks by grouping similar data in a cluster. This may result in the outliers to fall outside the cluster or may even go undetected.

We use binning method to reduce noise.

ii.   Data Transformation

Normalization helps the chosen attribute values to fall inside a little determined range, and discretization replaces the raw values of numeric attribute via conceptual ranges.

iii.   Data Reduction

Huge volume of data makes analysis harder. Data reduction techniques improve the storage effectively by reducing the unwanted data, thereby lowering analysis cost. Reducing the data size can be lossy or lossless process.

1. Data cube aggregation process to construction the data cube.
2. Attribute subset selection step helps us to choose the highly relevant attributes. Insignificant attributes can be discarded. Attribute with a p-value larger than the significance level may be useless. Only relevant features are extracted.
3. Numerosity reduction is a data reduction method, which replaces the unique information with the aid of smaller shape of data representation.
4. Dimensionality reduction is the process of reducing the wide variety of random variables or attributes under consideration. We employ principal component analysis (PCA).

1.4.3   Apply Machine Learning Algorithm and Prediction

Once the data are free from noise, desired features are extracted, and machine learning algorithm is applied to train the model. The proposed system uses the Heart Disease UCI data set from Kaggle website. This data set has fourteen attributes.

The attributes are shown below:

1. Age of the individual (age): The risk of developing cardio-vascular diseases increases with age, hence the age attributes is significant to make proper decisions.
2. Gender of the individual (gender): It is observed that men develop heart disease at an earlier age than women. Gender may help prediction process.
3. Chest pain type (cp): Four types of chest pain are considered:
    i)   Typical angina: Typical angina (TA) is a substernal chest pain triggered by bodily hard work or emotional trauma and calmed by rest or nitroglycerin. This condition occurs

when the heart muscle does not get enough oxygenated blood. Typical anginas radiate into organs, like arms, neck, and jaws, and are provoked by activity or exercise. It lasts for a short period. It is assigned as value 1.

ii) Atypical angina: Atypical angina shows symptoms like localized pain in a region and usually lasts for days. It is assigned as value 2.

iii) Non-anginal pains: the chest pain that look like heart pain in patients not suffering from heart disease. It is assigned as value 3.

iv) Asymptotic are those that do not cause or exhibit the symptoms. It is assigned as value 4.

4. Resting blood pressure value: Usually measured in mm Hg (trestbps). High levels of blood pressure can have adverse effect on arteries that supply blood to the heart eventually. Factors, such as cholesterol, obesity, and diabetes, act as additional risk factors.

5. Serum cholesterol in mg/dl (chol): Deposition of cholesterol results in narrowing of arteries. It is observed that higher levels of high-density lipoprotein (HDL) are harmless and higher levels of low-density lipoprotein (LDL) is harmful because it further increases narrowing of arteries, leading to risk of heart attack.

6. Fasting blood sugar (fbs): Insulin hormone secreted by pancreas helps in converting excess glucose to glycogen, thereby taking care of blood sugar level in the body. Insufficient amount of Insulin causes a rise in blood sugar level above 120 mg/dl. High levels of blood sugar leads to the risk of heart attack.

7. Resting electrocardiographic results (restecg)
   i) Normal condition is assigned the value 0.
   ii) Inherent myocardial diseases, electrolyte abnormalities, and drugs, such as digoxin and tricyclics, may result in having ST-T wave abnormality. It is assigned as value 1.
   iii) Thickening of walls of left ventricles and enlargement is called left ventricular hypertrophy, this may cause high blood pressure. It is assigned as value 2.

8. Maximum heart rate achieved (thalach): cardiovascular risk results in speeding up of heart rate.

9. Exercise induced angina (exang): the chest pain is normally experienced at the center of the chest. Intense pain may even extend to shoulders and hands. The pain related with angina can be mild or severe usually causing a feel of contractedness or squeezing.

10. ST despair prompted through exercising relative to rest (oldpeak): The incidence of down-sloping ST-phase depression at a lower workload computed in metabolic equivalents shows a worse analysis and greater probability of multivessel ailment. The duration of ST-phase depression is acute, as extended recovery after top strain is regular with a quality treadmill ECG stress test.

11. The slope of the peak exercise ST segment (slope): The ordinary ST section has a moderate upward concavity. Flat, depressed or downsloping ST segments may lead to coronary ischemia, which is caused by reduced blood flow in the coronary circulation through the coronary arteries. The upward slope is given as value 1. The flat slope is given as value 2. The down slope is given as value 3.

12. The number of major vessels (0–3) colored by fluoroscopy (ca)

13. Thalassemia (thal): thalassemia is a blood disease wherein the body makes a bizarre kind of hemoglobin. The normal, fixed defect, and reversible defect are assigned as values 3, 6, and 7, respectively.

14. Prediction attribute: the value 0 specifies harmless condition, and value 1 specifies harmful condition.

Threshold-based systems raise an alert when the measured value crosses the threshold. Raising an alert by considering the values obtained in the short span of time may raise unnecessary and frequent alerts, which may result in a greater number of false positives resulting in needless medical expenditures. Minor variations in attribute values that do not cause adverse effects on the health condition are mistaken as harmful signs. The proposed model considers several features that lead to alert and is flexible. To recollect the contemporary physiological condition of the patient, his/her previous five days medical record is considered from the date of alert issued. Alerts are allotted weights as 2, 1, 0 for high, medium, and low priority, respectively. We train the model with Kaggle heart disease data set and test the model with real-time patient data. We apply KNN and Naïve Bayes algorithm machine learning algorithms. Naïve Bayes algorithm is simple to implement and helps to determine the health status of the patient with a probabilistic approach. The KNN algorithm helps in determining the risk based on similarity measure.

1.5   Results

The heart disease UCI data set is used to train the model. The chi-squared attribute assessment with Waikato Environment for knowledge analysis equipment helps in deciding the most influencing variables among all the attributes in the data set. The attributes and its respective scores are given in Table 1.1.

The values obtained after the test show that the slope, exang, cp, old-peak, thalach, gender attributes are more significant in making decision over the rest. These variables are assigned with the weight 2 and remaining variables are assigned the weight 1.

Table 1.1   Attribute importance testing values.

Rank	Score	Attribute
1	109.4	10 slope
2	101.573	9 exang
3	91.531	3 cp
4	89.310	10 oldpeak
5	30.334	8 thalach
6	20.52	2 gender
7	0	4 tresbps
8	0	13 thal
9	0	7 restecg
10	0	5 chol
11	0	6 fbs
12	0	12 ca
13	0	1 age

The model was tested with real-time patient's sensory data. The data were collected from 70 individuals. We conduct the experiment with the assigned weights to check the accuracy with KNN and Naïve Bayes algorithm. Table 1.2 given below shows the accuracy of the parameters without weight and chi-squared parameter values. The confusion matrix for KNN and Naïve Bayes algorithm is shown in Table 1.3 and Table 1.4, respectively. Table 1.5 shows accuracy of the proposed system.

Table 1.2 Parameters with weights.

k	Parameter without weight	Chi-squared top parameters (1221111222111)	Chi-squared top 5 parameters (1121111122111)
k=15	78.93%	78.61%	78.80%
k=13	78.77%	78.25%	78.30%
k=11	78.67%	79.27%	79.15%
k=9	78.93%	78.03%	80.55%
k=7	77.23%	79.35%	78.21%
k=5	76.87%	79.75%	79.24%
k=3	78.57%	79.25%	78.34%
k=1	76.19%	77.55%	75.50%

Results Obtained by Applying KNN Algorithm

Table 1.3 Confusion matrix for KNN algorithm.

	Actual positive	Actual negative
Predicted Positive	32	10
Predicted Negative	4	24

Table 1.4 Confusion Matrix for KNN algorithm.

	Actual positive	Actual negative
Predicted Positive	22	15
Predicted Negative	19	14

$$True\ Positive\ Rate = \frac{True\ Positive}{True\ Positive + False\ Negative} => \frac{32}{32+4} = 0.888888$$

$$False\ Positive\ Rate = \frac{False\ Positive}{False\ Positive + True\ Negative} => \frac{10}{10+24} = 0.294117$$

Table 1.5 Accuracy table of proposed system with KNN and Naïve Bayes algorithm.

	KNN	Naïve Bayes
Accuracy	80%	52%

Results Obtained by Applying Naïve Bayes Algorithm

$$True\ Positive\ Rate = \frac{True\ Positive}{True\ Positive + False\ Negative} => \frac{22}{22+19} = 0.5368$$

$$False\ Positive\ Rate = \frac{False\ Positive}{False\ Positive + True\ Negative} => \frac{15}{15+14} = 0.5172$$

Result shows that the proposed system has donewell with KNN algorithm. KNN has outperformed the Naïve Bayes algorithm.

1.6   Future Enhancement

Remote patient monitoring system has changed the way of operation of conventional healthcare. The technological advancements and its impressive advantages have contributed significantly to the betterment of patient monitoring systems. A lot of work has been done in this regard and is still in progress. The accuracy of the sensors, development of applications that can run on mobile devices, and sophisticated devices have made the RPM system more usable and handier. Although the system has many positives, a lot of work needs to be done to overcome the challenges facing these systems. This experiment needs to be conducted with real-time data collected from a larger population to determine its effectiveness. Most of the systems collect data from user and rely on Internet connectivity to upload data to the server, where rest of the analysis takes place. This may cause a system to be unusable in a remote area with feeble Internet connectivity. An edge computing system is preferable to a cloud computing system as it results in lower delay. Home testing of significant biomarkers should be further explored.

1.7   Conclusion

In this paper, we have tried to depict the limitations of traditional health monitoring system, advantages of RPM system and its challenges. In our work we have explained in brief some of the commonly used machine learning algorithms used in RPM systems. We have proposed a model for heart disease–related RPM system where we considered several attributes that significantly contribute to heart failure and trained our model with heart disease Kaggle UCI data set by applying KNN and Naïve Bayes algorithm to classify the patient's health condition as risk or nonrisk. The threshold-based systems generate alarms even with minor deviation in values and may result in a greater number of false positives. The proposed model is flexible and raises an alert only when the abnormal condition is encountered repeatedly and hence results in lesser number of false positives. We also applied our model toKNN and Naive Bayes algorithm and compared their performance.

References

1. Petković, M., Remote patient monitoring: Information reliability challenges. *2009 9th International Conference on Telecommunication in Modern Satellite, Cable, and Broadcasting Services*, Nis, pp. 295–301, 2009.

2. Jeya Priyadharsan, D.M., Kabin Sanjay, K., Kathiresan, S., Kiran Karthik, K., Siva Prasath, K., Patient health monitoring using IoT with machine learning. *Int. Res. J. Eng. Technol. (IRJET)*, 06, 03, 7514–7520, Mar 2019.

3. Al-Naggar, N.Q., Al-Hammadi, H.M., Al-Fusail, A.M., AL-Shaebi, Z.A., Design of a Remote Real-Time Monitoring System for Multiple Physiological Parameters Based on Smartphone. *Hindawi J. Healthc. Eng.*, Article ID 5674673, 13, 2019. https://doi.org/10.1155/2019/5674673.

4. Padmashree, T., Cauvery, N.K., Anirudh, V.C., Kumar, P., Patient Health Monitoring System and Prediction using Data Analytics. *Int. J. Innov. Eng. Technol. (IJIET)*, 8, 162–166, 2017.

5. Kamel, M.B.M. and George, L.E., paper1-Remote Patient Tracking and Monitoring System. *IJCSMC*, 2, 12, 88–94, December 2013.

6. Kumar, P.P., Naidu, T.S., Vishnu, S., RemoteEcg Monitoring System by using Iot. *Int. J. Eng. Adv. Technol. (IJEAT)*, 9, 1S5, 71–73, December, 2019.

7. Qiu, Y., Liu, Y., Arteaga-Falconi, J., Dong, H., El Saddik, A., EVM-CNN: Real-Time Contactless Heart Rate Estimation from Facial Video. *IEEE Trans. Multimedia*, 21, 1778–1787, 2019,

8. Li, C., Hu, X., Zhang, L., The IoT-based heart disease monitoring system for pervasive healthcare service. *Procedia Comput. Sci.*, 112, 2328–2334, 2017.

9. Fayoumi, A. and BinSalman, K., Effective Remote Monitoring System for Heart Disease Patients,. *2018 IEEE 20th Conference on Business Informatics (CBI)*, Vienna, pp. 114–121, 2018.

10. Catarinucci, L., De Donno, D., Mainetti, L., Palano, L., Patrono, L., Stefanizzi, M.L., Tarricone, L., An IoT-Aware Architecture for Smart Healthcare Systems. *IEEE Internet Things J.*, 2, 515–526, 2015.

11. Nguyen, H.H. *et al.*, A review on IoT healthcare monitoring applications and a vision for transforming sensor data into real-time clinical feedback. *2017 IEEE 21st International Conference on Computer Supported Cooperative Work in Design (CSCWD)*, IEEE, 2017.

12. Bui, A.L. and Fonarow, G.C., Homemonitoring for heart failure management. *J. Am. Coll. Cardiol.*, 59, 2, 97–104, 2012.

13. Ka, G.S. and Varghese, A.R., Machine Learning based Health Monitoring System. *Mater. Today: Proc.*, 24, 1788–1794, 2020.

14. Yin, W., Yang, X., Zhang, L., Oki, E., ECG Monitoring System Integrated with IR-UWB Radar Based on CNN. *IEEE*, 2, 6344–6351, 2016.

15. Baucas, M.J. and Spachos, P., Speech Recognition Driven Assistive Framework for Remote Patient Monitoring. *Conference: 2019 IEEE Global Conference on Signal and Information Processing (GlobalSIP)*, November 2019.

16. Hassan, M.K. *et al.*, Intelligent hybrid remote patient-monitoring model with cloud-based framework for knowledge discovery. *Comput. Electr. Eng.*, 70, 1034–1048, 2018.

17. Stuntebeck, E.P., Davis II, J.S., Abowd, G.D., Blount, M., HealthSense: Classification of Health-related Sensor Data through User-Assisted Machine

Learning. *HotMobile '08: Proceedings of the 9th workshop on Mobile computing systems and applications*, pp. 1–5, February 2008.

18. Zhang, L., Yu, C., Jin, C., Liu, D., Xing, Z., Li, Q., Li, Z., Li, Q., Wu, Y., Ren, J., A Remote Medical Monitoring System for Heart Failure Prognosis. *Mob. Inf. Syst.*, Hindawi Publishing Corporation, Volume 2015, Article ID 406327, 1–12, 2015.

19. Boursalie, O., Samavi, R., Doyle, T.E., M4CVD: Mobile Machine Learning Model for Monitoring Cardiovascular Disease. *Proc. Comput. Sci.*, 63, 384–391, 2015.

20. Siva Priya, S., Shruthi, M.G., Sruthi, S., Patient health monitoring system. *IJARIIT*, 5, 2, 165–170, 2019.

21. Shameer, K. *et al.*, Predictive modeling of hospital readmission rates using electronic medical record wide machine learning: a case-study using Mount Sinai Heart Failure Cohort. *Pacific Symposium on Biocomputing 2017*, [parameters] https://towardsdatascience.com/heart-disease-prediction-73468d630cfc.

22. Medjahed, H. *et al.*, A pervasive multi-sensor datafusion for smart home healthcare monitoring. *2011 IEEE International Conference on Fuzzy Systems (FUZZ)*, IEEE, 2011.

23. Madhumita, K. and Gambhir, S., Leveraging machine learning for optimize predictive classification and scheduling E-Health traffic. *Recent Advances and Innovations in Engineering (ICRAIE)*, 2014, IEEE, 2014.

24. https://towardsdatascience.com/machine-learning-basics-with-the-k-nearest-neighbors-algorithm6a6e71d01761#:~:text=Summary,The%20k%2Dnearest%20neighbors%20(KNN)%20algorithm%20is%20a%20simple,both%20classification%20and%20regression%20problems.&text=In%20the%20case%20of%20classification,the%20one%20that%20works%20best

25. https://blog.jtiot.com/the-5-biggest-challenges-facing-remote-patient-monitoring

A Survey on Recent Computer-Aided Diagnosis for Detecting Diabetic Retinopathy

Priyadharsini C.[1]*, Jagadeesh Kannan R.[1] and Farookh Khadeer Hussain[2]

[1]Vellore Institute of Technology, Chennai, India
[2]University of Technology, Sydney, Australia

Abstract

Diabetic retinopathy (DR) is a complication that causes changes in blood vessels present in the retina, which leads to vision loss at later stages, and has no or lesser symptoms during the initial stages. Diabetic patients present around the globe are prone to DR, and it is one of the leading causes of vision loss. Various intelligent systems are continuously evolving to assist ophthalmologists in identifying the retinal abnormalities. In this research, recent computer-aided diagnosis (CAD) systems are analyzed based on the nature of data, recent approaches taken in classifying DR, performance comparison using statistical parameters, existing limitations, and challenges. The comparison results indicate that developing a precise CAD system in identifying DR is still an open research problem. The objective of this research is to survey recent research works, identify the gap, and provide useful insights that would help researchers working in this field to develop more efficient CAD systems.

Keywords: Diabetic retinopathy, deep learning model, convolution neural network, auto-encoders

*Corresponding author: priyadharsini.c2019@vitstudent.ac.in

R. Nidhya, Manish Kumar and S. Balamurugan (eds.) Tele-Healthcare: Applications of Artificial Intelligence and Soft Computing Techniques, (27–58) © 2022 Scrivener Publishing LLC

2.1   Introduction

Persons with diabetic mellitus develop progressive changes in the structure of retinal vasculature which is termed as diabetic retinopathy. Globally, the fifth major cause for blindness in the diabetic population and the working-age population is diabetic retinopathy [1]. At advanced stages, the symptoms of DR cause irreversible blood vessel changes leading to permanent loss of vision. However, if detected at an earlier stage, vision loss can be avoided. The reason for avoidable DR-associated vision loss becoming one of the major vision losses at a global scale is patients do not experience symptoms at an earlier stage, and it is time-consuming for the experts to understand the patient's medical conditions by evaluating retinal fundus images.

To aid retinal consultants and ophthalmologists in faster identification of people affected with DR, developing efficient and effective computer-aided or automated methods are essential needs of the hour. In recent years, the healthcare domain is benefitted by artificial intelligent models. The performance results of deep learning (DL) model to detect lung cancer, skin cancer, and cardiovascular disease were high, which prompted many researchers to apply various machine learning (ML) and DL models in the field of ophthalmology. Deep learning models showed better performance compared to ML models in identifying DR. Availability of powerful computation power, data, and different storage mechanisms helped in developing powerful DL models. Most of the recent research works focus on applying DL models, fine-tuning existing architectures, and using hybrid DL or DL and ML models. This paper aims at providing a survey on recent research contributions in identifying various tasks related to DR detection, challenges, and possible future directions.

Organization: The rest of the paper is organized as follows. Section 2.2 discusses the features and stages of DR. Sections 2.3 and 2.4 give the overview of DL models and data set, respectively. Followed by Section 2.5 that lists the performance metrics used by the researchers. Section 2.6 gives a survey of recent research works for various tasks involved in DR identification. Possible future directions are provided in Section 2.7, and finally, the conclusion is provided in Section 2.8.

2.2   Diabetic Retinopathy

2.2.1   Features of DR

To understand the progression and development of DR, it is important to know in detail about various symptoms in terms of its appearance, reason, and cause for its occurrence. The characteristics of each feature are as follows [2]:

- Microaneurysms (MA): microaneurysms are red spherical dots formed because of capillary wall outpouching. It is usually seen in the capillary nonperfusion area and macular area. Microaneurysms are the earliest symptoms of DR and easily visible in fluorescence angiography.
- Retinal hemorrhages (HMs): retinal HMs occur from capillary leakage. There are different types of retinal HMs—dot, blot, and flame HMs. Dot HMs appear similar to MAs but the size of it greatly varies with MAs.
- Retinal edema: the capillary leakage causes retinal thickening which is termed as retinal edema
- Hard exudates: hard exudates occur in circinate form or as clumps, and the patches are identified by yellowish-white waxy appearance.
- Cotton-wool spots: these superficial lesions are characterized by small whitish fluffy structure. The whitish appearance is because of excess axoplasmic flow at the nerve fiber infarct area.
- Venous abnormalities: venous abnormalities, such as dilatation, beading, and looping, occur near to the capillary nonperfusion area
- Intraretinal microvascular abnormalities (IRMA): IRMA is the closure of irregular fine red lines that connect venules and arterioles.
- Neovascularization: neovascularization is characterized by the multiplication or development of new vessels, either along the temporal retinal vessels or at the optic disk. Since the newly developed vessels are subtle and small, the capacity to handle the pressure required for the flow of blood is very less leading to blood leakage.

2.2.2   Stages of DR

Depending on the new vessel formation in blood vessels, DR is majorly classified as proliferative and nonproliferative DR (NPDR) [2]. The first phase of DR is nonproliferative where lesions occur in the retina leading to microvascular occlusion. The severity level in this stage varies from mild, moderate to severe NPDR. As the symptom progresses, new blood vessels start to proliferate leading to PDR causing vision loss. Table 2.1 and Figure 2.1 [3] shows the various stages of DR.

According to the ETDRS study, nonproliferative DR is classified as follows based on the severity level [2].

Table 2.1 DR classification.

Grade	Features
R0: No abnormalities	No abnormalities
R1: Mild NPDR	At least one microaneurysm, retinal hemorrhages, hard or soft exudates
R2: Moderate NPDR	Microaneurysms and/or dot and blot hemorrhages in at least 1 quadrant soft exudates (cotton wool spots)
R3: Severe NPDR	Anyone of the following 3 features is present (Known as the 4-2-1 rule) Microaneurysms and intraretinal hemorrhages in all 4 quadrants. Venous beading in 2 or more quadrants Moderate IRMA in at least 1 quadrant
R4: PDR	Any two of the features of the 4-2-1 rule is present

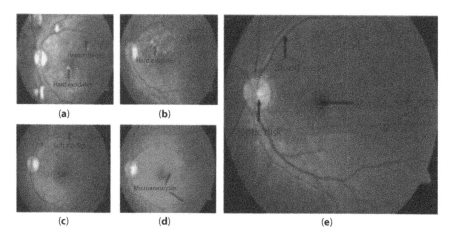

Figure 2.1 (a) PDR, (b) severe NPDR, (c) moderate NPDR, (d) mild NPDR, (e) normal retina.

2.3   Overview of DL Models

2.3.1   Convolution Neural Network

Convolution neural network (CNN) and its variations are the most widely used architecture among DL models when image data is considered. Each layer of CNN architecture in Figure 2.2 learns features of the image from low to high levels by performing a set of mathematical operations. Convolution, pooling, and fully connected layers are the three types of layers involved in this architecture.

Convolution layer performs a linear operation to extract the features. The sum of the product of elements is calculated by sliding over a small array of values called kernel over the input image pixels. The dimensionality of feature maps is reduced by a pooling layer. After performing a series of convolution and pooling, the output feature map is flattened by fully connected layers. Nonlinear activation functions are used according to the objective of the problem. AlexNet, GoogleNet, VGGNet, and ResNet are some of the often-used CNN models. The CNN models require large training data to attain proper convergence [5]. To overcome this issue, researchers either finetune pretrained CNN or use a pretrained CNN as a feature extractor [6].

The Table 2.2 provides the list of parameters and hyper-parameters involved in each layer of CNN

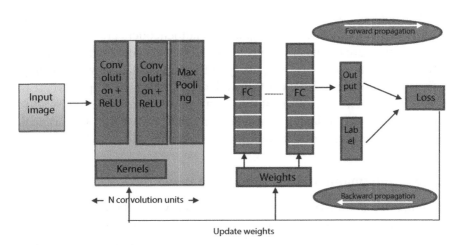

Figure 2.2 CNN architecture [4].

Table 2.2 Parameters and hyperparameters in CNN.

	Parameters	Hyperparameters
Convolution layer	Kernels	Number and size of kernels, activation function, stride, and padding values
Pooling layer	None	Stride, padding, pooling method, and filter size
Fully connected layer	Weights	Activation function and number of weights
Others		The architecture of the model type of loss function, regularization, and optimizer, value of learning rate and epoch, weight initialization mini batch size and data set splitting

2.3.2 Autoencoders

An autoencoder is a neural network that consists of encoder and decoder [7]. The encoder part tries to learn the latent space representation of the input image. And decoder part of the network reconstructs the input from the reduced representation. This architecture is generally used for dimensionality reduction or for image retrieval tasks where less and efficient features help in faster retrieval. Depending on the dimension of code generated, there are two types of autoencoders—under complete and regularized autoencoder. Regularized autoencoders are most used in practice, they are categorized into sparse, denoising autoencoders. Sparse autoencoders try to learn the sparsity of the representation by penalizing either the hidden unit biases or the hidden unit activation output, whereas denoising autoencoders corrupt the input at the initial stage itself by adding noise, learns the latent representation, and reconstructs the original input. Autoencoder is used to build stacked autoencoders (SAE).

2.3.3 Boltzmann Machine and Deep Belief Network

Boltzmann machine [8], otherwise called energy-based models discovers interesting features relating to the complex regularities present in training data. The underlying principle of Boltzmann architecture is based on the simulated annealing concept. It is the process of increasing the weights and drastically decreasing the weights so that the model reaches the global optimum. Many layers of feature detectors make the learning process slow. The Boltzmann machine is composed of neuron-like units that are symmetrically connected, which make probabilistic decisions on which neuron unit needs to be on or off. The output unit is not present as a separate unit. Only visible and hidden units are present. Depending on the weight updating mechanism, this model solves two problems—search problem and learning problem. In the search problem, the weights are fixed, whereas minor weight update mechanism is carried out in learning problem.

Restricted Boltzmann machine [8] is a modified version of the Boltzmann machine where nodes across visible and hidden units are connected. And nodes within the visible or hidden layer are not connected to other nodes of the same layer. The network formed by stacking up of multiple RBMs, fine-tuning using gradient-descent, and backpropagation is called deep belief network.

2.4   Data Set

In this section, an overview of publicly available data sets for DR detection and its details are discussed. Broadly grading of DR images is based on two types of annotation—image level annotation and pixel level annotation.

Data sets labeled with image-level annotations are:

1. MESSIDOR [9] data set consists of 1200 TIFF images out of which 800 are dilated images and 400 are nondilated images. Images are of resolution 1440×960, 2240×1488, and 2304×1536. Expert ophthalmologists annotated the retinal images to grade DR and identify the risk of Macular edema at severity levels of 4 and 3, respectively.
2. KAGGLE [10] is a large data set that consists of 80,000 JPEG images intended for identifying no, mild, moderate, severe NPDR, and PDR.
3. EyePACS-1 [11] consists of 9,963 images in which the graders graded the images for each lesion type and for identifying referable DR. Online grading template was used by graders to grade each lesion type as yes, no or cannot grade.

Data set labeled with pixel-level annotations are:

4. E-Ophtha [12] is annotated to identify MAs and exudates (EX). It consists of 148 MAs, 47 EXs, 233 normal non-MA, and 35 normal non-EX images. Images are of resolution 2544×1696 and 1440×960 in JPEG format. And ground truth is in PNG format.

5. CHASE [13] data set consists of 28 images of resolution 1280×960 in JPEG and ground truth in PNG format to extract vessels

6. DIARETDB1 [14] consists of 5 normal retinal images and 84 images with minimum one NPDR symptom. 1500×1152 is the image resolution and Images, masks, ground truth are in PNG format. For each lesion type, expert ophthalmologists provided a lesion map

7. STARE [15] is a database with 402 images that shows 13 retinal diseases, vessel extraction, and optic nerve with images of resolution 605×700.

8. DRIVE [16] data set holds 33 normal images, seven early to mild NPDR with resolution 584×565 annotated to extract vessels. Images are in TIFF format; and ground truth, masks are in GIF format. DRiDB is annotated to identify MAs, hard and soft EXs, optic discs, macula, and HMs. It holds 50 images of resolution 720×576.

9. ARIA [17] data set is composed of 16 normal, 92 Age-related macular diseases (AMD), and 59 DR images with a resolution of 768×576. In TIFF format. This database can be used to learn Optic disk, fovea location, and vessel extraction.

10. REVIEW [18] data set contains 16 images for learning vessel extraction with varied resolutions of 3584×2438, 1360×1024, 2160×1440, and 3300×2600.

11. DRIONS-DB [19] data set consists of 110 images of resolution 600×400 in JPEG, and ground-truth value for the optic disc is in a text file.

2.5 Performance Metrics

In this section, various performance metrics used by researchers to check the efficiency of the model is listed.

Confusion Matrix: Most of the metrics are calculated from the confusion matrix. Confusion matrix used for classification task is an $n \times n$ matrix that shows the count of labels for all the combinations of predicted vs actual label classification as represented in Table 2.3. Here, "n" denotes the number of classes.

Table 2.4 lists various measures like accuracy, sensitivity, specificity, precision, F-score, and so on, are derived from the confusion matrix. Sensitivity and specificity measure the rate of correctly predicted positive and negative instances, respectively. These two measures play an important

Table 2.3 Confusion matrix.

	Actual positive	Actual negative
Predicted positive	True Positive (TP)	False Positive (FP)
Predicted Negative	False-negative (FN)	True negative (TN)

Table 2.4 Metrics calculated from confusion matrix.

Metrics	Formula
Accuracy	$Accuracy = \dfrac{(TP+TN)}{(TP+TN+FP+FN)} \times 100$
Sensitivity/true positive rate/ recall	$Sensitivity = \dfrac{(TP)}{(TP+FN)}$
Specificity/true negative rate	$Specificity = \dfrac{(TN)}{(TN+FP)}$
Precision/ positive predicted value	$Precision = \dfrac{(TP)}{(TP+FP)}$
F-score	$F\,score = \dfrac{2 \times Recall \times Precision}{(Recall + Precision)}$
Mathews correlation coefficient (MCC)	$MCC = \dfrac{(TP \times TN - FP \times FN)}{\sqrt{(TP+FP)(TP+FN)(TN+FP)(TN+FN)}} \times 100$

role in the healthcare domain. The higher the value, the better the model is. The table lists the formula for each measure.

The relationship between sensitivity and specificity is plotted using the Receiver operating characteristic curve. If the area under the curve (AUC) is closer to 1, then the model is better.

Peak signal to noise ratio (PSNR): The quality of the image reconstructed is measured using PSNR and mean square error (MSE) values.

$$PSNR = 10log_{10} \frac{(Peak\ value^2)}{(MSE)}$$

$$MSE = \frac{1}{mn} \sum_{i=0}^{m-1} \sum_{j=0}^{n-1} [I(i,j) - K(i,j)]^2$$

where I is an image of size m x n and K is the noise approximation.

Intersection over union (IOU), boundary-based evaluation, structural similarity index, dice similarity coefficient, Correlation coefficient, overlap score, G-means, balanced accuracy, overlapping error, and Kappa score are also other metrics that are found in research works to estimate the performance of the model.

2.6   Literature Survey

Depending on the importance of features for identifying DR stages, a survey of recent research works is grouped under the following categories: as shown in Figure 2.3 and the results obtained by the researchers are tabulated in Tables 2.5–2.9.

2.6.1   Segmentation of Blood Vessels

Maji *et al.* [20] performed pixel-wise segmentation to identify and segment vessel and nonvessel pixels using 12 CNN models with each CNN model formed with three and two convolution layers and fully connected layers, respectively.

Liskowski *et al.* [21] used zero-phase whitening, global contrast normalization techniques as a part of image preprocessing and augmentation using geometric transformations. The resultant image is fed into supervised deep CNN architecture to perform pixel-wise vessel segmentation and the model is evaluated using DRIVE, STARE, and CHASE data set.

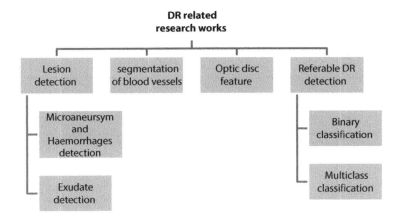

Figure 2.3 Categories of DR-related research works.

Wu *et al.* [22] estimated discriminative features and local structure distribution using CNN and nearest neighbor with Principal component analysis, respectively. A generalized probabilistic tracking framework using the resultant output from the previous stage was deployed to perform blood vessel segmentation and the DRIVE data set was used for evaluation.

Dasgupta and Singh [23] used the DRIVE data set. The authors extracted the green channel of the image, applied a set of preprocessing techniques like normalization, intensity scaling, gamma and contrast adjustment, combined FCN architecture with structure prediction, and segmented the vessels.

To segment blood vessels, Fu *et al.* [24] combined a fully connected network that produced a probability map of vessels and conditional random field for segmentation. Model evaluation was done using the DRIVE and STARE data set.

In the lower layers of FCN, Mo and Zhang [25] made the features more discriminative by introducing auxiliary classifiers. The training was carried out using transfer learning and the system was evaluated on CHASE, DRIVE, and STARE data set.

Tan *et al.* [26] converted the segmentation problem as a classification problem to identify optic disk, fovea, and blood vessel segmentation simultaneously. DRIVE data set was used and found that this model takes more computational time and is not feasible.

Maninis *et al.* [27] removed fully connected layers and added additional convolution layers after four convolution blocks in a pretrained VGG model. Model performance is evaluated using STARE and DRIVE.

Table 2.5 Research works on segmentation of blood vessels.

Research groups	Underlying principle	Models or methods	Data set	AUC	ACC	SN	SP	RPR
Maji *et al.* [20]	Pixel-wise segmentation to segment vessel and nonvessel pixels	12 CNN model	DRIVE	0.9283	94.7			
Liskowski and Krawiec [21]	Patch-based method	Deep CNN model	DRIVE STARE CHASE	0.9790 0.9928 96.96	95.35 97.29 .988	98.07 85.54 81.54	78.11 98.62 98.66	
Maninis *et al.* [27]	Image-to-image regression	Modification of Pretrained VGG architecture	DRIVE STARE					.822 .831
Wu *et al.* [22]	Estimating the distribution of local structure	CNN and PCA	DRIVE	.9701				

(*Continued*)

Table 2.5 Research works on segmentation of blood vessels. (*Continued*)

Research groups	Underlying principle	Models or methods	Data set	AUC	ACC	SN	SP	RPR
Dasgupta and Singh [23]	Segmentation task is assumed as a multi-label inference problem	FCN	DRIVE	95.33	.974	76.91	98.01	
Tan et al. [26]	Simultaneously segmented optic disc, fovea, and blood vessels	7-layer CNN	DRIVE			75.37	96.94	
Fu et al. [24]	To detect boundary or boundary detection task	FCN and conditional random field	DRIVE STARE		94.70 95.45	72.94 71.40		
Mo and Zhang [25]	Features were made more classifiable in lower layers	FCN	DRIVE STARE CHASE	.9782 .9885 .9812	95.21 96.76 95.99	77.79 81.47 76.61	97.80 98.44 98.16	

(*Continued*)

Table 2.5 Research works on segmentation of blood vessels. (*Continued*)

Research groups	Underlying principle	Models or methods	Data set	AUC	ACC	SN	SP	RPR
Maji *et al.* [28]	SDAE to learn features and random forest for classification	Unsupervised SDAEs and RF	DRIVE	.9195	93.27			
Roy and Sheet [29]	Domain adaptation approach incorporated	SAE-DNN	STARE	.912				
Li *et al.* [30]	Patches of a pixel were used with cross-modality data transformation	DAE	DRIVE STARE CHASE	.9738 .9716	97.29 96.28 95.81	75.6 77.26 75.07	98 98.79 97.93	

(*Continued*)

Table 2.5 Research works on segmentation of blood vessels. (*Continued*)

Research groups	Underlying principle	Models or methods	Data set	AUC	ACC	SN	SP	RPR
Lahiri *et al.* [31]	A probabilistic image map is generated and output of E-nets are combined using a convex weighted average	SDAE	DRIVE		95.3			
Fu *et al.* [24]	Segmentation problem is formulated as a boundary detection task	CNN and CRF	DRIVE STARE CHASE		95.23 95.85 94.89		76.03 74.12 71.30	

Table 2.6 Research works on optic disc segmentation.

Research groups	Data set	IOU	ACC	E	F	Other metrics
Optic disc segmentation						
Lim et al. [32]	MESSIDOR SEED-DB	0.888 0.916		0.112 0.0843		
Guo et al. [43]	DRISHTI-GS			.1225	93.73	
Tan et al. [26]	DRIVE		87.90			
Sevastopolsky [34]	DRION-DB RIM-ONE	.98 .98				Dice = .94 Dice = .95
Zilly et al. [40] (Multi-scale two-layer CNN)	DRISHTI – GS	.895			94.7	B = 9.1
Zilly et al. [41] (Ensemble learning of CNN)	DRISHTI – GS	.914			97.3	B = 9.9
Maninis et al. [27]	DRION-DB RIM-ONE					RP = .971 RP = .959
Shankaranarayana et al. [36]	RIM-ONE	.961			98.7	

(Continued)

Table 2.6 Research works on optic disc segmentation. (*Continued*)

Research groups	Data set	IOU	ACC	E	F	Other metrics
Optic disc segmentation						
Zhang et al. [37]	MESSIDOR					An average matching score of 85.4
Fu et al. [35]	ORIGA	.929		.071		
Srivatsava et al. [44]	Local Data Set			.097		
Optic disc localization						
Niu et al. [39]	ORIGA MESSIDOR		99.33 98.75			
Alghamdi et al. [38]	DRIVE DIARETDB1 MESSIDOR STARE		100 98.88 99.20 86.71			
Xu et al. [42]	ORIGA MESSIDOR STARE		100 99.43 89			
Zhang et al. [37]	MESSIDOR					MAP = 99.9

Table 2.7 Research work on exudate detection.

Research groups	Models or methods	Data set	SN	SP	ACC/AUC	F
Using segmentation/localization concept						
Prentasic and Loncaric [45]	11-layer CNN	DRiDB	78			78
Perdomo et al. [50]	Patch-based LeNet CNN	E-OPHTHA	99.8	99.6	ACC=99.6	
Gondal et al. [49]	CNN model plus CAM	DIARETDB1	HE=87, SE=80			
Quellec et al. [47]	CNN	DIARETDB1			AUC: HE=.735 SE=.809	
Without using segmentation/localization concept						
Gondal et al. [49]	CNN model plus CAM	DIARETDB1	HE=100, SE=90		AUC=.954	
Quellec et al. [47]	CNN	DIARETDB1			AUC: HE=.974 SE=.963	
Khojasteh et al. [46]	Patch-based ResNet and SVM	DIARETDB1 E-ophtha	99 98	96 95	ACC=98.2 ACC=97.6	

Table 2.8 Research work on Microaneurysms and Haemorrhages detection.

Research groups	Task	Models or methods	Data set	SN	SP	AUC	ACC
Using segmentation/localization concept							
Haloi [51]	MA	9-layer CNN	MESSIDOR, ROC	97	95	.982 .98	95.4
Van Grinsven [52]	HM	Selective sampling	Kaggle, MESSIDOR	84.8 93.1	90.4 91.5	.917 .971	
Gondal et al. [49]	HM, small red dots	CNN	DIARETDB1	HM=91 Small red dots=52			
Quellec et al. [47]	HM, small red dots	CNN	DIARETDB1			HM=.614 small red dots=.50	

(Continued)

Table 2.8 Research work on Microaneurysms and Haemorrhages detection. (*Continued*)

Research groups	Task	Models or methods	Data set	SN	SP	AUC	ACC
Orlando *et al.* [53]	MA, HM	HEF, CNN and RF	DIARETDB1 E-oph-tha	MA=48.83 HM=48.83 MA=36.80			
Shan and Li [54]	MA	Patch-based SSAE	DIARETDB1		91.6		91.38
Without performing segmentation/localization							
Gondal *et al.* [49]	HM, small red dots	CNN	DIARETDB1	HM=97.2 Small Red Dots=50			
Quellec *et al.* [47]	HM, small red dots	CNN	DIARETDB1			HM=.999 Small Red Dots=.912	
Orlando *et al.* [53]	Red lesion	HEF, CNN and RF	MESSIDOR	91.09	50	.08932	

Table 2.9 Research works on DR classification.

Research groups	Models or methods	Data set	AUC	ACC %	SN %	SP%
Gulshan et al. [55]	Transfer learning of Inception-V3 CNN model	EyePACS-1 MESSIDOR-2	0.991 0.990	-	90.3 87	90 98.5
Colas et al. [58]	End-to-end training of CNN model	Kaggle	0.946	-	96.2	66.6
Quellec et al. [47]	Transfer learning in ensemble network of CNN	DIARETDB1 Kaggle e-Ophtha	0.954 0.955 0.949	-	-	-
Costa and Campilho [59]	End-to-end CNN with SURF	MESSIDOR DR1 DR2	0.90 0.93 0.97	-	-	-

(Continued)

Table 2.9 Research works on DR classification. (*Continued*)

Research groups	Models or methods	Data set	AUC	ACC %	SN %	SP%
Pratt *et al.* [60]	End-to-end training of 13 layers of CNN	Kaggle	-	75	95	-
Gargeya and Leng [56]	End-to-end training of ResNet and gradient boosting tree	MESSIDOR-2 e-Ophtha	0.94 0.95	-	-	-
Ting *et al.* [63]	End-to-end training of CNN model	71896 images	0.936	-	90.5	91.6
Abramoff *et al.* [57]	End-to-end training of CNN model	MESSIDOR -2	0.980	-	96.8	87
Wang *et al.* [61]	Transfer learning in Zoom-in network	EYEPACS MESSIDOR	0.825 0.957	- 91.1	-	-
Mansour [62]	Transfer learning of AlexNet and SVM for classification	Kaggle	-	-	100	93

To learn the features, Maji *et al.* [28] used stacked denoising autoencoder (SDAEs) with 400 and 100 hidden neurons in first DAE and second DAE, classified the features using random forest, and evaluated the performance using DRIVE data set.

Roy and Sheet [29] used domain adaptation techniques in stacked autoencoder neural networks (SAE-DNN). After performing supervised learning in two hidden layers in SAE-DNN that are trained using the source domain and autoencoding mechanism, domain adaptation is applied during supervised fine-tuning and unsupervised weight adaptation. It is observed that applying domain adaptation techniques improved the result.

Li *et al.* [30] extracted patches of a pixel on the green channel of the image obtained using a supervised DL approach and employed Denoising autoencoders (DAEs) to form a vessel map from fundus images. CHASE, DRIVE, and STARE were used to assess the model.

2.6.2   Optic Disc Feature

Lim *et al.* [32] were the first to perform optic disc segmentation using a DL model by estimating the cup-to-disc ratio. The framework involves four stages—optic disk localization, enhancing relevant features, probability map formation from a pixel-level classification using CNN, and finally segmentation of probability map. Nine-layered CNN, MESSIDOR, and SEED-DB were used in this research.

Maninis *et al.* [27] made smaller modifications in the structure of VGG architecture to segment optic disc and blood vessels together. Feng *et al.* [33] used popular U-net architecture by employing residual blocks instead of convolution layers for segmenting optic disc and exudates together. Sevastopolsky [34] modified the convolution layers in U net architecture by reducing the filter numbers for segmenting both optic cup and disk. Fu *et al.* [35] used transfer learning in U shaped CNN along with polar transformation for segmenting optic discs and analyzed the performance using the ORIGA data set.

Shankaranarayana *et al.* [36] used ResNet for optic cup and disc segmentation and evaluated using the RIM-ONE data set. Resnet and generative adversarial networks were used to map the retinal images and segmentation map. The performance of this method is better even without applying any preprocessing steps.

Zhang *et al.* [37] deployed faster RCNN with the ZF net for optic disc localization. Hessian matrix to subtract the blood vessels in the bounding box and shape-constrained level algorithm for extracting boundaries of the optic disc is used. Kaggle data set for training and to test the MESSIDOR data set was used.

Series of CNN models were used by Alghamdi *et al.* [38] to detect abnormal optic discs after extracting, preprocessing, and normalizing candidate optic disc regions. Then in the second CNN module, the regions are classified into normal, abnormal, or suspicious. The system was evaluated using the local data set, STARE, MESSIDOR, DIARETDB1, and DRIVE data set.

Niu *et al.* [39] identified salient regions in the fundus image using a saliency-based visual attention model and then classified the regions using the CNN model for optic disc localization. ORIGA and MESSIDOR data set was used to test the performance.

Zilly *et al.* [40] trained the end-to-end model of multi-scale two layers CNN by converting the image to L*a*b color space to segment optic cup and disc. By the same authors [41], the same task was carried out by using a combination of entropy sampling and ensemble CNN models. In both the works, DRISHTI-GS data set was used

Xu *et al.* [42] calculated the pixel probability map by removing fully connected layers from the pretrained VGG model and connecting deconvolution layers to the last three pooling layers. The threshold function is applied to a probability map for localizing optic disc. Evaluating the model on STARE, ORIGA, and MESSIDOR data set showed that this method can correctly localize optic disc.

2.6.3   Lesion Detections

2.6.3.1   *Exudate Detection*

Prentasic *et al.* [45] used the idea of a probability map to detect exudates. The authors created a probability map of optic disc, vessels, bright border probability maps and combined them with the EX probability map obtained from 11-layer CNN. After fitting a parabola on the resultant probability map, the final exudate probability map is generated and used to detect Exudate. DRiDB database was used to evaluate the performance.

Analysis by Khojasteh *et al.* [46] on patch-based DL models using DIARETDB1 and e-ophtha data set showed that the combination of ResNet with SVM gave better results.

Quellec *et al.* [47] proposed visualization of the image as a heatmap using CNN techniques will help to detect lesions at the pixel level and at image level referable DR can be detected. Simonyan and Zisserman [48] used o_O CNN architecture for identifying DR and lesion simultaneously by generating heatmaps. Gondal *et al.* [49] also detected exudates along with other lesions using o_O CNN architecture. DR lesions are localized by removing dense layers from the CNN model and class activation map (CAM) to localize regions is achieved by adding the global average pooling (GAP) layer and classification layer after the last convolution layer. Kaggle data set was used for training and the performance was validated using DIARETDB1.

Permodo *et al.* [50] used the e-ophtha data set. The authors cropped the patches with exudates and performed classification by feeding the patches to LeNet architecture.

2.6.3.2 MA and HM

Haloi [51] classified each pixel as MA or non-MA by taking a window size of 129 × 129 and passed it to a nine-layer CNN architecture. The author used data augmentation and dropout training techniques as well and evaluated it on MESSIDOR and Retinopathy online challenge data set.

Grinsven *et al.* [52] used the CNN model and proposed a dynamic selective sampling strategy to select informative samples from the data set. This method considers only positive samples and extracts a patch size of 41 × 41 around HM and non-HM pixels. This method is evaluated on Kaggle and MESSIDOR data set.

Gond *et al.* [49], Quellec *et al.* [47]., Orlando *et al.* [53] detected lesions like exudates, HMs, small red dots, and referable DR simultaneously. Orlando *et al.* [53] followed a sequence of a process involving morphological operations, cropped patches of an image, extracted features like shape and intensity using CNN, fused, and passed it to a random forest model to create a probability map. The output is used to make image and lesion level decisions. Lesion evaluation was performed using DIARETDB1, e-ophtha data set, and performance of detecting referable DR was done using the MESSIDOR data set.

Shan and Li [54] created patches of the image without any preprocessing, extracted features using SSAE, classified the lesions as MA or non-MA using the SoftMax classifier. With 10-fold cross-validation and DIARETDB data set, the performance of the system was evaluated.

2.6.4 DR Classification

A study by Gulshan *et al.* [55] reported that CNN-based architecture gives high sensitivity and specificity in identifying referable DR. The Inception-v3 CNN-based model is used to learn the features using the EyePACS and MESSIDOR data set. Grageya and Leng [56] used the ResNet model to learn the features and gradient boosting classifier to classify DR into either normal or referable DR using the EyePACS data set. The model was evaluated on MESSIDOR-2 and e-ophtha data set as well. Abramoff *et al.* [57] used MESSIDOR-2 data set for training a supervised CNN model end-to-end to classify retinal images into normal or referable DR

Colas *et al.* [58] trained the CNN model end-to-end using the Kaggle data set to identify referable DR along with the location of lesions. Each image in the Kaggle data set is graded into five different stages by Ophthalmologists. Quellec *et al.* [47] also identified DR and lesions by generating heatmaps using CNN visualization techniques. The authors trained the model using transfer learning. Diabetic retinopathy is identified at image level and lesions are detected at a pixel level.

Costa *et al.* [59] used the bag of visual words concept. The authors encoded the extracted sparse or dense local features obtained from speeded-up robust features (SURF) using convolution operation, followed by a neural network to perform classification.

Pratt *et al.* [60] trained 13 layered CNN end-to-end using Kaggle data set to grade the DR into no, mild, moderate, severe, and proliferated DR. Wang *et al.* [61] incorporated the process of zooming the image by ophthalmologists with a network called zoom-in to look for lesions in their proposed architecture. The authors proposed an architecture based on a supervised CNN approach which consists of the main network pretrained from ImageNet and two subnetworks called attention network and crop-network. To evaluate the system EyePACS and MESSIDOR were used.

Mansour [62] applied image preprocessing techniques, performed background subtraction, localized blood vessels, reduced dimensionality using linear discriminant analysis, extracted the features using AlexNet, used SVM for classification on MESSIODR data set, and evaluated the performance.

2.7   Discussion and Future Directions

The performance of DL models provided a promising positive direction towards identifying lesions and classification of DR compared with hand-engineered models. From the literature survey, it can be observed that most of the research works are based on CNN models and there are fewer research works on identifying DR using other DL models. Analyzing the space and time complexity of the model on a large data set can help the researchers to identify best practices to employ developed models in real-time clinical practice. Some of the future directions could be combining

DL and ML models, analyzing images captured in different cameras, light conditions, in different color space, and resolution. The development of symptoms at every stage has a relation, gaining the domain knowledge from expert ophthalmologists and incorporating them in research will give a different approach to the problem and help in providing a solution that would benefit the clinicians.

2.8   Conclusion

Diabetic retinopathy is a complication that develops in the retina of diabetic patients which is silent at initial stages, grows rapidly, and causes irreversible changes at later stages. Early detection is crucial to avoid vision loss. Deep learning models perform better compared to conventional algorithms. So, in this paper, we focussed on DL models used in recent DR detection research works. In this survey paper, an overview of various DL models, most of the performance metrics, details about the data set was described initially, followed by various state-of-the-art techniques used by researchers were discussed in detail and the discussion section listed the challenges and possible future directions.

References

1. Lee, R., Wong, T.Y., Sabanayagam, C., "Epidemiology of diabetic retinopathy, diabetic macular edema and related vision loss". *Eye Vis.*, 2, 1, 1–25, 2015.
2. Khurana, A.K., *Comprehensive Ophthalmology*, Jaypee Brothers Medical Publishers, India, 7th ed., 2019.
3. Mateen, M., Wen, J., Hassan, M., Nasrullah, N., Sun, S., Hayat, S., "Automatic Detection of Diabetic Retinopathy: A Review on Datasets, Methods and Evaluation Metrics,". *IEEE Access*, 8, 48784–48811, 2020.
4. Togashi, K., Yamashita, R., Nishio, M., Do, R.K.G., "Convolutional neural networks: an overview and application in radiology,". *Insights Imaging*, 9, 4, 611–629, 2018. [Online]. Available: https://doi.org/10.1007/s13244-018-0639-9.
5. Liang, J., Tajbakhsh, N., Shin, J.Y., Gurudu, S.R., Hurst, R.T., Kendall, C.B., Gotway, M.B., "Convolutional neural networks for medical image analysis: Full training or fine tuning?". *IEEE Trans. Med. Imaging*, 35, 5, 1299–1312, 2016.
6. Bengio, S., Erhan, D., Bengio, Y., Courville, A., Mangazol, P.-A., Vincent, P., "Why does unsupervised pre-training help deep learning?". *J. Mach. Learn. Res.*, 11, Feb, 625–660, 2010.

7. Hinton, G.E., "Reducing the Dimensionality of Data with Neural Networks," *Sci. (80-.).*, 313, 5786, 504–507, Jul. 2006.

8. Courville, A., Goodfellow, I., Bengio, Y., *Deep Learning*, The MIT Press, Cambridge, Massachusetts, 2016.

9. Catherine Moulinoux, Jean-Claude Faure, and Witold Litwin, MESSIDOR system. In Proceedings of the 1981 ACM SIGSMALL symposium on Small systems and SIGMOD workshop on Small database systems (SIGSMALL '81), Association for Computing Machinery, New York, NY, USA, 130–135, 1981.

10. "Kaggle dataset: Diabetic Retinopathy Detection," 2015, https://www.kaggle.com/c/diabetic-retinopathy-detection/data (accessed Jul. 05, 2020).

11. Diabetic retinopathy screening, EyePACS, (8 May 2019), www.eyepacs.com/

12. E. Decencière, G. Cazuguel, X. Zhang, G. Thibault, J.-C. Klein, F. Meyer, B. Marcotegui, G. Quellec, M. Lamard, R. Danno, D. Elie, P. Massin, Z. Viktor, A. Erginay, B. Laÿ, A. Chabouis, TeleOphta: Machine learning and image processing methods for teleophthalmology, IRBM, 34, 2, 196–203, 2013, ISSN 1959-0318.

13. Owen, C.G.; Rudnicka, A.R.; Mullen, R.; Barman, S.A.; Monekosso, D.; Whincup, P.H.; Ng, J.; Paterson, C. Measuring retinal vessel tortuosity in 10-year-old children: Validation of the computer-assisted image analysis of the retina (CAIAR) program. IOVS 2009, 50, 2004–2010.

14. Kamarainen, T.K.K.K., Sorri, L., Pietil, A.R.V., Uusitalo, H.K.: the DIARETDB1 diabetic retinopathy database and evaluation protocol. In: *Proceedings of British Machine Vision Conference*, BMVA Press, pp. 15.115.10, 2007.

15. A. D. Hoover, V. Kouznetsova and M. Goldbaum, "Locating blood vessels in retinal images by piecewise threshold probing of a matched filter response," in IEEE Transactions on Medical Imaging, 19, 203–210, March 2000.

16. M. Niemeijer, J. J. Staal, B. V. Ginneken, and M. Loog, "DRIVE: digital retinal images for vesselextraction," 2004. http://www.isi.uu.nl/Research/Databases/DRIVE.

17. "Aria dataset.", Retinal image archive, 2006. http://www.eyecharity.com/aria_online.html (accessed Jul. 05, 2020).

18. Al-Diri, B., Hunter, A., Steel, D., Habib, M., Hudaib, T., Berry, S., "REVIEW - A reference data set for retinal vessel profiles,", in: *2008 30th Annual International Conference of the IEEE Engineering in Medicine and Biology Society*, pp. 2262–2265, Aug. 2008.

19. E.J. Carmona, M. Rincón, J. García-Feijoo and J. M. Martínez-de-la-Casa. Identification of the optic nerve head with genetic algorithms. Artificial Intelligence in Medicine, 43, 3, 243–259, 2008.

20. Maji, D., Santara, A., Mitra, P., Sheet, D., "Ensemble of Deep Convolutional Neural Networks for Learning to Detect Retinal Vessels in Fundus Images,", CoRR, pp. 1–4, Mar. 2016, arXiv:1603.04833. [Online]. Available: http://arxiv.org/abs/1603.04833.

21. Liskowski, P. and Krawiec, K., "Segmenting Retinal Blood Vessels With Deep Neural Networks,". *IEEE Trans. Med. Imaging*, 35, 11, 2369–2380, Nov. 2016.

22. Wu, A., Xu, Z., Gao, M., Buty, M., Mollura, D.J., "Deep vessel tracking: A generalized probabilistic approach via deep learning,", in: *2016 IEEE 13th International Symposium on Biomedical Imaging (ISBI)*, pp. 1363–1367, Apr. 2016.

23. Dasgupta, A. and Singh, S., "A fully convolutional neural network based structured prediction approach towards the retinal vessel segmentation,", in: *2017 IEEE 14th International Symposium on Biomedical Imaging (ISBI 2017)*, pp. 248–251, Apr. 2017.

24. Fu, H., Xu, Y., Wong, D.W.K., Liu, J., "Retinal vessel segmentation via deep learning network and fully-connected conditional random fields,", in: *2016 IEEE 13th International Symposium on Biomedical Imaging (ISBI)*, pp. 698–701, Apr. 2016.

25. Mo, J. and Zhang, L., "Multi-level deep supervised networks for retinal vessel segmentation,". *Int. J. Comput. Assist. Radiol. Surg.*, 12, 12, 2181–2193, Dec. 2017.

26. Tan, J.H., Acharya, U.R., Bhandary, S.V., Chua, K.C., Sivaprasad, S., "Segmentation of optic disc, fovea and retinal vasculature using a single convolutional neural network,", *J. Comput. Sci.*, 20, 70–79, May 2017. Available: http://arxiv.org/abs/1702.00509.

27. Maninis, K.-K., Pont-Tuset, J., Arbeláez, P., Van Gool, L., *"Deep Retinal Image Understanding,"*, pp. 140–148, 2016.

28. Maji, D., Santara, A., Ghosh, S., Sheet, D., Mitra, P., "Deep neural network and random forest hybrid architecture for learning to detect retinal vessels in fundus images,", in: *2015 37th Annual International Conference of the IEEE Engineering in Medicine and Biology Society (EMBC)*, pp. 3029–3032, Aug. 2015.

29. Roy, A.G. and Sheet, D., "DASA: Domain adaptation in stacked autoencoders using systematic dropout,", in: *2015 3rd IAPR Asian Conference on Pattern Recognition (ACPR)*, pp. 735–739, Nov. 2015.

30. Li, Q., Feng, B., Xie, L., Liang, P., Zhang, H., Wang, T., "A Cross-Modality Learning Approach for Vessel Segmentation in Retinal Images,". *IEEE Trans. Med. Imaging*, 35, 1, 109–118, Jan. 2016.

31. Lahiri, A., Roy, A.G., Sheet, D., Biswas, P.K., "Deep neural ensemble for retinal vessel segmentation in fundus images towards achieving label-free angiography,", in: *2016 38th Annual International Conference of the IEEE Engineering in Medicine and Biology Society (EMBC)*, pp. 1340–1343, Aug. 2016.

32. Lim, G., Cheng, Y., Hsu, W., Lee, M.L., "Integrated Optic Disc and Cup Segmentation with Deep Learning,", in: *2015 IEEE 27th International Conference on Tools with Artificial Intelligence (ICTAI)*, pp. 162–169, Nov. 2015.

33. Feng, Z., Yang, J., Yao, L., Qiao, Y., Yu, Q., Xu, X., "Deep Retinal Image Segmentation: A FCN-Based Architecture with Short and Long Skip Connections for Retinal Image Segmentation," In: Liu D., Xie S., Li Y., Zhao D., El-Alfy ES. (eds) Neural Information Processing. ICONIP 2017. Lecture Notes in Computer Science, Springer, Cham, 10637, 713–722, 2017.

34. Sevastopolsky, A., "Optic disc and cup segmentation methods for glaucoma detection with modification of U-Net convolutional neural network,". *Pattern Recognit. Image Anal.*, 27, 3, 618–624, Jul. 2017.

35. Fu, H., Cheng, J., Xu, Y., Wong, D.W.K., Liu, J., Cao, X., "Joint Optic Disc and Cup Segmentation Based on Multi-label Deep Network and Polar Transformation,", IEEE Transactions on Medical Imaging, vol. 37, no. 7, pp. 1597–1605, July 2018.

36. Shankaranarayana, S.M., Ram, K., Mitra, K., Sivaprakasam, M., "Fully Convolutional Networks for Monocular Retinal Depth Estimation and Optic Disc-Cup Segmentation, IEEE Journal of Biomedical and Health Informatics 23, 1417–1426, Feb 2019. Available: http://arxiv.org/abs/1902.01040.

37. Zhao, H., Chen, X., Zhang, D., Zhu, W., Shi, F., "Automatic localization and segmentation of optical disk based on faster R-CNN and level set in fundus image, in: *Medical Imaging 2018: Image Processing*, p. 65, Mar. 2018.

38. Alghamdi, H.S., Tang, H.L., Waheeb, S.A., Peto, T., "Automatic Optic Disc Abnormality Detection in Fundus Images: A Deep Learning Approach,", in: *Proceedings of the Ophthalmic Medical Image Analysis Third International Workshop*, pp. 17–24, Oct. 2016.

39. Niu, D., Xu, P., Wan, C., Cheng, J., Liu, J., "Automatic localization of optic disc based on deep learning in fundus images,", in: *2017 IEEE 2nd International Conference on Signal and Image Processing (ICSIP)*, pp. 208–212, Aug. 2017.

40. Zilly, J.G., Buhmann, J.M., Mahapatra, D., *"Boosting Convolutional Filters with Entropy Sampling for Optic Cup and Disc Image Segmentation from Fundus Images,"*, pp. 136–143, 2015.

41. Zilly, J., Buhmann, J.M., Mahapatra, D., "Glaucoma detection using entropy sampling and ensemble learning for automatic optic cup and disc segmentation,". *Comput. Med. Imaging Graph.*, 55, 28–41, Jan. 2017.

42. Xu, P., Wan, C., Cheng, J., Niu, D., Liu, J., *"Optic Disc Detection via Deep Learning in Fundus Images,"*, pp. 134–141, 2017.

43. Guo, Y., Zou, B., Chen, Z., He, Q., Liu, Q., Zhao, R., "Optic Cup Segmentation Using Large Pixel Patch Based CNNs,", in: *Proceedings of the Ophthalmic Medical Image Analysis Third International Workshop*, pp. 129–136, Oct. 2016.

44. Srivastava, R., Cheng, J., Wong, D.W.K., Liu, J., "Using deep learning for robustness to parapapillary atrophy in optic disc segmentation,", in: *2015 IEEE 12th International Symposium on Biomedical Imaging (ISBI)*, pp. 768–771, Apr. 2015.

45. Prentašić, P. and Lončarić, S., "Detection of exudates in fundus photographs using deep neural networks and anatomical landmark detection fusion,". *Comput. Methods Programs Biomed.*, 137, 281–292, Dec. 2016.

46. Khojasteh, P. et al., "Exudate detection in fundus images using deeply-learnable features,". *Comput. Biol. Med.*, 104, 62–69, Jan. 2019.

47. Quellec, G., Charrière, K., Boudi, Y., Cochener, B., Lamard, M., Deep image mining for diabetic retinopathy screening, *Medical Image Analysis*, 39, 178–193, 2017.

48. Simonyan, K. and Zisserman, A., "Very Deep Convolutional Networks for Large-Scale Image Recognition,", CoRR, abs/1409.1556, n. pag., 2015, [Online]. Available: http://arxiv.org/abs/1409.1556.

49. Gondal, W.M., Köhler, J.M., Grzeszick, R., Fink, G.A., Hirsch, M., *"Weakly-supervised localization of diabetic retinopathy lesions in retinal fundus images,"*, Jun. 2017, [Online]. Available: http://arxiv.org/abs/1706.09634.

50. Perdomo, O., Arevalo, J., González, F.A., "Convolutional network to detect exudates in eye fundus images of diabetic subjects,". Proc. SPIE 10160, 12th International Symposium on Medical Information Processing and Analysis, 101600T, Jan. 2017.

51. Haloi, M., "Improved Microaneurysm Detection using Deep Neural Networks,", ArXiv, abs/1505.04424, n. pag., May 2015. [Online]. Available: http://arxiv.org/abs/1505.04424.

52. van Grinsven, M.J.J.P., van Ginneken, B., Hoyng, C.B., Theelen, T., Sanchez, C., II, "Fast Convolutional Neural Network Training Using Selective Data Sampling: Application to Hemorrhage Detection in Color Fundus Images,". *IEEE Trans. Med. Imaging*, 35, 5, 1273–1284, May 2016.

53. Orlando, J., II, Prokofyeva, E., del Fresno, M., Blaschko, M.B., "An ensemble deep learning based approach for red lesion detection in fundus images,". *Comput. Methods Programs Biomed.*, 153, 115–127, Jan. 2018.

54. Shan, J. and Li, L., "A Deep Learning Method for Microaneurysm Detection in Fundus Images,", in: *2016 IEEE First International Conference on Connected Health: Applications, Systems and Engineering Technologies (CHASE)*, pp. 357–358, Jun. 2016.

55. Gulshan, V. et al., "Development and Validation of a Deep Learning Algorithm for Detection of Diabetic Retinopathy in Retinal Fundus Photographs,". *JAMA*, 316, 22, 2402, Dec. 2016.

56. Gargeya, R. and Leng, T., "Automated Identification of Diabetic Retinopathy Using Deep Learning,". *Ophthalmology*, 124, 7, 962–969, 2017.

57. Abràmoff, M.D. et al., "Improved Automated Detection of Diabetic Retinopathy on a Publicly Available Dataset Through Integration of Deep Learning,". *Investig. Opthalmology Vis. Sci.*, 57, 13, 5200, Oct. 2016.

58. Colas, E., Besse, A., Orgogozo, A., Schmauch, B., Meric, N., Besse, E., "Deep learning approach for diabetic retinopathy screening,". *Acta Ophthalmol.*, 94, n. pag., Oct. 2016. https://www.semanticscholar.org/paper/Deep-

Learning-Approach-to-Diabetic-Retinopathy-Tymchenko-Marchenko/
ad73322d6aa40779b7b39fd70f61a8935d6f360d

59. Costa, P. and Campilho, A., "Convolutional bag of words for diabetic reti-nopathy detection from eye fundus images,". *IPSJ Trans. Comput. Vis. Appl.*, 9, 10, Dec. 2017.

60. Pratt, H., Coenen, F., Broadbent, D.M., Harding, S.P., Zheng, Y., "Convolutional Neural Networks for Diabetic Retinopathy,". *Proc. Comput. Sci.*, 90, 200–205, 2016.

61. Wang, Z., Yin, Y., Shi, J., Fang, W., Li, H., Wang, X., "Zoom-in-Net: Deep Mining Lesions for Diabetic Retinopathy Detection,", ArXiv, abs/1706.04372, n. pag., 2017 Jun. 2017. [Online]. Available: http://arxiv.org/abs/1706.04372.

62. Mansour, R.F., "Deep-learning-based automatic computer-aided diagnosis system for diabetic retinopathy,". *Biomed. Eng. Lett.*, 8, 1, 41–57, Feb. 2018.

63. Ting, D.S.W. *et al.*, "Development and Validation of a Deep Learning System for Diabetic Retinopathy and Related Eye Diseases Using Retinal Images From Multiethnic Populations With Diabetes,". *JAMA*, 318, 22, 2211, Dec. 2017.

3

A New Improved Cryptography Method-Based e-Health Application in Cloud Computing Environment

Dipesh Kumar[1]*, Nirupama Mandal[1]† and Yugal Kumar[2]‡

[1]Department of Electronics Engineering, Indian Institute of Technology (ISM), Dhanbad, Jharkhand, India
[2]Department of Computer Science & Engineering, Jaypee University of Information Technology, Solan, Himachal Pradesh, India

Abstract

Nowadays, the world is moving toward the use of mobile apps and web applications for almost everything, which caused a surge in online data across the world. Cloud computing has proved to be a boon to the technology, which provides a dynamic infrastructure for applications, data, and file storage. To manage and provide better services to patients, various e-health applications have been developed. The e-Health applications based on a cloud computing environment allows healthcare services to monitor the health and health-related information of patients dynamically. However, with increasing online activities, the threat to data has also increased. Most of the applications are using old mechanisms to protect the data against any fraud and attack. e-Health data are very critical, so protecting the e-health data is a major area of concern. The main aim of this work is to provide a secure infrastructure for e-Health applications hosted in the cloud computing environment. In the proposed system, a patient's health data will be secured using HTTPS protocol. A new improved algorithm has been proposed for encryption and decryption of data. The proposed algorithm is based on asymmetric key encryption. The proposed encryption and decryption technique will be compared with existing encryption and technique used in the basic transposition method.

---

*Corresponding author: dipesh.kumar89@gmail.com
†Corresponding author: nirupama_cal@rediffmail.com
‡Corresponding author: yugalkumar.14@gmail.com

R. Nidhya, Manish Kumar and S. Balamurugan (eds.) Tele-Healthcare: Applications of Artificial Intelligence and Soft Computing Techniques, (59–84) © 2022 Scrivener Publishing LLC

The newly improved cryptography method has proven to be effective in terms of encrypting and decrypting the data at the sender's and receiver's end, respectively.

Keywords: Cloud computing, e-health, cryptography, encryption, decryption, ciphers

3.1   Introduction

The introduction of the concept of cloud computing has completely changed the storage capabilities and has allowed the mobility of applications throughout the globe. Cloud computing has played a major role in the development of online activities across the globe. It has allowed the applications to connect to the server across the globe and have increased security. The virtual cloud server provides better security measures as compared with physical servers and also is cost-effective. With the development of Internet facilities, the world has come very closer. Internet services and cloud computing environment has enabled applications to reach to the major number of populations across the globe. Several applications have been developed and hosted in the cloud computing environment. These applications have eased the life of the people. In the past few decades, it has been observed that there is an increase in health issues in major populations across the world. Also, with a busy schedule, it has become very difficult for an individual to take care of his health and that of their dependents. Also, healthcare infrastructure needs to be developed to support the overall population. The e-Health application has proved as a boon to monitor the health status of an individual. With the development of the cloud computing environment, the e-Health application has become an important tool to monitor the health record of the patient by PHR's and caretakers. The e-Health application also allows patients to get medical advice from doctors in case of any emergency. This application enables PHR's or healthcare centers to track the health record and medical history of the patient. The e-health application includes very personal data, like health records, medical history, transaction details, bank details, and so on, of the patient. With increasing technology, the volume of data across the Internet has increased in few decades. With the latest technologies, the threat to data across the Internet has also increased. Since e-Health applications include very personal and important data, major steps should be taken to secure the data. The transport layer is very important and is very prone to online attacks. In the transport layer, data transmission occurs from client to server over the Internet. To protect the data transmitted over the Internet in the transport layer, data should be secured properly. Cryptography has been proven very important in securing the data. Cryptography is a method to develop algorithms using codes to convert the message into ciphertext before sending the message to the receiver through network channels. Cryptography is also used to write algorithms to convert the ciphertext received at receivers to extract the original message. Various ciphers have been developed using the algorithm. These ciphers are included in digital certificates, which are used on the client and server-side for handshaking and encryption and decryption of message on sender's side and receiver's side, respectively.

With improving technology, the hackers also have enhanced their capability to decode the message in the transport layer which causes a major threat to the data used in the application. Another area of concern is the algorithms used in ciphers, the algorithms should be strong and must be complex enough to prevent any attack from a hacker, and it should present a challenge for hackers to decode it. The efficiency of the algorithm depends on the time it takes to encrypt and decrypt the message. In the proposed work, to avoid any attack from hackers, an improved algorithm has been proposed, which provides enough complexity to protect the data from hackers. In the proposed work, the proposed algorithm can encrypt the data sent by the sender to convert it into ciphertext. The decryption algorithm can fetch the original message from the ciphertext at the receiver's end. The time taken by the proposed algorithm to encrypt and decrypt the message is also recorded for further studies.

3.1.1 Contribution

The main contribution of the proposed approach is to provide a new improved cryptography algorithm. The proposed algorithm provides new and improved encryption and decryption technique. The proposed encryption and decryption technique can be used as a cipher in the application while creating digital certificates. As discussed in the introduction section, the e-Health applications are very critical applications that include various personal information related to patient health, should be secured properly to avoid any unforeseen activity with the patient's data. The cipher should include an algorithm that should not allow hackers to retrieve the original message from the ciphertext. Only the dedicated recipient should decode the ciphertext using the decryption algorithm at the receiver's end. The proposed cryptography method provides a new improved algorithm to encrypt the patient's data to create ciphertext at the sender's end and decrypt the ciphertext to extract the original text at the receiver's end.

3.2   Motivation

With increasing e-services across the world, the flow of messages across the servers has increased many folds in the last decade. In today's world, most of the activities are done online using the Internet, which poses a big threat to our data. While doing online activities, personal data are also got exposed over the Internet. With the cloud computing environment, online activities have got increased many folds, as cloud computing has fulfilled the demand for online activities to a great extent. From the literature survey, it has been observed that e-Health applications hosted in cloud computing environment has proved to be a boon to patient's and PHR's which allows the patient and healthcare agencies to track the health record of patients from anywhere across the globe. But with a lot of merits, most of the e-services including the e-Health application expose personal data over the Internet. The e-Health application stores patient's health records and all the patients ' all personal information. These personal details must be secured to avoid any misuse. With increasing online activities, hacker's attacks are also increasing day by day. With rapidly developing technology, hackers have also developed their skills to decode and hack the data available in the Internet and cloud environment. To avoid this attack, the cryptographic algorithms should be updated and modified regularly to provide a challenge to hackers to decode the data available in the transport layer. Motivated by the above, the new algorithms for encrypting and decrypting the data have been proposed to be used in cipher to secure the e-Health application.

3.3   Related Works

With the development of technology across the globe, the cloud has proved very useful in enhancing technology to the next level. Cloud has provided the freedom to developers and researchers to think beyond physical requirements, security, and cost while planning for any application. The various researcher has presented cloud computing as very useful to mobilize the technology across the globe. With enhanced technology, there is a need to monitor and secure mobile applications hosted in the cloud [1–4]. The Cloud computing environment has increased the development and use of mobile applications [5] across the globe. Mobile applications enable the user to perform their activity from the phone by connecting to the Internet. Mobile application hosted in cloud computing environment has enhanced the capability of mobile applications and allows them to store and save their data and access the data from anywhere across the globe with increased security and performance. The development of IoT devices has enhanced AI capabilities. The IoT devices and cloud computing environment has contributed to the development of e-Health applications [6, 7].

In the field of healthcare, e-Health application [8–10] has become very useful and efficient [11] for patients as well as for healthcare, caretakers, and PHR's. The e-Health applications allow the caretaker to monitor the health of the patient using IoT sensors at the patient's end. However, the e-Health applications face various issues as highlighted by various researchers in their work. Hiranya et al., has performed related issues in e-Health applications [12].

Researchers have given various studies in the field of healthcare management [13–19]. The major area of concern in e-Health applications hosted in the cloud is data security. Since, in the transport layer, data are transmitted from sender to receiver through a transmission channel, so there is a major chance of data thief or data modification by hackers. To protect the data of an e-Health application, cryptography [20] should be enhanced. Elmogy et al. has suggested a new cryptography algorithm based on ASCII code, but ASCII code is very easy to decode by hackers [21]. Harmouch et al. has proposed a new algorithm for dynamic algorithm [22], but this algorithm lacked proper efficiency in terms of the challenge it presents to hackers. Various concepts have been given in terms of ciphers to secure the communication between sender and receivers [23]. Ciphers have proved very useful in securing the message between sender and receiver in a network [24–26]. Ciphers include algorithms for encrypting and decrypting the messages in sender and receiver's end respectively. Umang et al. has proposed a transposition technique to encrypt the message at the sender's end before sending it to the messaging channel [27]. Various other researchers have given advanced forms of transposition cipher technique [28–30]. But transposition cipher alone is not enough to protect the data. Transposition ciphers are very common, and it is a simple technique to encrypt the data at the senders' end. Sajid et al. have proposed an image encryption technique for high-security transmission over a network [31], but the image encryption technique lacks efficiency. In addition to the above cipher techniques, Jaju et al. has given a modified RSA algorithm to enhance security for digital signature, but the RSA algorithm is a very common cipher that can be further modified and enhanced to create a more effective cipher [32]. AES is among the most common cipher technique, but it also lacks efficiency in terms of complexity these ciphers present to hackers so that hackers are not able to decode the ciphertext [33–36]. The cipher should include the algorithms which are capable of providing very complex encryption to plain text and convert it into ciphertext. Also, the cipher should be efficient enough to allow the receiver to decrypt the ciphertext to get the plain text. In the proposed work, a complex algorithm has been proposed which can encrypt the message and make the ciphertext very complex to avoid any attack by hackers.

3.4   Challenges

The major challenge of e-services is to secure the data across the Internet. As discussed in the introduction, e-Health applications using a cloud computing environment has proved to be very helpful to monitor and diagnose a patient. It has become very important to secure the data of e-Health applications hosted in the cloud computing environment. The e-Health application includes the patient's health record and patient's details which should be secured to avoid any unauthorized access. With developing technology, the e-Health applications must be enough security measures so that patient's data should be secured properly. Various ciphers provide various encryption and decryption algorithms, but the algorithms should be strong enough to secure the e-Health application. There is a need to develop a new improved algorithm to provide encryption and decryption of data efficiently. The encryption algorithm should be complex to generate complex ciphertext which will present difficulty to hackers to read the ciphertext. In the same way, the decryption algorithm should decrypt the ciphertext properly to fetch original text at the receiver's end without allowing any hacker's attack. In the proposed work, a new and improved encryption and decryption algorithm has been proposed which can be used in cipher for e-Health applications to secure patient data.

3.5   Proposed Work

In the proposed work, an advanced algorithm has been proposed which is used to secure the e-Health application. The proposed algorithm is used to secure the data of the e-Health application at the transport layer. Since the transport layer is very prone to attack, major steps have been taken to secure the data that are transmitted from client to server in an e-Health application. The e-health application includes very personal data so it should be secured properly.

In the proposed approach, a patient's clinical data is captured by using sensors and is send to a database hosted in a cloud computing environment. In Figure 3.1, a basic e-Health application architecture is shown. In the proposed e-Health application, sensors are used to capture patient's clinical data. The captured clinical data is sent to the mobile application. The mobile application works as a gateway. The mobile gateway sends the data to the cloud webserver through HTTPS protocol using RESTful web service. The webserver then communicates to the app server and the app server then communicates with the database server to store the data in a database hosted in the cloud computing environment.

The connection between e-health mobile application and cloud webserver is secured by using digital certificates. After the digital handshaking is completed and secured connection established between e-Health application and cloud webserver, the digital certificates use ciphers to encrypt the data before sending it to the messaging channel to cloud webserver. The original message is converted to ciphertext using the proposed encryption algorithm. This ciphertext is then sent to messaging channel. Messaging channel used in this simulation is JMS messaging tool. The ciphertext reaches to receiver's end and converted to plain text using the proposed decryption algorithm.

The process of converting the original message into ciphertext using a mathematical algorithm or arithmetical codes is called encryption. Extracting the original message from the received ciphertext at the receiver's end using a mathematical algorithm or arithmetical codes is called decryption. The complete process is known as cryptography.

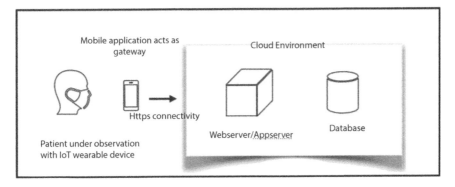

Figure 3.1 Basic architecture of e-health cloud environment.

3.6 Proposed Algorithm for Encryption

The proposed algorithm for encryption includes the following steps:

- Select a key of length N alphabets and place the text in a table of size N × 1
- Convert each letter into its ASCII code
- Add N (length of the text) to ASCII code of each alphabet
- Select a table of length n × p
- Assign each letter into each cell of the new table
- If the number of columns n is even, then cut the table from the middle and split the table into two half and merge to create a new table.
- The first half part will become the latter half of the new table and similarly, the latter half of the original table becomes the first half of the new table.
- If the number of columns is odd, then keep the middle column as it is and transverse the later columns to the first half of the new table and the first half to the latter half of the new table.
- Note down the elements of the cells of the new table vertically to get the encrypted ciphertext, which will be sent to the messaging channel to sender.

3.6.1 Demonstration of Encryption Algorithm

The proposed encryption method is explained in detail in the following section and steps are shown in Tables 3.1–3.7.

3.6.1.1 *When the Number of Columns Selected in the Table is Even*

Let us consider that the message sent from the e-Health mobile application to the cloud webserver and the proposed encryption method used as a cipher to encrypt the message.

Sample message string: **Patient Name—Charles**

Step I:
Count the number of letters in the message string including blank spaces and place each letter of the message in a table. Create a table of length 22 (string length of the sample message).

Table 3.1 Table creation when number of columns is even.

P	a	t	i	e	n	t		N	a	m	e		-		C	h	a	r	l	e	s

Step II:
Convert each alphabet into its respective ASCII code:

Table 3.2 Converting the alphabets into ASCII code.

080	097	116	105	101	110	116	32	078	097	109	101	32	95	32	067	104	097	114	108	101	115

Step III:
Add N that is 22 (length of message string) to each alphabet's ASCII code.

Table 3.3 Add N to each alphabet's ASCII code.

102	119	138	127	123	132	138	54	100	119	131	123	54	117	54	089	126	119	136	130	123	137

Step IV:
   Start transposition method. Choose a random table of column size n and place all the elements of step III to that table. Let us consider n=8.

Table 3.4 Start transposition method.

102	119	138	127	123	132	138	54
100	119	131	123	54	117	54	089
126	119	136	130	123	137		

Step V:
Since the number of columns is even, so split the table obtained in step IV into two equal parts:

Table 3.5 Split first part of the table.

102	119	138	127	123	132	138	54
100	119	131	123	54	117	54	089
126	119	136	130	123	137		

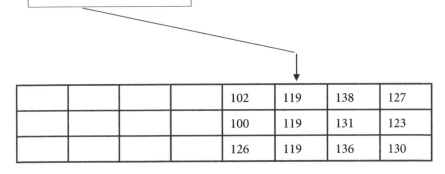

				102	119	138	127
				100	119	131	123
				126	119	136	130

Table 3.6 Split second part of the table.

102	119	138	127	123	132	138	54
100	119	131	123	54	117	54	089
126	119	136	130	123	137		

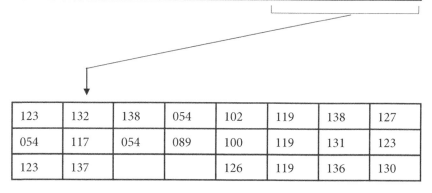

123	132	138	054	102	119	138	127
054	117	054	089	100	119	131	123
123	137			126	119	136	130

Step VI:
Take out all the elements from each column of Table 3.6 horizontally to obtain ciphertext:

Table 3.7 Ciphertext extraction.

123	132	138	054	102	119	138	127
054	117	054	089	100	119	131	123
123	137			126	119	136	130

123054123 132117137 138054154089 102100126 119119119 138131136 127123130

The final ciphertext obtained using the purposed encryption algorithms:

123054123132117137138054154 054089 102100126119119119913813 1136127123130

The above ciphertext is sent to the receiver through the JMS channel when the column length is considered in step IV as *even*.

3.6.1.2   When the Number of Columns Selected in the Table is Odd

When column length considered in step IV is odd then, step V is modified as shown in the below section:

Let us consider that the message sent from the e-Health mobile application to the cloud webserver and the proposed encryption method used as a cipher to encrypt the message.

Sample message string: **Patient Name: Charles**

Step I:
Count the number of letters in the message string including blank spaces and place each letter of the message in a table as shown in Table 3.8. Create a table of length 22 (string length of the sample message).

Table 3.8 Table creation when number of columns is odd.

P	a	t	i	e	n	t		N	a	m	e		:		C	h	a	r	l	e	s

Step II:
Convert each alphabet into its respective ASCII code as shown in Table 3.9:

Table 3.9 Converting the alphabets into ASCII code.

080	097	116	105	101	110	116	32	078	097	109	101	32	95	32	067	104	097	114	108	101	115

Step III:
Add N that is 22 (length of message string) to each alphabet's ASCII code as shown in Table 3.10.

Table 3.10   Add N to each alphabet's ASCII code.

102	119	138	127	123	132	138	54	100	119	131	123	54	117	54	089	126	119	136	130	123	137

Step IV:
Start transposition method. Choose a random table of column size n and place all the elements of step III to that table. Let us consider n=7.

Table 3.11 Start transposition method.

102	119	138	127	123	132	138	054	100
119	131	123	054	117	054	089	126	119
136	130	123	137					
C1	C2	C_3	C_4	C_5	C_6	C_7	C_8	C_9

Step V:

Create a new table with the same dimensions as shown in Table 3.11. The number of columns is odd, so the elements of the middle column, i.e., C_5 of Table 3.11 should remain at the same position, but all the elements of C_1-C_4 will move to C_5-C_9 of the new table as shown in Table 3.12. Similarly, all the elements of C_6-C_9 will move to C_1-C_4 of the new table as shown in Table 3.12.

Table 3.12 Split first part of the table.

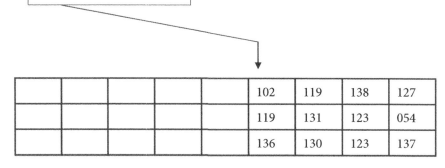

102	119	138	127	123	132	138	054	100
119	131	123	054	117	054	089	126	119
136	130	123	137					

					102	119	138	127
					119	131	123	054
					136	130	123	137

Table 3.13 Split second part of the table.

102	119	138	127	123	132	138	054	100
119	131	123	054	117	054	089	126	119
136	130	123	137					

132	138	054	100	123	102	119	138	127
054	089	126	119	119	119	131	123	054
					136	130	123	137

Step VI:

Take out all the elements from each column of Table 3.13 horizontally to obtain ciphertext.

Table 3.14 Ciphertext extraction

132	138	054	100	123	102	119	138	127
054	089	126	119	117	119	131	123	054
					136	130	123	137

| ↓ | ↓ | ↓ | ↓ | ↓ | ↓ | ↓ | ↓ | ↓ |

| 132 | 138089 | 054126 | 100119 | 123117 | 102119136 | 119131130 | 138123123 | 127054137 |

The final ciphertext obtained using the purposed encryption algorithm as shown in Table 3.14:

132054 138089 054126 100119 123117 10211913611913113O138123 123127054137

The above ciphertext is sent to the receiver through the JMS channel when the column length considered in step IV is *odd*.

3.6.2 Flowchart for Encryption

The encryption algorithm is shown in Figure 3.2 flowchart in this section.

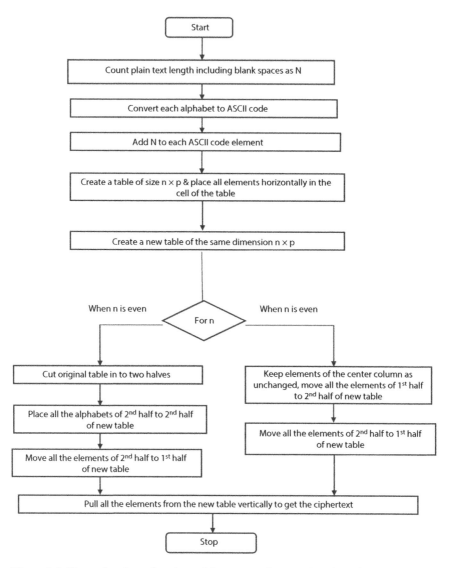

Figure 3.2 Figure showing a flowchart of the proposed encryption algorithm.

3.7   Algorithm for Decryption

- Select a table of n X m
- Fill each letter of ciphertext to each cell of the table.
- If the number of columns is even, then flip the table from the middle and place all the first half to the last half of the new table and the same for the second half to the first half of the new table.
- If the column count is odd, then keep the middle column as it is and move the first half to the second half of the new table and the second half to the first half of the new table.
- Count number of texts i.e. N
- Subtract N from each cell of the table
- Remove the ASCII code to get the exact alphabets.
- Take all the alphabets horizontally to get the exact original message i.e. plain text.

3.7.1   Demonstration of Decryption Algorithm

The proposed Decryption method is explained in detail in the following section.

3.7.1.1   *When the Number of Columns Selected in the Table is Even*

Let us consider the ciphertext received at the receiver's end is:

123054123132117137138054154 054089 102100126119119119113813 1136127123130

The received ciphertext will be converted to plain text using the proposed decryption method explained in the following section.

Step I:

Create a table of dimensions n × p and place each element of ciphertext vertically in the cells of the table.

Table 3.15 Table creation when number of columns is even.

123	132	138	054	102	119	138	127
054	117	054	089	100	119	131	123
123	137			126	119	136	130

Step II:
Cut the table shown in Table 3.15 into two equal parts and create another table of dimensions n × p and place the elements of the 1st half to 2nd half of the new table as shown in Table 3.16. Now, place the elements of the 2nd half to the 1st half of the new table as shown in Table 3.17.

Table 3.16 Split first part of the table.

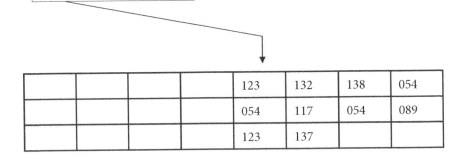

123	132	138	054	102	119	138	127
054	117	054	089	100	119	131	123
123	137			126	119	136	130

				123	132	138	054
				054	117	054	089
				123	137		

Table 3.17 Split second part of the table.

123	132	138	054	102	119	138	127
054	117	054	089	100	119	131	123
123	137			126	119	136	130

102	119	138	127	123	132	138	054
100	119	131	123	054	117	054	089
126	119	136	130	123	137		

Step III:
Subtract N from each element of Table 3.18. N is the total length of the original message.

Table 3.18 Subtract N from each element.

080	097	116	105	101	110	116	054
078	097	109	101	032	095	032	067
104	097	114	108	101	115		

Step IV:
Extract the original alphabets from the elements of the table by considering each element as ASCII code as shown in Table 3.19.

Table 3.19 Extraction of the original alphabets.

P	a	t	i	e	n	t	
N	a	m	e		:		C
h	a	r	l	e	s		

Step V:
Take out each element horizontally to get the plain text as shown in Table 3.20.

Table 3.20 Plain text extraction.

P	a	t	i	e	n	t		⟶	Patient
N	a	m	e		:		C	⟶	Name: C
h	a	r	l	e	s			⟶	harles

After decryption, the plain text received is **Patient Name : Charles**

3.7.1.2   *When the Number of Columns Selected in the Table is Odd*

Let us consider the ciphertext received at the receiver's end is:

132054 138089 054126 100119 123117 102119136119131130138123 123127054137

The received ciphertext will be converted to plain text using the proposed decryption method explained in the following section.

Step I:
Create a table of dimensions n × p and place each element of ciphertext vertically in the cells of the table.

Table 3.21 Table creation when number of columns is odd.

132	138	054	100	123	102	119	138	127
054	089	126	119	117	119	131	123	054
					136	130	123	137
C1	C2	C_3	C_4	C_5	C_6	C_7	C_8	C_9

Step II:
Since the number of columns is odd, so identify the column at center C_5. Now, create a new table of the same dimension and move the elements of column C_1–C_4 of Table 3.21 to column C_6–C_9 of the new table as shown in Table 3.22. Also, Move the elements of column C_6–C_9 of Table 3.21 to column C_1–C_4 of the new table.

Table 3.22 Split first part of the table.

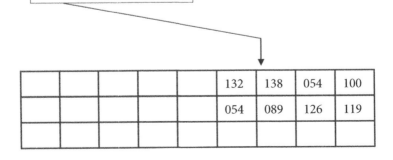

Table 3.23 Split second part of the table.

132	138	054	100	123	102	119	138	127
054	089	126	119	117	119	131	123	054
					136	130	123	137

102	119	138	127	123	132	138	054	100
119	131	123	054	117	054	089	126	119
136	130	123	137					

Step III:

Extract original letters by considering each element as ASCII code in Table 3.23 as shown in Table 3.24.

Table 3.24 Extract original letters by considering each element as ASCII.

P	a	t	i	e	n	t		N
a	m	e		:		C	h	a
r	l	e	s					

Step IV:

Take out each alphabet horizontally to get plain text as shown in Table 3.25.

Table 3.25 Plain text extraction.

P	a	t	i	e	n	t		N	→ Patient
a	m	e		:		C	h	a	→ Name: C
r	l	e	s						→ harles

After decryption, the plain text received is patient name: Charles

3.7.2   Flowchart of Decryption Algorithm

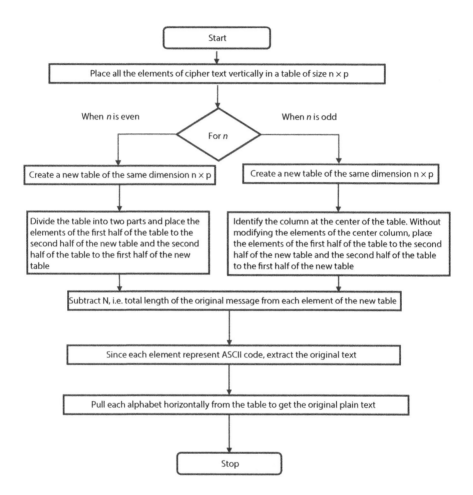

3.8   Experiment and Result

The proposed cryptography method is applied to sample messages to convert the plain text into ciphertext using an encryption algorithm. Also, the time taken by the encryption algorithm to convert the plain text to ciphertext is recorded:

Table 3.26 Time taken for encryption.

Plain text	Cipher text	Time (in a sec)
Patient name is John	118051 129114 135051 051093 099099 130116116123135128129124118	0.00167
Local Address—abcd	127134 055051 084114 119116 095119 117130133118118118119116134	0.00156
Permanent Address—pqrs	119136135132123136123137137 1321 37 102138137123088117136122054 131122134	0.00210
Hospital name—city	124118 135114 116051 127088 091051 124130097135134116137131128	0.00111

The proposed decryption algorithm is applied to decrypt the ciphertext obtained in Table 3.26 and also time is taken by the proposed algorithm to decrypt the ciphertext is recorded.

Table 3.27 Time taken for decryption.

Cipher text	Plain text	Time (in a sec)
127134 055051 084114 119116 095119117130133118118118119116134	Patient name is John	0.00215
119136135132123136123137137 132137 102138137123088117136122054131122134	Local Address- abcd	0.00176
124118 135114 116051 127088 091051124130097135134116137131128	Permanent Address- pqrs	0.00112
118051 129114 135051 051093 099099130116116123135128129124118	Hospital Name- City	0.00196

3.9   Conclusion

The e-Health application hosted in a cloud computing environment has proved to be very useful to monitor the health record of the patient. The e-Health application has allowed the healthcare center's and caretakers to monitor their patients remotely to avoid any emergencies. With increasing online activities and the flow of the high volume of data across Internet networks, it has become very critical to secure the patient's data in an e-Health application hosted in the cloud computing environment. In the proposed work, a new and improved cipher has been proposed which will not allow any hacker to hack the ciphertext and extract the plain text. The proposed encryption algorithm has three levels of encryption, the first level of encryption is converting the plain text into their relative ASCII value. The second level of encryption is adding the value equal to the string length to the result of ASCII code for each alphabet. The third level of encryption is the advanced form of transposition cipher which differs from normal transposition cipher as it has different operations for odd and even number of table column selected by the user as discussed in the sections above. $(x + \alpha)^n = \sum_{k=0}^{n} \binom{n}{k} x^k \alpha^{n-k}$ These three levels of encryption will provide difficulty to the hackers to extract the plain text as compared to any other cipher. The time taken by the algorithm to complete the encryption and decryption process is in milliseconds as demonstrated and shown in Table 3.26 and Table 3.27. In further studies, apart from e-Health applications, the proposed algorithms can be also be used in ciphers while creating SSL connectivity between two applications.

References

1. Jayathilaka, H., Krintz, C., Wolski, R., "Detecting Performance Anomalies in Cloud Platform Applications". *IEEE Trans. Cloud Comput.*, 8, 3, 764–777, July-Sept. 1, 2020.
2. Da Cunha Rodrigues, G., Calheiros, R.N., Guimaraes, V.T., Santos, G.L.D., de Carvalho, M.B., Granville, L.Z. *et al..*, "Monitoring of cloud computing environments: Concepts solutions trends and future directions". *Proc. 31st Annu. ACM Symp. Appl. Comput*, pp. 378–383, 2016, [online] Available: http://doi.acm.org/10.1145/2851613.2851619.
3. Pai, P.P., Sanki, P.K., Sahoo, S.K., De, A., Bhattacharya, S., Banerjee, S., "Cloud computing-based Non-Invasive Glucose Monitoring for Diabetic Care". *IEEE Trans. Circuits Syst. I Regul. Pap.*, 65, 2, 663–676, Feb. 2018.

4. Gu, C., Li, Z., Huang, H., Jia, X., "Energy Efficient Scheduling of Servers with Multi-Sleep Modes for Cloud Data Center". *IEEE Trans. Cloud Comput.*, 8, 3, 1, 833–846, 2020.

5. Dr.Islam, M.D.R. and Mazumder, T., "Mobile application and its global impact". *Int. J. Eng. Technol.*, 10, 6, 72–78, January 2010.

5. Atayero, A.A., Williams, R., Badejo, J.A., Popoola, S.I., "Cloud-based IoT-enabled solid waste monitoring system for smart and connected communities". *Int. J. Civ. Eng. Technol.*, 10, 2, 2308–2315, 2019.

6. Farahani, B., Firouzi, F., Chang, V., Badaroglu, M., Constant, N., Mankodiya, K., "Towards fog-driven IoT eHealth: Promises and challenges of IoT in medicine and healthcare". *Future Gener. Comput. Syst.*, 78, 659–676, January 2018.

7. Selvaraj, S. and Sundaravaradhan, S., Challenges and opportunities in IoT healthcare systems: A systematic review. *SN Appl. Sci.*, 2, 1, 139, 2020.

8. Kadhim, K.T., Alsahlany, A.M., Wadi, S.M., Kadhum, H.T., "An Overview of Patient's Health Status Monitoring System Based on Internet of Things (IoT)". *Wirel. Pers. Commun.*, 114, 2235–2262, 2020.

9. Mukhopadhyay, A., Sreenadh, M., Anoop, A., "eHealth Applications: A Comprehensive Approach". *2020 International Conference on Emerging Trends in Information Technology and Engineering (ic-ETITE)*.

10. Baccar, N. and Bouallegue, R., "A new web-based e-health platform". *014 IEEE 10th International Conference on Wireless and Mobile Computing, Networking and Communications (WiMob)*.

11. Singh, I., Kumar, D., Khatri, S.K., "Improving The Efficiency of E-Healthcare System Based on Cloud". *2019 Amity International Conference on Artificial Intelligence (AICAI)*.

12. Jayathilaka, H., Krintz, C., Wolski, R., "Detecting Performance Anomalies in Cloud Platform Applications". *IEEE Trans. Cloud Comput.*, 8, 3, July-Sept. 1, 764–777, 2020.

13. Jemal, H., Kechaou, Z., Ayed, M.B., Adel, M., Cloud Computing and Mobile Devices Based System for Healthcare Application. *IEEE International Symposium on Technology in Society (ISTAS) Proceedings*, 2015.

14. Farahani, B., Firouzi, F., Chang, V., Badaroglu, M., Constant, N., Mankodiya, K., "Towards fog-driven IoT eHealth: Promises and challenges of IoT in medicine and healthcare". *Future Gener. Comput. Syst.*, 78, 659–676, January 2018.

15. Shah, S.T.U., Yar, H., Khan, I., Ikram, M., Khan, H., "Internet of Things-Based Healthcare: Recent Advances and Challenges", in: *Applications of Intelligent Technologies in Healthcare*, pp. 153–162, Springer, Cham, 2019.

16. Gil, D., Ferrández, A., Mora-Mora, H., Peral, J., "Internet of things: A review of surveys based on context-aware intelligent services". *Sensors*, 16, 7, 1069, July 2016.

17. Bhatt, C.M., Dey, N., Ashour, A., *Internet of Things and Big Data Technologies for Next Generation Healthcare*, vol. 23, Springer, Cham, 2017 https://doi.org/10.1007/978-3-319-49736-5 vol. 23, Springer, Cham, 20.

18. Farahani, B., Firouzi, F., Chang, V., Badaroglu, M., Constant, N., Mankodiya, K., "Towards fog-driven IoT eHealth: Promises and challenges of IoT in medicine and healthcare". *Future Gener. Comput. Syst.*, 78, 659–676, January 2018.

19. Shah, S.T.U., Yar, H., Khan, I., Ikram, M., Khan, H., "Internet of Things-Based Healthcare: Recent Advances and Challenges", in: *Applications of Intelligent Technologies in Healthcare*, pp. 153–162, Springer, Cham, 2019.

20. Davies, D., "A brief history of cryptography", in: *Information Security Technical Report*, vol. 2, pp. 14–17, 1997.

21. Elmogy, A., Bouteraa, Y., Alshabanat, R., Alghaslan, W., "A New Cryptography Algorithm Based on ASCII Code". *2019 19th International Conference on Sciences and Techniques of Automatic Control and Computer Engineering (STA)*.

22. Harmouch, Y. and El-Kouch, R., "A New Algorithm for Dynamic Encryption". *Int. J. Innov. Appl. Stud.*, 10, 1, 305–312, 2015.

23. Adams, C., "Designing against a class of algebraic attacks on symmetric block ciphers". *Int. J. Appl. Algebra Eng. Commun. Comput.*, 17, 17–27, 2006.

24. Sharma Prabhjot, N. and Kaur, H., "A Review of Information Security using Cryptography Technique". *Int. J. Adv. Res. Comput. Sci.*, 8, Special Issue, 323–326, 2017.

25. Tayal, S., Gupta, N., Gupta, P., Goyal, D., Goyal, M., "A Review paper on Network Security and Cryptography". *Adv. Comput. Sci. Technol.*, 10, 5, 763–770, 2017.

26. Prajapat, S. and Thakur, R., "Time variant approach towards symmetric key". *Proceedings of SAI 2013*, IEEE, pp. 398–405, 2015.

27. Bhargava, U., Sharma, A., Chawla, R., Thakral, P., "A new algorithm combining substitution & transposition cipher techniques for secure communication". *2017 International Conference on Trends in Electronics and Informatics (ICEI)*, IEEE.

28. Fernando, M.G.Z., Sison, A.M., Medina, R.P., "Securing Private Key using New Transposition Cipher Technique". *2019 IEEE Eurasia Conference on IoT, Communication, and Engineering (ECICE)*.

29. Bhargava, U., Sharma, A., Chawla, R., Thakral, P., "A new algorithm combining substitution & transposition cipher techniques for secure communication". *Proc. - Int. Conf. Trends Electron. Informatics ICEI 2017*, vol. 2018-Janua, pp. 619–624, 2018.

30. Rihartanto, R., Supriadi, S., Utomo, D.S.B., "Image Tiling Using Columnar Transposition". *2018 International Conference on Applied Information Technology and Innovation (ICAITI)*.

31. Sajid, M., Khizrai, Q., Bodkhe, P.S.T., "Image Encryption using Different Techniques for High-Security Transmission over a Network". *Int. J. Eng. Res. Gen. Sci.*, 2, 4, 299–306, 2014.

32. Jaju, S.A. and Chowhan, S.S., "A Modified RSA algorithm to enhance security for digital signature". *2015 Int. Conf. Work. Comput. Commun. IEMCON,* 2015.

33. Soliman, S.M., Magdy, B., El Ghany, M.A.A., "Efficient Implementation of the AES algorithm for security applications". *2016 29th IEEE International System-on-Chip Conference (SOCC).*

34. D'souza, F.J. and Panchal, D., "Advanced encryption standard (AES) security enhancement using hybrid approach". *2017 International Conference on Computing, Communication, and Automation (ICCCA).*

35. Qadir, A.M. and Varol, N., "A Review Paper on Cryptography". *2019 7th International Symposium on Digital Forensics and Security (ISDFS).*

36. Hasan, Z., Agrawal, C.P., Agrawal, M.A., "Online Transaction Security Enhancement": An Algorithm Based on Cryptography". *2019 International Conference on Issues and Challenges in Intelligent Computing Techniques (ICICT) .*

4

Cutaneous Disease Optimization Using Teledermatology Underresourced Clinics

Supriya M.*, Murugan K., Shanmugaraja T. and Venkatesh T.

KPR Institute of Engineering and Technology, Coimbatore, India

Abstract

Access to dermatologists is limited for disadvantaged patients, who may receive suboptimal dermatologic care from nonspecialists. We assessed if teledermatology could improve primary care provider (PCP) delivered care for cutaneous disease at a clinic serving uninsured patients. Utilizing the American Academy of Dermatology's free Access Dermatology program, we offered store-and-forward teledermatology to PCPs, who initiated consultations at will during clinical care independent of the study. We, respectively, analyzed all consultations and collected patient age, teledermatology diagnosis, time to teledermatology reply, time to next dermatology appointment, as well as PCP and teledermatologist-proposed care plans. Retrospective analysis of 131 consults revealed a 37-hour mean teledermatology response-time versus a 14-day appointment wait ($p < 0.00001$). Teledermatologist provided a definitive care plan without in-person evaluation for 82 (65%) of completed consults and recommended interimtreatments while awaiting appointments in 15 cases, thus accelerating care plan delivery in 97 cases (76%). The triage decision rate differed among diagnostic categories; deferral to in-person evaluation was more frequent for neoplasms ($p < 0.0001$). When PCPs specified preconsult treatment plans, 82% differed from teledermatologist-advised management. Following teledermatologist recommendations would have changed the clinical course in 70% of cases, potentiallyavoiding suboptimal care, including inappropriate cortical-steroids, antimicrobials, and emergency room referrals. We found teledermatology can effectively guide PCPs in resource-limited settings by accelerating delivery of dermatologist-recommended care plans for uninsured patients. Expanding teledermatology for PCPs in underresourced clinics has the potential to improve treatment of cutaneous disease by nonspecialists and to mitigate suboptimal care for disadvantaged patients.

*Corresponding author: supriyavimala@gmail.com

R. Nidhya, Manish Kumar and S. Balamurugan (eds.) Tele-Healthcare: Applications of Artificial Intelligence and Soft Computing Techniques, (85–100) © 2022 Scrivener Publishing LLC

Keywords: Clinical outreach, dermatology, healthcare access, healthcare disparities, store-and-forward, teledermatology, telemedicine, underserved

4.1 Introduction

While skin issues are a common cause for skin problems, for visiting a provider of healthcare [1, 2], including in charitable clinics, four access to dermatologists are needed for patients. In the western world, it is restricted, and this has an overwhelming impact on disadvantaged, uninsured, and underinsured individuals. Accordingly, these vulnerable groups are more nondermatologists, likely to receive treatment for cutaneous disease providers of primary care, which could result in suboptimal performances. The rise of teledermatology has a realistic approach for reducing this gap in healthcare.

Lack of timely and secure access to underresourced clinic consultation with a dermatologist [3], and the importance of the feedback of a specialist in such settings have been highlighted in studies that show that diagnoses and therapies suggested by primary care provider (PCP) and teledermatologists differ greatly for cutaneous problems. Previous studies have shown that teledermatology has remote dermatologists that can direct PCPs through outreach programs caring for needy patients who otherwise would not receive treatment. Application of teledermatology in reality, PCP perception of dermatological conditions has been enhanced [4] and accelerated provision of care, [5] which could enhance patient delivery of quality of life [6]. In addition, the outreach of teledermatology will have a substantial economic impact by avoiding more expensive costs of receiving dermatological services, such as emergency care visit.

The aim of our research is to determine whether PCP-delivered teledermatology treatment for patients may improve the lack of access to dermatologists with an emphasis on their potential to minimize procedures that are suboptimal. To that end, a partnership was evaluated for voluntary academic teledermatology outreach and health clinic for the metropolitan poor serving solely uninsured patients [7]. Using the American Academy of Dermatology (AAD) store-and-forward platform for teledermatology, PCP consultations were examined, respectively, to assess the possible effect of remote control input from dermatologists on time-to-care and leadership plans in the case of cutaneous illness.

4.2   Materials and Methods

4.2.1   Clinical Setting and Teledermatology Workflow

All PCPs offered free of charge and voluntary participation in the portability of AAD health insurance store-and-forward compliant and trans-
parency act-compliant access teledermatology platform. The enrolees have
been given a one-time in-person demonstration or an explanatory power
point file. The PCPs may use access to apply consultations via a smartphone application or a web-based application platform. The electronic consult method for teledermatology PCPs were encouraged to include patient
age, gender, a focused history of dermatological worry, and the patient's
photograph findings of physical examinations [8]. No other patient information identifiers have been collected. Alternatively, PCPs were asked to
have differentials of their own until receiving a teledermatologist's diagnosis and treatment plantips, including whether the patient was going to
be referred in the absence of an ER or urgent care center consultation of
teledermatology.

All PCP-submitted consultations were evaluated by one of the consultants. Several voluntary remote board-certified dermatologists at
Pennsylvania University, after an e-mail receipt notification of the first
available teledermatologists for each new appointment, the consultation
will be requested and a reply provided as time allowed, solely for the purpose of guiding patients. Regardless of the study, treatment teledermatologists have been invited to include a diagnosis and a course of treatment,
including a recommendation as to whether an in-person assessment by a
dermatologist is needed.

4.2.2   Study Design, Data Collection, and Analysis

With the permission of the Institutional University of Pennsylvaniaa case
management commission examined, sequence of all consultants in teledermatology (N = 131) was obtained between January 2013 and November
2017. Consultations on teledermatology are deemed complete if at least
one photograph was uploaded by the PCP and the teledermatologist will
furnish every treatment strategy. Data extracted for each consultation
completed included patient's age and gender, time of consultation submis-
sion, time of response from the consultant, as well as PCP and teledermatologist proposed treatment and diagnosis blueprints [9]. To measure
the mean and median, these data used time-to-reply for consultation with

teledermatology versus waiting. As reported, time for the next dermatology clinical schedule compares the values using signed-ranked test.

For all consultations, the average deferral rate was estimated for the number of completed cases in which teledermatologists involved are dependent on recommended in-person assessment. The number for neoplasms, deferrals, and no deferrals were measured. Compared with non-neoplasms and compared using the same Fisher's test, the justification for the in-person assessment was identified. From the strategy of the teledermatologist, the uncertainty diagnosis (in-person visualization suggested prior todiagnosis) or stated criteria for a nonselective operation will be carried out in the dermatology clinic (e.g., biopsy of lesions, into destruction). Teledermatology has been considered to speed up treatment delivery if (i) a definitive treatment plan by a teledermatologist or (ii) any provisional treatment plan [10]. The teledermatologist was advised to start when the patient was awaiting for dermatology, the PCP nomination.

For each case where the recovery plan has been specified by the treatment plan, the PCP submitted proposal was classified by PCP (N = 72), C.L.S. treatment was based solely on the reference to the recommended teledermatologist as reported in access dermatology, the treatment plan. The PCP plans were deemed to be distinct from those of the teledermatologists, if any of them (i) included some particular treatment/plan that the teledermatologist did not suggest or (ii) any other treatment/plan was excluded, which the teledermatologist suggested. Examples of PCP tactics found to be overtreatment of an antibiotic, an antiviral agent, an anti-mycotic agent, or a corticosteroid, if none of these were specifically present, the teledermatologist suggested it. The analysis accepted the university (Protocol 832136) institutional review board of Pennsylvania.

4.3   Proposed System

4.3.1   Teledermatology in an Underresourced Clinic

Improving access to consultation with dermatologists in a primary clinic setting for treatment that serves vulnerable people, a nonprofit, with PCPs community health clinic that exclusively takes care of uninsured citizen patients, many of whom are Latino immigrants who face all kinds of problem barriers to healthcare [11]. Enrolment in PCPs was provided inaccess to request consultations in the field of teledermatology during their regular clinical care course "Substances and Processes." A board-certified organization volunteer dermatologist responded to consultations to direct

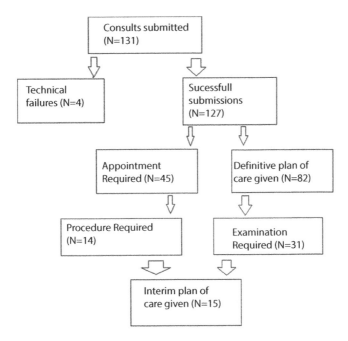

Figure 4.1 Teledermatology consult.

independent PCPs of the analysis. To identify the viability of store-and-forward, we studied teledermatology in this environment and teledermatology consultations over the course of the duration for analysis (Figure 4.1). Of all the consultations (N = 131) requested, we observed that the 97% completion rate for teledermatologists were acquired historical and photographic data to supply a reply. This means that after a minimum of path, PCPs were able to use the access successfully. Just four instances (3%) were considered technical, failures of these were attributable to early photograph omission, the introduction of the software, which banned teledermatologists, from offering any particular instructions.

4.3.2   Teledermatology Consultations from Uninsured Patients

The patients included in our 131 case series were 63% male, and they were 31.7 years old on average (range, 1–92 years). All were missing health benefits, a prerequisite to be taken care of all. To describe the essence of the skin problems that drive teledermatology consultation, each of the consultations completed (N = 127) was classified as centered on the diagnosis suggested by teledermatologists (Table 4.1). The most common diagnosis of infectious skin (18%, 23/127) was fungal or viral infections, such as tinea or verrucae, and hair disorders have also been suspected (7%, 9/127).

Table 4.1(a) Teledermatology consult characteristics.

Characteristics	N=131
Sex	
Male	83 (63%)
Female	48 (37%)
Age (years)	
Average (±SD)	31.7 (±10.9)
Range (IQR)	1–92 (25–37.5)

Table 4.1(b) Diagnostic category.

Diagnostic category	Number of cases (%)	% Deferred to in-person
Inflammatory eruptions	55 (43%)	24% (13/55)
Nonpigmented neoplasms	25 (20%)	64% (16/25)
Infectious diseases	23 (18%)	30% (7/23)
Hair disorders	9 (7%)	11% (1/9)
Pigmented neoplasms	7 (6%)	71% (5/7)
Pigmentary disorders	4 (3%)	50% (2/4)
Other	4 (3%)	25% (1/4)
Total	127	35% (45/127)

SD, standard deviation; IQR, interquartile range.

4.3.3   Teledermatology for Patients Lacking Access to Dermatologists

We evaluated whether teledermatology consultations produced by PCP were sufficient for remote dermatologists to be allowed to deliver clear care plans based on the history given photographs. Of the consultations done, in 65% (82/127) of cases, teledermatologists decided that initially, an in-person evaluation was not needed, and a conclusive evaluation care plan was provided to the PCP via remote delivery. Even if it was difficult for teledermatologists to make a definitive treatment plan, they have been able to recommend aninterim therapy, which could be begun immediately by means of interim therapy in 33% (15/45) of cases referred to an in-person case, the PCP appointment. In complete teledermatology, the operation of a dermatologist-recommended treatment plan for 76% (97/127) of this study's patients has accelerated.

Of the 35% (45/127) of cases referred for in-person reference, the reasons behind this decision were the diagnosis and appointment. An uncertainty needs evaluation (24% of all examinations), events (31/127) or a nonselective procedure prerequisite (11% in all cases, 14/127), such as destruction of the lesion.

The level of deferment to in-person assessment varies, which is centered on the diagnosis category that was made by the teledermatologist (Table 4.2). While teledermatologists have recommended in-person review of 71% pigmented animal neoplasms and 64% of nonpigmented neoplasms, 11% just hair diseases, and 24% of inflammatory eruptions needed appointment to a dermatologist, the discrepancy between the 66% (21/32) deferral averages for every neoplasm, which is statistically equivalent to 25% (24/95) for nonneoplasms, is important (p value < 0.0001, Fisher exact test).

Both patients must wait in the absence of teledermatology for the next dermatology clinic in person to receive input specialist [12, 13]. Quantifying

Table 4.2 Teledermatology timing and deferral rate.

Disease category	Deferral rate (%)
Neoplasms	21/32 (66%)
Non-neoplasms	24/95 (25%)
Fisher's exact test	$p<0.0001$
Time to specialist input (Days)	Average (±SEM)
Teledermatology	1.6 (±0.3)
In-person appointment	13.9 (±0.9)
Wilcoxon signed-rank test	p< 0.00001

SEM, standard error of the means.

the effects of teledermatology, we measured the time-to-care for patients, the average time for teledermatology consultations to answer and compared this with the average time for the next in-person to wait monthly dermatology consultation (Table 4.2) Clinic. A mean response to teledermatology period of 1.6 days was considerably shorter than the wait for an appointment, i.e., a period of 13.9 days. Through consultation with teledermatology, dermatologist's average decrease in wait time the input was 12.3 days (296 h; SEM, 22days).

4.3.4 Teledermatologist Management from Nonspecialists

Primary care providers were required to include their consultants when submitting a consultation of the patient's suggested course of treatment if teledermatology was not available. Compared with specific PCP-reported results, the preconsult recovery plans (N = 72), suggested by teledermatologists in 82% (59/72) of cases, differed, focusing on the importance of expert reviews for management cutaneous sickness. For primary care providers in the remaining cases (N = 55), a clear plan was given, or they clearly mention that they would be referred to dermatology.

Analyzing all cases completed (N = 127), we find that implementation of the recommendations was delivered via teledermatology. It would have resulted in a big 70% (89/127) of the cases, which are shifts in the patient's course of treatment. The possible suboptimal results were further defined by using those 89 cases that would have happened if the PCP proposed the technique, which was adopted in the absence of advice given by teledermatology at the specialist level (Table 4.3). We have listed PCP-proposed proposals in 27% (34/127) of the cases, under treatment; examples include failure to treat a suspected infection, a sufficiently strong topical corticosteroid, or a systemic inflammatory agent. On the other hand, we considered PCP-proposed overtreatment of plans in 11% of the cases (14/127); examples included unnecessary use of antifungal agents, oral antibiotics, corticosteroids, or systemic [14].

In 26% (33/127) of the cases, the receipt of a treatment plan by the patient in the absence of teledermatology. This would have simply been postponed in those situations. It was the PCP strategy to refer to the dermatology clinic but the teledermatologist advised an interim therapy that could be promptly started or given more rapid reassurance distribution [15]. In the latter instances, teledermatology permitted the clinic to assign its restricted specialist appointments more efficiently to those patients really need an in-person examination by a dermatologist.

Table 4.3 Outcomes.

Potential result of PCP plan	N (% of complete results)
Undertreatment	34 (27%)
Weak topical corticosteroid	11 (8.7%)
Missed infection	7 (5.5%)
Missed referral	7 (5.5%)
Suboptimal topical agent	7 (5.5%)
Suboptimal acne regimen	2 (1.6%)
Overtreatment	14 (11%)
Antifungal	7 (5.5%)
Antibiotic	4 (3.1%)
Antiviral	1 (0.8%)
Oral corticosteroid	1 (0.8%)
Potent topical steroid	1 (0.8%)
Delay of care	33 (26%)
Unnecessary ER referral	8 (6%)
Total	89 (70%)

PCP, primary care provider; ER, emergency room.

Dermatologist finally tested whether the proposed disposition could have been altered for the patient by using teledermatology.

In eight instances (6.3%), PCPs suggested that the patient would have been referred to an ER or urgent care facility consultation in the absence of teledermatology [16, 17]. These findings stress the potential for teledermatology to have a good effect on the use of healthcare services for cutaneous sickness.

4.3.5   Segment Factors of Referring PCPs and Their Patients

We led hour-long meetings with 10 PCPs who allude patients to teledermatology consistently and who serve a normal total reference base of

2,760 teledermatology cases yearly. A lot of overviewed PCPs detailed that they rehearsed in federally qualified health centers. With respect to their patients' socioeconomics, the PCPs revealed that patients are from assorted racial and ethnic foundations, are basically poor by government principles and are uninsured or underinsured. When asked how they invested their energy expertly, this gathering of PCPs detailed that they spent a mean of 74% of their expert time in all medication, 4% of their time in teledermatology and 17% of their time in organization. The PCPs detailed that they have been occupied with teledermatology in California for a mean of 4.79 a long time (standard deviation, 5 years) [18]. The vast majority of PCPs revealed utilizing S&F teledermatology and 20% of PCP announced utilizing LI teledermatology. Of the 80% of PCPs, who have been engaged with S&F teledermatology, 62% made formal preparations in telemedicine.

4.3.6   Teledermatology Operational Considerations

When solicited, 100% of PCPs reacted that expanding access for the patients was the essential explanation that they partook in teledermatology. At the point, when we asked the essential consideration, 40% of the PCPs revealed that they have no particular staffing necessity. Among the remainder of the PCPs, the detailed utilizing medical care experts, everything being equal, including doctors, mid-level suppliers, clinical collaborators, or nonmedical work force, to help with various parts of the teledermatology activity. Ordinarily, there are no devoted timetables for S&F teledermatology, and patients get their pictures taken at the hour of their essential consideration visit. When questioned about the additional obligation of conveying teledermatologists' suggestions with patients, 90% of PCPs invited this additional obligation.

4.3.7   Instruction of PCPs

At the point when we asked PCPs whether their arrangement of dermatologic issues has improved due to the accessibility of teledermatology administration, 100% of PCPs detailed that their agreement has improved and expanded. Moreover, they detailed that the kinds of skin issues for which they make a teledermatology reference have changed after some time. Although PCPs alluded respectably testing yet basic skin infections at the start of the reference timeframe, the reference rate for regular skin sicknesses declined after some time as they figured out how to oversee them through teledermatology [19, 20].

4.4   Challenges

When we asked the essential consideration of doctors, the estimation of S&F teledermatology for their medical populace is 100% detailed and announced that they might want to see more teledermatology administration given to the medical patients. Besides, if more teledermatologists were accessible, 90% PCPs revealed that they would allude more patients to teledermatologists. The essential consideration of doctors were approached to distinguish factors significant to the achievement of a teledermatology activity [21–23]. The PCPs announced the accompanying two factors as being vital to an effective teledermatology activity: convenient admittance to dermatologists (60%) and collegial PCP–dermatologist connections that take into consideration discourse on persistent issues (40%).

We requested that PCPs distinguish the most testing parts of taking an interest in teledermatology. The PCPs distinguished the accompanying challenges: actualizing dermatologists' proposals (40%), disturbances in their work stream because of joining teledermatology (40%), and troubles in capturing skin injuries (20%). At long last, the PCPs were asked which aspect of teledermatology activity required improvement [24–26]. The PCPs announced improvement in work process (30%), decline in meeting cost (30%), quicker turnaround time for counsels (20%) [27], improvement in correspondence with the dermatologist (20%) and innovative upgrades (10%) [28].

4.5   Results and Discussion

Ubiquitous smartphones fitted with cameras provide the opportunity to give remote dermatologists high-quality images to review and provide PCPs with clinical advice with good accuracy in diagnosis and high customer satisfaction. This technology has the power to speed up the provision of advice from dermatologists to nonspecialists who care about dermatologist's disadvantaged populations and suboptimal mitigation cutaneous disease management. Consequently, we found that treatment options suggested by teledermatologists vary. The bulk of patients will have altered management as significantly suggested by PCPs.

Our research confirms that cutaneous disease is usually found in the skin. The findings were close to those of previous research and were used in primary care. Looking in practice at the breakdown of dermatological diagnoses, the main diagnostic community was found to be eczema in its different types. Exanthemata (15.9%), impetigo (7.6%), and 19.2% of the total (5.1%).

It could have contributed to major healthcare reforms, more judicious use of antimicrobial agents and antimicrobials, like avoidance of referrals from intensive care. Our analysis shows how teledermatology consultation can be stored and implemented to help underresourced PCPs working in clinics, which also have restricted expert access. Still teledermatology may be found to be used as a triage mechanism, reducing the number of in-person patients needing assessment and could considerably shorten the patient queue. Awaiting appointments for dermatology that can become volunteer run specialty outreach clinics, it was very long.

4.5.1   Challenges of Referring to Teledermatology Services

The effects of review exhibit that 100% of overviewed PCPs find teledermatology is very significant. Our overview explained that the essential explanation of PCPs take an interest in teledermatology reference to open the entryways of admittance to dermatology administrations for their patients. Expanding admittance to strength care, taking an interest in teledermatology gives an instructive occasion to essential care doctors. After some time, as their profundity of information has expanded, these PCPs who routinely take an interest in the teledermatology reference measure have figured out how to oversee basic skin conditions themselves. Furthermore, we required less dermatological references. While improving medical services access and giving instructive occasions to alluding doctors, teledermatology may likewise assist with lessening the medical services cost to society as PCPs figure out how to oversee testing cases of regular skin illnesses and as people who some time ago could not have acquired dermatology care get treatment during the prior, additional treatable phases of their skin infections.

Although our study's size and unique setting can limit its size, even our relationship gives considerable insight into the cutaneous diseases seen inclinic that serve uninsured patients particularly Latino patients. Although data on race and ethnicity were not specifically available, the availability of Spanish-speaking language collected in our research Spanish-focused society and medical workers certainly, outreach services in our case, improved the representation of Latino patient'sseries and affected the diagnosis distribution. Until inquiry, pre inquiry the Latino population has been revealed in the United States faces various challenges to pursuit and acquisition of healthcare in the U.S., including expenses, legal fees, status, travel, prejudice, and language. Although previous studies have documented detailed dermatologic studies, there are problems facing Latino workers in rural areas, particularly in rural areas. Our teledermatology relationship, agricultural ecosystems, PCPs helped us to evaluate dermatological consultation from an inner city public health clinic with a strong emphasis on supporting the Latino urban culture.

Our research was based on a collaboration with a community health organization, clinic in an urban environment, but expanding access to access. The shortage of dermatologists employed in remote rural areas can also beresolved by specialist feedback through teledermatology platforms. In fact, previous studies have shown that teledermatology has programs of outreach similar to ours have increasedentry to care at the specialist level in rural areas of the United States and resource-limited remote areas of Countries, travelling in person to see urban experts. In addition, though our median is pending, our in-person dermatologist examination lasted 14 days. This underestimates the wait time of on-site volunteer clinic. In the United States where a new patient is waiting for the average, the visit to dermatology was found to be more than a month. The consequent delay in treatment further underlines the future importance of care using teledermatology systems for triagedermatological consultation to help prioritize more patients. Urgent cutaneous eruptions or lesions that involve expedited eruptions or lesion referrals from experts.

In summary, we have demonstrated that voluntary consultation inteledermatology programs, such as ours, can offer a lot efficiently. Specialist level advice is required for PCPs caring for uninsured people populations, which typically have cutaneous problems. The scalability and sustainability of outreach to teledermatology, especially it can be logistically demanding when volunteer-dependent. Even though different organizations have outlined plans for expanding services for teledermatology, in addition to access Community Healthcare's Dermatology extension outcome program and separate outcomes in the United States, international collaboration networks have grown effectively by PCP to specialist advice via electronic consultation with dermatologists off-site via its platform. The AAD actively includes and enrols PCPs who work in hospitals.

The low incidence of malignant tumours seen in primary care indicates that we accept the recommendations of the National Institute for Health and Clinical Excellence that indicates that the management of most skin cancers in secondary care should take place. It will focus education programmes on separating benign from malignant skin tumours. It also helps to minimise excessive secondary care.

Serve patients with restricted access to dermatology to pair them with one another with accredited volunteer teledermatologists in their state and to train users to use the free access dorm platform. We are hoping that our findings will promote engagement in teledermatology outreach attempts that have the ability to broaden access to dermatologists tips for vulnerable patients who do not want toreceive specialist-level treatment, which may ultimately help to reduce differences of dermatology of healthcare.

References

1. Wilmer, E.N. *et al.*, Most common dermatologic conditions encountered by dermatologists and nondermatologists. *Cutis*, 94, 285–292, 2014.
2. Kerr, O.A. *et al.*, The profile of dermatological problems in primarycare. *Clin. Exp. Dermatol.*, 35, 380–383, 2010.
3. Lowell, B.A. *et al.*, Dermatology in primary care: prevalence and patient disposition. *J. Am. Acad. Dermatol.*, 45, 250–255, 2001.
4. Ayoubi, N. *et al.*, Dermatologic care of uninsured patients managed at free clinics. *J. Am. Acad. Dermatol.*, 81, 433–437, 2019.
5. Resneck, J.S., Jr., Isenstein, A., Kimball, A.B., Few Medicaid and uninsured patients are accessing dermatologists. *J. Am. Acad. Dermatol.*, 55, 1084–1088, 2006.
6. Mulcahy, A. *et al.*, Variation in dermatologist visits by sociodemographic characteristics. *J. Am. Acad. Dermatol.*, 76, 918–924, 2017.
7. James, W.D., The use of technology in providing dermatologic care to vulnerable populations. *Cutis*, 89, 53–54, 2012.
8. Chansky, P.B., Simpson, C.L., Lipoff, J.B., Implementation of a dermatology teletriage system to improve access in an underserved clinic: a retrospective study. *J. Am. Acad. Dermatol.*, 77, 975–977, 2017.
9. Nelson, C.A. *et al.*, Impact of store-and-forward (SAF) tele-dermatology on outpatient dermatologic care: a prospective study in an underserved urban primary care setting. *J. Am. Acad. Dermatol.*, 74, 484.e1–490.e1, 2016.
10. Uscher-Pines, L. *et al.*, Effect of tele-dermatology on access to dermatology care among Medicaid enrollees. *JAMA Dermatol.*, 152, 905–912, 2016.
11. Armstrong, A.W. *et al.*, Tele-dermatology operational considerations, challenges, and benefits: the referring providers' perspective. *Telemed. J. eHealth*, 18, 580–584, 2012.
12. Murugan, K., Daniel, F., Shanmugaraja, T., Siddharthraju, K., Dhivya Devi, R., Supriya, M., A critical review on medical image processing techniques. *J. Crit. Rev.*, 7, 5, 576–580, 2020.
13. Naka, F., Lu, J., Porto, A., Villagra, J., Wu, Z.H., Anderson, D., Impact of dermatology eConsults on access to care and skin cancer screening in underserved populations: a model for tele-dermatology services in community health centers. *J. Am. Acad. Dermatol.*, 78, 293–302, 2018.

14. Mohan, G.C., Molina, G.E., Stavert, R., Store and forward tele-dermatology improves dermatology knowledge among referring primary care providers: A survey-based cohort study. *J. Am. Acad. Dermatol.*, 79, 960–961, 2018.

15. Piette, E., Nougairede, M., Vuong, V., Crickx, B., Tran, V.T., Impact of a store-and-forward tele-dermatology intervention versus usual care on delay before beginning treatment: a pragmatic cluster-randomized trial in ambulatory care. *J. Telemed. Telecare*, 23, 725–732, 2017.

16. Whited, J.D., Quality of life: a research gap in teledermatology. *Int. J. Dermatol.*, 54, 1124–1128, 2015.

17. Yang, X., Barbieri, J.S., Kovarik, C.L., Cost analysis of a store and forward tele-dermatology consult system in Philadelphia. *J. Am. Acad. Dermatol.*, 81, 758–764, 2019.

18. Warshaw, E.M., Gravely, A.A., Nelson, D.B., Reliability of store and forward tele-dermatology for skin neoplasms. *J. Am. Acad. Dermatol.*, 72, 426–435, 2015.

19. Warshaw, E.M. *et al.*, Accuracy of tele-dermatology for pigmented neoplasms *J. Am. Acad. Dermatol.*, 61, 753–765, 2009.

20. Barbieri, J.S. *et al.*, Primary care providers' perceptions of mobile store-and-forward teledermatology. *Dermatol. Online J.*, 21, pii13030/qt2jt0h05w, 2015.

21. Edison, K.E., Ward, D.S., Dyer, J.A., Lane, W., Chance, L., Hicks, L.L., Diagnosis, diagnostic confidence, and management concordance in live-interactive and store-and forward teledermatology compared to in-person examination. *Telemed. J. E Health*, 14, 889–895, 2008.

22. Krupinski, E., Burdick, A., Pak, H. *et al.*, American Telemedicine Association's practice guidelines for teledermatology. *Telemed. J. E Health*, 14, 289–302, 2008.

23. Johnson, M. and Armstrong, A., Technologies in dermatology: Teledermatology review. *G. Ital. Dermatol. Venereol.*, 146, 143–153, 2011.

24. Pathipati, A., Lee, L., Armstrong, A., Healthcare delivery methods in teleder-matology: Consultative, triage and direct-care models. *J. Telemed. Telecare*, 17, 214–216, 2011.

25. Pak, H., Edison, K., Whited, J., *Teledermatology: a user's guide*, Cambridge University Press, New York, 2008.

26. Warshaw, E.M., Hillman, Y.J., Greer, N.L. *et al.*, Teledermatology for diag-nosis and management of skin conditions: A systematic review. *J. Am. Acad. Dermatol.*, 64, 759–772, 2011.

27. Edison, K.E. and Dyer, J.A., Teledermatology in Missouri and beyond. *Mo. Med.*, 104, 139–143, 2007.

28. Group ATATSO (American Telemedicine Association Teledermatology Special Interest Group), *ATA U.S. Teledermatology Program Survey 2003*, American Telemedicine, Washington, DC, 2018.

5

Cognitive Assessment Based on Eye Tracking Using Device-Embedded Cameras via Tele-Neuropsychology

Shanmugaraja T.*, Venkatesh T., Supriya M. and Murugan K.

KPR Institute of Engineering and Technology, Coimbatore, India

Abstract

A significant issue to address the ageing population increases widespread screening for cognitive impairment, a lack of medical centers to get the needs for self-assessment is grooming in current scenario. Long distributed evaluations using webcam eye following information, visual paired comparison (VPC) tasks, could enhance permission to external, intermittent testing for cognitive cancelling than more confirmation against medical-grade eye follower is needed. The evaluations are done over three visits by collecting VPC data from 18 participants, aged 50 years and older, and possessing regular cognitive ability to show the equivalence between the current automatic point device for eye follower measures received by means of a laptop-bedded. The eye tracker information was collected through the program of the manufacturer, and the webcam data were computed using a new method. Programmatic marking of VPC webcam data showed clear associations with the medical lens. Average VPC showed efficiency correlation over all periods (s = 0.96; R1 s = 0.95; R2 s = 0.89; R3 s = 0.98; t's< 0.002). Correlation of results over time was stable as well (s = 0.87; R1 s = 0.86; R2 s = 0.90; R3 s = 0.91; t's < 0.002). The average difference of each device's output data was 0.00. These findings indicate that device-based cameras are a valid and versatile option for gaze-based tasks of assessment of cognitive function to conventional laboratory-based equipment. For tele-neuropsychology, validation of this approach reflects significant technical advancements.

Keywords: E-health, m-health, tele-health, tele-medicine, tele-neurology

Corresponding author: shanmugarajatsr@gmail.com

R. Nidhya, Manish Kumar and S. Balamurugan (eds.) Tele-Healthcare: Applications of Artificial Intelligence and Soft Computing Techniques, (101–116) © 2022 Scrivener Publishing LLC

5.1   Introduction

Alzheimer's disease and associated dementias reflect one of the greatest modern public health issues of time [1, 2]. Early detection of symptoms is essential [3]; however, there is inadequate healthcare infrastructure at present. To fulfil the in-person screening demand, visual type of eye tracking-based paired comparison tasks, cognitive test has been shown to be reliable in detecting older adults [4–7]. Traditionally, study settings have been small because technical criteria are relevant to eyetracking collection of data.

Webcams found in laptops, tablets, and smartphones are inexpensive and easily accessible alternative for the remote eye-tracking metric array for VPC tasks, but more validation against eye trackers of clinical grade is needed. Previous study reveals evidence of concept for using embedded neuropsychological webcams neuropsychiatric evaluations and neuropsychiatric evaluations [8]. As such, we established a method for collecting data on gaze position and period from device-imbedded cameras and algorithms used for machine learning to create models of individualized scoring. The main idea was to identify equivalence of VPC data between types of camera to validate potential apps in remote configurations.

5.2   Materials and Methods

When deciding the pieces of the system and the camera of the two predefined eyes afterward, we would illustrate how the experiment progress of the VSC challenge involves the graphical configuration, data assurance, and rating processes for each eye unit located around the globe. Device model, device portrayals, the information obtained are analyzed, and the fragment is closed.

5.3   Framework Elements

A person's eye advancements were stored using a Tobi X2-60 tracking camera (Tobi AB, Stockholm) and using an underlying camera (Apple, Cupertino, CA).

5.3.1   Eye Tracker Camera

Framework inspected on 60 Hz, look points were resolved by overall places, which include eyeball and understudies focuses. Members are situated

27 crawls on 19-inch level board screen which shows the up gradation. Ball movement information was monitored.

5.3.2   Test Construction

Visual-matched correlation assignments utilize recognizable and novel visual upgrades. A normal VPC method includes an acclimation stage and a test stage. During the underlying acclimation stage, subjects were given sets of indistinguishable visual improvements for a fixed timeframe. At evaluation stage, this follows a postponement of any one among stable or unstable timeframes; ideals are given extra combinations of visual upgrades, which incorporates one boost from the acclimation stage (recognizable upgrade) upgrade. A proportion of taking a gander at the boost comparative with all out review duration for the test created curiosity inclination mark.

The development of task utilized in investigation is just 5 minutes adjusted adaptation of a 30-minute task created. The test comprised 20 preliminaries, every preliminary containing an acclimation stage and a test stage. Like the Gola and associates work worldview, acquaintance and monitoring stages are also not successive (Figure 5.1).

During the acclimation stage, the member appeared in a succession sets of indistinguishable pictures. At the last of the test, the evaluation stage happens, in that the member demonstrated other succession sets of pictures, each pair comprises a picture from the acclimation stage and a novel picture. The test stages appeared after all acclimation stages and switch request. Upgrades comprised highly contrasting, high difference pictures

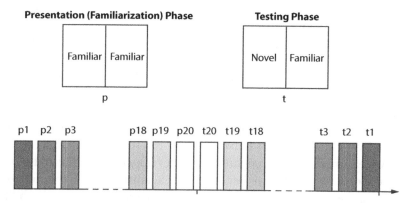

Figure 5.1 Familiar phase and test phases.

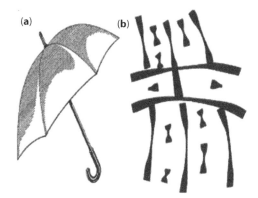

Figure 5.2 VPC stimuli (a) nameable, (b) unnameable.

estimating various unusual measurements. Remarkable pictures are utilized for every preliminary (Figure 5.2).

Participants from various areas were employed from a hospital and Boston Hospital of Massachusetts. Information was given by all participants and met inclusion requirements for the age of 50 years with normal scores cognitive status telephone interview [9]. During three in-clinic visits, the participants completed a 5-minute VPC mission (baseline (T1), week 1 (T2) and week 6 (T3)), simultaneously, using both the external eye-tracking camera to record (Tobi X2-60; Tobi AB, Stockholm, Sweden) and embedded with laptop camera (Apple MacBook Air laptop 13-inch; Cupertino, Apple, CA).

Validity and reliability of VPC for visual evaluation memory and cognitive deficiency have previously been established [10, 11]. In brief, respondents were shown a series of two similar side-by-side photographs (20 trials) during the familiarization process and were watched for 5 seconds (Figure 5.3). Twenty trials were presented with one previously presented test stage, displayed image, and one new image side by side.

The vision algorithm predicted the position of the gaze and plotted it on the plane, then quantified as "right," "left," or "none." The merged classifications were "right" and "left," depending on the location of the novel and familiar images. The quantity of time spent seeing the new pictures was separated. A novelty preference (NP) score was generated from either image type, as a percentage. Twenty tests were included in each VPC mission, and variable delay tests between 2 and 168 seconds (mean scores for NP). A measure of visual recognition was developed across the 20 test trials. The scores for the NP are benchmarked against levels of possible success. Scores near the opportunity stage (50%) are symptomatic of disability, and higher ratings are representative of normal function [12].

Figure 5.3 Test pictures from the acclimation stage (a), during which two indistinguishable pictures are introduced next to each other, and the test stage.

The data for the eye tracker were analyzed by the software, and the details from the webcam were secured by a new algorithm. The covariance between output information from VPC from review of the clinical-grade eye tracker and the webcam product-moment correlations with a person was calculated. In correlations by person, each participant has been created through each for the 20 trials (Figure 5.4), and overall VPC results in three points in time. There have been paired sample *t* tests used to evaluate the equivalence of data obtained by the webcam and the clinical-grade eye tracker. Paired-sample mean score differences were examined by *t*-tests across the 20 specific trials, and the overall level of success means each of the time points, over time, and collapsed punctuates.

Figure 5.4 Test pictures from the acquaintance stage during which one picture from the acclimation stage is introduced close to a novel picture.

5.3.3   Web Camera

The company's 1.4 GHz speed PC- Intel's 4GB 1,536 MB of DR3 and 1.600MB Intel HD Graphics 5,000 Graphics Card, with a specification generation 5,000. During the test recording, the PC's video target was 640 to 480. Three human coders, the phase-of-calibration video, analyzed the individual frames manually and evaluated all modulated packets (30/s). Evaluation of each modification frame is carried out by monitoring the bandwidth of the calibration frames and comparing them. The only distinction was with the ball on the left or the ball on the left. If 90% or higher did not attain accurate individual precision of the programed monitored frames, the coding does not exceed 90% or higher. The video during the calibration process was replicated. Frames with a ball is omitted in the centre of the frame (top, centre and bottom vertically) (Figures 5.3, 5.4). No calibration data were available, incorporated into the test protocol.

5.3.4   Camera for Eye Tracking

Two values were used at the end of the calibration point and are to be used as precision steps. The following are:

1. RMSE—is a mistake specified for every point. Each point of view is measured as the Cartesian interval between the point and the location of the ball for calibration.
2. Performance, a measured value dependent on Tobi's X2-60 SDK/API validation codes. Where either value is calibrated to a certain level (0.10 for the first threshold), 0.15 was calibrated to RMSE and 0.15 was calibrated to the second and 0.8 to the first and 0.7, respectively, to the second calibration. To ensure correct gaze positions measurement, the calibration has been replicated with two additional calibration times for consistency. The calibration results were not incorporated into the experiment.

5.4   Proposed System

5.4.1   Camera for Tracking Eye

The subjects were recorded by a Tobi X2-60 eye tracking device during the configuration and testing period, which records 60 Hz (60/s) eye view data.

The Tobi Pro SDK, the raw Tobi info, has been obtained in programmatic terms. In two distinct "coordinate systems," each data are displayed, and the active monitor coordinates the eye gaze data reported by the Tobi. The ADCS is a 2D computer coordinating the display of the notebook, an upper left edge and the lower right end of the screen.

The 3D UCS synchronization domain uses added coordinates. Information by the participant's own eye position enables, for instance, a correct measurement of the eye and the screen distance and hence the normal sight for each respondent. Each of the data points was an approximate angle between the left and the right eyes. We have taken the center of the two key elements as the last indicator for this date (Figure 5.5). This was the default environment in Tobi Pro as well.

In each Tobi information, point-coordinated information was used to test the "authenticity script" and used to ascertain "whether certain the eye tracker notice is provided for an eye truly begins from that eye" (eye not found). If the legitimacy code for both eyes is 4, the information point has

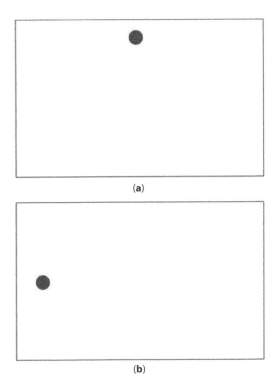

(a)

(b)

Figure 5.5 (a) Centre of the top. (b) Middle left.

been omitted. Naturally, research preparations were prohibited if unprotected codes of validity barred exceeding 4 s.

5.4.2   Web Camera

The topics were registered and checked via the PC camera during the change. For our own account, we used a pretty decent flash video recorder (NFVR), which was migrated to our own web application (AWS) for the corresponding flash video (FLV) occasion. The metadata was introduced into the FLV video for both modification and monitoring to ensure communication with the video boxes and the validation data. In addition, a secure evidence base has been placed with special preliminary information. Meta examples include times where the orientation ball travels from one to the other and when the test items occur and are protected.

5.4.3   Scoring

The essential exhibition metric for VPC undertakings is oddity inclination, which is the current examination level of time. The member spends taking a gander at the novel picture contrasted and the natural picture. In this line, the score for curiosity inclination was calculated as (time seeing novel picture) for each preliminary test (total time seeing either picture). The last score for a complete evaluation was the medium score for each of the 20 provisional findings, with respect to curiosity.

5.4.4   Eye Tracking Camera

For every preliminary, we set up a rectangular zone-of-interest border around every one of the combined pictures. This square shape was of fixed size and somewhat bigger than the picture, it includes some blunder information. In any introductory, the curiosity tendency (time focused on new picture) has been documented/(total time focused on by the same token picture). Time spent survey images, which depend on the overall time of fixation with the Tobi X2-60 programming, were calculated.

5.4.5   Web Camera Human-Coded Scoring

The details captured by the web camera was isolated in singular boxes. The cases were organized and categorized using the FLV metadata during the video collection through preliminary checking. Details on web cameras were broken down using three different rates: 10 diagrams each second,

5 diagrams per second, and 3 diagrams per second. At that point, the prepared information was analyzed by three free human coders on the edge of each outline premise to ascertain if the subject looked on either side of the screen or right again, or under no other heading. The "neither one of the options" coding was proposed to outlines whether the member was closing the eyes or whether vision was impotent is needed to render the eye ball unclear from other part of the body.

In either case, as the member seemed to look to the focus of the screen, the normal coding agents instructed to choose the right or left side (since they were likely not really taking a gander at the middle). The individual assessments rendered the lion's choice for each picture. If single coder judged the block to the two others judged the image to be "right," the last scoring is "correct." Then, for each preliminary assessment, the consolidated "left," "right," "correct," "novel," and "recognizable" assessments were meant by which picture of the pair was a novel picture. The oddity score was the level of edges, the participants were regarded as taking a gander on the new side for each preliminary assessment.

Curiosity Preference = (# of "novel" outlines)/(complete # of "novel" outlines + # of "recognizable" outlines).

5.5   Subjects

A more developed adult clinically resident network was selected from science-intrigued volunteers at the Brigham Research and Treatment Centre.

The inquiry was verified thru the General Unit by the Associate Human Testing Council of the Institutional Oversight Board (IRB). The topics underwent IRB-affirmed educated consent techniques, and both topics gave composed and informed consent for the interest of the inquiry. Prohibition criteria have included a history of substance abuse, drug misuse, brain injury, or current significant physical or psychiatric condition. Both subjects complied with integration laws old enough (over 50 years) and intellectual status by the age-specified criteria in the cognitive status telephone interview (TICS). No previous PC information was required.

5.5.1   Characteristics of Subject

All respondents were mentally average citizens, with a mean age of 68.7 ± 7.6 years (territory, 54–97). The mean training cycles completed were 15.6 ± 2.8 (territory, 12–20) for the studies of 58.5% female (31 subjects), respectively. Because of the wear down and specialized problems, information from 44 subjects at point 1, 36 topics was made visible at number 2, and information retained by 38 subjects at point 3 are made visible.

5.6   Methodology

Themes were approached to engage in three facility visits as part of a broader conference for the analysis of longitudinal performance on paper-pencil and detailed psychological assessments. After the primary tour, the second visit took place several weeks and the third one month and a half after the main visit. The first 30-minute VPC mission with the standard camera eye after eye and the 5-minute division with a synchronous snap, all using the composite camera and the tacit web general, was tested during the main visit. The 5-minute form was monitored during the subsequent visits. Toward the start of any VPC mission organization, it was told that the subjects were taking pictures "as though staring at the TV," and they would appear on the television.

5.6.1   Analysis of Data

Investigations into IBM SPSS version 21.0 were performed. At all times, interpreters were polled using Siegel and Castellan's kappa count to grasp webcam scoring. The dependability of Pearson's second item relationships was tested inside the web camera. Every second, knowledge was broken down using a subset test by members (n = 25) as set sets of 10, 5, and 3 outlines were prepared. The dependency on Pearson's object second ratio was tested between the Tobi X2-60 Eye after a Camera and the web camera using 3 FSPs. Cohen's criterion was used to determine the consistency of those associations as small, medium, 0.30, or higher, with connection coefficients about 0.10. Chi-square research measured the recurrence of information quality problems in each of the three periods and the recurrence of information quality issues in conjunction with the camera and corresponding web camera.

5.7   Results

Eighteen participants have completed all three visits, and the study included them. The 61% female cohort was with an average age of 67 to 76 years and 72% Caucasian and schooling for 16.6 to 2.4 years, 116,645 frames in total have been analyzed. Automated gaze position and gaze positioning scoring duration data revealed from the webcam-based VPC task effective comparisons with the clinical-grade eye tracker. Figure 5.6 indicates the average per-participant and per-trial results output at each point of time on the VPC task for both styles of camera and indicates the overall success level of the trial and means of the VPC mission at each point of time and collapsed for time points. Pearson average output correlation was robust at all time points: r = 0.95 (T1 r = 0.97; T22 r = 0.97; T22 r = 0.95). T3 r = 0.97; p's < 0.001). Pearson Association Performance was also stable across time points: r = 0.888 (T1 r = 0.85; T2 r = 0.89; p < 0.001; T3 r = 0.92).

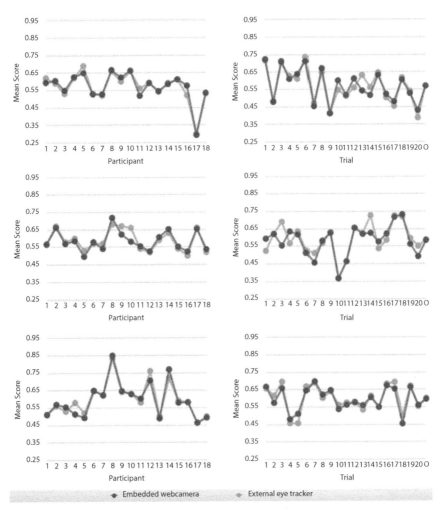

Figure 5.6 Mean score vs trial participants graph of embedded and external web camera.

Differences in mean between the performance data of each system gains 0.00 (Figure 5.6).

Figure 5.6 NP scores between the embedded webcam and the external eye tracker at the participant and trial stage. Scores are displayed as mean scores NP at participant level at (a) time 1 (b) time 2 (3) time mean trail level NP at (d) time 1 (e) time 2, (f) time 3.

5.8 Discussion

The findings indicate equivalence between data collected in a clinical-grade eye tracker and webcam for a VPC memory function evaluation mission. Such knowledge supports the use of device-embedded webcams for the processing of data by VPC, representing in the field of conditions, a significant technological advance. By the use of webcams, we can record the participants.

These variables may be the eyes, face, and surroundings, then assess which can preserve the validity of the results. Webcams give a specific method for verifying personal identification and administration during remote testing. Our observations lay the groundwork for the simultaneous selection. Along with other results, eye-tracking metrics, such as keystrokes and taps based on the haptic, allow remote multimodal cognitive and behavioral assessment typing data [13–15]. In addition to cognition assessment, a range of clinical activities and VPC duties are successfully deployed and also includes schizophrenia [16], suicidal minorities, autism, ideation [17, 18]. The ubiquity of cameras integrated with smartphones indicates the eye tracking data methods for remote collection. It can be disseminated worldwide, allowing evaluation in environments and lack of standard health infrastructure.

The limited sample size and the limitations of this analysis include the participant's relative homogeneity. The inclusion, however, is larger; overall of three time points, the data offer a larger sample for technical output validation. Additionally, the study included trial-level data to minimize smoothing effects associated with the vector for the NP result. Another such limitation of this study is the processing of in-clinic data. It is the primary importance of the device-embedded cameras and data acquisition remotely. Furthermore, in-clinic effectiveness future rationale is important to justify the act in remote configurations.

Merged and merged. Scores for (a) trial-level and (b) run-level data are given. Paired t-test outcomes in a nonsignificant mean difference of 0.00 for individual and combined time points and colour open online photos.

The omnipresence of such technologies is incorporated in the focus points in the use of an intrinsic web camera. The limited effort is made to acquire and integrate web-based cameras into task plans and the general ease of their operation and assistance [19]. With regard to the previously mentioned cameras, today's eye of high casing rates requires broad arrangement and coordination with ideal quality of information, and those systems need a consistent execution. The findings of this analysis confirm these factors, which indicate that the high business eye rate following the camera has higher recurrence than the inherent web camera.

The specialized capacity of people using business grade eye trackers is additionally a part in the recurrence of specialized issues. It is imperative to bring up the preparation of people to physically score information from the web camera in addition to the related expenses and counting preparing time. One bit of leeway managed by the utilization of a web camera is the chance of inconspicuous information catch of eye developments. Petridis and partners exhibited a strategy online, obtaining the understudy size utilizing a web camera (Figure 5.7), while such uses in the eye following may bear the cost of more prominent biological legitimacy. The clinical

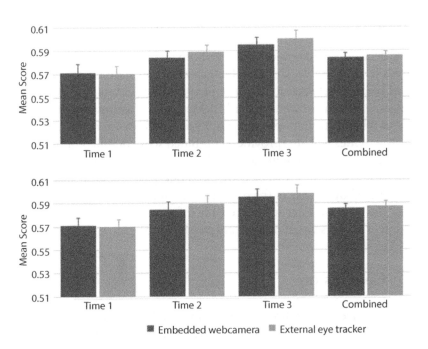

Figure 5.7 Mean NP scores over time points between embedded webcams and external eye trackers.

estimation of setup eye following builds the assessing parts of cognizance inside a conventional testing climate.

The challenges of camera use in web eye following countenances are the absence of clearness with respect to its utility across contrasting undertaking plans. Many examination of eye following assignment plans incorporate estimation of various eye following highlights, for example, look area, look obsessions and reobsessions vertical, and even saccadic developments, just as an understudy estimation (e.g., distance across, enlargement). The base edge rate needed for precise information investigation and scoring is very likely the factor and ward upon the particular assignment worldview and the particular eye following highlights of interest [20]. While the flow research has exhibited the capacity to dependably catch explicit highlights, for example, look area and understudy distance across the number of highlights. The highlights are restricted, and concurrent assortment of numerous highlights stays an unmistakable bit of leeway of business grade research eye trackers. On a basic level, similar calculations utilized in R&D eye follower programming can be given to extricate value-based visual element information from cameras. At instance, distinguishing proof of packet angle parts of the eye (e.g., student) considers the assessment and extraction of the student and understudy centroid as explicit highlights.

Using those equations, the amount of highlights obtained by a web camera may be improved. This examination proves that the score accuracy on a VPC decisive worldview of 3–60 FPS both on human and robotic scoring systems is comparable. Comparable examinations investigate the evaluation of balance between job requirements, are important for the creation of edges, and can be seen in the historical use of company eyes trailing cameras when entering web cameras. Execution measurements on the eye during activities will also provide a combined score of different highlights. To construct the affectability and explicitness of a PCP task, for instance, further experiencing growers with moderate psychological disorder are characterized by the use of the mixture of excitement, obsessions, and saccades. The base rates needed for reliable information research and the calculation of various visual outputs are possibly subject to special highlights.

5.9   Conclusion

The acceptance of asynchronous webcam-based cognitive tests access will significantly increase access to neuropsychological assessment. For the rising population, in particular, risk of older adults far from dementia. The therapeutic usefulness of method of this longitudinal ongoing studies may be carried out in other populations provided more validations and verifications are in force.

References

1. Lyketsos, C.G. and Miller, D.S., Addressing the Alzheimer's disease crisis through better understanding, treatment, and eventual prevention of associated neuropsychiatric syndromes. *Alzheimers Dement.*, 8, 60–64, 2012.
2. Alzheimer's Association, Alzheimer's disease facts and figures. *Alzheimers Dement.*, 14, 367–429, 2018.
3. Brookmeyer, R., Gray, S., Kawas, C., Projections of Alzheimer's disease in the United States and the public health impact of delaying disease onset. *Am. J. Public Health*, 88, 1337–1342, 1998.
4. Loewensteinm, D.A., Curiel, R.E., Duara, R., Buschke, H., Novel cognitive paradigms for the detection of memory impairment in preclinical Alzheimer's disease. *Assessment*, 25, 348–359, 2018.
5. Crutcher, M.D., Calhoun-Haney, R., Manzanares, C.M., Lah, J.J., Levey, A.I., Zola, S.M., Eye tracking during a visual paired comparison task as a predictor of early dementia. *Am. J. Alzheimers Dis. Other Demen.*, 24, 258–266, 2009.
6. Zola, S.M., Manzanares, C.M., Clopton, P., Lah, J.J., Levey, A.I., A behavioral task predicts conversion to mild cognitive impairment and Alzheimer's disease. *Am. J. Alzheimers Dis. Other Demen.*, 28, 179–184, 2013.
7. Lagun, D., Manzanares, C., Zola, S.M., Buffalo, E.A., Agichtein, E., Detecting cognitive impairment by eye movement analysis using automatic classification algorithms. *J, Neurosci. Methods*, 201, 196–203, 2011.
8. Murugan, K., Daniel, F., Shanmugaraja, T., Siddharthraju, K., Dhivya Devi, R., Supriya, M., A critical review on medical image processing techniques. *J. Crit. Rev.*, 7, 5, 576–580, 2020.
9. Knopman, D.S., Roberts, R.O., Geda, Y.E., Pankratz, V.S., Christianson, T.J.H., Petersen, R.C. *et al.*, Validation of the telephone interview for cognitive status-modified in subjects with normal cognition, mild cognitive impairment, or dementia. *Neuroepidemiology*, 34, 34–42, 2010.
10. Bott, N., Madero, E.N., Glenn, J., Lange, A., Anderson, J., Newton, D. *et al.*, Deviceembedded cameras for eye tracking–based cognitive assessment: Validation with paper-pencil and computerized cognitive composites. *J. Med. Internet Res.*, 20, e11143, 2018.
11. Seligman, S.C. and Giovannetti, T., The potential utility of eye movements in the detection and characterization of everyday functional difficulties in mild cognitive impairment. *Neuropsychol. Rev.*, 25, 199–215, 2015.

12. Bott, N.T., Lange, A., Rentz, D., Buffalo, E., Clopton, P., Zola, S., Web camera based eye tracking to assess visual memory on a visual paired comparison task. *Front. Neurosci.*, 11, 370, 2017.

13. Feenstra, H.E.M., Vermeulen, I.E., Murre, J.M.J., Schagen, S.B., Online cognition: Factors facilitating reliable online neuropsychological test results. *Clin. Neuropsychol.*, 31, 59–84, 2017.

14. Crump, M.J.C., McDonnell, J.V., Gureckis, T.M., Evaluating Amazon's Mechanical Turk as a tool for experimental behavioral research. *PloS One*, 8, e57410, 2013.

15. Kokkinakis, D., Fors, L.K., Bjorkner, E., Nordlund, A., Data collection from persons with mild forms of cognitive impairment and healthy controls Infrastructure for classification and prediction of dementia, in: *Proceedings of the 21st Nordic Conference on Computational Linguistics*, Association for Computational Linguistics, Gothenburg, Sweden, pp. 172–182, 2017, [Internet]. Available at www.aclweb.org/anthology/W17-0220 (last accessed November 14, 2018).

16. Pierce, K., Marinero, S., Hazin, R., McKenna, B., Barnes, C.C., Malige, A., Eye tracking reveals abnormal visual preference for geometric images as an early biomarker of an autism spectrum disorder subtype associated with increased symptom severity. *Biol. Psychiatry*, 79, 657–666, 2016.

17. Ross, R.G., Harris, J.G., Olincy, A., Radant, A., Eye movement task measures inhibition and spatial working memory in adults with schizophrenia, ADHD, and a normal comparison group. *Psychiatry Res.*, 95, 35–42, 2000.

18. Tsypes, A., Owens, M., Gibb, B.E., Suicidal ideation and attentional biases in children: An eye-tracking study. *J. Affect. Disord.*, 222, 133–137, 2017.

19. Chhaya, R., Weiss, J., Seffren, V., Sikorskii, A., Winke, P.M., Ojuka, J.C. *et al.*, The feasibility of an automated eye-tracking-modified Fagan test of memory for human faces in younger Ugandan HIV-exposed children. *Child Neuropsychol.*, 24, 686–701, 2018.

20. Forssman, L., Ashorn, P., Ashorn, U., Maleta, K., Matchado, A., Kortekangas, E. *et al.*, Eye-tracking-based assessment of cognitive function in low-resource settings. *Arch. Dis. Child*, 102, 301–302, 2017.

6

Fuzzy-Based Patient Health Monitoring System

**Venkatesh T.[1]*, Murugan K.[1], Supriya M.[1], Shanmugaraja T.[1]
and Rekha Chakravarthi[2]**

*[1]KPR Institute of Engineering and Technology, Coimbatore, India
[2]Sathyabama Institute of Science and Technology, Chennai, India*

Abstract

Because of exponential growth and rapid modernization in urban areas, here is a disparity in the socioeconomic urban and rural populace. As per World Health Organization (WHO), the doctor to patient ratio (DPR) is 1:1000. It is an apprehensive task for a doctor to monitor health concerns of the patients. The time spent by a doctor to a patient is an average of 7 to 10 minutes, where most of the time, the doctors are busy in taking notes of the symptoms or feeding the data to the healthcare system. The smart devices and computational intelligence (CI) and soft computing techniques (SCT) may help the doctors to monitor the data of their patients suffering with various healthcare issues and also to diagnose and to provide state-of-the-art treatment. The collected data may be used by the conglomeration of doctors for their superfluous analysis and predictions, local government authorities may use the data to improve sanitation and controlling the outbreak of epidemics and also for other healthcare predictions. Applying SCT, identification of correlated features, feature ranking or importance, and feature selection are performed on UCI machine learning data sets, and also, classification and prediction are performed on the data sets to examine the accuracy of the predictions for the classification algorithms—RPART, KNN, and SVM.

Keywords: Heart rate, systolic blood pressure, temperature, Sp02, API

*Corresponding author: venkatt87@gmail.com

R. Nidhya, Manish Kumar and S. Balamurugan (eds.) Tele-Healthcare: Applications of Artificial Intelligence and Soft Computing Techniques, (117–158) © 2022 Scrivener Publishing LLC

6.1   Introduction

In developing countries, ageing and rising population have become a serious concern as medical costs and demand for health services are increasing. In recent decades, there has been a steady growth in the ageing population. For the last 50 years, there have been three times the number of older people, and over the next 50 years, they will increase more [1]. Figure 6.1 shows a comparison between the growth rates of older populations to total population.

The application of computer platforms in healthcare systems and of wireless communication technology improves the quality of healthcare services for millions of people worldwide. It also helped to better manage the medical supplies, medical diagnoses, patient record administration, and healthcare services. However, following indoor patient conditions, more nursing time is still being expended, and the few hospital beds are physically filled and more expendable and more money are being consumed.

As patient records are becoming an important part of healthcare, they have had an effect on the safety, cost and quality of healthcare. The technology for creating, distributing, storing, and maintaining health data for patients is evolving rapidly. Progresses in the health information system can enable patients and caregivers access data electronically from anywhere.

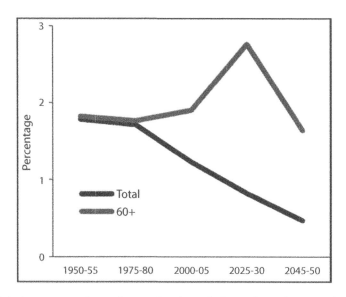

Figure 6.1 Average annual growth rate of total population and population aged 60 years or older.

To achieve these advantages, a basic necessity infrastructure that can support the use of electronic health information based in patients; that goes beyond the constraints of any particular provider, health plan, or delivery system [2]. In hospitals, there are tending to be many independent networks of medical knowledge supporting departments, health centers, surgeries, and laboratories. For example, the radiology may be isolated from the database maintained by the main information system of the hospital by its own application system.

6.1.1   General Problem

Patients in hospital or other healthcare facilities monitoring means that they are not mobile or able to walk or step around the hospital bed. Patients need to be monitored constantly and if critical, nurses should notify the in-call doctors because the doctors could react late and cause poorer quality of treatment. To provide patient care of a higher level, a better and effective monitoring system is required from anywhere.

Hospitals and healthcare facilities have long used comprehensive and autonomous medical information systems that assist a wide number of care providers. The primary factor is the need to consolidate the health records and files of patients so that various healthcare organizations and services are able to share and share current status and health data of patients for immediate and reliable diagnosis and treatment.

A mobile RFID intelligent patient surveillance and diagnosis system has been built in this research to support mobile healthcare and clinical decision support applications. It includes a medical recording system which diagrams patients and provides them with electronic health records. There is a fluid logic foundation algorithm. The medical history for the patient and the flip-flop logic base system are used to transmit alarms and alerts to custodians for any anomalies. The system can be used to track patients indoors and outside in particular chronically diseased patients.

6.1.2   Existing Patient Monitoring and Diagnosis Systems

Understanding observing framework is a framework that comprises different gadgets that are utilized to screen the patients' status, for example, the heart ECG sign alarms the medical care takers if there is an abnormality [3]. These frameworks are required in circumstances where the patient is in a dangerous condition or basic physiological state or has constant sicknesses, for example, diabetes [4, 5] and hypertension [6, 7]. Such frameworks are arising because of the expanded medical care needs of a maturing populace, new remote advances, better video and checking advances, diminishing medical care assets and demonstrated cost-viability. It is not new in medical services; it began in 1625 with the estimate of internal heat level and pulse. New innovations have been created after World War II and a huge measure of various kinds of observing can be created [8]. Many existing wired and remote patients' observing frameworks are accessible in the market today. Anyway, remote innovations are making strides because of its versatility, size, sturdiness, cost, and simplicity of establishment [9–20]. Coming up next is a writing overview to the absolute latest and poplar frameworks.

6.1.3   Fuzzy Logic Systems

"Fuzzy logic is a type of many-esteemed rationale; it manages thinking that is fixed or inexact instead of fixed and precise. Fuzzy logic factors may have a reality esteem that ranges in degree somewhere in the range of 0 and 1." It is basically a decision reached by a standard based calculation, "Fuzzy logic," utilizing etymological factors that are used to frame enrollment capacities (MFs), which could conceivably have covering limits. The contribution to the standard base could conceivably have supreme qualities, for example, yes or no, 0 or 1; in this way, the qualities can be shifted somewhere in the range of 0 and 1. The calculation filters all the information/s esteems and creates yield choice mirroring the status of the checked item/s, i.e., the Fuzzy rationale framework is a basic, decision-based framework that can be utilized to screen natural boundaries that could be troublesome or difficult to display with straightforward direct arithmetic.

Fuzzy logical algorithms have shown a potential to enhance the performance of clinicians by imitating human thinking processes under complex circumstances and performing repetitive tasks, which humans are inappropriate for. The sensor information was used to change insulin infusion rate to decide whether responses to ordinary "inputs," such as daily insulin, food, and exercise could be handled. The mean absolute percentage error between the blood glucose values expected and present was found to be over 10%. A clinically feasible method utilizing an internal blood glucose monitoring system was also established in another study. With a specialist fluid logic algorithm, the machine has been able to track the glucose and change the insulin level.

The disadvantages outlined so far include times where FL systems do not meet normal human output, and this also leads to inadequate programming (a professional diabetologist also needs to lay down the rules on the actions of an experienced system). Fuzzy logic is very well adapted for medical control systems because the criteria are often narrowly diagnosed, such as one physician I consider to be ill and one who is considered very ill. Fuzzy logic is a medical control system. A customized design of hardware and software can deliver a high degree of functionality and reliability. These systems use many input sensors to track critical sings such as levels of blood glucose as shown on Figure 6.2. To monitor the amount of insulin to be supplied, the data obtained are compared with each other. This redundancy decreases the probability of errors in the system.

The implementation of the Fuzzy logic Blood Glucose Monitoring is shown in Figure 6.3. The author identified the use of fugitive logic techniques to build a framework for decision support, which will enable postprandial glycaemia optimization in patients with type one diabetes. This method takes into account the form of food, glycemia, and insulin

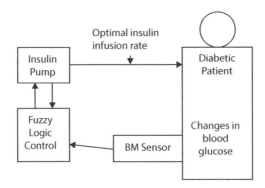

Figure 6.2 Closed loop feedback system.

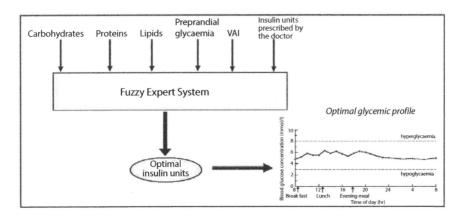

Figure 6.3 Fuzzy logic blood glucose monitoring.

resistance taken by patients. The findings have been very positive. The device indicated that insulin units should be changed correctly before a meal.

Fuzzy logic has also been used to identify heart disease. The device registered on a VA basis. Long Beach and Cleveland Foundation Database of the Medical Center. The system includes 13 inputs, including chest pain sort, BP, BS, HR, cholesterol, and a patient's cardiac disease performance. The system has been developed software with Matlab. Test results revealed that this system was much better than a nonexpert urologist, and approximately 94%, as did the expert.

Other medical applications, for example, the FL application for medical option in intensive care units (ICU) have documented the application of Fuzzy logic. The machine uses two inputs: MAP and Hourly Urine Production (HUO) mean blood pressure. The inputs are used for deciding how each calculation can change the intravenous fluid rate (IFR). A method has been built in that can be used for medical diagnosis. It uses fugitive logic design: the fugitive, the inferior motor, the basis for the law and the deflation, which gives the entries of five inputs: the protein, the red blood cell, and lymphocytes. The formulation of the rule-based engine was using a MATLAB simulation. The results of the simulation are in line with estimated results based on the design. This study aims at creating a control mechanism that improves the efficiency of the diagnosis of a human brain condition.

6.2   System Design

Practical and nonpractical determinations ought to be investigated to plan a solid, versatile, safe ease, and low-energy utilization framework. This segment portrays the utilitarian and nonuseful details of the proposed structure. The general design is intended to fulfill these details.

6.2.1   Hardware Requirements

The gadget particulars can be better chosen and asset streamlined by designers. In this framework, particulars set the attributes and administrations to be offered by a wireless monitoring system and the limitations to be upheld by them. This part exhibits the useful and nonutilitarian determinations of the proposed structure.

6.2.1.1   Functional Requirements

In a software engineering context, the functional requirements define the set of particular tasks or behaviors a producer must perform. In a software engineering context, the functional requirements specify what a system should do: the key criteria for this projects are the remote acquisition of the vital signals of a patient, which are assessed using RFID-based sensors, the evaluation of patient health status with a fluid logical algorithm, the documentation of patient health records in medical electronics and alerting caregivers to their patient status. It also requires a Web-based tool to coordinate and view sensor data collected. Additional feature specifications are:

    I.   organizing and locating readers to a fixed data set in a particular arrangement;

    II.   to gather readings from nodes in the network of wireless sensors;

    III. registration activities that include.

6.2.1.1.1   Staff Registration
Each staff member must have an account to use the monitoring system. The username, password, and staff ID are issued to each employee. Minimal personal data, such as first, last, and telephone numbers, are needed.

6.2.1.1.2   Patient Registration
Patients should be enrolled in a system and profiled and stored in a database for their information. Provided a patient ID, a tempering tag ID, a blood pressure tag ID, a SPo_2 tag ID, and a blood sugar tag ID, the personal details of the patient should be registered. A certain employee should also be allocated to them.

6.2.1.1.3   Deletion of Patients
Workers should be able to profile, load, and unload patients.

6.2.1.1.4   Cancellation of Staff Member Grant
Links to the system should be refused to unauthorized workers.

6.2.1.1.5   Details of Logging
Only approved staff individuals could sign in, screen, and track patients
    IV. Collecting patients' vital signs

The vital signs of RFIDs are read by various means, including

- **Data collection from temperature sensor (wrist band)**
  We have RFID bracelets linked to sensors for temperature. We must have a multi-tag scanner, so that several tags can be read at the same time.
- **Data collection from blood pressure meters**
  The device must also read frames that are bound to the sensor by an RFID tag.
- **Data collection from blood sugar meters**
  The device also must read frames that are linked to a blood sugar sensor by an RFID tag.
- **Data collection from SPo$_2$meters**
  The device must also read frames that are attached to a SPo$_2$ sensor using an RFID tag.
- **Data storing**
  All readings of data are considered essential and appropriate for patient monitoring. Data must always be saved in a database for this purpose.

6.2.1.1.6   Data Displaying—Patient Data
Clinical work force can see patients' individual data and information accumulated. Information will be shown in a few arrangements as indicated by the users' demand. Users will have the option to pick whether they need to see patients' assembled information utilizing the electronic application or the work area application and to determine the time-frame they need to screen. Persistent determination is finished by entering a patient ID. Staff individuals can see patients' temperature, circulatory strain, SPo$_2$, pulse, and glucose.

6.2.1.1.7   Exploiting of Staff's Data
Personnel must be able to access personal details of other personnel, for example, telephone numbers, in the event of an emergency. The selection of staff members is carried out by choosing an employee from a list with the names and personnel ids of all staff members (SIDs).

6.2.1.1.8   Staff Alertion
If anomalies were found in patient data, the employees would be notified by means of an SMS. With our fluctuating logic engine, we can see if the status of a patient is normal, low risk, or dangerous.

6.2.1.2   *Nonfunctional Specifications*

Nonfunctional specifications define restrictions or limitations in product execution. The nonfunctional specifications for this project included the following:

6.2.1.2.1   Accessibility

The dispersed existence of transmission lines is the reason for creating a web interface for providing users with information. These interfaces are accessible from any location on the Web and are compatible with most web browsers with no specialized software installed to display data.

6.2.1.2.2   Scalability

The utilization of an electronic instrument to picture the movement of the remote sensor networks was an endeavor to improve the adaptability of the quantity of clients who can get to the framework. Moreover, the framework is versatile to oblige extra patients. A peruser is fit for perusing and preparing 100 labels at the same time. What is more, numerous perusers can be utilized in the framework.

6.2.1.2.3   Privacy

To keep the framework sheltered and secure, the user, regardless of whether a specialist or a medical caretaker, must enter a legitimate username and secret word each time he/she needs to get to the framework. This measure is taken to ensure the specialist understands privacy. None of the data can be refreshed without the best possible security prerequisites. When all is said and done, data cannot be refreshed, as data are not entered by the attendants or specialists but instead sent by the RFID labels to the peruser and the peruser to the customers.

6.2.1.2.4   Usage of Software

The framework must be user-friendly and easy to use. It should be difficult for no or few doctors/nurses to use the system.

6.3   Software Architecture

The components that comprise the system's software architecture are shown in Figure 6.4. There are five main components to the Mobile Patient

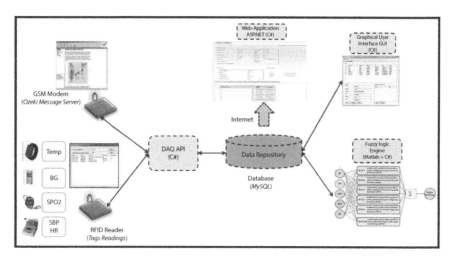

Figure 6.4 System software architecture.

Monitoring System (MPMS). Components together ensure that the entire system operates effectively and reliably. These modules include the API, MySQL DataBase Manger, DataAcquiry Unit (DAQ), Fuzzy Logic Matlab Code, GUI, C# Code and a web application using both C# and HTML Codes. The MPMS consists of all five program components that function collectively. After the system was set up, tests were performed to validate general robustness, reliability, and so on of the established framework. In the indoor office environment, the device test was carried out. The following paragraphs explain the specifics for each part of the program.

6.3.1   The Data Acquisition Unit (DAQ) Application Programmable Interface (API)

The Data Acquisition Unit (DAQ) Application Programmable Interface (API) permits connecting with the peruser to gather the information and show them on the API screen. It is the front-end control and checking interface utilized by framework administrators. It incorporates a wide range of presentations that permit administrators to screen patients' fundamental signs. The API was actualized dependent on the API that was given by Summit.co (a program needed to collaborate with the peruser). Summit.co is the organization that gave the RFID items. Additional functionalities to the code were added and acclimated to suit and satisfy the prerequisites of the framework. The API was written in C#, and it permits administrators to see continuous patient information. It has the accompanying functionalities:

a) Finding a tag type;
b) Extracting temperature, blood pressure, SPo_2, glucose and heart rate frames got by a RFID reader,
c) Finding comparing understanding from label ID,
d) Rearranging the crucial signs esteems to be viable with the orchestrated information base tables
e) Inserting the crucial signs esteems in table, and
f) Triggering an alert if there should be an occurrence of any anomalies. Anomalies are examined in a later area.

At the point when the API is first dispatched, the checking screen is shown. The observing screen shows ongoing crucial signs data for each

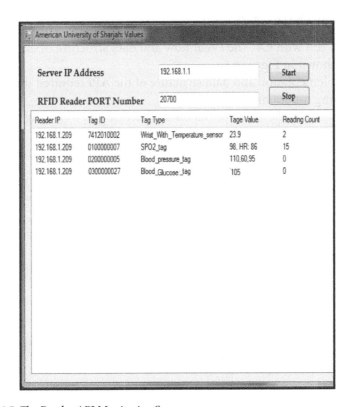

Figure 6.5 The Reader API Monitoring Screen.

patient in the framework. A depiction of the observing screen is appeared in Figure 6.5.

This covers the following fields:

> Server IP address
> Port number- Monitoring RFID
> Port number- Reader
> Display panel
> IP Reader
> Tag ID
> > Temperature Sensor
> > BP Monitor
> > SP02 Gauge
> > Diabetes Monitoring
> Tag value
> Reading Count

6.3.2   Flowchart—API

The API is run with C#. The event flow and data structure of the API program are shown in Figure 6.6.

The implementation and data structure of the API required the usage of the following functions:

To implement the API and its data structure the following functions have been used:

➢ DBConnect()
➢ Initialize()
➢ OpenConnection()
➢ CloseConnection()
➢ StopListen()
➢ ListenState()
➢ ReceiveData()
➢ GetChtName(TagFormatClass.TagType_tagType)
➢ BufferData_Analyze(Byte[] _byteBuffData)
➢ GetTemperature(string _strDataSection)
➢ SetBGSensorCoordinates(string_strDataSection,string-tagID,ref TagFormatClass_tagData)

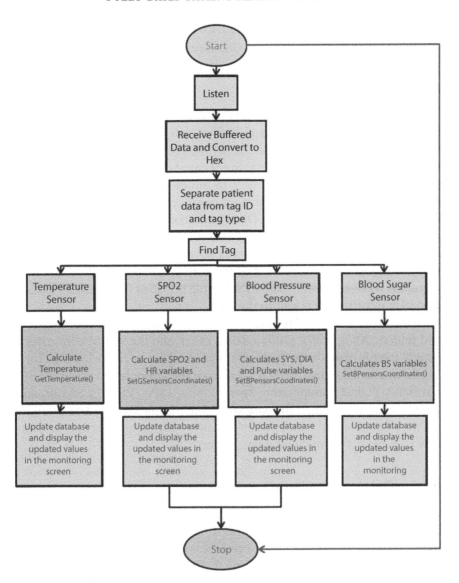

Figure 6.6 API sequence.

6.3.3 Foreign Tag IDs

The RFID tags' ID's are certainly dangerous that are not traced to a specific patient and accessed by a reader. If we allow for storage of the data being sent by tags along with the other read values in our database tables, we would have an excess of data and a lot of memory wasted. To stop this as soon since they were identified, the frames were dropped.

6.3.4 Database Manager

The System Database Manager (SDBM) is responsible for developing and maintaining the entire patient and staff records, including the database for vital signs. For patient accessed, the SDBM generates a configuration files along with time and date log data. In the event that a device failure occurs, each log file is modified in real time to mitigate data loss. The GUI sends a data packet from its current patient question into SDBM containing all the patient data obtained. The SDBM reads the data and adds them to the relevant patient log file. The SDBM also processes requests for data made by the GUI. When an operator seeks a patient's history, the SDBM retrieves the information and transfers it to the display interface. When this data request is received by the SDBM, the log file is loaded into memory and all data base information is sent to the GUI.

In the GUI, even the SDBM can be used when removing patient log files and folders. An operator sends a delete order, and the SDBM eliminates a patient log file from the patient's vital sign database or entire log directory. In addition to data from RFID readers from the sensor blood pressure (BP) SBP/DBP, PULSE (temperature sensor), SPo_2 (SPo_2/PULSE) Sensor, and blood sugar/sugar sensor the database is built using MySQL data database for stored patient and personnel information. The architecture of the database is illustrated in the following chapters.

6.3.5 Database Designing

A database is required to save all patients and personnel records and data read by the sensors. The database was introduced with a MySQL database that is compatible with C#, as we can access the database via C#. There are 24 tables for the system's database called "Hospital." Initially, a diagram was created to help organize the relationship between individuals. Figure 6.7 demonstrates the relationship between different entities, followed in the next subsection by the definition of and entity.

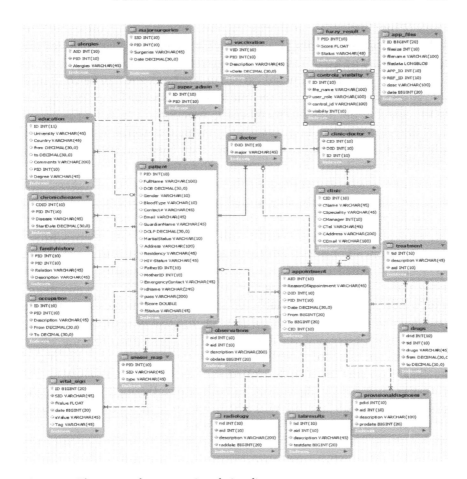

Figure 6.7 The proposed system entity relation diagram.

6.3.6   The Fuzzy Logic System

6.3.6.1   Introduction to Fuzzy Logic

One of the core concepts of fuzzy logic is the membership standard defined by the use of the fuzzy input set to "fuzzify" any data point. The device designer decides the Input fuzzy collection for division into attribute values of the full range of potential input values. A minimum and maximum range of input value is available for each membership function, either 0 or 1. Various forms, including trapezoidal, Gaussian, and triangular, for the feature set, can be used. Trapezoidal and triangular shaped member functions are the most common and easy to understand, and can be combined into an awkward set by setting the minimum input value for every function to the center of the previous membership function.

"Fuzzy logic is a multipurpose logic, which concerns with inference which is either set or approximate rather than fixed and true. Fuzzy logic variables can be valid to a degree ranging from 0 to 1." It is simply a conclusion drawn by a computer program that recognizes that not all values, such as yes or no, 0 or 1 are absolute to enable calculations to differ from 0 to 1.

The fugitive logic system is a simple, control-based system, which can be used to track biological systems with simple linear mathematics, which would be difficult or impossible to model. Fuzzy logic systems have shown a capacity to enhance the efficiency of a clinician by imitating human cognitive processes and conducting repetitive activities in dynamic situations, which individuals are not suitable for. In the fields of medical diagnostics, treatment of diseases and patient pursuit, the use of computer technology has today increased considerably. While these environments where computers are used are incredibly complex and unpredictable, the use of intelligent systems has been developed, such as fused logic, artificial neural networks, and genetic algorithms. In both books, the fugitive rationale is based on the MPAS. The MPAS is a basic reference for medical and hospital personnel to easily assess a patient's disease.

6.3.6.2   The Modified Prior Alerting Score (MPAS)

The modified prior alerting score (MPAS) is a guide for patients' bedside assessment and is based on five physiological parameters: systolic blood pressure, heart rate, breathing rate, temperature, and AVPU score (A to "warning," V to "repressed to verbal stimulus," P to "repressive stimulation." The ability of an MPAS to recognize surgical patients that may benefit from intensive care was shown in 2000, despite relative divergence from normal blood pressure and urine production. In 2001, patient admissions were validated with the MPAS. A research was developed in 2006 to evaluate the capacity of MPAS (Table 6.1) to classify at-risk patients and to assess MPAS' viability as a screening method to initiate early identification and hospital admission. It could be used to classify patients clinically unsuccessful and who require immediate intervention quickly. During diagnosis and transport, MPAS can be used for the monitoring of medical patients. It has been shown that MPAS is effective at

Table 6.1 The modified prior alerting score.

MPAS							
Risk Band / Vital Sign	Low 3	Low 2	Low 1	Normal 0	High 1	High 2	High 3
Systolic BP	SBP <75	70<SBP <85	80<SBP <100	95<SBP <199		SBP>185	
Heart Rate		HR<50	45<HR <60	53<HR <100	95<HR <110	105<HR <130	HR >125
SPO2	SPO2 <85	83<SPO2 <90	87<SPO2 <95	SPO2 >93			
Temperature		T<36.5		36<T <38.5		T>38	
Blood Sugar	BS<66	63<BS <72		70<BS <110		106<BS <150	BS >140

decreasing mortality risks and disease opportunities in patients whose health is increasingly declining.

For this activity, the MPAS score was determined using various parameters as shown in Table 6.2. The criteria used are: systolic blood pressure (SBP), cardiac rate (HR), saturating oxygen (SPo$_2$), body temp (TEMP),

Table 6.2 AVPU/GCS score using MPAS.

MPAS	+3	+2	+1	0	+1	+2	+3
Systolic blood pressure	<70	70-80	81-100	101-199		≥200	
Heart rate		<40	41-50	51-100	101-110	111-130	>130
Respiratory Rate		<9		9-14	15-20	21-29	≥30
Temperature		<35	35.1-36	36.1-38	38.1-38.5	>38.5	
AVPU/GCS score	<9	9-13	14	A/15	V/Confused	P	U

The score is calculated by measuring the five parameters as above and adding together the assigned score for each physiological value.

AVPU – Alert, Verbal, Pain, Unresponsive; GCS – Glasgow Coma Scale.

and blood sugar (BS). Experts in the area of feedback is delegated to the diagnosis of know-how associated with the Rashid Centre for Diabetes and Research (RCDR).

6.3.6.3   Structure of the Fuzzy Logic System

This section explains the fuzzy system of logic. Figure 6.8 demonstrates the fundamental framework of our system. The fuzzy logic system uses 5 input characteristics and 1 output characteristics. Systemic blood pressure (SBP), heart rate (HR), oxygen saturation (SPo_2), body temperature (TEMP), and blood sugar (BS) are the areas of input (attributes). The field performance applies to the case of the patient (risk group).

Information flows from right to left, data processing referring to five inputs contributing to one output. One of the most critical features of fuzzy logic schemes is the parallel design of the rules. The rationale is smooth from the regions where the action of the machine dominates by just one

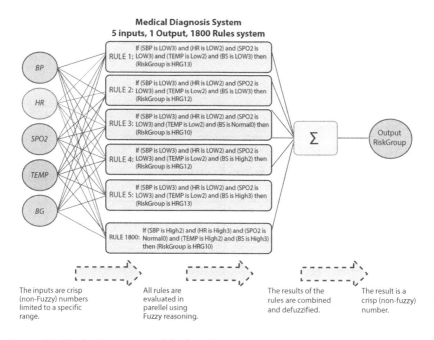

Figure 6.8 The basic structure of the fuzzy logic system.

norm, rather than a sharp flipping between various modes on the basis of breakpoints. The measures that are taken to create a fluctuating logic system including a fluent system design for experts are defined in the following paragraphs: membership functions, fuzzy rule base creation, fuzzification and defuzzification.

6.3.7 Designing a System in Fuzzy

In the design of expert systems the usual steps taken involve specifying the input and output variables, the choice of acceptable membership features and the development of a fuzzy database of rules. The following are the elements.

6.3.7.1 Input Variables

Blood Pressure: The outcomes can quickly be modified by varying values of blood pressure. We use systolic blood pressure in this region. The variable input is split into five fuzzy sets. These sets are (low-3, low-2, low-1, normal-0, high-2), and the five fuzzy sets have trapezoidal membership functions. The SBP ranges of each fuzzy set are seen in Table 6.3. Blood pressure field membership functions are shown in Figure 6.9.

Heart rate: we use six fuzzy sets for this input area (low-2, low-1, normal-0, high-1, high-2, and high-3) on the basis of the MPAS scoring system and the guidance of the specialist. The six fuzzy sets are trapezoidal in their

Table 6.3 The SBP ranges that correspond to each fuzzy set.

Input field	Range	Fuzzy sets
SBP	<75	Low 3
	70-85	Low 2
	80-100	Low 1
	95-199	Normal- 0
	>185	High 2

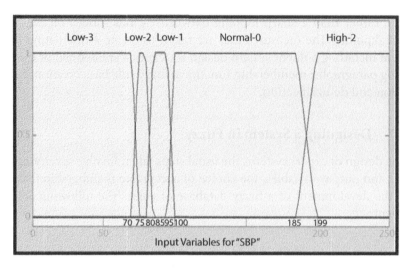

Figure 6.9 Membership functions of SBP parameter.

membership features. The HR values were defined similar to the SBP using Table 6.4. The HR ranges that match each set are shown in Table 6.4. Figure 6.10 indicates the heart rate membership features.

Table 6.4 The HR ranges that correspond to each fuzzy set.

Input field	Range	Fuzzy sets
	<50	Low 2
	45-60	Low 1
	53-100	Normal- 0
Heart rate HR	95-110	High 1
	105-130	High 2
	>125	High 3

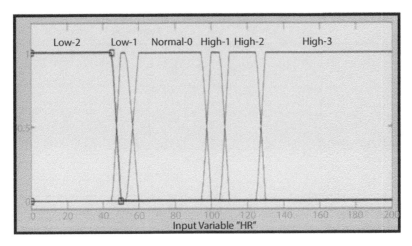

Figure 6.10 Membership functions of the Heart Rate HR parameter.

SPo₂: The oxygen saturation in the blood of the patient is a value for this area. We have four language variables in this area (low-3, low-2, low-1, and normal). We have four linguistic sets. All values above 95 (>95) are undeniably regarded as natural. These fuzzy sets have been described in Table 6.5. The fuzzy sets have trapezoidal membership features, and Figure 6.11 shows them.

Temperature: We have three fuzz sets (Low-2, Normal-0, High-2) in this region. These fuzzy sets have been described in Table 6.6. These fuzzy

Table 6.5 The SPo₂ ranges that correspond to each fuzzy set.

Input field	Range	Fuzzy sets
SPO2	<85	Low 3
	83-90	Low 2
	87-95	Low 1
	>93	Normal- 0

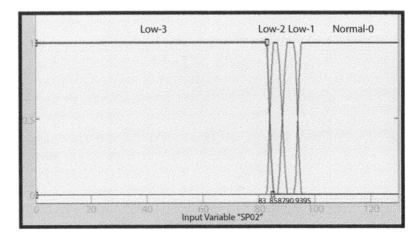

Figure 6.11 Membership functions of the SPo2 parameter.

Table 6.6 The Temp ranges that correspond to each fuzzy set.

Input field	Range	Fuzzy sets
	<36.5	Low 2
Temperature	36-38.5	Normal 0
	>38	High 2

sets have trapezoidal membership features. Figure 6.12 defines these membership features.

6.3.7.2 The Output Variable

The performance of the fuzzy logic engine is defined in this paragraph. There is a "risk group" performance variable that corresponds to the amount of risk in the case of a patient. It is between 0 and 15. The greater the benefit, the greater the patient's health risk. In this method we have 15 fuzzy sets (NRM, LRG 1, LRG2, LRG3, LRG4, HRG5, HRG6, HRG7, HRG8, HRG9, HRG10, HRG11, HRG12, HRG13, and HRG14) for the variables risk group performance. These sets are triangular membership functions. Table 6.7 and Figure 6.13 show descriptions of the membership features.

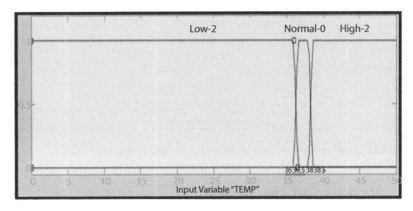

Figure 6.12 Membership functions of the heart rate TEMP parameter.

Table 6.7 The output variable (Riskgroup) ranges that correspond to each fuzzy set.

Output field	Range	Fuzzy sets
Risk Group	0<RG<0.5	NRM
	0.5<RG<1.5	LRG 1
	1.5<RG<2.5	LRG 2
	2.5<RG<3.5	LRG 3
	3.5<RG<4.5	LRG 4
	4.5<RG<5.5	HRG 5
	5.5<RG<6.5	HRG 6
	6.5<RG<7.5	HRG 7
	7.5<RG<8.5	HRG 8
	8.5<RG<9.5	HRG 9
	9.5<RG<10.5	HRG 10
	10.5<RG<11.5	HRG 11
	11.5<RG<12.5	HRG 12
	12.5<RG<13.5	HRG 13
	13.5<RG<14	HRG 14

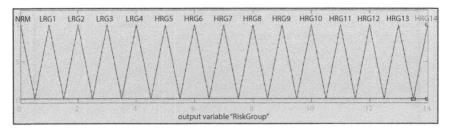

Figure 6.13 Membership functions of the output variable (risk group) field.

6.4   Results and Discussion

In setting up a secure surveillance system, close cooperation in a medical center is an essential step. To gather adequate data from various types of patients, diverse health conditions and various age ranges, ongoing monitoring should be carried out. This helps to take any detail into account and combine a common set of laws with a device thinking process. As a first step, short-term tests have been carried out to determine the functionality of the processes and to figure out the weak points of the system to ease the future. This section represents a brief profile of the patients involved in the studies and data collection findings. This would be the next move in testing to use the same data obtained to verify the Fuzzy logic engine for RFID framework devices.

6.4.1   Hardware Sensors Validation

A design for data collection was used for the collection of data regarding participants of varying ages. Blood pressure (BP), cardiac velocities (HR), blood oxygen levels (SPo$_2$), temperature (TEMP) level, and blood sugar (BS) levels were calculated by participant. This design required data to be obtained from various participants using own devices (RFID tags) of the proposed framework and using RCDR devices. The concept used the data obtained to test and verify the medical devices of the proposed system by comparing the findings to RCDR devices.

The method of evaluating the participants was carried out in two phases to achieve the goals of this report. First for the center devices, the nurse tested the primary signs of the participants and then with the proposed method devices measured the signs again. Finally, the findings were matched between the two separate instruments. Tables with the patient name, age, gender, height, weight, and BMI are included in the findings of the experiment.

6.4.2   Implementations, Testing, and Evaluation of the Fuzzy Logic Engine

A comparison of the status of the risk groups proposed in the fuzzy expert system (DSS) is the assessment of the fuzzy expert system with the status of the risk groups implied in the MPAS scoring system. This section contains tests in 35 patients, of which 26 are RCDR patients and 8 are expected. The 26 RCDR patients are similar who volunteer for the machine instruments to be validated. The data from these patients are also used for the assessment of the fugitive logic engine. The following table summarizes the details and the outcomes received from the patients. The experimental data contain:

1. Vital signs of RCDR patients assessed by RFID sensors are,
   - temperature value
   - SBP value,
   - heart rate value,
   - SPo_2 value,
   - blood sugar value.
2. The outcomes from the condition and ranking of the patients are determined using the MPAS score system. These findings are known as the true results of the system.
3. The outcomes of the risk group status and score of patients were determined with the fluid logical engine. A connection between the performance of the system scoring MPAS and the fuzzy logic comes is then prepared to test the fuzzy logic engine of the system.

It summarizes the results of the analysis for the fluid validation of the logic engine. The findings are grouped in three groups shown in Table 6.8: regular, low-risk and high risk group (HRG). The following are presented in this table. The classification of these groups depends on the outcome. A combination of the risk group status indicated by the fuzzy expert system (decision aid) and the risk group status is based on the MPAS rating system in the assessment of the Fuzzy expert system. Figure 6.14 indicates the disparity between the multiple case scores determined with the MPAS scoring system and the judgement supporting system in the 2D-Cloumn table.

Table 6.8 A comparison between the MPAS results and the Fuzzy Logic results.

| Patient | Vital signs | | | | | | Results | | | |
| | RCDR | | | | | | Using MEWS | | Using fuzzy logic | |
Num	Temp	SBP	HR	SPO2	BS		Status	Score %	Status	Score %
NORMAL (NRM)										
1	37	161	62	97	72		NRM	0	NRM	0.28636
2	36.59	121	79	97	103.5		NRM	0	NRM	0.2863636
3	37	120	65	95	88		NRM	0	NRM	0.2863636
4	37.5	170	80	96	102		NRM	0	NRM	0.28636
5	38.1	127	89	98	89.46		NRM	0	NRM	0.846875
Low Risk Group (LRG)										
6	37.5	139	70	98	120.42		LRG	2	LRG	2.49545
7	37	135	92	96	138		LRG	2	LRG	2.49545
8	37	120	71	98	119.52		LRG	2	LRG	2.49545
9	36.1	129	88	97	134.28		LRG	2	LRG	3.9477273

(Continued)

Table 6.8 A comparison between the MPAS results and the Fuzzy Logic results. (Continued)

| Patient | Vital signs | | | | | | Results | | | | |
| Num | RCDR | | | | | | Using MEWS | | Using fuzzy logic | |
	Temp	SBP	HR	SPO2	BS		Status	Score %	Status	Score %
10	38.2	117	63	98	115		LRG	2	LRG	3.378
11	37	180	92	97	226		LRG	3	LRG	3.504545
12	37	134	84	100	163.26		LRG	3	LRG	3.504545
13	37.5	175	70	97	167		LRG	3	LRG	3.5045455
14	37	184	75	96	156		LRG	3	LRG	3.504545
15	37	144	87	97	206		LRG	3	LRG	3.504545
16	37	147	88	97	277		LRG	3	LRG	3.504545
17	38.2	118	92	96	165		LRG	3	LRG	4.3361224
18	38.2	132	82	95	160.38		LRG	3	LRG	4.3361224
19	37	180	96	98	201		LRG	3	LRG	3.7772727
20	36.6	137	96	100	204		LRG	3	LRG	3.7772727

(Continued)

Table 6.8 A comparison between the MPAS results and the Fuzzy Logic results. (*Continued*)

| Patient | Vital signs | | | | | | Results | | | | |
| | RCDR | | | | | | Using MEWS | | Using fuzzy logic | |
Num	Temp	SBP	HR	SPO2	BS		Status	Score %	Status	Score %
21	36.6	181	58	96	181		LRG	3	LRG	3.8530675
22	37	151	56	98	237.42		LRG	3	LRG	4.0543478
23	37	118	84	94	161		LRG	3	LRG	4.005
24	37	96	55	96	68		LRG	3	LRG	3.8185096
High Risk Group (HRG)										
25	39	137	92	96	253.44		HRG	5	HRG	5.4954545
26	40	134	76	97	184		HRG	5	HRG	5.4954545
27	39	159	65	96	416.7		HRG	5	HRG	5.4954545
28	41	187	87	97	161		HRG	5	HRG	5.9342466
29	38.3	73	97	97	145		HRG	5	HRG	6.9822222
30	37.5	86	48	88	69		HRG	6	HRG	6.5539024
31	38.6	190	120	94	120		HRG	6	HRG	7.8737903

(*Continued*)

Table 6.8 A comparison between the MPAS results and the Fuzzy Logic results. (*Continued*)

| Patient | Vital signs | | | | | | Results | | | |
| | RCDR | | | | | | Using MEWS | | Using fuzzy logic | |
Num	Temp	SBP	HR	SPO2	BS		Status	Score %	Status	Score %
32	38.6	190	127	94	120		HRG	6	HRG	8.3566148
33	38.6	76	40	80	60		HRG	10	HRG	10.5
34	40	300	135	94	160		HRG	10	HRG	10.995

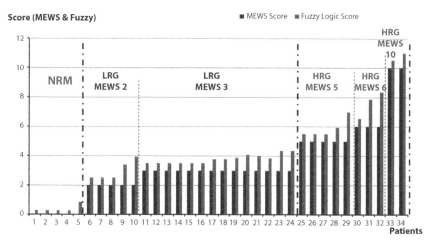

Figure 6.14 2D-Cloumn chart for the different cases scores calculated by the MPAS scoring system and the decision support system is shown.

The MPAS scoring system and based on the same collection of data is the reference score used for assessing the decision support system. The estimated significance of the MPAS scoring system reveals the degree to which the two schemes agree. The faded expert method will it is clear, deliver the same score as the MPAS score system in nearly every situation. The system shall be used in the period between two hospital visits as a support system for tracking patients with chronic diseases.

6.4.3   Normal Group (NRM)

The device was checked with five cases in this type. The four first cases have regular vital signs (the five inputs are normal), while the five cases have 4 normal vital signs and 1 fugitive vital sign. The first four cases are identical. The value of the temperature is from Average to High 2. The MPAS score was found to be 0 (Status: Normal) for all five of these cases, meaning that the five patients had normal signs of life. But the outcomes of the Fuzzy logic indicate a score of 0.286 in the first four patients, and 0.847 in the fifth instance, which distinguishes the 5th from the other. The reference chart for the Normal case is seen in Figure 6.15.

6.4.4   Low Risk Group

The device was checked with 19 cases in this type. The first five incidents fall into the category of low risk group (LRG) 2 and the next 14 fall into the

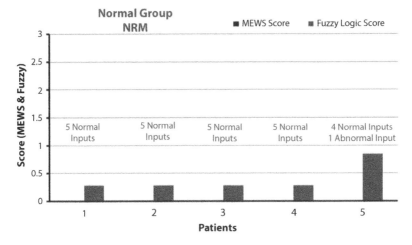

Figure 6.15 The NRM case comparison graph.

category of LRG 3. The first three patients in group LRG 2 have an abnormal input and four regular inputs; the second two have a single abnormal input, a fluid input and three normal inputs. The findings of MPAS revealed a score of 2; in the first three instances, the last two differ in Fuzzy Logic. The comparative diagram of the LRG2 case is seen in Figure 6.16.

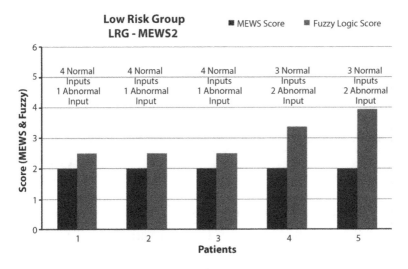

Figure 6.16 The LRG2 case comparison graph.

Figure 6.17 describes the following 14 LRG3 instances and demonstrates Fuzzy Logic differences in outcomes derived from the MPAS scoring system.

Two patient 4 and one patient 5, as seen in Table 6.9, are patients with three regular inputs (SBP, HR, SPo$_2$) and two irregular inputs (temperature and BS); however, the conceptual scoring is distinct. The steps of measuring their scores must be outlined to illustrate this discrepancy, so that the rules are defined and the variations between scores are clarified.

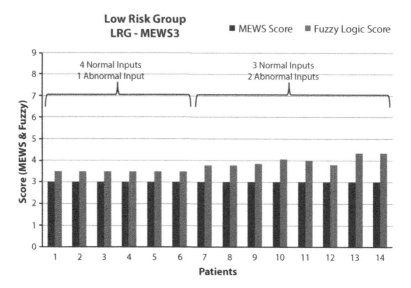

Figure 6.17 LRG3 case comparison graph.

Table 6.9 Patient 4 and 5 vital signs, MPAS and Fuzzy Logic scores.

	RCDR					Using MEWS		Using Fuzzy with overlap	
	Temp	SBP	HR	SPO2	BS	Status	Score %	Status	Score %
Patient 4	36.1	129	88	97	134.28	LRG	2	LRG	3.948
Patient 4	38.2	117	63	98	115	LRG	2	LRG	3.378

Table 6.10 The degree of membership for each input for patient 4.

SBP		HR		SPO2		TEMP		BS	
Input variable	Membership Value	Input variable	Membership Value	Input variable	Membership Value	Input variable	Membership Value	Input variable	Membership Value
LOW 3	0	Low 2	0	Low 3	0	Low 2	0.8	LOW 3	0
LOW 2	0	Low 1	0	Low 2	0	Normal 0	0.2	LOW 2	0
LOW 1	0	Normal 0	1	Low 1	0	High 2	0	Normal-0	0
NORMAL 0	1	High 1	0	Normal 0	1			High 2	1
HIGH 2	0	High 2	0					High 3	0
		High 3	0						

Table 6.11 The degree of membership for each input for patient 5.

SBP Input variable	Membership Value	HR Input variable	Membership Value	SPO2 Input variable	Membership Value	TEMP Input variable	Membership Value	BS Input variable	Membership Value
LOW 3	0	Low 2	0	Low 3	0	Low 2	0	LOW 3	0
LOW 2	0	Low 1	0	Low 2	0	Normal 0	0.6	LOW 2	0
LOW 1	0	Normal 0	1	Low 1	0	High 2	0.4	Normal 0	0
NORMAL 0	1	High 1	0	Normal 0	1			High 2	1
HIGH 2	0	High 2	0					High 3	0
		High 3	0						

The structure is based on 1800 rules as mentioned earlier, and each rule depends on solving the entries into several ambiguous linguistic sets. The data must be fluctuated by both of these language sets before the laws can be tested. For each feedback for patients 4 and 5, Table 6.10 and Table 6.11 indicate the rate of membership.

In conjunction with the rules, the device will attach the weights from above to the membership function. Just two rules (rules 1254 and 1259) fire or not have zero outcomes from the 1800 rules picked. This makes the amount of fuzzy Output Response magnitudes to be deduced, combined and defuzed to return the real crypted output only to "LRG2" and "LRG4," In this list of laws, the inputs are logically connected to the output response values of all predicted inputs by using the AND operator. The results are then combined in a logical sum for each member function. For each output member element, a firing intensity is determined. It only remains to combine these logical sums to generate the crisp output in a defuzzification phase. For each performance membership feature for patient 4 and patient 5, Tables 6.12 and 6.13 indicate the firing power and centroid.

The tables reveal that for the patient 4, the firing strength of the LRG4 is greater than that of the LRG2, while for patient 5, the firing strength of the LRG4 is less than the LRG2. Thus, it is rational for patients 4 to have higher performance score (risk group) than 5. Defluence is obtained by comparing the results of a lowering method with the estimation of the "fuzzy centroid" of the region. The results are then determined. Each output member's weighted strengths are multiplied and summarized by their

Table 6.12 The firing strength and centroid for each output membership function for patient 4.

Rule #	Operators	Strength	Centroid
Rule 1249	If (SBP is Normal 0) and (HR is Normal 0) and (SPO2 is normal 0) and (Temp is Low 2) and (BS is High 2) then (RiskGroup is LRG 4)	1&1&1&0.8&1 = 0.8	LRG 4→ 0.8 Centroid = 4.5
Rule 1254	If (SBP is Normal 0) and (HR is Normal 0) and (SPO2 is normal 0) and (Temp is Low 2) and (BS is High 2) then (RiskGroup is LRG 4)	1&1&1&0.2&1 = 0.2	LRG 2→ 0.2 Centroid = 2.5

Table 6.13 The firing strength and centroid for each output membership function for patient 5.

Rule #	Operators	Strength	Centroid
Rule 1254	If (SBP is Normal 0) and (HR is Normal 0) and (SPO2 is normal 0) and (Temp is Normal 0) and (BS is High 2) then (RiskGroup is LRG 2)	1&1&1&0.6&1 = 0.6	LRG 2→ 0.6 Centroid = 2.5
Rule 1259	If (SBP is Normal 0) and (HR is Normal 0) and (SPO2 is normal 0) and (Temp is High 2) and (BS is High 2) then (RiskGroup is LRG 4)	1&1&1&0.4&1 = 0.4	LRG 4→ 0.4 Centroid = 4.5

respective output member's center points. The risk group performance of patients 4 and 5 is seen in Equations 6.1 and 6.2, respectively.

$$Risk\ group = \frac{((0.8 * 4.5) + (0.2 * 2.5))}{(0.8 + 0.2)} = 4.1 \tag{6.1}$$

$$Risk\ group = \frac{((0.6 * 2.5) + (0.4 * 4.5))}{(0.6 + 0.4)} = 3.3 \tag{6.2}$$

The risk-group ranking of patient 4 based on these findings is 4.1, closer to LRG 4 and better than patient 5, which is weaker than patient 4, and 3.3 based on these results. Back in Table 6.4, patient 4 and patient 5 simulation figures were 3,378 and 3,948. Table 6.14 displays the simulated

Table 6.14 Comparison of calculated and simulated results of the fuzzy logic system for patients 4 and 5.

Results	Patient 4	Patient 5
MATLAB Simulation	3.948	3.378
Calculated Values	4.1	3.3
Difference	0.512	0.078
Error %	1.75	0.34

and measured effects. The outcome discrepancy is due to the machine delay involved.

6.4.5   High Risk Group (HRG)

The device was checked with 10 cases in this type. The first five events fell under HRG5, the next three are under HRG6, and the last two fall under HRG10. The comparison of the MPAS scoring system and the fluctuating outcomes for the HRG are seen in Figures 6.18, 6.19, and 6.20.

This segment discussion reveals that the ranges can be more accurately separated by the fluffiness of the MPAS method and it is simple to find the number of variables that lead to the shift in performance. Furthermore, it is easier to use 15 outputs than the three outputs, because they have a more accurate output. We will also note that the system of Fuzzy logic was better than the system of MPAS scoring.

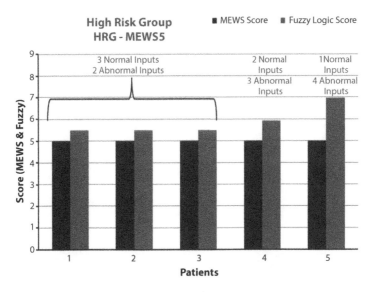

Figure 6.18 The HRG5 case comparison graph.

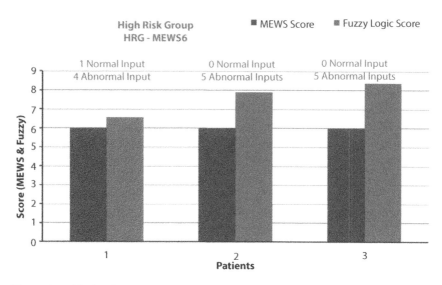

Figure 6.19 The HRG6 case comparison graph.

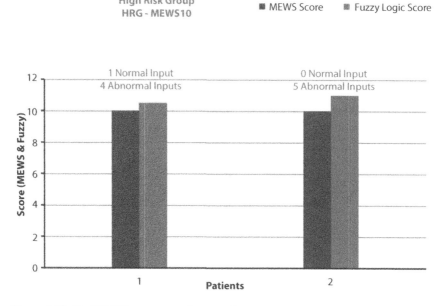

Figure 6.20 The HRG10 case comparison graph.

6.5   Conclusions and Future Work

6.5.1   Summary and Concluding Remarks

The present study has been undertaken to develop an interactive RFID healthcare application for home or in the hospital. This interface enables patients to be mobile during testing and recording reading of their vital signs. A diagnostic framework based on Fuzzy logic techniques complements the platform. The machine increases the ability of workers to control patients' vital signs across various places and medical institutions or at home. It involves crucial sign tracking and alarming, web-based surveillance systems and assisting regulatory clinical decisions in multiple settings. Critically sick patients are constantly tracked with the goal of reducing the risk of extreme harm occurring from slow healthcare delivery.

We also assume that the technology can be applied to the rest of medical fields and combined with other information systems in hospitals. The new framework should provide healthier and safer facilities for the healthcare sector by incorporating more medical centers into the system.

6.5.2   Future Directions

Potential avenues for future study include:

- decrease the specimen size from 26 to a larger collection to improve device checking and precision. A wider patient pool provides more possible disease possibilities and thus a greater coverage of both options.
- to build the Fuzzy logic method to know irregular (Ex. temperature) variables.
- ethnicity and age considerations should be integrated into decision making.
- the findings of the proposed method affirm the utility of fluids in patient surveillance but must also be checked in real-time to demonstrate their entire therapeutic worth.

References

1. Desa, United Nations Population Division, "II. Magnitude And Speed Of Population Ageing - World Population Ageing 1950–2050", in: *Nations, World Assembly On Ageing—2016*, Population Division, Desa, United.

2. *"Defining Key Health Information Technology Terms"*, Department Of Health & Human Services, Office Of The National Coordinator For Health Information Technology, USA, April 28, 2018.

3. Berg, J., *"Current Aad Future Possibilities of Medical Informatics"*, Tromso University, Norway, Spring, 2010.

4. Laguna, J., López, S., Fontecha, J., Fuentes, C., Hervás, R., De Ipiña, D.L., Bravo, J., Villarreal, V., "A Proposal For Mobile Diabetes Self-Control: towards A Patient Monitoring Framework,", in: *Lecture Notes in Computer Science 5518Iwann*, pp. 869–876, 2019.

5. Mcisaac, W.J., Tisler, A., Irvine, M.J., Saunders, A., Dunai, A., Rizo, C.A., Feig, D.S., Hamill, M., Trudel, M., Cafazzo, J.A., Logan, A.G., "Mobile phone–based remote patient monitoring system for management of hypertension in diabetic patients". *Am. J. Hypertens. (Ajh)*, 20, 942–948, 2017.

6. Polk, T., Hande, A., Bhatia, D., Walker, W., "Remote Blood Pressure Monitoring Using A Wireless Sensor Network", in: *IEEE Sixth Annual Emerging Information Technology Conference*, 2017.

7. Yan, Z., Shi, J., Kandachar, P., Freudenthal, A., Jiang, J., "A mobile monitoring system of blood pressure for underserved in china by information and communication technology service,". *IEEE Trans. Inf. Technol. Biomed.*, 14, May 2017.

8. Benyo, B., Varady, P., Benyo, Z., "Patient monitoring on industry standard fieldbus", in: *The First Joint Bmes/Embs Conference*, Atlanta, Ga, Usa, 2007.

9. Figueiredo, C.P., Mühle, C., Ruff, R., Mendes, P.M., Hoffmann, P., Becher, K., "Design and realization of a wireless sensor gateway for health monitoring,", in: *32nd Annual International Conference Of The IEEE EMBS*, Buenos Aires, Argentina, August 31 - September 4, 2016.

10. Blanckenberg, M.M., Scheffer, C., Rademeyer, A.J., "Wireless Physiological Monitoring System For Psychiatric Patients", in: *31st Annual International Conference Of The IEEE EMBS*, Minneapolis, Minnesota, USA, September 2-6, 2019.

11. Besar, R., Tan, Y.S., Tee, K.H., Ong, K.C., Kho, T.K., *"Bluetooth-Enabled Ecg Monitoring System"*, Malaysia, 2006.

12. Choi, B.H., Seo, J.W., Sohn, R.H., Ryu, M.S., Yi, W., Park, K.S., Choi, J.M., "A System For Ubiquitous Health Monitoring In The Bedroom Via A Bluetooth Network And Wireless Lan", in: *26th Annual International Conference Of The IEEE Embs*, San Francisco, Ca, Usa, September 1-5, 2004.

13. Ekström, M., *"Small Wireless Ecg With Bluetooth™ Communication To A Pda"*, Thesis, (Msc, Mälardalen University, 2006.

14. Bai, Y.-W. and Yang, D.-C., "Mobile Blood-Glucose Monitoring Of An Integrated Health Information Management System,", in: *In IEEE International Conference On Consumer Electronics (ICCE)*, 2012.

15. Cho, J., Choi, J., Nam, T., Park, J., "A Zigbee Network- Based Multi-Channel Heart Rate Monitoring System For Exercising Rehabilitation Patients", in: *IEEE*, 2007.

16. Roffia, L., Lamberti, C., Salmon, T., Auteri, V., "Zigbee-Based Wireless Ecg Monitor", in: *Computers In Cardiology*, 2007.
17. Luo, Y.-L., Chang, Y.-S., Lin, Y.-H., Li, W.-J., "A Wireless Blood Pressure Monitoring System For Personal Health Management,", in: *32nd Annual International Conference Of The IEEE EMBS*, Buenos Aires, Argentina, August 31 - September 4, 2010.
18. Chambers, D., Rotariu, C., Frehill, P., "Using Zigbee To Integrate Medical Devices", in: *29th Annual International Conference Of The IEEE EMBS Cité Internationale*, Lyon, France, August 23-26, 2007.
19. Choi, J.S. and Zhou, M., "Performance Analysis Of Zigbee-Based Body Sensor Networks", in: *IEEE International Conference on Systems, Man and Cybernetics*, 2010.
20. Wood, A., Selavo, L., Cao, Q., Fang, L., Doan, T., He, Z., Stoleru, R., Lin, S., Stankovic, J.A., Virone, G., "An advanced wireless sensor network for health monitoring", in: *IEEE*, 2005.

7

Artificial Intelligence: A Key for Detecting COVID-19 Using Chest Radiography

C. Vinothini[1]*, P. Anitha[2], Priya J.[3], Abirami A.[2] and Akash S.[2]

[1]Department of Computer Science and Engineering, Dayananda Sagar College of Engineering, Bengaluru, Karnataka, India
[2]Department of Computer Science and Engineering, Dr. N.G.P Institute of Technology, Coimbatore, Tamilnadu, India
[3]Department of Information Technology, Bannari Amman Institute of Technology, Sathyamangalam, Tamilnadu, India

Abstract

An impending branch of computer science is artificial intelligence. It plays an important role in the construction of smart machines that are capable of performing sophisticated operations. One of the key characteristics of artificial intelligence is its ability to make decisions on its own and rationalize the solution, helping us to achieve a certain goal. Our human race has faced many threats in the form of epidemics and pandemics, which have proved to be almost incurable in the past. Nevertheless, science and its evolving technologies have given us some hope to fight such threats. One such pandemic that our human race is facing in the current times is COVID-19. This deadly disease is rapidly spreading across the whole world endangering the lives of humans. Amid the chaos, we desperately need to stop the spread, or at least take adequate counter-active measures to detect this virus at its early stage. Deep learning, a subset of artificial intelligence provides many models which helps in the automation of the task of detecting viruses in humans mainly with the help of image processing. In detecting COVID-19, deep learning is a breakthrough, which has helped us in our proposed system. This system makes use of chest radiographs (CXR) to detect the presence of the virus in the human body thereby lowering the risk of spread which is fairly high in manual detection methods. The CXRs are one of the most common imaging tests in the clinical field, which helps in detecting the presence of cold, cough, shortness of breath in the lungs, and so on. The proposed model is very efficient when it comes

*Corresponding author: vinuchidambaram@gmail.com

R. Nidhya, Manish Kumar and S. Balamurugan (eds.) Tele-Healthcare: Applications of Artificial Intelligence and Soft Computing Techniques, (159–178) © 2022 Scrivener Publishing LLC

to detecting problems in the lungs with the help of image processing. We propose an improvised neural network derived from the Convolutional Neural Network which works similar to the human brain structure to detect and process the CXR images efficiently and at faster rates. The neural network mimics the functioning of the brain, where self-learning and decision making are its key features. The image data sets are a collection of CXR images which have a RGB value of 1. This approach is proven to be safer and better than the manual testing methods that are currently deployed. As the traditional methods for detecting COVID-19 virus is tedious, and not fairly accurate, automating this task can help in giving accurate results with reduced risk of spread of disease through physical contact.

Keywords: Artificial intelligence, COVID-19 virus detection, chest radiographs, Convolutional Neural Network (CNN), deep learning

7.1   Introduction

Coronavirus disease (COVID-19) is an infectious disease caused by a newly discovered coronavirus, which is genetically related to severe acute respiratory syndrome coronavirus (SARS-CoV-2). In a short period, the spread of this virus is evident over the nation, recording 40.1 million cases worldwide. It has led to 1.11 million deaths, as of October 19, 2020. The virus that causes COVID-19 is predominantly transmitted through droplets which are generated when an infected person coughs, sneezes, or exhales. The virus is highly contagious and instantaneous actions need to be taken to identify the presence of the virus at the primary stage. The qualitative test of nucleic acid to find the presence of SARS-CoV-2 RNA in test specimens is done by reverse transcription polymerase chain reaction (RT-PCR) that is best performed using nasopharynx samples compared with the throat samples that are taken to examine the presence of the virus. Various other tests including Isothermal amplification assays, antigen tests, and antibody tests [14] are also conducted to detect the presence of the virus in human beings but all these involve too much physical presence and hence tend to increase the risk of spread. Surveys and studies have proved that most of the COVID-19 infected patients were also diagnosed with pneumonia [5]. This supports the idea of chest computed tomography (CT) screening on the patients to confirm the infection. However, amidst the rapid increase in COVID-19 patients, this method would only be a burden to the radiology department of various hospitals and laboratories, thus seeking the need of a more efficient approach. Bilateral, peripheral consolidation, and ground glassopacities are the common ways in which CXRs can be categorized.

Nevertheless, it can be put together that CXR image findings have a lesser sensitivity than primary RT-PCR testing (69% vs 91%, respectively). Even though the sensitivity is low, CXR irregularity could be identified in 9% of patients whose initial RT-PCR was negative. Amid the growing pandemic as a grave threat to the human race, CXR images will play a major role in detecting COVID-19 virus at an early stage, provided the methods are improved to attain higher efficiency [6].

As of now, CXR cannot completely replace RT-PCR, nevertheless, it is a way to prioritize patients' treatments as the indication of pneumonia is a common symptom among majority of the patients who have been tested positive with COVID-19 virus, which in turn will help the hospitals to administer all the cases in a better way. Moreover, adopting this method can help in saving medical resources for those who are genuinely in need, as pneumonia is a bacterial infection [17] which occurs frequently, and excluding these patients will help in faster diagnosis of COVID-19 affected patients [23]. Scientific innovations have paved the way for the evolution of new techniques which can identify the presence of COVID-19 virus using CXR images [5]. Although this field of research is still ongoing, we wish to explore this on a deeper level. As we can notice bilateral involvement, peripheral distribution and ground-glass opacification (GGO) in the distribution of COVID-19 virus patterns, a thoroughly designed neural network will be able to detect similar findings successfully [1, 7]. We aim to explore different biological markers used in analyzing CXR images namely, cardio-thoracic ratio, lung area intensity distribution, and so on [3, 4, 11]. The study states that there exists a remarkable contrast in the patch-wise intensity distribution, co-relating to the radiological discoveries of the localized intensity variations in the CXR images. The discoveries help us propose an improvised convolutional neural network architecture, which will help us classify the images with high accuracy providing efficient results at faster rates. Many novel neural network models have been developed for various diseases, including malaria and pneumonia, which provided adequate results and helped a lot. We wish to implement the knowledge of these models to develop an improvised neural network, efficient enough to detect COVID-19 in patients at an early stage to improve the medical situation and contribute to early recovery of patients. The existing model that helps in detecting COVID-19 in patients using CXR images (Figure 7.1) works on a smaller data set, and is limited in many ways. Our proposed architecture helps in clarifying all the drawbacks that were present in the existing model, thereby being more efficient and reliable in real-time usage.

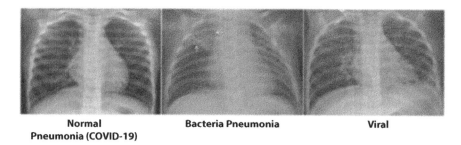

Normal   **Bacteria Pneumonia**   **Viral**
Pneumonia (COVID-19)

Figure 7.1 A sample of CXR images.

One of the key aspects of using such architecture is the automatic detection of important features without human supervision, learning distinctive features of the given data set on its own. Moreover we can see that the network detects and corrects the spatial errors on its own without any additional aids thereby contributing to a refined output. With our improvised architecture we show that our work outputs higher efficiency and accuracy, compared to the existing model.

7.2   Related Work

7.2.1   Traditional Approach

History reveals that a lot of research work has been done in this field which has introduced various methods, such as classification, clustering, and optimization methods. With the advancement in technology the assistance of computers have been coupled along with these methods which has helped in detecting a lot of disease causing viruses including the detection of pneumonia in lung images [19]. M Cocklin *et al.* [19] had proposed an image processing system for digital Chest X-Ray images in 1984. However, the times were not developed to handle, such a tedious task, considering the hardware and software capabilities.

Mathias Prokop *et al.* [20] discussed about the different principles of image processing in digital chest radiography. They used spatial frequency and gradation as their key parameters for processing the images. Many of these methods related to traditional theories and early agemachine learning approach, including thresholding algorithms, geometrical features, texture features or statistical methods. Although these methods provided adequate results, they required knowledge beforehand, the preprocessing was quite complex, and were able to work only on small data sets, thereby narrowing down reliability.

7.2.2   Deep Learning–Based Approach

Over the past few years, Deep Learning approaches [15], like Convolutional Neural Network models have been prominent in the field of Machine Learning [8, 9]. It dates back to the 1990s, where researchers made use of CNN models to perform speech recognition and text recognition. Later on, it was also used for handwriting recognition, image recognition, gene sequence analysis and disease analysis. Alex Krizhevsky, in 2012 proposed AlexNet for natural image classification. It is a deep CNN model which gained a fair amount of fame in the ILSVRC challenge. AlexNet drastically improved the efficiency CNN models in the classification of natural images [23].

Later, many novel and efficient models, such as ResNet, DenseNet, and Dual Path Networks (DPN) were developed [1, 3, 10, 12, 13, 16]. In the recent years, CNN models have helped a lot in medical image analysis including pneumonia detection, malaria detection, and so on. Pranav Rajpurkar *et al.* [1] used an algorithm which consisted of 121 layers of convolution, which had a 76.8% accuracy in detecting pneumonia in CXR images [2]. Lakhani and Sundaram [2] are the two people who embedded the AlexNet and GoogLeNet neural networks with data augmentation. This was done without any pretraining to obtain an area under the curve (AUC) of 0.94–0.95. Mask-RCNN, a deep neural network, was used by Jaiswal *et al.* which employs both global and local characteristics for pulmonary image segmentation combined with image augmentation, along with dropout and L2 regularization, for pneumonia identification achieved an area under the curve (AUC) of 0.95. These deep learning approaches [15] required less information prior to preprocessing, were able to train on large data sets and had prominent applications almost everywhere. However, in the previous studies on pneumonia lung image classification, researchers generally used original and simple CNN network for experiments. Various efficient strategies can be used in image classification which was proposed recently, and with slight variations, higher accuracy and efficiency can be expected. Our proposed architecture is inspired by the above mentioned related works, which aims for higher efficiency and better performance, compared to the methods used before.

7.3   Materials and Methods

7.3.1   Data Set and Data Pre-Processing

The data set was obtained from National Institutes of Health (NIH), and Kaggle. The image data set consisted of different images: normal CXR images, Pneumonia contained CXR images, and COVID-19 CXR images. The image data set is classified into three subsets: test, train, val. As the name suggests, test subset contains images that are used to test our model, train subset contains images that are used to train our model, and val subset contains images which are used for validation of our model. The images were labeled by the authors for the purpose of image processing. Natural language processing (NLP) was used by the authors to create these labels for all these images. NLP assisted to retrieve data from the radiological reports. These labels are expected to be more than 90% accurate and will serve the purpose of our training, testing and validation. The purpose of choosing these data sets was the availability of these data sets publically for any research group and also that the images were labeled with all the necessary details for the research purpose. Before curating the data set, we had pediatric CXR images included in it. To avoid any form of biasing in the network, we excluded the pediatric images.

Several methods are used over these images for data augmentation which include rotation, zooming, shifting and horizontal flip. These augmentation methods are applied after the commencement of the training process, before each cross-validation. Each subset contains three folders labelled: Normal, Pneumonia, COVID-19. As per Table 7.1, there are a total of 29879 images as of now, out of which we have 620 images relating to COVID-19, 11504 Pneumonia associated images, and 17015 normal images. We wish to increase the size of the data set as much as possible for better accuracy and efficiency of the model. We can see in the table given (Table 7.2), that the existing model uses 15043 images in total, to train, test and validate their model.

The existing model [3] uses a data set consisting of normal images, Pneumonia images, and COVID-19 images, a detailed description of which is given below:

Table 7.1 Data set in proposed model.

Data set	Normal	Pneumonia	COVID-19	Total
Training	17015	11504	620	29229
Validation	150	150	25	325
Testing	150	150	25	325
Total	17405	11804	670	29879

Table 7.2 Data set in existing model.

Data set	Normal	Pneumonia	COVID-19	Total
Training	8651	5812	160	14623
Validation	100	100	10	210
Testing	100	100	10	210
Total	8851	6012	180	15043

7.3.2 Proposed Model

Our proposed model is an improvised version of the existing Deep Learning model used for analyzing CXR images to detect COVID-19 [1]. The model uses three layers of convolution, along with a ResNet layer and an Xception layer [22]. This is different from the basic convolutional model that is generally used, which only has layers of convolution for image processing. In this architecture (Figure 7.2), input information enters the subsequent layers, to realize the integration of feature flow, with reduced loss of information transfer and avoiding the problem of gradient disappearance. Compared to natural image recognition, detecting COVID-19 infected CXR images is quite a difficult task, as not only the shape of the infected tissues is changeable, but also the ambiguous boundary between infected tissues and normal tissues could differ [18, 20]. The deep learning network focuses on critical factors or core areas to improve the performance. It understands the key features of COVID-19 affected CXR images, thereby improving the efficiency of the entire model. The different layers in the network include: Three convolutional layers each layer accompanied by a ReLU layer and a Softmax layer, a ResNet layer, and an exception layer. The convolutional layer is said to be the major element of a Convolutional Neural Network. It has different parameters, such as a set of filters or kernels, which have the capability of self-learning, with a small receptive field. They extend throughout the complete depth of the input volume. For every forward pass that the network initiates over the input volume, each of the filters is convolved across the height and width of the volume. During this process, the dot product between the input and the entries of the filter is calculated, resulting in an activation map of the filter which is 2-dimensional in nature. Hence, the network is able to acknowledge the filters that operate when it detects a particular type of feature at a spatial position in the input. Another key element of the network is the rectified linear unit, often referred to as ReLU. It utilizes the nonsaturating activation function. It effectively discards the negative values from the activation map by changing their values to zero.

This unit tends to enhance the overall network's decision making abilities and functionalities, thereby improving the nonlinear properties without governing the receptive fields of the network's layer of convolution. Another important function that needs to be spoken of is the softmax function, which is a generalized form of the logistic function with a multi-dimensional nature. It is frequently used in multinomial regression and also as the last activation function of a neural network to anneal the output of the network as a probability distribution over the speculated classes of outputs. An additional layer used is the ResNet. It is the abbreviation of Residual Neural Network. It develops on constructs acquired from pyramid cells in the cerebral cortex of the human brain. It achieves this by making use of skip connections, or shortcuts to skip a few layers. This layer is often utilized to increase the learning speed, by means of diminishing the effect of disappearing gradients, by transmitting between less numbers of layers.

The additional Exception layer used lightens the network which makes use of depth wise convolution followed by a pointwise convolution. The three hyper parameters that govern the convolution layer's output volume's size are: depth, stride and zero-padding. The first hyper parameter, the depth, is responsible of the count of the neurons present in the layer that connect common regions of the input volume. The neurons present in the layer gain an understanding of how to activate themselves for various features in the input. For instance, considering that the first convolutional layer gets the raw image as its input, then various neurons next to the dimensional depth may get actuated in the existence of different aligned edges, or color smears. The stride is responsible for managing the functionality of the depth columns across the assigned spatial dimensions that is the width and height. As the stride takes the value 1, the filters progress with the interval of one pixel. This process, however results in heavy

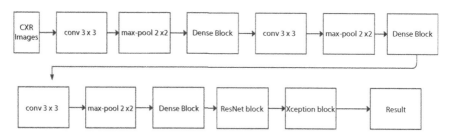

Figure 7.2 Architecture of proposed model.

overlapping of the receptive fields between the depth columns followed by large volumes of output. When the stride changes to 2, the filter moves at the interval of 2 pixels.

The overwhelming benefit of increasing the stride length is that the overlapping of the receptive fields gets reduced and the output volume thus generated has compact spatial dimensions. It is advantageous at times to add zeros to the input on the boundary of the input volume.

The third important hyperparameter is the size of the padding. It gives access to the spatial size of the output volume. At times, it is required to specifically maintain the spatial size of the input volume. The output volume's spatial size can be calculated using a function which takes in the parameters as stated below:

Input volume size V, the kernel field size of the neurons present in the layer of convolution F_s, the stride used to for the application A_s, and the quantity of zero padding Z_p used on the boundary. The formula used for computing the number of neurons that can accompany in a given volume is:

$$\frac{V - F_s + 2Z_p}{A_s} \tag{7.1}$$

Suppose, the value obtained is a noninteger, then we can say that the neurons cannot be aligned to be positioned in the input volume in a uniform manner and that the strides are erroneous. Basically speaking, changing the zero padding to be $Z_p = (F_s - 1)/2$ when the stride acquires the value $A_s = 1$ results in the similar size of the input volume and output volume when compared spatially. Nevertheless, it is not always needed to make use of all the neurons present in the preceding layer. For example, a designer designing a particular neural network designer may resolve to make use of just a part of padding, and not use it completely. Another layer that plays a crucial role in our model is the pooling layer. It functions independently over the input's depth and changes the size of it in a spatial manner. It resamples the input given to it in a nonlinear manner. It makes use of multiple nonlinear functions to implement the pooling process. The pooling layer splits the input image into a collection of disjoint rectangles, and for each of the region thus formed; the layer outputs the maximum value. One of the most common functions that is used is the max pooling function. The benefit of using a pooling layer is that it reduces the number of parameters that are used, and effectively decreases the spatial size of the input given to the layer for processing. These layers are often inserted between each layer of convolution, accompanied by a ReLU layer.

Even though the recent trends in neural networks is of incorporating smaller filters, thereby discarding the pooling layers, the functionality of pooling layer proves to be of great significance in image detection and therefore helps us a lot in our architecture.

The most usual form of this layer is one with a 2×2 filter size used with a stride of 2 over every depth portion in the input by a value of 2 through the width and height, thereby removing three-fourth of the activation:

$$g_{A,B}(A_S) = \max_{x,y=0}^{1} A_{S_{2A+x,2B+y}} \tag{7.2}$$

In this instance, all the operations are over 4 numbers, and hence it has no effect over thedepth dimension.

One of the key benefits of our proposed model is its dense layer. It gives a unique architecture (Figure 7.3) to our model as there exists a stark contrast between a convolutional layer and a dense layer. As the dense layer learns from its previous layer, unlike the convolutional layer which uses consistent features with a minimal field of reception, it helps a lot in learning fast and providing better results. Here, every neuron is connected to one another, that is, each of the neurons get the input from the neurons in the preceding layer, and hence the network is densely connected.

ReLU adopts the activating function which is nonsaturating in nature:

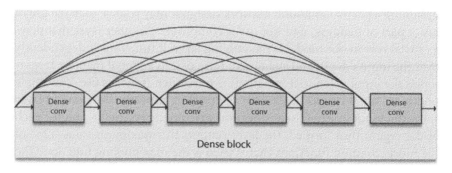

Figure 7.3 Architecture of a dense block [23].

$$f(a) = \max(0, a) \tag{7.3}$$

ResNet propagates forward by skipping intermediary layers. For single skips, the layers may be indexed either as **i** − 2 to **i** or as **i** to **i** + 2. Given a weight matrix $V^{i-1,i}$ for connection weights from layer **i** − 1 to **i**, and a weight matrix $V^{i-2,i}$ for connection weights from layer **i** − 2 to **i**, then the forward propagation would be:

$$x^i := f(V^{i-1,1}.x^{i-1} + y^i + V^{i-2,\,i}.x^{i-2}) \tag{7.4}$$

$$:= f(A^i + V^{i-2,i}.x^{i-2}) \tag{7.5}$$

where:
x^i the activation (outputs) of the neurons in layer **i**, f the activation function of the layer **i**,
$V^{i-1,i}$ the weight matrix for the neurons between layer **i**-1 and **i** and

$$A^i = V^{i-1,\,i}.x^{i-1} + y^i \tag{7.6}$$

In general case this would be expressed as:

$$x^i := f\left(A^i + \sum_{h=2}^{H} V^{i-h,i}.x^{i-h} \right) \tag{7.7}$$

When it propagates forward:

$$v^{i-1,i} := -1 \frac{\partial R^i}{\partial v^{i-1,i}} = -1 x^{i-i}.e^i \tag{7.8}$$

where:
l, a learning rate (l<0),
e^i, the error signal of neurons at layer **i**, and
x^i_l the activation of neurons at layer **i**.

The depth wise separable convolution layer [21] is what powers the Exception. The heightand weight after applying a layer of convolution is obtained by:

$$\frac{\text{height} = (\text{height} - \text{size of filter} + 2^*\text{padding}) + 1}{\text{Stride}} \qquad (7.9)$$

$$\frac{\text{height} = (\text{height} - \text{size of filter} + 2^*\text{padding}) + 1}{\text{Stride}} \qquad (7.10)$$

For segmentation purposes we used Mean Absolute Error loss function which gave us nearzero error for both training and testing phases.

$$EL(p,\hat{p}) = \frac{1}{S}\sum_{1=0}^{S}|p - \hat{p}_i| \qquad (7.11)$$

where $\hat{p}$ is the predicted value.

ALGORITHM
1. Proposed Model:

Step 1: Load test images and train images separately for processing. The pixel values of allthe images are stored in a matrix format.
Step 2: Resize test images and train images by reducing its width and height and preservingthe aspect ratio.
Step 3: Convert test images and train images into numerical arrays for efficient and fastprocessing.
Step 4: Shuffle the numerical array of train images to avoid ambiguity.
Step 5: Split the train images into two: test and train for providing input to the neuralnetwork.
Step 6: Provide the input to the neural network and process the data set.
Step 7: Compile the neural network model to introspect the result and evaluate it.
Step 8: Output the summary to check the accuracy of the neural network model.

2. Neural Network:

Step 1: The resized test images and train images are passed as input to the first convolutionallayer which uses a kernel size of 3 and a 3×3 mask. The output of the convolutional layer ispassed to the Dense Block to connect all the sublayers used in the convolutional layer together to achieve the required output.

Step 2: The Output of the convolutional layer is now passed into the ResNet layer which incorporates the Batch Normalization technique to alter the input and augment the performance of the network. In addition to the Batch Normalization technique, this layer also makes use of Kernel regularizer and Activity regularizer to minimize the weight and bias of the output.

Step 3: The final layer, Xception layer is used, which utilizes three channels to operate on theinput in two manners: Depth wise and Point wise.

7.4 Experiment and Result

7.4.1 Experiment Setup

The CXR image data was segmented into subsets and labelled by NIH and Kaggle. All theimages relate to real life patients; therefore, all our experiments are based on the patient level. We hold the opinion that the model trained and evaluated on the patient level is of more practical significance and closer to reality. In this study, we use Accuracy, Sensitivity, Specificity and F1 value (F1-score) as evaluation criteria for the experimental result, which are defined as follows:

$$\text{Accuracy} = P_t/(N_t + P_f + P_t + N_f) \tag{7.12}$$

$$\text{Sensitivity} = P_t/(P_t + N_f) \tag{7.13}$$

$$\text{Specificity} = N_t/(N_t + P_f) \tag{7.14}$$

$$\text{F1\_score} = 2P_t/(2P_t + Pf + N_f) \tag{7.15}$$

where P_t stands for true positive, N_t is true negative, P_f is false positive, and N_f is false negative. In the training process, the epoch is a set of 100, the batch is a set of 64, we set the learning rate to 0.01 with the momentum parameter of 0.9, the loss function is set to categorical cross-entropy and the optimizer is set to Adam.

The data set is split into three subsets, the train subset, the test subset and the val subset. The images in the train and test subsets are then read and stored into two different lists. After this, we resize the images by shrinking it according to our needs. Then the lists containing thepixel level data of the images is converted into 2-dimensional numeric arrays.

Now we come to the part where we split the data for training and testing. We take 25% of the data set for testing, and 75% for training. Our model starts its functioning with the activation of the first layer of convolution.

The convolutional layer applies a filter to the given input which gives rise to an activation. This process, when repeated outputs an activation map, or a set of them, whichcan be termed as a feature map. The feature map shows the positions of the features that it detected from the input, and also indicates its strength [24]. The first layer consists of 128 filters. The filters are reduced exponentially for the next two convolution layers. The improvement in the architecture of the network provides us with the ability of working with large number of filters under an image classification problem. This enhances the ability of themodel to automatically learn from larger data sets to provide better efficiency. We alsoincorporate 3 strides and a ReLU activation function. Then we make use of a MaxPooling layer which helps in the reduction of the spatial dimensions of the output volume. The use of strides is to determine the "step" of the convolution across the horizontal and vertical axis of the input volume. At the end of this process, we use an optimizer (in our case we used "Adam") to optimize the output. The whole process is repeated 3 times, with different values of filters at the time of initialization of each convolutional layer, for attaining the bestaccurate result possible.

After the end of the processing using the convolutional layer, we add a layer of Residual Neural Network, commonly called "ResNet." ResNet makes use of a function called "regulazier" which is applied onto the parameters used in the different layers of the network during the optimization process. These values are appended to the loss function of thenetwork. At the end, we include another layer for computation, called the Exception layer. This layer consists of four blocks, each block having three layers of convolution accompaniedby a ReLU activation function and a batch normalization function for each of the layers. There are two additional blocks that control the flow of the data. After the whole process is finished, the output is regularized, and batch normalization function is activated. The summary of the model summarizes the whole process. The different layers used in our proposed network tend to complicate the architecture, with different layers stacked up together into a single network.

Even though there are many layers used, they are efficiently utilized during the training process, to yield the desired results. This experiment is implemented in a Keras framework of 2.4.3 based on TensorFlow-GPU 2.3.0 written in Python 3.7.6 under Windows system consisting of 16 GB RAM, 8th Gen Intel i5 Processor, and a NVIDIA GTX 1050 GPU.

7.4.2   Comparison with Other Models

In our study, we adopt Accuracy, Sensitivity, Specificity, and F1-score as the evaluation criteria. Table 7.4 shows the average metric scores of the comparative methods. To evaluate the performance of different classification methods, we train and evaluate several representative CNN models on the same data, including DL COVID-19 and COVID-Net. We implemented codes of these two CNN networks and evaluated the performances in our experimental condition. The performance metrics helps us determine the loss in our network and introspect the same with the networks used for comparison. It gives us a clear idea of how well our network performs in contrast to the State of the Art (SOTA) methods that already exist. All experiments are performed in the same environment and evaluated on the same data set. We compared our proposed model, with different networks to evaluate our network'sperformance.

Starting off, we can see from the Table 7.3 that COVID-Net has an accuracy of 82.7%, Sensitivity of 80.1, Specificity of 91.2 and an F1-Score of 78.8. FC DenseNet67 has an accuracy of 81.8, sensitivity of 73.1, 91.5 of specificity, and 74.3% of F1-score. Looking at FC DenseNet103, we can see that it is 88.9% accurate, 83.4% sensitive, 96.4% specific, and has an 59.3% F1-score. U-Net gives 85.9% accuracy, 82.3% sensitive toward the data set, 95.3 specific and has a F1-score of 82.5.

Table 7.3 Comparison with other networks.

Networks	Accuracy	Sensitivity	Specificity	F1 score
COVID-Net	82.7	80.1	91.2	78.8
U-Net	85.9	82.3	95.3	82.5
FC DenseNet67	81.8	73.1	91.5	74.3
FC DenseNet103	88.9	83.4	96.4	84.4
Proposed method	91.1	86.6	97.2	87.1

Table 7.4 Comparison with existing networks.

Networks	Accuracy	Sensitivity	Specificity	F1 score
Existing method	70.7	92.5	89.7	59.3
Proposed method	91.1	86.6	97.2	87.1

7.5 Results

Table 7.4 shows the average metric scores of the comparative methods. Compared with the other models, our model achieved superior performance, obtaining the accuracy of 97.47%, sensitivity of 97.78% and specificity of 97.07%, which means that our proposed architecture is more suitable for the task of detecting COVID-19 from CXR images. The size of the patch used has an adverse effect on the performance of the model. To calculate this, wetested the model with different patch sizes, like 112 × 112, 224 × 224, and 448 × 448. The results were not at all satisfying with the patch size of 112 × 112. However, that was not the case with the patch size of 448 × 448. We could note that we obtained up to par results with the patchsize of 224 × 224, even though the accuracy was a bit lower than that of the patch 448 × 448. Therefore, from Table 7.5, we can say that decreasing the size of the patch points out to be a major downside, but increasing it does not seem to do much of a help either.

Hence we tested different patch sizes, and chose the one lying in the middle of both the patch sizes. We have compared the performance of our model using a global patch and a local patch. The graph shown above depicts the absolute performance of the model, on the basis of global and local patches.

These patches help determine the loss in pixels, whilst training the images and help to find these missing regions. These approaches are named so as they function on the global and local region of the images.

The **x-axis** of the graph shows the proportion of training data that we are taking, which lies between 0% and 100%, which is scaled to be within the range of 0 and interpreted with thevalues between 0 and 1. The **y-axis** depicts the accuracy of the model, the range of which is between 0 and 1 interpreting the percentage (0% to 100%). We start off with 10% data, and at this level, the absolute performance of the global patch is around 60% and that of the local patch is around 40%. As the training data are increased in proportion, we can see the gradual change In the absolute performance

Table 7.5 Classification results using different patch sizes.

Patch size	Accuracy	Sensitivity	Specificity	F1 score
112 × 112	81.2	77.3	94.4	78.6
224 × 224	91.1	86.6	97.2	87.1
448 × 448	94.3	83.2	96.6	82.2

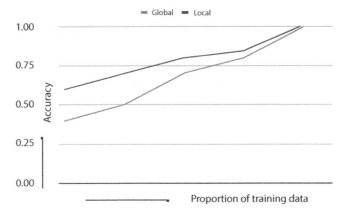

Figure 7.4 Absolute performance.

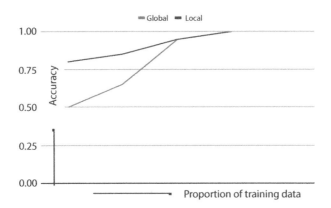

Figure 7.5 Relative performance.

(Figure 7.4) toward the positive side, indicating that the model performs better as the proportion of the training data is increased. The same can be seen inthe case of relative performance (Figure 7.5).

7.6   Conclusion

COVID-19 has become a global pandemic in such a short period that it should be taken seriously and we all need to be cautious about it at all times. In such times, it is difficult to visit hospitals physically and spend time there for manual tests. The use of CXR images for diagnosis of COVID-19 proves to be of great help. As the traditional methods used for diagnosis are not enough for clinical purposes, we need to make use of artificial intelligence to improve the performance of these methods. During the development of our model, we realized how complicated the architecture was becoming, and hence we tried our best to optimize the whole network to diminish erroneous situations and bring out the best result possible. As the traditional methods used for diagnosis are not enough for clinical purposes, we need to make use of artificial intelligence to improve the performance of these methods. Even though collecting large CXR images is difficult due to the nature of the pandemic, training a deep neural network is a tough task.

However, with the help of NIH and Kaggle, we could collect ample images for training, testing and validation of our model. Our proposed model shows outstanding performance in classifying COVID-19 infected CXR images, has higher precision and faster convergence speed. Our experiments show that neural network based image detection methods are very promising for detecting COVID-19 in patients. In the future, we hope that our proposed model can be deployed in areas with poor medical conditions and medical facilities. It will greatly reduce the burden on doctors and increase the speed of diagnosis, and alleviate the harm caused by the emerging pandemic.

References

1. Rajpurkar, P., Irvin, J., Zhu, K., Yang, B., Mehta, H., Duan, T., Ding, D., Bagul, A., Ball, R.L., Langlotz, C., Shpanskaya, K., Lungren, M.P., Ng, A.Y., CheXNet: Radiologist-Level Pneumonia Detection on Chest X-Rays with Deep Learning. *Comput. Vis. Pattern Recognit.*, 1711.05225, 1–7, 25 Dec 2017.
2. Lakhani, P. and Sundaram, B., Deep Learning at Chest Radiography: Automated Classification of Pulmonary Tuberculosis by Using Convolutional Neural Networks. *Radiology*, 2, 2017 Aug, Epub 2017 Apr 24. PMID: 28436741, 284(), 574–582.
3. Wong, H.Y.F. *et al.*, Frequency and distribution of chest radiographic findings in COVID-19 positive patients. *Radiology*, Art. no. 201160, Mar. 2020.
4. Oh, Y., Park, S., Ye, J.C., "Deep Learning COVID-19 Features on CXR Using Limited Training Data Sets". *IEEE Trans. Med. Imaging*, 39, 8, 2688–2700, Aug. 2020.
5. Brown, P.D. and Lerner, S.A., Community-acquired pneumonia. *Lancet*, 352, 9136, 1295–1302, 1998.

6. Farooq, M. and Hafeez, A., COVID-ResNet: A deep learning framework for screening of COVID19 from radiographs, *The Lancet*, 352, 1295–1302, 2020. arXiv:2003.14395. [Online]. Available: http://arxiv.org/abs/2003.14395.

7. Franquet, T., Imaging of pneumonia: Trends and algorithms. *Eur. Respir. J.*, 18, 196–208, 2001.

8. Kallianos, K., Mongan, J., Antani, S., Henry, T., Taylor, A., Abuya, J., Kohli, M., How far have we come? Artificial intelligence for chest radiograph interpretation. *Clin. Radiol.*, 74, 338–345, 2019.

9. Hosny, A., Parmar, C., Quackenbush, J., Schwartz, L.H., Aerts, H.J., Artificial intelligence in radiology. *Nat. Rev. Cancer*, 18, 500–510, 2018.

10. Wang, Y., Wang, C., Zhang, H., Ship classification in high-resolution SAR images using deep learning of small datasets. *Sensors*, 18, 2929, 2018.

11. Roy, S. *et al.*, Deep Learning for Classification and Localization of COVID-19 Markers in Point-of-Care Lung Ultrasound. *IEEE Trans. Med. Imaging*, 39, 8, 2676–2687, Aug. 2020.

12. Ouyang, X. *et al.*, Dual-Sampling Attention Network for Diagnosis of COVID-19 From Community Acquired Pneumonia. *IEEE Trans. Med. Imaging*, 39, 8, 2595–2605, Aug. 2020.

13. Wang, X. *et al.*, A Weakly-Supervised Framework for COVID-19 Classification and Lesion Localization From Chest CT. *IEEE Trans. Med. Imaging*, 39, 8, 2615–2625, Aug. 2020.

14. Eisenstadt, M., Ramachandran, M., Chowdhury, N., Third, A., Domingue, J., COVID-19 Antibody Test Vaccination Certification: There's an app for that. *IEEE Open Journal of Engineering in Medicine and Biology*, 1, 148–155, 2020.

15. Jamshidi, M. *et al.*, Artificial Intelligence and COVID-19: Deep Learning Approaches for Diagnosis and Treatment. *IEEE Access*, 8, 109581–109595, 2020.

16. Hu, S. *et al.*, Weakly Supervised Deep Learning for COVID-19 Infection Detection and Classification From CT Images. *IEEE Access*, 8, 118869–118883, 2020.

17. MDPI and ACS Style, Luján-García, J.E., Yáñez-Márquez, C., Villuendas-Rey, Y., Camacho-Nieto, O., A Transfer Learning Method for Pneumonia Classification and Visualization. *Appl. Sci.*, 10, 2908, 2020.

18. Udugama, B., Kadhiresan, P., Kozlowski, H.N. *et al.*, Diagnosing COVID-19: The Disease and Tools for Detection. *ACS Nano*, 14, 4, 3822–3835, 2020.

19. Cocklin, M., Gourlay, A., Jackson, P., Kaye, G., Miessler, M., Kerr, I., Lams, P., An image processing system for digital chest X-ray images. *Comput. Programs Biomed.*, 19, 1, 3–11, 1984.

20. Ciresan, D., Meier, U., Masci, J., Gambardella, L.M., Schmidhuber, J., Flexible, High Performance Convolutional Neural Networks for Image Classification (PDF). *Proceedings of the Twenty-Second International Joint Conference on Artificial Intelligence*, vol. 2, pp. 1237–1242. Retrieved 17 November 2013, 2011.

21. Chollet, F., Xception: Deep Learning with Depth wise Separable Convolutions, in: *IEEE Conference on Computer Vision and Pattern Recognition*, 2017.

22. Krizhevsky, A., Sutskever, I., Hinton, G.E., Imagenet classification with deep convolutional neural networks, in: *Advances in neural information processing systems*, pp. 1097–1105, 2012, https://doi.org/10.1145/3065386.

23. Brownlee, J., Image Classification, Object Detection, and Face Recognition in Python, in: *Deep Learning for Computer Vision, Machine Learning Mastery*, 2019.

24. Quan, Q., Wang, J., Liu, L., An Effective Convolutional Neural Network for Classifying Red Blood Cells in Malaria Diseases. *Interdiscip. Sci.*, 217–225, 2020. https://doi.org/10.1007/s12539-020-00367-7.

8

An Efficient IoT Framework for Patient Monitoring and Predicting Heart Disease Based on Machine Learning Algorithms

Shanthi S.[1]*, Nidhya R.[2], Uma Perumal[3] and Manish Kumar[4]

[1]Department of CSE, Malla Reddy College of Engineering and Technology, Hyderabad, Telangana, India
[2]Department of CSE, Madanapalle Institute of Technology & Science, Andhra Pradesh, India,
[3]Department of Computer Science, Jazan University, KSA, Saudi Arabia
[2]School of Computer Science and Engineering, Vellore Institute of Technology, Chennai, Tamil Nadu, India

Abstract

One of the major technologies, which support healthcare industry and its applications in the current scenario, is the Internet of Things (IoT). The IoT plays a vital role in the field of health services by interconnecting various resources involved in the medical field and provides more secure, smart and effective services to the general community. Many advanced sensors are available right now in the market that can be wearable or can be implanted into the human body and the purpose of which is to observe the health of the patients continuously, collect their data and transfer the patient's health-related data to the medical server. Machine learning along with IoT is being extensively used in the field of health sector and medical diagnosis. With the improvement in the technology, we could predict the diseases forehand and can able to predict the seriousness of the problem. The IoT framework is used for collecting the heartbeat, blood pressure, and temperature of a person via the sensor deployed in the human body and using machine learning algorithm to predict the heart disease of a particular person and also to analyze the current health condition of a particular person. Cleveland heart diseases data set is being used here for predicting the heart disease and the collected patient information is used for finding out the prediction of diseases. Comparison of four

---
*Corresponding author: shanu_shivak@yahoo.com

R. Nidhya, Manish Kumar and S. Balamurugan (eds.) Tele-Healthcare: Applications of Artificial Intelligence and Soft Computing Techniques, (179–200) © 2022 Scrivener Publishing LLC

machine learning algorithms, namely Naïve Bayes Algorithm, Decision Trees, KNN and logistic regression, is carried out. Proposed method combines both IoT and machine learning concepts and is used to provide efficient and effective remote health monitoring for patient, determine whether a patient is having a particular disease or not as well as to provide a quick solution to the patients in case of some emergency situation, which requires immediate doctor attention. The proposed method is very effective and helps in predicting the heart diseases at a very early stage.

Keywords: Remote patient monitoring, IoT, Naïve Bayes algorithm, decision trees, logistic regression, K-Neighbor classifier

8.1   Introduction

With the advancement of the technology, remote health monitoring system has become one of the easiest and fastest ways to assess the health of a patient. It is a very important area, which gains more attention in the recent years. Remote healthcare ranges from monitoring elderly people, children's, chronic patients, accident victims, and so on. Instead of the patient meeting the doctor directly, health-related parameters are measured continuously by means of using sensors and then the data are processed and forwarded to the medical server. There are varieties of sensors available in market for monitoring various essential signs such as temperature, blood pressure, glucose levels in blood, pulse rate, and so on. Wireless body Area Networks play a major role in the current scenario. It is capable of collecting real-time information continuously and could carry out the continuous monitoring of the patients. WBAN is mainly used in mainly used in monitoring the patients, especially the chronic disease patients. WBAN is basically a short range wireless technology. The tiny sensors are implanted into human body capable of capturing the information about the patient and communicating among them and among processor wirelessly within a short range of distance. In remote patient monitoring system, medical information about the patients can be collected automatically by using sensors and can be communicated and processed by the medical team.

Figure 8.1 shows a typical architecture diagram of WBAN-based healthcare monitoring system. The body consists of various sensors/actuators and body control unit (BCU). Sensors gather the information such as blood pressure, temperature, pulse oximeter for oxygen levels and pulse rate, ECG for heart beats, EEG for detecting brain waves, EMG for

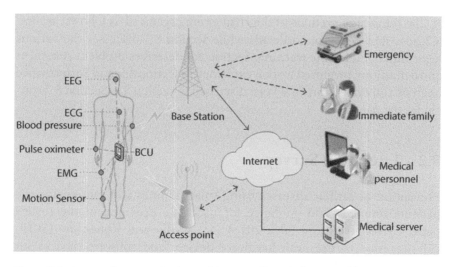

Figure 8.1 A general communication architecture of a typical WBAN-based healthcare monitoring system [43].

measuring muscle response, and so on, and pass this information to the BCU. Actuators are nodes which are responsible for carrying out the work based on the instructions from sensors or from BCU. The BCU work is to gather all the information from all the sensors and then to transmit the information to the base station and then to the medical server and medical personnel either local or remote along with the patients record history. From the base station, the information is transferred to the family members and depending on the emergency situation informed to the ambulance person also. The doctor can access and process the data and can provide the timely help to the patients [1].

Internet of Things consists of sensors, processors and communications hardware, and all these put together results in gathering data transmit the data and perform actions on data on the environment. The concept of IoT connects devices, which are in remote and can be accessed remotely via the use of wireless technology [2]. Algorithms in machine learning have been extensively used in many domains, such as healthcare, social media, transportation, and so on, and have become inseparable from our regular life. Machine learning has started influencing the healthcare industry much more when compared with the olden days [3]. It has an outstanding improvement in the area of medical images reconstruction, brain segmentation, identifying body organs and classification, and so on.

The remaining sections of the chapter are organized as follows: section 8.2 describes background details while section 8.3 discusses the various algorithms of machine learning. Section 8.4 describes problem statement and definitions, proposed work is explained in section 8.5, and Performance analysis and evaluation have been discussed in section 8.6. Section 8.7 concludes the paper.

8.2 Literature Survey

Prevention of cardiac diseases using smart phones and monitoring the patients remotely and guidance for users are provided in the review paper by (Nguyen and Silva 2016) [4]. Szydlo and Koneiczny (2015) [5] suggested to use both hardware devices and software devices for tele-monitoring the various hearts based diseases. Lanata *et al.* (2015) used autonomous nervous systems for variability detection for ECG and heart rate [6]. In Kozlovszky *et al.* (2015) using off-the-shelf sensor sets the various heart diseases are being monitored [7]. Ricci *et al.* discussed about the implantable electronic devices and its performance and analysis [8]. Ramesh *et al.* discussed about the various states the mobile device can be based on the charging level of the mobile [9]. He discussed about the blood pressure monitoring and ECG. Optimization features and data storage are explained.

Many aged people suffer because of chronic diseases and it creates burden on the health services. To overcome various health-related problems we are in need of a system which will automatically take care of the patients diagnose them and inform the doctors about the situation of the patients [10]. This is the driving force behind the remote patient monitoring system. The wearable devices play a very important role in the current market in healthcare sectors, and it helps to monitor and track the patients very easily [11]. The healthcare market will have a steep rise in the market in 2023.

The IoT along with machine learning does a crucial part in the healthcare service providers, and it helps the patients to monitor them regularly for chronic disease management and helps in taking immediate treatments for the patients. Many IoT-enabled medical devices are presently obtainable now in the market and they are used to gather the information about the patient, and it plays a major role in curing chronic diseases and for providing preventive care [12–14]. Machine learning provides good outcomes in predicting the clinical data when compared with that of the traditional process. Machine learning is good at processing enormous amount of data, and it converts it into necessary healthcare information, which is more useful to the doctors and patients can be predicted the diseases priorly and proper preventive mechanism can be taken care for the patients. Machine Learning tries to help the doctors in better analysis and to improve the satisfaction of the patients [15–17]. Disease identification and diseases diagnosis became very ease with machine learning.

Majid [18] in his paper discussed the usage of mobile for acquiring the patient data remotely using Bluetooth. Bluetooth is used to transfer the data from the medical device to the storage. The data is stored remotely in server. Amir Hoshang Kioumars, 2014 [19] proposed the effective device for monitoring the temperature and heartbeat. He proposed using zigbee technology and AT micro controller for communication purpose of transmitting the heath data of patients. Deo Shao, 2012 [20] keeps track of the data already available in the hospitals and provide the statistics of health data of patients. Patient's medical history is also maintained. Al-Majeed et al. [21] proposed using IoT devices for home telehealth system. Firouzi [22] proposed using smart sensors in the field of healthcare applications. Hassanalieragh [23] discussed the current problems confronted by the IoT devices and proposed solutions to overcome these issues. Jabbar [24] proposed an IoT semantic-based interoperability model (IoT-SIM), which is used to work among heterogeneous IoT devices in the field of healthcare. Maktoubian and Ansari [25] discussed about monitoring system for solving the issues related to security and privacy of healthcare IoT devices. Mutlag et al. [26] presented a detailed literature review of using fog computing in the healthcare IoT devices. Shakeel [27] proposed a deep Q-network for limiting malware attacks in healthcare IoT devices.

Akhbarifar [28] proposed secure IoT data management for predicting the various combinations of hypertension, hypercholesterolemia, and heart disorder using data mining methods. Simanta Shekhar Sarmah [29] used DLMNN classifier to predict heart disease. PDH-AES technique is used for secure data transfer, and it yielded better results when compared to AES algorithm.

8.3 Machine Learning Algorithms

Machine learning algorithms are generally categorized into unsupervised learning, supervised learning, semisupervised learning, and reinforcement learning [30].

1) **Unsupervised learning**: This technique generally makes use of unlabeled data. The most used unsupervised learning methods include feature selection and clustering. This technique is also used for detecting the anomalies [31]. Some of the examples of unsupervised learning methods in healthcare industry includes such as prediction of diabetes, prediction of heart diseases, hepatitis diseases and chronic diseases. Mostly clustering [32] and dimensionality reduction technique is used [33].

2) **Supervised Learning**: Here labeled data are being used and its map the link between the inputs and outputs. In classification techniques the output is discrete and in regression the output will be a continuous value. Some of the examples in healthcare include classifying the various diseases related to lungs [34], identification of organs from human body [35, 37].

3) **Semisupervised Learning**: These techniques are a combination of both labeled and unlabeled data and generally the labeled data are of small amount and the unlabeled data are of larger amount. Methods which utilize both these types of data are called as semi-supervised learning methods and they will neither be supervised nor unsupervised. This technique is most widely used in healthcare due to very few labeled data available. Semi-supervised learning is used in medical image segmentation and recognizing the activity [38].

4) **Reinforcement Learning**: With a given set of observations, actions and rewards these methods try to acquire a policy function in reply to the actions which have been carried out over a period of time falls under the category of reinforcement learning (RL) [39]. RL plays a major role in the disease diagnosis.

8.4   Problem Statement

The need for Remote patient monitoring is increasing day by day, particularly for chronic diseases such as heart diseases. There is a necessity to reduce the risk factors and try to monitor the patients remotely and send their reports to the doctors for assessment. At the same time, using the machine learning algorithms and try to predict and diagnose the possibility of getting heart diseases based on the patient health data and the heart disease data set which is being used and take precautionary measures. The IoT is being used for collecting the patient-related data from various sensors and for transmitting the data to the cloud server from the local storage and four machine learning algorithms are being considered for predicting heart diseases Naïve Bayes, logistic regression, K-neighbors classifier and Decision Tree Algorithm. Compared the performance measure of the four algorithms and provided the accuracy of prediction.

8.5   Proposed Work

Proposed system provides a platform for monitoring the patients remotely and to predict the heart diseases by using IoT along with machine learning algorithms.

The proposed work consists of four steps:

- Collection of values through sensor nodes
- Data storage in cloud
- Prediction of data with machine learning algorithms

  1. Data cleaning and data preparation.
  2. Splitting of data.
  3. Training the data.
  4. Testing the data.
  5. Accuracy calculation.

8.5.1   Data Set Description

The data set used for predicting heart disease (Figure 8.2) is obtained from Cleveland data set. (https://www.kaggle.com/ronitf/heart-disease-uci/version/1). This data set is obtainable from Kaggle data set repository and is an open source. The data set includes a total 14 columns with 13 variables which are independent and 1 target variable (dependent). It has 303 rows. The description of the variables is provided in Table 8.1.

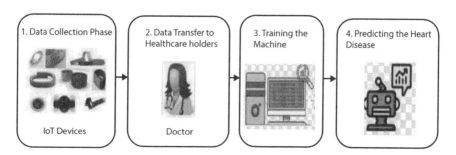

Figure 8.2 Prediction of heart disease using machine learning algorithm.

Table 8.1 Attributes of data set for heart diseases.

S. no	Name of the variable	Type of variable	Description
1.	Sex	Discrete	Male=1 and female =0
2.	Age	Discrete	patient Age
3.	Fbs	Discrete	fasting blood sugar true=1; false =0;
4.	Chest Pain	Continuous	Type of chest pain
5.	Trestbps	Continuous	blood pressure
6.	Chol	Continuous	Cholesterol value
7.	Exang	Discrete	exercise induced angina yes=1; no=0;
8.	Restecg	Continuous	electrocardiographic results
9.	Thalach	Continuous	heart rate maximum
10.	Oldpeak	Continuous	Depression
11.	Ca	Discrete	number of major vessels (0-3)
12.	Slope	Discrete	slope of the peak
13.	Thal	Discrete	3 = normal; 6 = fixed defect; 7 = reversible defect
14.	Num	Discrete	heart disease diagnosis

8.5.2 Collection of Values Through Sensor Nodes

This data collection step involves gathering the individual person's physiological data gathered from the IoT sensor devices and is of wearable type by the humans. Those devices (wearable) attached to the individual human body are responsible for collecting the clinical data of patients in a constant and continuous manner. The clinical values retrieved by the sensors are stored in the database in a continuous fashion. When the clinical value exceeds the normal limit, then the information is sent to the family members as well to the doctor and a copy of the information is stored in the

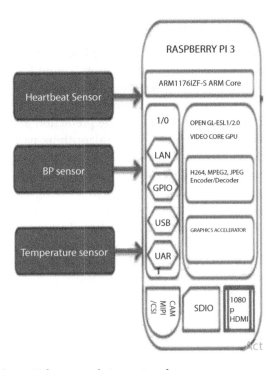

Figure 8.3 Raspberry Pi for accumulating patient data.

database. Three sensors, such as heartbeat sensor, BP sensor, and temperature sensor are being used here for collecting the clinical values. These sensors can be implanted into the human body, or a wearable type of device can be attached to the human body. Arduino Uno is utilized for monitoring the health parameters of the body and for extracting the information from the sensors. Raspberry Pi (Figure 8.3) is used to accumulate the collected data into its server and later transfer the data to the cloud server.

8.5.3   Storage of Data in Cloud

Internet of Things generally has the intention of sending the collected clinical data in a continuous manner. So the clinical data are transmitted and stored in the cloud storage, Google Firebase. Google firebase supports both mobile and web application development. The data stored in the database can be remotely accessed. The clinical data are sent to the doctors for verification and for providing immediate solution [42].

8.5.4   Prediction with Machine Learning Algorithms

Cleveland heart diseases data set is being used here for detecting the heart disease, and the collected patient information is used for finding out the prediction of diseases. Training data and test data are being considered here for analyzing the heart disease. The patient's clinical data are evaluated against the training data, and results of the prediction are provided here. We have considered four machine learning algorithms, namely Naïve Bayes Algorithm, Decision Trees, K-Neighbors classifier, and logistic regression. This proposed method provides efficient and effective remote health monitoring for patient, determine whether a patient is having a particular disease or not as well as to provide a quick solution to the patients in case of some emergency situation, which requires immediate doctor attention [36].

The clinical values so far collected in the cloud are used for analysis purpose. To make the predictions, the system should be trained using the sample values. Cleveland heart diseases data set is being used here for making the predictions (Figure 8.4). Accurate predictions can be obtained only when the training data are more. The larger the training data, the more the accuracy is. The data that are collected and tested till before should be included in the training data set and the data obtained right now is the data that need to be tested. Since the data set and also used the current data the training data will become more and more accurate the predictions are.

8.5.4.1   Data Cleaning and Preparation

The first step is to have a reliable data set for better results. In many cases, the data sets may contain duplicate values, missing values, and errors, which may lead to erroneous results. To get better quality of the data,

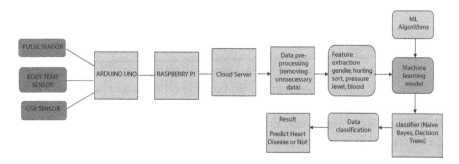

Figure 8.4 Proposed system of patient monitoring and prediction.

as well as results, have employed the data cleaning process. This process involves removing of null values and values which have incomplete data. Data cleaning is performed by using Null Removal method and eliminating features. The data set considered is not having any missing values and no need of removing any rows from the data set.

8.5.4.2   Data Splitting

It involves the process of splitting the data into Training phase and testing phase. Seventy percent of the data are considered for training and testing is carried out with 30% of data.

8.5.4.3   Training and Testing

Training data are trained using various machine learning algorithms. The target value is chosen and is used for measuring the accuracy approximately and thereby assessed the different machine learning models. Estimating the determining value is useful for us to predict whether the patient is affected by heart disease or not. Next, separate the numerical features from categorical features. Then, the relation between the categorical features in various plots is shown, and trying to figure out or rather observe the influence of those categorical features in the actual determining variable "diagnosis." SciKit Learn library is used, and a general function for training our models is formulated. The model is evaluated, whether the model overfits or underfits the data (so-called bias/variance tradeoff), then split the data then test and train them in the ratio of 70:30. Then create a model to run all the algorithms.

8.5.5   Machine Learning Algorithms

8.5.5.1   Naive Bayes Algorithm

Naïve Bayes falls under supervised learning algorithm, and it is based on Bayes Theorem. It is used for solving most of the classification Problems. Mainly, it is used in text classification and a high-dimensional training data set is involved. This algorithm is one of the simple, effective, and fastest algorithms for making quick predictions. It is generally called as probabilistic classifier, due to the probability of a particular object it predicts. Bayes theorem is utilized to determine probability of a hypothesis with prior knowledge. It is based on the conditional Probability [40].

Likelihood   class prior probability

$$P(C/X) = \frac{P(X/C) * P(C)}{P(X)}$$

Posterior
Probability

Predictor Prior
Probability

(8.1)

$$P(c|X) = P(x_1|c) \times P(x_2|c) \times \cdots \times P(x_n|c) \times P(c)$$ (8.2)

- $P(c|x)$ = posterior probability of class(target) given predictor (attribute)
- $P(c)$ = prior Probability of class
- $P(x|c)$ = likelihood , probability of predictor given class
- $P(x)$ = prior probability of predictor

Advantages of Naïve Bayes algorithms' performance are appreciable in multiclass prediction. When the independence assumption holds, this algorithm performs well when compared with other algorithms. This algorithm performs well with categorical input values when compared with that of numerical values. Naive Bayes is used in predicting real-time scenarios, multiclass prediction, classification of text, filtering of spams, analysis of sentiments, recommender system, and so on.

8.5.5.2   Decision Tree Algorithm

Decision Tree (DT) is a type of supervised learning algorithm. Equally numerical and categorical type of data is being used. Decision Tree is dependent on definite conditions, and it provides a categorical output, such as true or false, yes or no, 0 or 1. Decision Tree Algorithm is widely used in handling medical data set. For handling medical data set, the DT Classification algorithm is widely used (Figure 8.5) [40].

Information Gain:

Information Gain = Class Entropy – Entropy Attributes

Class Entropy:

$$(Pi + Ni) = -\frac{P}{P+N}\log_2\frac{P}{P+N} - \frac{N}{P+N}\log_2\frac{N}{P+N}.$$ (8.3)

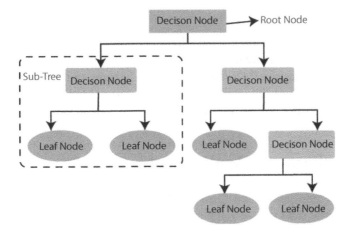

Figure 8.5 Representation of a decision tree.

Here => P, Possibilities of Yes. => N, Possibilities of No.
Entropy Attributes:

$$\text{Entropy attribute} = \sum \frac{Pi + Ni}{P + N}. \tag{8.4}$$

This model represents the data set in the format of a tree. This is the reason for high accuracy in Decision Trees. Mainly three nodes are involved in the analysis of decision tree:

- Root node—this main node
- Interior node—takes care of dependent variables
- Leaf node—result node

8.5.5.3   K-Neighbors Classifier

The K-Neighbors Classifier is based on the majority vote of neighbors. A different type of classification is used by this classifier. The neighbors that are close are given more weight age when compared with the neighbors who are more distant [40]. "d" represents the distance measured between vector and neighbor, and the weight is generally represented as 1/d. It works on concept that is used for the purpose of learning and is based on instance. The estimation also happens during the classification. The accuracy obtained for the above data set is 0.75.

8.5.5.4   Logistic Regression

Logistic regression is mostly used when the target variable is of categorical type. Dependent variable is modeled using logistic function. The accuracy of logistic regression is 0.85. The parameters X-train and Y-train are fed as input to the method. Fit () and X-test and Y-test are fed to method. Score () to compute the score for logistic regression model [41].

8.6   Performance Analysis and Evaluation

Authors have implemented this paper with heart disease data set is gathered from the data centre Kaggle [11] and can be obtained from https://www.kaggle.com/ronitf/heart-disease-uci/version/1. The motive of preferring these data sets is that the data gathered from huge heart disease patients' databases. Particularly, the data set considered is fitting to the numerous age groups of heart patients. The sample heart disease data set considered for experimental analysis is given in Table 8.1.

The diagnosis is the class label in the data set, and it consists of 2 values (0 and 1) in which 0 indicate not-heart disease patients and 1 represents heart patients.

Naïve Bayes, logistic regression and K-neighbor classifier and Decision Tree classifier is implemented using the specified data sets and are trained to run on the machine to produce the outcome of the particular person whether he is affected by heart disease or not. The results justifies the possible factors, which are responsible for heart diseases and also predict at what exact age the person is going to be affected by heart diseases (Figure 8.6.) Two factors are of more important and considered for prediction analysis: cholesterol and heart beat rate in the human body. The outcome is shown by using two colors, such as green and orange, as shown in the report. The prediction is depicted in Figure 8.7.

	age	sex	cp	trestbps	chol	fbs	restecg	thalach	exang	oldpeak	slope	ca	thal	target
0	63	1	3	145	233	1	0	150	0	2.3	0	0	1	1
1	37	1	2	130	250	0	1	187	0	3.5	0	0	2	1
2	41	0	1	130	204	0	0	172	0	1.4	2	0	2	1
3	56	1	1	120	236	0	1	178	0	0.8	2	0	2	1
4	57	0	0	120	354	0	1	163	1	0.6	2	0	2	1

Figure 8.6 Reading the data values.

Attribute wise graph plotting

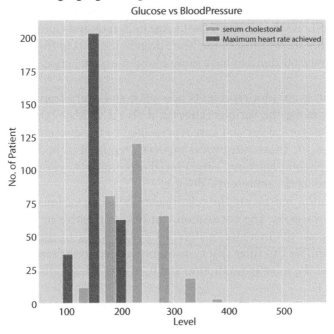

Figure 8.7 Level vs. no of patient.

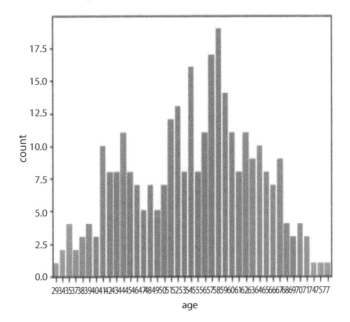

Figure 8.8 Count vs. age.

Count plot shows the count of observations in each categorical bin using bar. Figure 8.7 represents the level in x-axis and number of patient in Y-axis. Figure 8.8 shows the count plot with Age in X-Axis and Count in Y-Axis.

Figure 8.9 shows most of the heart disease patients in their age of upper 40s and lower 60s tend to have more blood pressure between 130 mm and 150 mm.

The histogram plot represents how each and every feature and label is scattered among the various ranges and also it validates the necessity for scaling. Categorical variables are represented by the discrete bars as shown in Figure 8.10. These categorical variables required to be handled before applying machine learning. Target variable represents 2 classes 0 represents "no disease" and 1 represents "disease."

Correlation represents the relationship between various features or to the target variable. The correlation can have a positive or negative value depending on the increase or decrease in one value of the feature. From the diagram, we can infer that cp is highly related to the target variable. cp contributes the most in prediction and presence of heart diseases shown in Figure 8.11.

Confusion matrix true positive, true negative, false positive and false negative values for Naïve Bayes and decision tree classifier are shown in Figure 8.12.

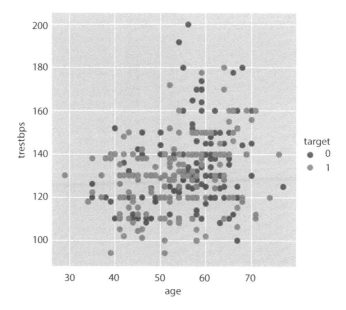

Figure 8.9 Age vs. trestbps.

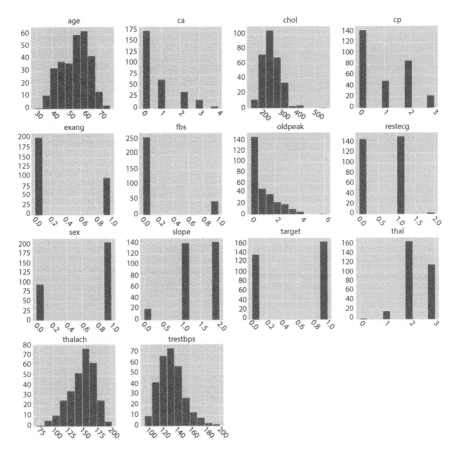

Figure 8.10 Graphs of various attributes.

Table 8.2 Accuracy of models with all features.

Models/no. of runs	RUN1	RUN2	RUN3	RUN4	RUN5
Naive Bayes	0.88	0.88	0.88	0.88	0.88
Decision Tree	0.75	0.75	0.73	0.73	0.73
KNN	0.75	0.75	0.75	0.75	0.75
Logistic Regression	0.85	0.85	0.85	0.85	0.85

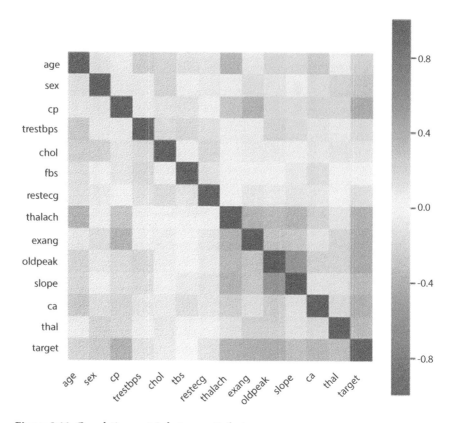

Figure 8.11 Correlation matrix between attributes.

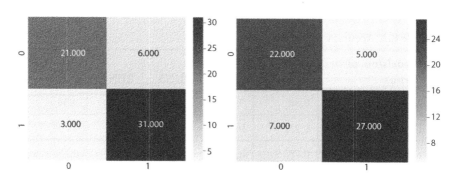

Figure 8.12 Confusion matrix with Naïve Bayes (i) and decision tree (ii).

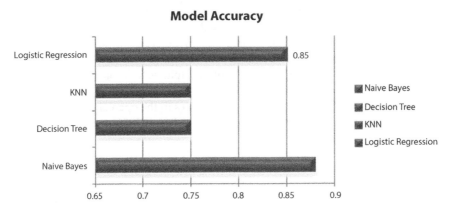

Figure 8.13 Comparative result of algorithms.

8.7 Conclusion

Various supervised and unsupervised machine learning algorithms used in predicting heart diseases are analyzed. Four algorithms Naïve Bayes, Logistic Regression, KNN, and DT are used for predicting heart diseases (Figure 8.13 and Table 8.2). The same data set is applied to all the four algorithms in order to analyze the best algorithm in terms of accuracy. Naive Bayes is proven to be the best classification algorithm with 88% accuracy when compared to DT algorithm. Naive Bayes can get all probabilities since it treats all members of a class as independent. We can observe that Naïve Bayes is showing good results, and DT is approximately correct and not accurate. Thus naïve Bayes is good for handling clinical data. In future the machine learning algorithms can be used to predict or diagnose various diseases. Future work can be extended to other machine learning algorithms and parameter tuning can be used to improve the accuracy of the algorithm.

References

1. Aleksandar, M., Chris, O., Emil, J., Wireless Sensor Networks for Personal Health Monitoring: Issues and an Implementation. *Comput. Commun.*, 29, 2521–2533, 2006.
2. Khan, S.F., Healthcare Monitoring System in Internet of Things (IoT) by Using RFID. *The 6th International Conference on Industrial Technology and Management*, 2017.

3. Abd, D.H., Alwan, J.K., Ibrahim, M., Naeem, M.B., "The Utilisation of Machine Learning Approaches for Medical Data Classification", in: *Annual Conference on New Trends in Information & Communications Technology Applications*, March 2017.

4. Nguyen, H.H. and Silva, J.N.A., Use of smartphone technology in cardiology. *Trends Cardiovasc. Med.*, 26, 4, 376–386, 2016.

5. Szydlo, T. and Koneiczny, M., Mobile devices in the open and universal system for remote patient monitoring. *IFAC-PapersOnLine*, 48, 4, 296–301, 2015.

6. Lanata, A. *et al.*, Complexity index from a personalized wearable monitoring system for assessing remission in mental health. *IEEE J. Biomed. Health Inf.*, 19, 1, 132–139, 2015.

7. Kozlovszky, M., Kovacs, L., Karoczkai, K., Cardiovascular and diabetes focused remote patient monitoring, in: *VI Latin American congress on biomedical engineering CLAIB 2014*, Paraná, Argentina, 29, 30 & 31 October 2014 Springer International Publishing, Cham, pp. 568–71, 2015.

8. Ricci, R.P. *et al.*, Effectiveness of remote monitoring of CIEDs in detection and treatment of clinical and device-related cardiovascular events in daily practice: the homeguide registry. *Europace.*, 15, 7, 970–977, 2013.

9. Ramesh, M.V., Anand, S., Rekha, P., A mobile software for health professionals to monitor remote patients, in: *2012 Ninth international conference on wireless and optical communications networks (WOCN)*, pp. 1–4, 2012.

10. The W.H.O, *Ageing and health*, World health organization, 20185 February, Available from https://www.who.int/news-room/fact-sheets/detail/ageing-and-health.

11. Mordor Intelligence, *Wearable Sensors Market-Segmented by Type of Sensor (Temperature, Pressure, Motion), Application (Health and Wellness, Safety Monitoring, Sports, and Training), and Region-Growth, Trends, and Forecast (2018 -2023)*, 2018, Mordor Intelligence, April, Available from: https://www.mordorintelligence.com/industry-reports/global-wearable-health-sensors-market-industry.

12. Yin, Y. *et al.*, The Internet of things in healthcare: An overview. *J. Ind. Inf. Integr.*, 1, 3–13, 2016.

13. Ghani, A., *Healthcare electronics—A step closer to future smart cities*, ICT Express, 5, 4, 256–260, 2018.

14. Yeole, A.S. and Kalbande, D.R., Use of Internet of Things (IoT) in Healthcare: A Survey, in: *Proceedings of the ACM Symposium on Women in Research 2016*, ACM, Indore, India, pp. 71–76, 2016.

15. Callahan, A. and Shah, N.H., Chapter 19 -Machine Learning in Healthcare, in: *Key Advances in Clinical Informatics*, A. Sheikh, (Eds.), pp. 279–291, Academic Press, 2017.

16. Al-Janabi, S. *et al.*, Survey of main challenges (security and privacy) in wireless body area networks for healthcare applications. *Egypt. Inform. J.*, 18, 2, 113–122, 2017.

17. Mohammadzadeh, N. and Safdari, R., Patient Monitoring in Mobile Health: Opportunities and Challenges. *Med. Arch.*, 68, 1, 57–60, 2014.

18. Al-Taee, M.A., Jaradat, N.A., Abu Ali, D.M., "Mobile Phone-Based Health Data Acquisition System Using Bluetooth Technology,". *IEEE Jordan Conference*, Amman, pp. 6–8, Dec. 2011.

19. Kioumars, A.H., *"Wireless data acquisition and monitoring for healthcare services systems,"*, pp. 50–145, Massey University, 2011.

20. Shao, D., *"A Proposal of a Mobile Health Data Collection and Reporting System for the Developing World,"*, pp. 43–57, Malmö University, 2012.

21. Al-Majeed, S.S., Al-Mejibli, I.S., Karam, J., "Home telehealth by internet of things (IoT),", in: *Proceedings of the 2015 IEEE 28th Canadian Conference on Electrical and Computer Engineering (CCECE)*, Halifax, Canada, May 2015.

22. Firouzi, F., Internet-of-things and big data for smarter Healthcare: From Device to Architecture. *Appl. Anal.*, 78, 2, 2018, 583–586, 2018.

23. Hassanalieragh, M., "Health monitoring and management using Internet-of-Things (IoT) sensing with cloud-based processing: opportunities and challenges,", in: *Proceedings of the 2015 IEEE International Conference on Services Computing*, New York, NY, USA, July 2015.

24. Jabbar, S., "Semantic interoperability in heterogeneous IoT infrastructure for healthcare,". *Wirel. Commun. Mob. Comput.*, 2017, Article ID 9731806, 10, 2017.

25. Maktoubian, J. and Ansari, K., "An IoT architecture for preventive maintenance of medical devices in healthcare organizations,". *Health Technol.*, 9, 3, 233–243, 2019.

26. Mutlag, A.A., Abd Ghani, M.K., Arunkumar, N., Mohammed, M.A., Mohd, O., "Enabling technologies for fog computing in healthcare IoT systems,". *Future Gener. Comput. Syst.*, 90, 62–78, 2019.

27. Shakeel, P.M., "Maintaining security and privacy in healthcare system using learning based deep-Q-networks,". *J. Med. Syst.*, 42, 10, 186, 2018.

28. Akhbarifar, S., Javadi, H.H.S., Rahmani, A.M. *et al.*, A secure remote health monitoring model for early disease diagnosis in cloud-based IoT environment. *Pers. Ubiquit Comput.*, 2020. https://doi.org/10.1007/s00779-020-01475-3.

29. Sarmah, S.S., An Efficient IoT-Based Patient Monitoring and Heart Disease Prediction System Using Deep Learning Modified Neural Network. *IEEE Access*, PP, 99, 1–1, July 2020.

30. Kumar, P.M. and Gandhi, U.D., A novel three-tier Internet of Things architecture with machine learning algorithm for early detection of heart diseases. *Comput. Electr. Eng.*, 222–235, 2017.

31. Chandola, V., Banerjee, A., Kumar, V., "Anomaly detection: A survey,". *ACM Comput. Surv. (CSUR)*, 41, 3, 15, 2009.

32. Pandey, A.K., Pandey, P., Jaiswal, K., Sen, A.K., Datamining clustering techniques in the prediction of heart disease using attribute selection method. *International Journal of Science, Engineering and Technology Research (IJSETR)*, 14, 16–17, 2013.

33. Polat, K. and Guneş, S., "Prediction of hepatitis disease based on principal component analysis and artificial immune recognition system,". *Appl. Math. Comput.*, 189, 2, 1282–1291, 2007.

34. Shen, W., Zhou, M., Yang, F., Yang, C., Tian, J., "Multi-scale convolutional neural networks for lung nodule classification,". in: *in International Conference on Information Processing in Medical Imaging*, Springer, pp. 588–599, 2015.

35. Yan, Z., Zhan, Y., Peng, Z., Liao, S., Shinagawa, Y., Zhang, S., Metaxas, D.N., Zhou, X.S., "Multi-instance deep learning: Discover discriminative local anatomies for bodypart recognition,". *IEEE Trans. Med. Imaging*, 35, 5, 1332–1343, 2016.

36. Alloghani, M., Al-Jumeily, D., Mustafina, J., Hussain, A., Aljaaf, A.J., "A systematic review on supervised and unsupervised machine learning algorithms for data science,". in: *Supervised and Unsupervised Learning for Data Science*, pp. 3–21, Springer, 2020.

37. Sohail, M.N., Ren, J., Uba Muhammad, M., "A euclidean group assessment on semi-supervised clustering for healthcare clinical implications based on real-life data,". *Int. J. Environ. Res. Public Health*, 16, 9, 1581, 6 May 2019.

38. Mahapatra, D., "Semi-supervised learning and graph cuts for consensus based medical image segmentation,". *Pattern Recognit.*, 63, 700–709, 2017.

39. Sutton, R.S., Barto, A.G. *et al.*, *Introduction to reinforcement learning*, vol. 2, MIT Press, Cambridge, 1998.

40. Almustafa, K.M., Prediction of heart disease and classifiers' sensitivity analysis. *BMC Bioinf.*, 21, 278, 2020. https://doi.org/10.1186/s12859-020-03626-y.

41. Uddin, S., Khan, A., Hossain, M. *et al.*, Comparing different supervised machine learning algorithms for disease prediction. *BMC Med. Inform. Decis. Mak.*, 19, 281, 2019. https://doi.org/10.1186/s12911-019-1004-8.

42. Prabhakaran, V.M., Balamurugan, S., Charanyaa, S., Data Flow Modelling for Effective Protection of Electronic Health Records (EHRs) in Cloud. *Int. J. Innov. Res. Comput. Commun. Eng.*, 3, 1, 77–84, January 2015.

43 Shihong Z., Yanhong X., Honggang W., Zhouzhou L., Shanzhi C., Bo H., A survey on secure wireless body area networks, Security and communication networks, vol. 2017, Article ID 3721234, 9 pages, 2017. https://doi.org/10.1155/2017/3721234.

9

BABW: Biometric-Based Authentication Using DWT and FFNN

R. Kingsy Grace[1]*, M.S. Geetha Devasena[1]† and R. Manimegalai[2]‡

[1]Department of Computer Science and Engineering,
Sri Ramakrishna Engineering College, Coimbatore, India
[2]Department Computer Science and Engineering,
PSG Institute of Technology and Applied Research, Coimbatore, India

Abstract

In this digital era, information security and authentication are crucial. Traditional, as well as modern, methods of identification are not capable of protecting the vast amounts of confidential data that exist worldwide. Conventional identification methods, such as passwords, secret codes, and personal identification numbers are compromised easily and also easily shared, observed, stolen, or forgotten. However, a possible alternative in determining the identities of users is to use biometrics. The brain wave as a biometric for authentication has several advantages that it cannot be stolen or replicated. Even differently abled persons shall comfortably use brain wave authentication systems rather than other authentication systems. Thus, brain wave authentication becomes one of the competing authentication systems and paves way for promising research. The brain wave signal that echoes the brain activity is captured by Electroencephalogram. Although the acquisition of EEG signal is feasible with advancement of technology, the development of authentication system using brain waves poses many challenges because of the nature of the brain waves activity of human beings. The proposed automatic biometric-based user recognition uses brain waves activity for authentication. The acquisition of EEG signal is done and compressed using discrete wavelet transform (DWT). The Feed Forward Neural Network (FFNN) is used for pattern matching in order to provide accurate results. The accuracy of proposed BABW algorithm is 87.7% and is better than other algorithms in the literature.

*Corresponding author: kingsygrace.r@srec.ac.in
†Corresponding author: msgeetha@srec.ac.in
‡Corresponding author: drrm@psgitech.ac.in

R. Nidhya, Manish Kumar and S. Balamurugan (eds.) Tele-Healthcare: Applications of Artificial Intelligence and Soft Computing Techniques, (201–220) © 2022 Scrivener Publishing LLC

Keywords: Cognitive biometrics, authentication, brain computer interface, electroencephalogram, discrete wavelet transform, feed forward neural network, password, EEG signal

9.1 Introduction

Standout among the most imperative parts of any system is to recognize its owner with the help of any authentication system. Usually, authentication systems use passwords in the form of text and that are helpless against various types of assaults. Authentication systems protect the user's data from unauthorized access. There is ground-breaking number of ways used for authenticating systems using password, and the most important methods are in Shen *et al.* [1]. The authentication passwords are easily memorized, and the users are not using regularly [2], at the same time, the passwords are elapsed from memory because of various passwords for different accounts [3]. New authentication systems are increased day by day to protect the users with the help of biological and behavioral patterns of the users.

There are two types of biometric user recognition. The first type is based on distinguishing behavioral patterns, such as (*i*) gait, (*ii*) signature, (*iii*) keyboard typing, (*iv*) lip movement, (*v*) hand-grip. The second type is a person's physiological traits, such as (*i*) face, (*ii*) voice, (*iii*) iris, (*iv*) fingerprint, (*v*) hand geometry, (*vi*) electroencephalogram-EEG (*vii*) electrocardiogram (ECG) (*viii*) ear shape, (*ix*) body odor, (*x*) body salinity, and (*xi*) vascular [4]. Some of the weaknesses for commonly used biometric methodology are: iris recognition requires high-cost equipment for data collection and parsing. Finger printing requires placing the finger or hand on the sensor correctly. A signature will be modified in most of the cases. Background noise is a big problem in voice matching [5]. Fingerprinting and iris scanning technologies are used worldwide in air ports and other places to identify persons for security. In many cases [6–8] biometric recognition provides less security and is easily forged or embezzled. User identification plays a major role in securing computer resources. Individual authentication should be strong to protect resources [9, 10]. Natural user interface (NUI) technology could be used to communicate with the computer through (*i*) gestures, (*ii*) voice, (*iii*) expressions, (*iv*) emotions, and (*v*) thoughts. The brain wave of a person is not able to known by the other people, it is a good solution to the other biometric authentication techniques like fingerprint, face, and iris patterns as passwords [11]. Brain wave signals are used for authentication systems with the help of thoughts. Brain signals are more unique when compared to other physiological traits and behavioral patterns.

There are many literatures available based on biometric modalities like fingerprint, iris, voice, or face. From the literature, plainly brainwave of each individual is one of a kind and electroencephalogram (EEG) is useful for biometric recognition in this present day [12–18]. Person authentication using brain wave has excellent applications in brain computer interface (BCI) systems and at the same time improving the efficiency and accuracy of the systems are critical. Brain wave signal biometry open up new research directions in this AI era and provides enhanced applications in the forthcoming years with the authentication-related applications in (*i*) mobile devices, (*ii*) virtual reality, (*iii*) augmented applications, (*iv*) headsets, and (*v*) Internet.

9.2   Literature Survey

This section discusses the related works on the use of brain waves for user identification. Usually brain waves are investigated to learn brain ailment such as (*i*) epilepsy, (*ii*) spinal cord injuries, (*iii*) Alzheimer's, (*iv*) Parkinson's, (*v*) schizophrenia, and (*vi*) stroke. Brain computer and brain machine interface systems use brain signals for various entertainment applications. Campisi *et al.* have proposed brain wave-based user authentication [4] automatically. The proposed method captures brain signals as ECG signals using superficial scalp electrodes. The captured signals are classified using K-nearest neighbor algorithm and trained using neural network for identification.

Kusuma Mohanchandra *et al.* have proposed a new modality to authenticate a person using brain wave [19]. The authors also have developed an application to unlock and lock screen using brain wave. The proposed system uses Emotiv headset to capture the unique brain wave signals of human beings. It consists of 14 sensors to get enhanced signal features. Power spectral density for intermingle signals are calculated. After classifying alpha, beta, and gamma signals in the brain signals, the proximity value is computed. If the proximity value is equal or greater than 0.78, it is assumed to be a matched pattern in the proposed system.

Marcel and Millan have investigated the utilization of brain movement as another model for individual authentication. The proposed framework by Marcel and Millan [20] consists of the steps, such as (*i*) brain wave signal recording, (*ii*) training the collected data, and (*iii*) identifying the client. The brain wave signal recording is done many times to get correct signal. The posteriori model adaptation is applied to train the collected signal. Then, the client model is implemented using adaptation technique. Likelihood is the parameter used for measuring the client identity. The identity is accepted when the likelihood is higher, and the identity is rejected when the likelihood is lower. The proposed method identifies some mental activities of the user are more fitting for authentication than the others.

Soni *et al.* have proposed a two-level authentication process in Soni *et al.* [21]. The first level uses brain wave authentication, and the second level authentication uses a pass key. The proposed system gets the pass key when the first level is authenticated. There are three parts in the proposed system, such as: (*i*) brain computer interface (BCI), (*ii*) level differentiator unit (LDU), and (*iii*) checker module. The BCI module consists of brain wave sensors to get the brain signals. The received brain signals are converted into packets and transferred to LDU. The LDU having the responsibility to match the existing pattern with the generated pattern. A subsystem has developed to generate the pass key using advanced RISC machines (ARM) [21].

Angkraingkij have introduced a biometric system using EEG [22]. The EEG signal frequency range is 0 to 100 Hz. It is classified as five classifications, namely, (*i*) delta, (*ii*) theta, (*iii*) alpha, (*iv*) beta, (*v*) gamma. To remove the nose from the EEG signals, the proposed technique used Independent Component Analysis (ICA) which is based on SOBIRO algorithm. From the outcomes unmistakably the proposed authentication framework works well with Delta range EEG signal. Reshmi *et al.* have discussed a technique [16] for user identification using brain signals. The brain signals are EEG signals that are captured using FMRI, which is a brain imaging method. The proposed system captured brain waves using Emotiv EPOC EEG neuro headset [23], which has 14 electrodes and two sensors. Brain wave authentication is advantageous over other biometric technologies because of its features, such as (*i*) uniqueness, (*ii*) robustness to spoofing attacks, (*iii*) continuous identification, and (*iv*) never produce duplicate signal. Ramaswamy has proposed an authentication system to reduce False Accept Error (FAE) and false reject error (FRE), which is based on brain waves. The proposed two-way authentication system has fourfold validation procedure to validate the system [24]. The proposed system is applicable to the individuals based on the thought process of them. The proposed system is tested for five subjects, and all the five subjects are proved to be correct with some thought process. From the outcomes, obviously, the proposed twofold strategy is highly suited for avoiding fraud. The proposed system is tested as a pilot but requires an elaborate research with more subjects for implementing in real time.

Jenkins *et al.* have proposed EEG-UAC for biometrics [25]. The user access control (UAC) is combined with electroencephalogram (EEG) to get better authentication. The EEG-UAC requires steps using memory recall for testing. The proposed system uses brain wave biometrics. The proposed system is similar to iris recognition. The EEG is the additional layer to the proposed system. Like iris, the EEG is taken number of times to process. The PIN for this system is generated using RSA algorithm. The proposed system was tested with three users initially. The number of sessions for each user is 25, and the number of images in each session is 30. Initially, the proposed system is tested using MATLAB and later on in test bed for checking its scalability.

Alariki *et al.* have a detailed literature survey on EEG-based biometric. The EEG-based research projects are reviewed according to their performance. Alariki *et al.* [26] provide a classification on the features used for the authentication of EEG and fNIRS signals. The efficiency of the biometric is increased by collecting the brain signals using EEG and fNIRS. It is also noted that the SVM classification plays a better role in classification of brain signals.

Barkadehi *et al.* [27] provides a review on authentication systems. Different authentication systems are classified according to their type of usage and the categories. Advantages and disadvantages of different classification systems are identified. Svogor and Kisasondi have proposed a future authentication system using EEG which is having two factors for authentication of any system [28]. Because of the stress of humans, it is difficult to get the same EEG signal. The EEG sensor is also used to provide additional information to create password. The cracking of the password is very difficult in the proposed system because of the combination of EEG and password.

The summary of different EEG-based biometric Systems is shown in Table 9.1. The summary table comprises of the EEG-based biometric techniques accessible in the literature. The comparison of different methods is based on the algorithms used, type of tools used for brain wave acquisition, parameters considered, number of data set used, and the performance of the system.

Table 9.1 Summary on EEG-based biometric systems.

Literature Reference	Algorithm/Method	Tools used	Encryption	Parameters used	Number of data set	Performance
Gui, Q., Z. Jin and W. Xu, 2014 [29]	Ensemble Averaging, Neural Network	EEG headset	Not Mentioned	Accuracy, Number of Neurons	32	High accuracy when neurons are increased
Gui, Q., Z. Jin, M.V.R. Blondet, S. Laszlo and W. Xu, 2015 [6]	Euclidean Distance (ED) and Dynamic Time Warping (DTW)	EEG headset	Not Mentioned	Accuracy	30	Good Accuracy
Thorpe, Van Oorschot and Somayaji (2005) [30]	Feasible Pass-thoughts-Based System	EGG device Pin pattern	Yes	Not Mentioned	P300 potentials	Viable and useful new form of authentication
Svogor and Kisasondi (2012) [28]	EEGPass algorithm	EGG device	Yes	Not Mentioned	1	Search space for attacker is high
Abo-Zahhad, Ahmed and Abbas (2015) [31]	Levinson-Durbin and Burg algorithm	EGG device Eye blink	Not Mentioned	Correct Recognition Rate	10	Accuracy is improved by 99.8%.
Ruiz-Blondet, M.V., Z. Jin and S. Laszlo, 2016 [32]	CEREBRE (Cognitive Event RElated Biometric REcognition) Protocol	EEG headset	Yes	accuracy	50	100% Identification Accuracy

(Continued)

Table 9.1 Summary on EEG-based biometric systems. (*Continued*)

Literature Reference	Algorithm/Method	Tools used	Encryption	Parameters used	Number of data set	Performance
Kang, J.H., C.H. Lee and S.P. Kim, 2016 [33]	Support Vector Machine (SVM)	EEG headset	Not Mentioned	Feature, Channel, CI value	7	Feature Selection accuracy of 94.9% & Biometric Accuracy of 85.5%
Bashar, M.K., I. Chiaki and H. Yoshida, 2016 [34]	**Feature Extraction Methods** Multiscale Shape Description (MSD), Multiscale Wavelet Packet Statistics (WPS) and Multiscale Wavelet Packet Energy Statistics (WPES) **Classification Method** Support Vector Machine (SVM)	EEG headset	Not Mentioned	TPR, FNR, Accuracy	9	Accuracy of 94.44%

9.3 BABW: Biometric Authentication Using Brain Waves

Brain wave-based authentication is recently a new addition to the conventional authentication techniques. It involves the use of electrical activity in brain to confirm a person's identity. The proposed work BABW is based on such authentication by classification and feature extraction of data. The EEG databases [35, 36] are obtained for a particular person either in normal condition or a patient who has epilepsy, coma or any disorders, physically challenged persons' data information are collected and created a database for person authentication. The EEG data are then preprocessed and input signal for the data is obtained. During preprocessing, the noise from the EEG signal is removed to urge closer to the actual neural signals. DWT reduces the computational time which renders it far more suitable for discrete signal and is employed for signal coding and often used as a preconditioning for data compression. FFNN can learn without anyone else and produce the yield that isn't restricted to the info gave to them. So the Discrete wavelet transform (DWT) is applied to the compressed signal and the feature extracted signal is subjected to FFNN and compare with the database templates for authentication.

The Steps involved in the Proposed Biometric Authentication using Brain Waves System is shown in Figure 9.1. The proposed BABW brain

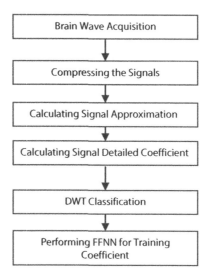

Figure 9.1 Steps involved in the proposed biometric authentication using brain waves system.

wave-based authentication involves the following: (*i*) data acquisition process (DAQ), (*ii*) preprocessing, (*iii*) feature extraction, (*iv*) classification, and (*v*) authentication process. Generally, various methods are used for capturing brain wave signals. NeuroSkyMindWave headset is used by the proposed system [4]. It is a noninvasive method of EEG recordings which are captured with electrodes fixed in scalp. Usually ECG signals are nonlinear and nonstationary. To remove the interference while capturing the brain wave signals, they are subject to preprocessing. Noise and artifacts are removed during preprocessing. The EEG signals are transformed to frequency domain from time domain. The EEG signals are compressed at a medium level or band pass level frequency where low frequency of noise and artifacts are neglected.

From the preprocessed ECG signals, the features are extracted using Discrete Wavelet Transform (DWT). Decomposition of DWT is shown in Figure 9.2. Wavelet analysis used to express the ECG signal as a linear combination of set of functions by shifting and expanding the original wavelet. The low-pass filter *lp* and high pass filter *hp* are the factors of discrete wavelet transform. The wavelet function w_i and the scale function s_i are the two important functions, which are used for processing and are defined in equation (9.1) & (9.2).

$$w_i = 2_i/2\; lp_i(k-_{2i}l) \tag{9.1}$$

$$s_i = 2_i/2\; hp_i(k-2_il) \tag{9.2}$$

where the value $\dfrac{2i}{2}$ is an normalization used for input, the scale parameter is k and interpretation parameter *is g*, respectively. The decomposition of DWT is described in equation (9.3) & (9.4).

$$a(k)(g) = x(k)^* \, w_i \tag{9.3}$$

$$d(k)(g) = x(k)^* \, s_i \tag{9.4}$$

where the approximation coefficient is a(k)(g) and the detail coefficient is d(k)(g). The input EEG signal is decomposed into various bands of frequency and is categorized into high-pass and low pass filter signal. Figure 9.2 depicts the decomposition. The mother wavelet is denoted by *x[n]*, high-pass filter is denoted by *hp[n]* and the low pass filter is denoted by *lp[n]*. The decomposition level is selected as 3 as lack of useful frequency

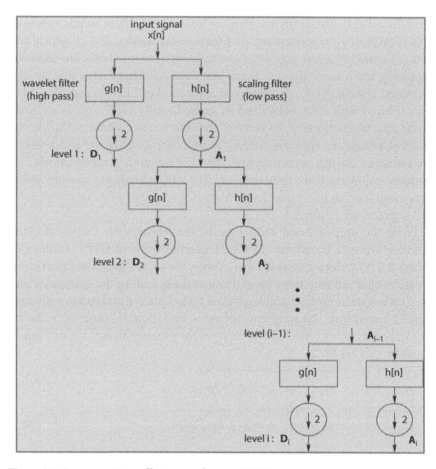

Figure 9.2 Decomposition of brain signals using DWT.

components in EEG signals above 30 Hz. At A3 level, the wavelet decomposition with respect to input signal is obtained.

Feature extracted data are classified to generate templates. The templates already available in the database of particular person are to be identified and compared with input EEG data and authentication is made. By comparing, it authenticates the access of a person to the system. The extracted features have been used as the inputs to design the neural network models. The input database is separated into two sets as training set and testing set.

Neural network is an amazing asset for catching and addressing complex input/output associations. Desire to develop an artificial system similar to human brain is the motivation for development of neural network. Feed Forward Neural Network (FFNN) [37] model have been used for training.

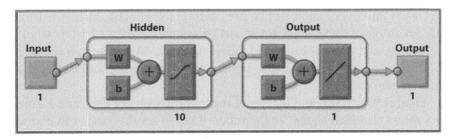

Figure 9.3 Training using feed forward neural network.

The FFNN with one hidden layer is trained utilizing an error back feed forward network. The fundamental setup as a rule comprises of the layers, such as (*i*) input layer, (*ii*) hidden layer, and (*iii*) output layer. Feed forward networks frequently have a minimum of one hidden layers of sigmoid neurons followed by an output layer of linear neurons. The fastened weight coming up with from the input area to the output area is finished by FFNN. The weights of a FFNN square measure fastened when coaching, therefore, the condition of any vegetative cell is completely set by the input-output style and not the underlying and past conditions of the vegetative cell, so such networks square measure is named static neural networks. The structure of a FFNN is shown in Figure 9.3.

The final step of the proposed system BABW is authentication. The brain wave signal is read from the user who is trying to access the system. The user has to think the word that is recorded previously as pass-thought. The collected signals are processed to find the maximum and minimum coefficient in the signal. These coefficients are matched with the trained data. If the matching is successful, the user is recognized and can access the system. If authentication fails, the user cannot access the system.

9.4   Results and Discussion

The EEG signals that are assembled from a public and openly accessible data set [38] and used to execute and test the proposed framework. The EEG signals were initially procured utilizing the 64-channel BCI2000 framework [39] with a sampling rate of 160 Hz, and EEG signals were referred to the normal of the earlobe electrodes. Fourteen different runs are conducted on the original data set. The various conditions considered for experiment includes (*i*) resting state, both (*ii*) eyes-open and (*iii*) closed. A set of imaginary and real numbers are acquired from 109 subjects.

For each and every subject, five nonoverlapping epochs is recorded for all conditions. Along these lines, 2048 examples extricated from whole recording, and they are examined independently. MATLAB programming is utilized for recording the EEG information from Neurosky headset and further processing.

Figures 9.4(a), (b), and (c) depict the preprocessing of data, and Figure 9.5 shows classified signal. The number of iterations that occurs in neural network training is called Epochs. Figure 9.6 shows the result of neural network training. It shows whether the neural network training is done. Mean square error indicates the error occurred during training. The accuracy on different data samples of proposed system is shown in Table 9.2. The efficiency of the implemented brain wave authentication DWT-FFNN is compared with the algorithms in the review in terms of accuracy and found to be better in Table 9.3.

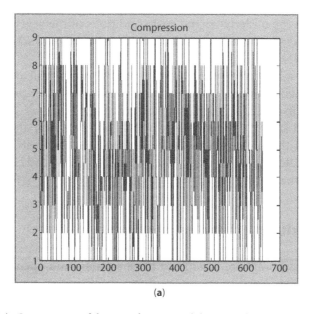

(a)

Figure 9.4 (a) Compression of the input brain signal during authentication.

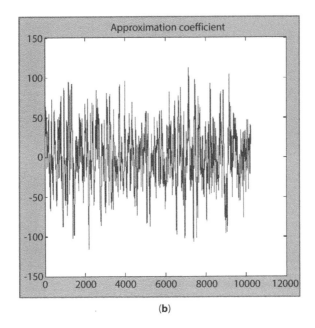

(b)

Figure 9.4 (b) Brain signal after approximation.

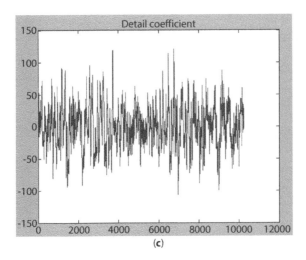

(c)

Figure 9.4 (c) Calculating detailed coefficient in the brain signal.

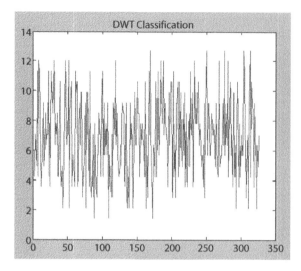

Figure 9.5 Brain signal classification using DWT.

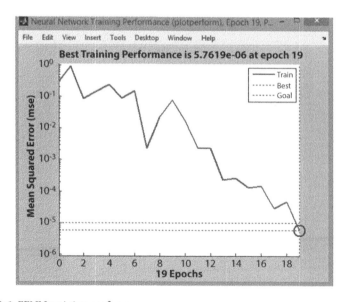

Figure 9.6 FFNN training performance.

Table 9.2 Accuracy on different samples

Description	Data sample 1	Data sample 2	Data sample 3
Number of Times Data Trained	10	10	10
Number of Times Data Tested	6	8	5
Number of Times Accurate Result Obtained	5	8	4
Accuracy	83.33	100	80

Table 9.3 Performance of the proposed method.

Researches	Method	Accuracy
Heger *et al.* (2013)	Naïve Bayes	80%
Blondet *et al.* (2015)	Cross-correlation	84%
Gui *et al.* (2016)	Euclidean distance	80%
Proposed Method	DWT-FFNN	87.7%

9.5   Conclusion

The proposed biometric system BABW recognizes users using brain waves. Recent studies in the literature proved that brain waves are different from person to person and they are unique. Individual authentication expects to acknowledge or dismiss an individual and guaranteeing a personality. The brain waves are captured using NeuroSky Mind Wave headset and are preprocessed to remove noise. The preprocessed signal is classified using

DWT and is given as input to the FFNN. The user is authenticated if the brain wave signal of the person is matched with the trained data. The user access to the system will get rejected if the brain wave signal of the person does not match with the trained data. Recognizing user using brain waves is very reliable and more secured than any other biometric systems. It can be used in important security applications, such as in banks, military, private sectors, and so on. Brain wave-based biometric system is the emerging new technique for user authentication. The trained signal is matched with the data in the data base to approve authentication. The proposed system provides 83% accuracy for samples 1, 100% accuracy for samples 2, and 80% accuracy for samples 3. In future work, recognition and verification of the proposed system can be increased by using additional features in the input data set. The EEG data can be collected from individuals using Mind Wave kit which contains 32 electrodes for better accuracy. The proposed system, Biometric authentication using brain waves can be combined with other biometric identification systems, such as face, speech for more security.

References

1. Shen, C., Yu, T., Xu, H., Yang, G., Guan, X., User Practice in Password Security. *J. Comput. Secur.*, 61, 130–141, August 2016.
2. Shen, H., Kumar, N., He, D., Shen, J., Chilamkurti, N., A security-enhanced authentication with key agreement scheme for wireless mobile communications using elliptic curve cryptosystem. *J. Supercomput.*, 72, 9, 3588–3600, September 2016.
3. Nicholson, J., Coventry, L., Briggs, P., Faces and Pictures: Understanding Age Differences in Two Types of Graphical Authentication. *Int. J. Hum. Comput. Stud.*, 71, 10, 958–966, October 2013.
4. Campisi, P. and La Rocca, D., Brain waves for automatic biometric-based user recognition. *IEEE T. Inf. Foren. Sec.*, 9, 5, 782–800, 2014.
5. Shankar, S., A Review on the Challenges Encountered in Biometric Based Authentication Techniques. *Int. J. Adv. Res. Comput. Sci.*, 2, 6, 129–134, 2014.
6. Gui, Q., Jin, Z., Blondet, M.V.R., Laszlo, S., Xu, W., Towards EEG biometrics: Pattern matching approaches for user identification, in: *Proceedings of the IEEE International Conference on Identity, Security and Behavior Analysis*, IEEE Xplore Press, Hong Kong, China, pp. 1–6, 2015.
7. Ruiz Blondet, M.V., Laszlo, S., Jin, Z., Assessment of permanence of non-volitional EEG brainwaves as a biometric, in: *IEEE International Conference on Identity, Security and Behavior Analysis (ISBA 2015)*, Hong Kong, pp. 1–6, 2015.

8. Fraschini, M., Hillebrand, A., Demuru, M., Didaci, L., Marcialis, G.L., An EEG-Based Biometric System Using Eigenvector Centrality in Resting State Brain Networks. *IEEE Signal Process. Lett.*, 22, 6, 666–670, June 2015.

9. Hema, C.R., Paulraj, M.P., Kaur, H., Brain signatures: A modality for biometric authentication, in: *2008 International Conference on Electronic Design*, pp. 1–4, 2008.

10. Liew, S.H., Choo, Y.H., Low, Y.F., Yusoh, Z.I.M., Yap, T.B., Muda, A.K., Comparing Features Extraction Methods for Person Authentication Using EEG Signals, in: *Pattern Analysis, Intelligent Security and the Internet of Things. Advances in Intelligent Systems and Computing*, A. Abraham, A. Muda, Y.H. Choo (Eds.), vol. 355, 2015.

11. Thomas, K.P. and Vinod, A.P., Biometric identification of persons using sample entropy features of EEG during rest state. *IEEE International Conference on Systems, Man, and Cybernetics (SMC)*, 2016.

12. Meisheri, H., Ramrao, N., Mitra, S.K., Multiclass Common Spatial Pattern for EEG based Brain Computer Interface with Adaptive Learning Classifier. *Pattern Recognit. Lett.*, 1–8. arXiv preprint arXiv:1802.09046, 2018

13. Faber, P.L., Travis, F., Milz, P., Parim, N., EEG microstates during different phases of Transcendental Meditation practice. *Cogn. Process.*, 18, 3, 307–314, April 2017.

14. Paranjape, R.B., Mahovsky, J., Benedicenti, L., Koles, Z., The Electroencephalogram as a Biometrics. *Proc. Canadian Conf. Electrical and Computer Eng.*, 2, 1363–1366, 2001.

15. Vogel, F., The Genetic Basis of the Normal Human Electroencephalogram (EEG). *Hum. Genet.*, 10, 91–114, 1970.

16. Ravi, K. and Palaniappan, R., Leave-one-out authentication of persons using 40Hz EEG oscillations, in: *International Conference on Computer as a Tool*, Belgrade, Serbia & Montenegro, 2005.

17. Poulos, M., Rangoussi, M., Chrissikopoulos, V., Evangelou, A., Parametric person identification from the EEG using computational geometry, in: *IEEE International Conference on Electronics, Circuits and Systems*, Pafos, Cyprus, 1999.

18. Parajanpe, R., Mahovsky, J., Benedicenti, L., Koles, Z., The electroencephalogram as a biometric, in: *Canadian Conference on Electrical and Computer Engineering*, vol. 2, pp. 1363–1366, 2001.

19. Mohanchandra, K., Lingaraju, G.M., Kambli, P., Vinay, K., Using Brain Waves as New Biometric Feature for Authenticating a Computer User in Real-Time. *Int. J. Biom. Bioinf.*, 7, 1, 49–57, 2013.

20. Marcel, S. and R. Millan, J., Person Authentication Using Brainwaves (EEG) and Maximum A Posteriori Model Adaptation. *IEEE Trans. Pattern Anal. Mach. Intell.*, 29, 4, 743–752, 2007.

21. Soni, Y.S., Somani, S.B., Shete, V.V., Biometric user authentication using brain waves, in: *Proceedings of the International Conference on Inventive Computation Technologies (ICICT)*, Coimbatore, India, vol. 2, pp. 1–6, 2016.

22. Angkraingkij, P., Significant Frequency Range of Brain Wave Signals for Authentication, in: *Software Engineering, Artificial Intelligence, Networking and Parallel/Distributed Computing 2015. Studies in Computational Intelligence*, R. Lee, (Ed.), vol. 612, Springer, Cham, 2016.

23. Reshmi, K.C., Ihsana Muhammed, P., Priya, V.V., Akhila, V.A., A Novel Approach to Brain Biometric User Recognition, Global Colloquium in Recent Advancement and Effectual Researches in Engineering, Science and Technology. *Proc. Technol.*, 25, 240–247, 2016.

24. Ramaswamy, P., Two-Stage Biometric Authentication Method using Thought Activity Brain Waves. *Int. J. Neural Syst.*, 18, 01, 59–66, 2008.

25. Jenkins, J., Sweet, C., Sweet, J., Noel, S., Szu, H., Authentication, Privacy, Security can Exploit Brainwave by Biomarker, in: *Independent Component Analyses, Compressive Sampling, Wavelets, Neural Net, Biosystems, and Nanoengineering XII*, H. Harold, L.D. Szu (Eds.), vol. 9118, Proc. of SPIE, Baltimore, Maryland, United States, 2014.

26. Alariki, A.A., Ibrahimi, A.W., Wardak, M., Wall, J., A Review Study of Brian Activity-Based Biometric Authentication. *J. Comput. Sci.*, 14, 2, 173–181, 2018. DOI: 10.3844/jcssp.2018.173.181.

27. Barkadehi, M.H., Nilashi, M., Ibrahim, O., Zakeri Fardi, A., Samad, S., Authentication Systems: A Literature Review and Classification. *Telemat. Inform.*, 35, 1491–1511, 2018.

28. Svogor, I. and Kisasondi, T., Two factor authentication using EEG augmented passwords, in: *Proceedings of the International Conference on Information Technology Interfaces*, ITI, IEEE, Zoran, pp. 373–378, 2012.

29. Gui, Q., Jin, Z., Xu, W., Exploring EEG-based biometrics for user identification and authentication, in: *IEEE Signal Processing in Medicine and Biology Symposium (SPMB)*, IEEE, Philadelphia, PA, USA, pp. 1–6, 2014.

30. Thorpe, J., Van Oorschot, P.C., Somayaji, A., Pass-thoughts: Authenticating with our minds, in: *Proceedings of the 2005 Workshop on New Security Paradigms*, pp. 45–56, Association for Computing Machinery, New York, NY, United States, 2005, https://doi.org/10.1145/1146269.1146282.

31. Abo-Zahhad, M., Ahmed, S.M., Abbas, S.N., A new multi-level approach to EEG based human authentication using eye blinking. *Pattern Recognit. Lett.*, 0, 1–10, 2015. https://doi.org/10.1016/j.patrec.2015.07.034.

32. Ruiz-Blondet, M.V., Jin, Z., Laszlo, S., CEREBRE: A novel method for very high accuracy event-related potential biometric identification. *IEEE Trans. Inf. Foren. Sec.*, 11, 1618–1629, 2016.

33. Kang, J.H., Lee, C.H., Kim, S.P., EEG feature selection and the use of Lyapunov exponents for EEG-based biometrics, in: *Proceedings of the IEEEE MBS International Conference on Biomedical and Health Informatics*, pp: 228–231, IEEE Xplore Press, Las Vegas, NV, USA, 2016.

34. Bashar, M.K., Chiaki, I., Yoshida, H., Human identification from brain EEG signals using advanced machine learning method EEG-based biometrics,

in: Proceedings of the IEEE EMBS Conference on Biomedical Engineering and Sciences, pp. 475–479, IEEE Xplore Press, Kuala Lumpur, Malaysia, 2016.

35. Kumari, P. and Vaish, Dr. A., Brainwave Based Authentication System: Research Issues and Challenges. *Int. J. Comput. Eng. Appl.*, IV, I & II, 89–108, 2014.

36. Poulos, M., Rangoussi, M., Alexandris, N., Evangelou, A., Person Identification from the EEG using nonlinear signal classification. *Methods Inf. Med.*, 41, 64–75, January 2002.

37. Architecture of FFNN. https://openi.nlm.nih.gov/detailedresult.php?img= PMC3942393_TSWJ2014-908140.003&req=4.

38. EEG Motor Movement/Imagery Dataset—PhysioNet. http://physionet.org/ pn4/eegmmidb/.

39. Brain-Computer Interface (BCI) Dataset Collection Software, BCI2000 software. http://www.bci2000.org/.

10

Autism Screening Tools With Machine Learning and Deep Learning Methods: A Review

Pavithra D.[1]*, Jayanthi A. N.[2], Nidhya R.[3] and Balamurugan S.[4]

[1]Department of Information Technology, Dr. N. G. P. Institute of Technology, Coimbatore, Tamilnadu, India
[2]Department of Electronics and Communication Engineering, Sri Ramakrishna Institute of Technology, Coimbatore, Tamilnadu, India
[3]Department of Computer Science and Engineering, Madanapalle Institute of Technology and Science, Madanapalle, Andhra Pradesh, India
[4]Intelligent Research Consultancy Services, Coimbatore, Tamilnadu, India

Abstract

Autism spectrum disorder (ASD) is the most challenging developmental disorder that affects the social skills, language—communication, imagination of the child. Moreover, children with autism have repetitive behavior patterns, attention deficit, anxiety, self-injury, sameness, abnormal sleep patterns, aggression that leads to behavioral issues. Each child differs in symptoms, and they vary from mild to severe autism. Early diagnosis and treatment help the child to come over the situation. Autism spectrum disorder is diagnosed using assessment tools called ASD screening tools, used by the medical staff with the support of parents/caregivers. There is much research for improving the accuracy and classification of ASD using computational intelligence. This paper is a review of different screening tools and machine learning methods for ASD diagnosis.

Keywords: Autism, machine learning, ASD screening tools, Quantitative Checklist for Autism in Toddlers (Q-CHAT), Autism Screening Instrument for Educational Planning (ASIEP-3), Childhood Autism Rating Scale (CARS-2), Early Screening of Autistic Traits (ESAT), autism behavior checklist, ISAA

---

*Corresponding author: pavimba07@gmail.com

R. Nidhya, Manish Kumar and S. Balamurugan (eds.) Tele-Healthcare: Applications of Artificial Intelligence and Soft Computing Techniques, (221–248) © 2022 Scrivener Publishing LLC

10.1   Introduction

"Autism", the word comes from the Greek word autos, which means self. This was used by psychiatrist Leo Kanner in his first clinical setting (1943). After a year (1944), Hans Asperger, an Austrian pediatrician named children as "autistic psychopathology" who have repetitive, restrictive, and stereotypical behavior patterns. They also have impairment in occupational, social, and other functional activities. They lack in language and cognitive skills of their appropriate age (DSM-IV, 1994). Both of them describe that children with autism have difficulties in cognitive, behavior, social, and communication. Finally, in 1911, a Swiss psychiatrist Eugene Bleuler termed the word "autism" to indicate the state of social withdrawal [64].

Autism is a pervasive developmental disorder that causes impairment in speech, social, and cognitive skills varying from mild to severe [1]. The term "spectrum" describes the variations in the developmental disabilities among the children, no two children with ASD are unique in their problems. According to 2018 survey report of the Center for Disease Control and Prevention, every 1 in 54 children are identified with autism spectrum disorder (ASD) and it prevails in all racial, ethnic, and socio-economic groups. Autism spectrum disorder occurs in boy children than girls. Many studies in Europe, North America, and Asia identified that the prevalence of ASD is between 1% and 2%. Nearly 17% of children with age group 3 to 17 years are identified with developmental disorder by their caretakers in the study period of 2009 to 2017, that includes attention-deficit/hyperactivity disorder (ADHD), ASD, cerebral palsy, and blindness. Early detection can help the children to sort out the risk factors and may help to lead a normal life.

Present autism screening tools employ questionnaires with rules to classify and grade the cases. The quality of the outcome depends on the subjective contribution of the professional and the interpretation of the clinical staff and caretakers/parents. There are several screening tools like Autism Childhood Autism Rating Scale (CARS), Autism Diagnostic Observation Schedule (ADOS), Autism Diagnostic Interview—Revised (ADI-R), and so on. Generally, ASD symptoms are shown in the first three years of life. Apart from monitoring the behavior of the child, it cannot be diagnosed at this age. This can be initiated by intelligent algorithms like deep learning and machine learning.

Machine Learning is a research area based on artificial intelligence, database, and mathematics that discover accurate models from the existing data sets [2, 3]. A major task in ML is learning from the existing data set,

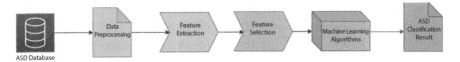

Figure 10.1 Steps for classifying ASD using machine learning algorithm.

which is called supervised learning. In this, model is built using the existing data set which is called training set. The built model is evaluated using a set of data, known as test data to measure its performance. In ML when there is no target value, a grouping of instances is done, and this method is called clustering. Prediction without discovering any patterns is termed unsupervised learning. ML increases the prediction or diagnosis of the cases more accurately and efficiently. These models that are derived from ML do not replace clinician rather it guides to improve the decisions of ASD diagnosis. Much research has been conducted using ML in the classification and prediction of autism. It not only improves the performance of screening or diagnosis but also provides valuable information regarding the classification. The general steps for ASD classification using Machine Learning techniques are depicted in Figure 10.1.

Deep learning (DL) is another AI technique that depicts the brain working of humans for processing the data, even when they are unstructured, unlabeled, and diverse. Deep learning is also termed as deep neural networks (DNNs) because it mainly involves neural network architecture where deep represents the depth of the hidden layers. Performance of DL increases with the number of data, and most of the time, the features for training the model are selected by the model itself. DL in the medical field enhances the accuracy and speed of diagnosis.

10.2 Autism Screening Methods

Many screening or diagnostic tools are available to grade ASD. Some of them are CARS, ADOS, ADI-R. These are more time consuming as they have long questionnaires and rating methods. It also requires experienced clinicians and administrators [4]. Other than clinical tools, there are many tools developed by psychologists and neurologists. These tools help the caregivers, parents, and therapists to identify the autistic qualities in the children. Tools like Modified Checklist for Autism in Toddlers (M-CHAT), Autism Spectrum Quotient (AQ) contains questions to discriminate against autism with others [5, 6]. Much research has been done to identify the effectiveness and efficiency of the ASD screening tools

[7, 8]. Nevertheless, limited studies have been performed to discover the strengths and weaknesses of ASD screening tools [9–11]. Some of the studies focused on comparing the performance concerning sensitivity and specificity, others focused on early identification in toddlers. This part is to identify the merits and shortcomings of each screening method.

10.2.1   Autism Screening Instrument for Educational Planning—3rd Version

Autism Screening Instrument for Educational Planning—3rd Version (ASIEP-3) by David A. Krug (2008) is an individually administered tool to evaluate autistic children and create an instructional plan appropriate to the child. This tool can be used for 0 to 2 years and 11 to 13 years of age in children. It contains five aspects of behavior Autism Behavior Checklist (ABC), vocal, interaction, educational assessment, and prognosis of learning rate. The duration to complete the assessment for ASIEP-3 is about 90 to 120 minutes, which is longer than CHAT [11].

10.2.2   Quantitative Checklist for Autism in Toddlers

Quantitative CHecklist for Autism in Toddler (Q-CHAT) is the oldest among all the screening methods. It is used for early detection of autism, at the age of 18 to 24 months developed by Allison *et al.* (2008). CHAT was developed in 2001 and Q-CHAT is the modified version including items related to language, social interaction, and repetitive behavior. Robins *et al.* [65] developed M-CHAT-R/F, a modified version of Q-CHAT as the performance was low concerning sensitivity. It is a two-stage screening tool to diagnose ASD. Initially, CHAT and M-CHAT contain 20 Likert scale based questions, which took 20 to 25 minutes to complete. Then M-CHAT was reduced to 10 questions to identify the presence of autism traits in a short period [12]. The Chinese version of Q-CHAT, CHAT-23 was developed to screen children at the age of 16 to 30 months. The recent version of Q-CHAT, 10-Q-CHAT is developed in many languages for the use of clinicians all over the world. This has been an acceptable version of Q-CHAT as its performance is 91% in sensitivity and 98% in specificity.

10.2.3   Autism Behavior Checklist

Autism Behavior Checklist is dealing with the behavior of the child. It was developed by Krug *et al.*, in 1980 [66], part of ASIEP's third version. It was designed such that a parent or caretaker, familiar with the child can complete ABC and then can consult the physician for further analysis. It can be used only with children of age 3 years and older. It contains 57 items classified into five categories, such as sensory, relating to environment, object and body usage, language and communication, and finally social skills. Each item is scored in the range of 1-4 based on the children's behavior. Campbell *et al.* (2006), analyzed the performance of ABC with 167 sample cases revealed that there was 80% accuracy with 77% sensitivity, 91% specificity [13].

10.2.4 Developmental Behavior Checklist-Early Screen

Developmental Behavior Checklist-Early Screen (DBC-ES; Gray & Tonge [67], autism diagnosing tool formed from the Developmental Behaviour Checklist Parent/Primary Caregiver Report (DBC-P). It contains 17 items from the original checklist and is used to screen children of 18 to 48 months. The DBC-P was developed for children with age 4 to 18 years to identify the behavior and emotional problems. DBC-ES was developed for infants (18–48 months) in 2007 by Gary *et al.* This tool was accepted for parent/caregiver administered autism screening tool for identifying the children with cerebral frailties and provides performance with 83% sensitivity and 48% specificity [14].

10.2.5 Childhood Autism Rating Scale Version 2

Childhood Autism Rating Scale–Second Edition (CARS-2), developed by Eric Schopler *et al.* to assess the children at the age of 2 years and older. It is a 15-item rating scale to diagnose autism among other developmental delays. It uses 4-point rating scale based on the frequency and duration. This includes three forms: the standard version rating booklet (CARS2-ST), similar to original CARS and used for children younger than 6 years with communication difficulties or below-average IQ, the high functioning version rating booklet (CARS2-HF), for assessing children who verbally fluent of 6 years and older with IQ above 80 and a questionnaire for parents and caregivers (CARS2-QPC), unscored scale to use with CARS2-ST and CARS2-HF. The 15 item scale is about relating people, emotional response, imitation, body and object use, adapting to change, visual, listening, touch, smell, taste, fear, communication, activity level, and general impressions. The validity test for CARS-2 was performed, which showed specificity 87% and sensitivity of 81%.

10.2.6   Autism Spectrum Screening Questionnaire (ASSQ)

Ehlers and Gillberg designed a screening tool to identify the prevalence of autism among the children and further in collaboration with Lorna Wing developed a tool to identify Asperger's syndrome. This method contains 27 items with a rating 0 to 2, and this can be used for screening children aged 7 to 16 years. When the score exceeds the threshold value, then the child has the symptoms of ASD and other developmental problems. Einfeld and Tonge performed the test for the threshold of 13, which resulted in 90% of accuracy. Adachi *et al.*, 2018 tested psychometric properties for young children in Japan with a cutoff of 7, resulted in 93% sensitivity and 84% specificity [14].

10.2.7   Early Screening for Autistic Traits

Early Screening for Autistic Traits (ESAT) screening method was developed for infants of 0 to 36 months to identify the autistic characters among other developmental disorders. It mainly focused on neurodevelopmental issues in infants. In 2006, Dietz *et al.* developed an ESAT diagnosing checklist containing 14 items related to the behavior of the child such as attention, playing, reactions, communication, eye contact, social. This checklist contains only YES or NO questions, which takes nearly 10 to 15 minutes of the survey [15]. Infants scored high in ESAT, who are susceptible to ASD and other developmental disabilities, this tool does not distinguish infants younger than 25 months. Few children who scored less in ESAT was identified with ASD in later stages [16].

10.2.8   Autism Spectrum Quotient

In 2001, Dr. Simon Baron-Cohen published autism spectrum quotient in the autism research center, Cambridge, UK. This contains nearly fifty questions including the areas of imagination, attention, communication, and social skills. This tool was mainly designed to identify the symptoms of autism in adults with average intelligence. Each item was identified either of response: "Definitely Agree," "definitely disagree," "slightly agree," "slightly disagree," the final score was between 0 and 50. The higher the score is the higher the autism symptoms. In 2012, Allison, *et al.*, revised the version as AQ-10 adult, with shortened questions and the same type of response. The score calculated follows the handcrafted diagnosis rule and when it is above a threshold value of six then the individual is considered to have autism and other developmental problems [17]. In 2008, Auyeung *et al.* proposed a validity test for AQ with a cutoff of 32, which resulted in 77% sensitivity and 74% specificity [18].

10.2.9   Social Communication Questionnaire

The Social Communication Questionnaire (SCQ) is a 40-item screening method to identify ASD symptoms. Each item has the response of yes/no with one point for abnormal behavior and 0 for normal behavior within 15 minutes of assessment time [19]. There are two versions of SCQ, namely lifetime and current. The SCQ-lifetime analyzes the complete history of the child, whereas SCQ current analyzes the behavior of the child in the past 3 months. When the score is beyond the cutoff and analyzed for ASD, the SCQ-current analysis is used for setting goals for the development of the child. Social Communication Questionnaire was analyzed for an optimum cutoff score of 22 and revealed 75% sensitivity and 60% specificity [19].

10.2.10   Child Behavior Check List

Child behavior check list (CBCL) was developed by Tomas Achenbach in 1991 for identifying developmental problems for children aged 6 to 18 years. There are two forms of Child Behavior Checklist: preschool and school age. The preschool version was developed with 100 questions with three responses, 0 to 2, it covers children of age 1 and a half to 5 years. The school-age version contains 118 items with the same response for the age group of 6 to 18 years. This version covers problems related to aggressiveness, attention deficit, anxiety, social skills, depression, somatic problems, thought problems. These items are categorized into internalizing and externalizing problems. In 2013, Bordin *et al.,* performed the validity of CBCL for Brazilian children, which provided high sensitivity and specificity for identifying behavioral disorder children [20].

10.2.11   Indian Scale for Assessment of Autism

Indian Scale for Assessment of Autism (ISAA) is an Indian diagnostic tool for identifying autism for children from age of 3 to 22 years, developed by the National Trust, Ministry of Health and Family Welfare, and Ministry of Social Justice and Empowerment of the Government of India. This tool was developed mainly for Indian children to cover variable literacy levels, culture, and languages. This tool was used to identify the severity levels of the children. It is a 40-item questionnaire with a five-point scale ranging from 1 to 5, categorized into six major domains: emotional, social response, communication, behavior, sensory, and cognitive. Time taken to complete the assessment is 20 to 30 minutes with a minimum score of 40 to declare as no-autism and a maximum score of 200 for severe autism. In 2015, Sharmila *et al.*, performed diagnostic accuracy for children aged 2 to 9 years and reported 93.3% sensitivity and 97.4 specificity [21].

Table 10.1 provides a summary of all the ASD diagnosing tools with their performance and time for diagnosing. The ASD tool's performance depends on accessibility, popularity, comprehensibility, administrative methods, and timing.

10.3   Machine Learning in ASD Screening and Diagnosis

Machine learning is a statistical method that uses data for accurate prediction and classification. ASD diagnosis is a complex problem that needs accurate classification to provide proper therapy for the children. This section discusses the application of various machine learning algorithms for ASD screening and diagnosis.

Ridwah *et al.* proposed a fuzzy system to identify the level of autism using a two-step process, namely data acquisition and fuzzy system. The system contains four steps from fuzzification, analyzing the rules developed, aggregating the rules, and finally, defuzzification. The author used different screen tools like CHAT, M-CHAT, ABC, ADI for data acquisition, and diagnosing the level of autism. The result obtained indicates that the fuzzy system performs accurately in diagnosing the level of ASD [22].

The author has compared six machine learning algorithms like Decision tree, Random Forest (RF), support vector machines (SVMs), Logistic Regression, Categorical Lasso, and Linear discriminant analyses to differentiate ASD and ADHD using the behavior exhibited by the children. Social Responsiveness Scale was used with 65 features and tested for 2925 individuals and identified 5 of 65 behavior set is sufficient for distinguishing ADHD and ASD. This resulted in an accuracy of 96.5% [4]. Bone *et al.* developed an ML algorithm to diagnose ASD. They used Social Responsiveness Scale (SRS) scores and ADI-R of 1726 individuals with and without ASD. The algorithm was based on a robust ML classifier and SVM, which resulted in 89.2% sensitivity and 59% specificity [23].

Ilias *et al.* [24] tested the performance of SVM and neural networks for classifying ASD from normal children using gait patterns. They have used kinetic, temporal-spatial, and kinematic gait patterns and identified a combination of three patterns results in better classification with 95% accuracy.

Table 10.1 Summary of ASD screening tools.

ASD tool	Items in the tool	Age of the children	Time for diagnosis	Sensitivity (in %)	Specificity (in %)	References
CHAT	14	Toddlers (8–24 months)	15 mins	40	98	Cohen et al., 1992
Modified Checklist for Autism in Toddlers, Revised (M-CHAT-R)	20	Toddlers (16–30 months)	20 mins	-	-	Diana Robins, Deborah Fein & Marianne Barton, 2009
Q-CHAT	25	Toddlers (18–24 months)	20 mins	88	91	Allison et al., 2012
CHAT-23	23	Toddlers (16–30 months)	20 mins	84	85	Wong et al., 2004
ABC	57	Children (3–14 years)	30 mins	77	91	Krug et al., 2008
ASIEP-3	47	Toddler and children (2–13 years)	Varies	100	81	Krug et al., 2008

(Continued)

Table 10.1 Summary of ASD screening tools. (*Continued*)

ASD tool	Items in the tool	Age of the children	Time for diagnosis	Sensitivity (in %)	Specificity (in %)	References
CARS-2	15 (2 version)	Children (version 1: <6 years, version 2: 6–13 years)	20 mins	81	87	Schopler *et al.*, 2009
Developmental Checklist-Early Screen (DBD-ES)	17	Toddlers (18–48 months)	15 mins	83	48	Gray & Tonge, 2005
ESAT	14	Toddlers (16–30 months)	15 mins	88	14	Dietz *et al.*, 2006
Autism Spectrum Screening Questionnaire (ASSQ)	27	Children and Adolescent (7–16 years)	15 mins	91	86	Ehlers *et al.*, 1999
AQ	50	Adult (>18 years)	30 mins	93	52	Baron-Cohen *et al.*, 2001

(*Continued*)

Table 10.1 Summary of ASD screening tools. (*Continued*)

ASD tool	Items in the tool	Age of the children	Time for diagnosis	Sensitivity (in %)	Specificity (in %)	References
SCQ	40	<4 years	20 mins	75	60	Rutter *et al.*, 2003
CBCL	100	Children (6–18 years)	40 mins	75	82	Achenbach, 1991
ISAA	40	Children and adolescent (3–22 years)	20 mins	93.3	97.4	Sharmila *et al*, 2014

Authors have proposed, DNN with a novel feature selection (DNN-FS) algorithm for identifying ASD using brain FC patterns. Here, they have compared with and without feature selection method with DNN, which resulted in providing better accuracy of 86.36% for DNN-FS. They have used three hidden layers with 150 nodes and Autism Brain Imaging Data Exchange (ABIDE) data set [25]. The authors have classified autistic children using magnetoencephalography (MEG) signals, the features used are power and phase of neural oscillations. They have proposed a phase angle clustering with an ANN classifier and found that PAC yields better accuracy than power spectral density (PSD) of 88.20%. They also have identified PSD features that are dominant in the right hemispheres of the brain, whereas PAC identifies autism attributes in the whole brain [26]. Xu *et al.* proposed to characterize ASD from normal children using function near-infrared spectroscopy time series in the brain. They have proposed a DL model with long short-term memory (LSTM) and convolutional neural network and achieved better classification with 97.1% sensitivity and 94.3% specificity. They also identified that changes in oxy-hemoglobin and deoxy-hemoglobin results in weaker logical thinking with high memory power and continued to be in random shocks [27]. Haweel *et al.* classified ASD children based on the severity level using task-based functional magnetic resonance imaging (fMRI) data with a speech experiment to get the features. Feature extraction is done using general linear model, and classification with grading was performed using recursive feature elimination and RF algorithm, which resulted in an accuracy of 72% [28]. The author compared the performance of four machine learning algorithms (NB, SVM, k-NN, and RF) with grade of the ASD children. They have used the ISAA data set of 100 children, and the experiment was performed using Weka 3.9 tool kit with 10-fold cross-validation (CV). The accuracy of the RF algorithm (93.3%) was better than other machine learning algorithms [29]. Baadel *et al.* performed autism classification by combining clustering and classification. The data are collected using ASD tests, which combine Q-CHAT 10 and AQ-10 Child screening tools. OMCOKE clustering algorithm, which is based on the K-means clustering algorithm, is used as an initial phase to cluster ASD data into two clusters, then different classification algorithms, like PART, RF, RIPPER, Artificial Neural Network (ANN), and random trees were performed. The accuracy of all the algorithm has been improved by applying clustering before classification, clustering algorithm reduced the data dimensionality and streamlined the data based on important features that resulted in minimum rules generated for the classifiers [30].

Vaishali *et al.* proposed a method with a binary firefly algorithm for feature selection. This algorithm selected an optimal of 11 of 21 features from the data set. The data set used here is from the UCI repository. The classification is performed using two algorithms, namely SVM and Multilayer Perceptron. Both the algorithms are compared with each other and identified that SVM has better accuracy than MLP [31].

The authors have proposed a logistic regression model for screening adult ASD. The most predictive and feature identification is performed to get the optimal features for ASD diagnosis for adults and adolescents. The feature examinations were done with the help of Chi-Square Testing (CHI) and Information Gain (IG) methods. Further, classification was performed using logistic regression (LR). The performance of the model has better accuracy, specificity, and sensitivity [32].

Altay and Ulas compared two ML algorithms, namely k-nearest neighbor (kNN) and linear discriminant analysis (LDA) for diagnosing ASD. The LDA algorithm performed with better accuracy of 90.8% when compared to kNN, which resulted in an accuracy of 88.5%. Linear discriminant analysis attained a sensitivity of 0.9524 and specificity of .08667, whereas kNN obtained 0.9762 sensitivity and 0.80 specificity. F-measure obtained for the LDA algorithm is 0.9091 and 0.8913 for kNN [33].

In this work, the authors compared eight ML algorithms for the ADOS data set of 4540 individuals. They have considered modules 2 and 3 of ADOS. The features identified for module 2 are 9 of 28 and for module 3, it is 12 of 28. These identified features produced 98.27% of accuracy for detecting ASD for module 2 and 97.66% of accuracy for module 3. They have concluded with a 55% reduction in the feature set for better classification of ASD [34].

The SVM algorithm was used to identify the autism spectrum by using 2,500 records for both training and testing. The records collected were based on ADI-R and ADOS scales. The result indicated that a minor combination of both the scale features would increase the performance. This modified approach improved the sensitivity from 85.6% to 94.3% and specificity of 80.9% to 89.3% with a minimum number of features. Feature selection is done using the Greedy backward-elimination method. Training of SVM is performed by the linear kernel, as well as a radial basis function (RBF) kernel [35].

Parikh et al. identified the prognostic power of personal characteristic data (PCD) for improving the diagnosis of ASD. They have extracted nearly six PCD features from 851 subjects from ABIDE data set. Nine supervised algorithms were used to analyze the data and the performance was measured by sensitivity, specificity, the area under the receiver operating characteristic curve (AUC), and accuracy. Nine models with identified six features resulted in the best performance for a neural network with a mean AUC of 0.646 followed by the kNN with a mean AUC of 0.641 with six PCD features. With these features, discriminative features like neuro-imaging can be added to have an automatic machine learning ASD diagnosis model [36].

Machine learning classifiers are used to detect autism through their imitation. Here, the authors have investigated the use of data-driven machine learning models in addressing problems related to discriminative test conditions and kinematic parameters for classifying ASC and neurotypical controls. Nearly 40 kinematic parameters were identified from eight imitation conditions through the machine learning model. Out of which two most optimal imitation conditions with nine significant kinematic parameters were recognized and compared with standard attribute evaluators. The result proved the likelihood of using machine learning models for analyzing high-dimensional data for the autism diagnosis. The classifiers used were the SVM and Naïve Bayes, which resulted in an accuracy of 86.7% [37].

Martial *et al.* proposed a method to identify the modifications in community patterns in operational networks under ASD. Community pattern quality metrics were used to design controls and machine learning classifiers were used to detect ASD. The model was tested on 6 publicly available data sets with 235 subjects. ML methods like Naive Bayes (NB), Logistic Regression (LR), kNN, SVM, LDA, and Classification and Regression Trees (CART) were used, and the performance was measured using precision, recall, F-measure, and accuracy [38].

In this paper, the authors have extended the already proposed work for adults and adolescents with module 4 of ADOS. The SVM algorithm is used to scrutinize whether ASD detection can be enhanced by extracting the behavioral features from ADOS module 4. They have tested with 673 high-functional adolescents, 385 adult data, and 288 patients identified as ASD with no psychiatric diagnoses. The result showed a good performance in terms of sensitivity and specificity equal to existing ADOS analyses with a minimized feature set of five behavioral features for different age groups, including adults and adolescents [39].

Sharma (2019) proposed a method for detecting ASD using Correlation-based Feature Selection (CFS) subset selection with Greedy Stepwise (GS) feature selection technique known as CFS-GS technique in the machine learning model. The optimal features are selected using CFS-GS. This proposed algorithm was tested for three data sets of different age groups and different machine learning algorithms. The performance was measured using sensitivity, specificity, and accuracy. For child data, when the proposed selector used with NB and Stochastic Gradient Descent classifier, the result obtained was 100% in terms of accuracy, sensitivity, and specificity.

There was a notable performance increase when used with other classifiers for adolescent data like 100% sensitivity and specificity for K-star and random tree classifiers. Certain classifiers yield nearly 100% sensitivity and accuracy for the adult data set [40].

Authors have proposed an ML model that combines RF-CART and RF-Iterative Dichotomiser 3 (ID3). The data set used for evaluation was 250 real clinical data set with AQ-10 data set that contains both the categories with and without autism. The result showed the proposed model had a better performance in terms of false positive rate (FPR), precision, accuracy, sensitivity, and specificity [41].

Wall *et al.* (2012) experimented Alternative decision Tree (ADTree) for detecting ASD in short screen time. The ADI-R scale was used with 891 individuals' data with the AQ-10 data set, the proposed model achieved 92.26% accuracy for the child, 93.78% accuracy for adolescent, and 97.10% for the adult data set. The main issue was an inadequate real data set [42].

Kanimozhiselvi and Pratapproposed a Po-LVQ neural network, i.e., possibilistic-Linear Vector Quantization neural network for grading ASD in children. The model graded the level of ASD as "normal," "mild-moderate," "moderate-severe," "severe." This model produced an accuracy of 95%, and this can be suggested for grading ASD in autism assessment support system [43].

Authors have used ANN for ASD diagnosis. Here, they have used 10 questions including age, gender, and presence of jaundice as input attributes. The ANN model contains the input layer, hidden, and output layer. The input layer takes the features as input and the hidden layers perform the actual operation using weights and bias. Finally, the hidden layer directs them to an activation function as their output. The tested model performs better in terms of average error rate and good accuracy [44].

Thabtah and Peebles proposed a new ML model named Rules-Machine Learning that detects ASD by providing better knowledge about the rules, which can be analyzed by the domain experts for clarification regarding the classification. Results were tested on three data sets related to children, adolescents, and adults, which proved a better performance than Boosting, Bagging, decision trees, and rule induction in terms of accuracy, sensitivity, harmonic mean, and specificity [45].

Ayşe Demirhan offered a rapid and accurate ASD diagnosis using SVM, kNN, and RF machine learning algorithms for adolescent data. Ten-fold CV was used for this binary classification and obtained an accuracy of 95%, 89%, and 100% for SVM, kNN, and RF, respectively. The RF performed better than the other two algorithms resulting in 100% specificity and sensitivity [46].

Table 10.2 Comparison of machine learning algorithms.

Ref.	Machine learning method	Data set used	Performance
[22]	Fuzzy System	CHAT, M-CHAT, ABC, ADI	Better Accuracy
[23]	Decision tree, RF, SVM, Logistic Regression, Categorical Lasso and Linear discriminant analysis	Social Responsiveness Scale (SRS) scores and ADI-R	89.2% sensitivity and 59% specificity
[24]	SVM and neural network	Gait Patterns	95% accuracy
[25]	DNN-FS	ABIDE data set	Accuracy of 86.36%
[30]	OMCOKE clustering algorithm	Q-CHAT 10 and AQ-10	Sensitivity and Specificity of 86.3% and 87.5%
[31]	SVM and MultiLayer Perceptron	UCI repository	MP performs better than SVM
[34]	eight ML algorithms	ADOS	98.27% of accuracy for detecting ASD for module 2 and 97.66% of accuracy for module 3.
[35]	SVM	ADI-R and ADOS	Improved the sensitivity from 85.6% to 94.3% and specificity of 80.9% to 89.3% with minimum number of features.

(Continued)

Table 10.2 Comparison of machine learning algorithms. (*Continued*)

Ref.	Machine learning method	Data set used	Performance
[36]	Nine supervised algorithms	ABIDE (Autism Brain Imaging Data Exchange) data set	Neural network with mean AUC of 0.646 and k-NN with a mean AUC of 0.641 with six PCD features
[37]	SVM and Naïve Bayes	Kinematic parameters	Accuracy of 86.7%
[39]	SVM algorithm	Module 4 of ADOS	Sensitivity of 86.5%
[41]	RF-ID3 and RF-CART	AQ-10 data set and 250 real data set	Accuracy of 96.2%
[42]	Alternating Decision Tree (ADTree)	AQ-10 data set	Accuracy of 92.26%, 93.78%, and 97.10% for child, adolescent and adult respectively.
[46]	SVM, kNN, and RF	ASD adolescent scan data	Accuracy of 95%, 89%, and 100% for binary classification with 10-fold CV for SVM, kNN, and RF methods respectively
[48]	kNN, the SVM method and the RF method	ASD data sets such as children, adolescences and adults.	RF-100% accuracy, executed 100 times
[49]	SVM, J48, BVM, and Decision tree	CARS	SVM provides high accuracy 95–97% and low error rate.

The authors have proposed an ML-based model for early detection of ASD. Feature transformation was performed using sine function and Z-score transformations. The SVM classifier showed a better result for toddler data sets while Ada-boost provided the best results for children and adult data sets. Glm-boost performed better for the adolescent data set. The analysis continued by combining many feature selection techniques with Z-score–transformed data sets for detecting ASD factors in toddler, child, adolescent, and adult data sets. This indicated that when machine learning methods are optimized correctly, they can provide better prediction in ASD traits and can be used in early diagnosis [47].

UğurErkan and Dang analyzed the existing ML algorithms, such as kNNs, SVM method, and the RF method for detecting ASD traits in children, adolescences, and adults data sets. The training and testing data were obtained randomly from the existing database. The classification models were executed 100 times for randomly selected parts of the data. the empirical result showed that SVM and RF performed better than kNN in detecting ASD. The RF algorithm had better classification accuracy than the other two algorithms for all the three data sets [48].

The authors have compared the existing ML algorithms for data collection with preprocessing and classification of ASD with the levels. The results showed that SVM, J48, BVM, and Decision tree performed better for analyzing the behavioral and learning skills of ASD. SVM resulted in better accuracy of 95% to 97% and a lower error rate. The algorithm mainly focused on social relationships and reciprocity, emotional responsiveness, speech-language and communication, behavior patterns, cognitive components, and sensory aspects [49].

Table 10.2 presents the comparison of all the machine learning methods discussed above with the techniques, data set used, and the performance obtained.

10.4   DL in ASD Diagnosis

Deep learning algorithms make the classification of data a step forward than supervised machine learning algorithms. It can be used for analyzing more complex data. DL involves minimal human involvement for extracting the most optimal features by using an unsupervised learning strategy. This method would help in an exploratory search on clinical data that leads to fewer errors. This section deals with the application of DL methods to diagnose ASD traits.

The authors have used CNN for detecting autism traits. The proposed CNN architecture contains a convolutional layer followed by a max-pooling layer and a fully connected layer. The max-pooling layer is preceded by a hidden layer that would find the optimal features to avoid overfitting problems. A dropout regularization is performed after the max-pooling layer to reduce the nodes to 25% for training. At last, the output node is combined to fully connected layer that is used for classification. The proposed model has tested for ABIDE I data set with preprocessing that includes a correction for motion, normalization of voxel intensity, and slice timing correction. The result obtained by the model had an accuracy of 70.22% for detecting ASD traits using ABIDE data set [50].

Misman *et al.* applied a DNN for classifying ASD. The data set used was two ASD adult screening data sets. Initially, preprocessing was performed to handle the variable reduction, missing values, label encoding, and normalization. The model contains two main hyper-parameters, namely the number of nodes and number of layers, which has to be optimized for getting better accuracy. The presented DNN model obtained good accuracy in classifying ASD for the attributes of patients' behavior and clinical information.

The authors have proposed a DL-based multimedia data mining for diagnosing ASD traits. The model used a LSTM networks for speech activity detection (SAD) and speaker diarization patterns that produce the vocal turn-taking metrics. They have also proposed a novel pipeline method for predicting ADOS-2 Calibrated Severity Scores (CSS) of Social Affect (SA). The model was examined using data of 33 children with autism by extracting their linguistic patterns from their conversations by the diagnosticians in the clinical environment. The obtained results were compared with the language acquisition system, Language ENvironment Analysis (LENA), and other algorithms. The proposed model produced a good result of R^2 measures in identifying the severity of ASD when compared with other algorithms [51].

Authors have intended to develop a new model for verbal protest recognition that can be adapted for ASD children. There are two techniques, namely Gaussian Mixture Model (GMM) with stacking and CNN trained on Log Mel-Filter Banks (LMFB). The proposed model was examined for accuracy that mainly focuses on false-positive rates and data set biases minimization by introducing noise and input perturbation [52].

Rathore *et al.* compared three existing algorithms namely, neural networks, SVMs, and RFs for classifying ASD using three topological features—persistence diagrams, persistence images, and persistence landscapes. They have also proposed a hybrid approach that augments the topological features with functional correlations. The result obtained indicates that a simple three-layer neural network (NN) produces an accuracy of 69.2% for classifying autism using ABIDE data set [53].

Authors have projected a bioinformatics-based framework named *Prioritization* of *Autism-genes* using *Network-based Deep-learning Approach* (PANDA) to classify ASD-genes with the human genome based on gene-gene pattern interactions and topological similarity of the gene in the interaction network. The model trains the DL graph classifier by the human molecular interaction network that is used to predict and rank the autism gene associated with every node of the network graph. *Prioritization* of *Autism-genes* using *Network-based Deep-learning Approach* produces a gene prioritization ranking list, which is validated with an independent large-scale exome-sequencing study that results in the top 10% of PANDA-ranked genes that were found appreciably enriched for autism society. The model produced a better classification accuracy of 89% than the existing machine learning algorithms [54].

Suman Raja and Sarfaraz Masood compared the existing algorithms, SVM, kNN, Naïve Bayes, Logistic Regression, NN, CNN for identifying ASD among children, adults, and adolescents. The algorithms were tested on publicly available clinical data sets for the three categories. The data set for children contains 292 instances and 21 attributes. Data set for adolescents consists of 104 instances and 21 attributes. For the adult data set, there were 704 instances with 21 attributes. The result obtained after handling missing values proved that CNN had better ASD classification than other algorithms with high accuracy of 99.53%, 98.30%, 96.88% for adults, children, and adolescents, respectively [55].

The authors have examined the use of a novel DL neural network architectures for identifying whether the child has visual concentration during the therapy sessions. To evaluate this model, videos were collected from the clinical environment in an unconstrained setting that resulted in low-resolution videos from the camera of the robot in child-robot interaction [56].

Niu *et al.* proposed an automated multichannel deep attention neural network (DANN) for ASD diagnosis. This model integrates multiple layers of neural networks, attention mechanism, and feature fusion that capture the inter-relationships in multimodality data. The model was evaluated for ABIDE repository with 809 subjects, where 408 ASD patients and 401 other developmental controls. The result indicated a better classification accuracy than other DL models [57].

Eslami & Saeed proposed the Auto-ASD-Network model to identify the subjects with ASD from healthy subjects using fMRI data. MLP with two hidden layers is used in this model and SMOTE algorithm is used to generate artificial data and avoid overfitting by doing data augmentation. The reduction in the overfitting problem would increase the classification accuracy of the model. Further analysis was performed by feeding the discriminative power of features extracted using MLP to the SVM classifier. The hyperparameters of the SVM classifier is optimized using Auto-Tune Models (ATM). The empirical result showed better classification accuracy than other models [58].

Tao & Shyu identified a model named SP-ASD Net to identify whether the observer is typically developed (TD) or has ASD, based on the scan path of the observer's gazing at the given image. The model combines both CNNs and LSTM networks. The model was better in classifying ASD using the gazing movement of the eye [59].

Rad *et al.* (2015) proposed a DL model that uses the Stereotypical Motor Movement (SMM) pattern for identifying ASD traits. The model uses CNN for a feature extraction procedure that transforms the multi-channel accelerometer signal into a reduced set of features. Finally, SVM classified is as applied to identify the new representation of signal into SMM and no-SMM classes. The model resulted in nominal accuracy in identifying ASD using the stereotype behavior [60].

Shahamiri & Thabtah proposed a novel ASD screening method that alternates the conventional scoring methodology using a DL model. The model contains a mobile application with the user interface for capturing answers for the questionnaire data; an intellectual ASD detection web service that integrates with a CNN which is trained by historical ASD cases; finally, the data are stored in a database that is used for training CNN. The obtained model was evaluated on a publicly available large ASD data set for adult, adolescent, child, and toddler cases [61].

The authors have proposed a new DL method for SMM identification using CNN in time and frequency domains. The intrasubject SMM variability was solved by the proposed CNN by setting the parameters after analyzing the SMM signals. This idea made the model outperform the existing methods [62].

The authors have applied the DNN architecture to analyze the performance of the DNN model for ASD diagnosis in terms of classification accuracy by using two ASD adult data sets. The results are compared with the existing machine learning method, SVM. The accuracy obtained by the DNN model in ASD classification for the first and second adult data set is 99.40% and 96.08%, respectively, whereas SVM obtained an accuracy of 95.24% and 95.08%. Empirical results proved that ASD cases can be classified accurately by implementing the DNN model [63].

10.5   Conclusion

The most important issue in ASD research is to improve the diagnosis performance with the existing tool to have faster and specific services. This can be done by improving the accuracy of the diagnosis, reducing the time for assessment, choosing the right scale for diagnosis, and also considering the sensitivity and validity of the data. Machine learning methods and DL algorithms have been applied for ASD diagnosis, which reduced the time of diagnosis by identifying the strong features in the existing tools. This paper analyzed different ASD screening methods for the criterion, such as time taken to complete the test, age, number of items included, performance based on specificity and sensitivity. Later, we focused on different machine learning and DL algorithms in the diagnosis of ASD using different forms of data.

References

1. Pennington, M.L., Cullinan, D., Southern, L., Defining autism: variability in state education agency definitions of and evaluations for Autism Spectrum Disorders. *Autism Research and Treatment*, p.327271, 2014.
2. Qabajeh, I., Thabtah, F., Chiclana, F., A dynamic rule-induction method for classification in data mining. *J. Manage. Anal.*, 2, 3, 233–253, 2015.
3. Mohammad, R.M., Thabtah, F., McCluskey, L., Intelligent rule-based phishing websites classification. *IET Inf. Secur.*, 8, 3, 153–160, 2014.
4. Duda, M., Ma, R., Haber, N., Wall, D.P., Use of machine learning for behavioral distinction of autism and ADHD. *Transl. Psychiatry*, 9, 6, e732–e732, 2016.
5. Baron-Cohen, S., Wheelwright, S., Skinner, R., Martin, J., Clubley, E., The autism-spectrum quotient (AQ): Evidence from asperger syndrome/high-functioning autism, malesand females, scientists and mathematicians. *J. Autism Dev. Disord.*, 31, 1, 5–17, 2001.
6. Scott, C., Baron-Cohen, F., Bolton, S., Brayne, P., The CAST (childhood Asperger syndrome test)- preliminary development of a UK screen for mainstream primary-schoolage children. *Autism*, 6, 1, 9–31, 2002.
7. Sappok, T. *et al.*, Diagnosing autism in a clinical sample of adults with intellectual disabilities: How useful are the ADOS and the ADI-R?. *Res. Dev. disabilities*, 34, 5, 1642–1655, 2013.
8. Matson, L., Hattier, J., Williams, M., How does relaxing the algorithm for autism affect DSM-V. *J. Autism Dev. Disord.*, 42, 8, 1549–1556, 2012.
9. Stewart, L.A. and Lee, L.C., Screening for autism spectrum disorder in low- and middle-income countries: A systematic review. *Autism*, 21, 5, 527–539, 2017.

10. Zwaigenbaum, L., Bauman, M., Stone, W., Al, E., Early identification of autism spectrum disorder: recommendations for practice and research. *Pediatrics*, 136, Supplement 1, S41–S59, 2015.

11. Soleimani, F., Khakshour, A., Abasi, Z., Khayat, S., Ghaemi, S.Z., Azam, N., Golchin, N.A.H., Review of autism screening tests. *Int. J. Pediatr.*, 2, 4.1, 319–329, 2014.

12. Allison, C. *et al.*, The Q-CHAT (quantitative checklist for autism in toddlers): a normally distributed quantitative measure of autistic traits at 18–24 months of age: preliminary report. *J. Autism Dev. Disord.*, 38, 8, 1414–1425, 2008.

13. Eaves, R.C., Campbell, H.A., Chambers, D., Criterion-Related and construct validity of the pervasive developmental disorders rating scale and the autism behavior checklist. *Psychol. Sch.*, 37, 4, 311–321, 2000.

14. Einfeld, B. and Tonge, S., Developmental Behaviour Checklist (DBC). *West. Psychol. Serv.*, 2002.

15. Dietz, C., Swinkels, S., Daalen, E.V., Engeland, H.V., Buitelaar, J.K., Screening for autistic spectrum disorder in children aged 14–15 months : Population screening with the Early Screening of Autistic Traits Questionnaire (ESAT). Design and general findings. *J. Autism Dev. Disord.*, 36, 6, 713–722, 2006.

16. Lord, C. and Luyster, R., Early diagnosis and screening of autism spectrum disorders. *Medscape*, 10, 2, 2005.

17. Allison, C., Auyeung, B., Baron-Cohen, S., Toward brief 'red flags' for autism screening: the short autism spectrum quotient and the short quantitative checklist for autism in toddlers in 1,000 cases and 3,000 controls [corrected]. *J. Am. Acad. Child Adolesc. Psychiatry*, 51, 2, 202–212, 2012.

18. Auyeung, B., Baron-Cohen, S., Wheelwright, S., Allison, C., The autism spectrum quotient: Children's version (AQ-Child). *J. Autism Dev. Disord.*, 38, 7, 1230–1240, 2008.

19. Rutter, M., Bailey, A., Lord, C., The social communication questionnaire manual. *United States Am. West. Psychol. Serv.*, 2003.

20. Bordin, I.A., Rocha, M.M., Paula, C.S., Teixeira, M.C., Achenbach, T.M., Rescorla, L.A., Silvares, E.F., Child behaviour checklist (cbcl), youth self report (ysr) and teacher's report form (trf): an overview of the development of the original and Brazilian versions. *Cadernos de saúde pública*, 29, 13–28, 2013.

21. Mukherjee, S.B., Malhotra, M.K., Aneja, S., Chakraborty, S. and Deshpande, S., Diagnostic accuracy of Indian Scale for Assessment of Autism (ISAA) in chidren aged 2-9 years. *Ind. Ped.*, 52, 3, 212–216, 2015.

22. Isa, N.R.M., Yusoff, M., Khalid, N.E., Tahir, N., Nikmat, A.W.B., Autism severity level detection using fuzzy expert system, *2014 IEEE Int. Symp. Robot. Manuf. Autom. IEEE-ROMA* 2014, pp. 218–223, 2015.

23. Bone, D., Bishop, S., Black, M.P., Goodwin, M.S., Lord, C., Narayanan, S.S., Use of machine learning to improve autism screening and diagnostic instruments: effectiveness, efficiency, and multi-instrument fusion, *J. Child Psych. Psychiatry*, 57, 8, 927–937, 2016.

24. Ilias, S., Tahir, N., Jailani, R., Zawiyah, C., Hasan, C., Classification of autism children gait patterns using neural network and support vector machine. In: *2016 IEEE Symposium on Computer Applications & Industrial Electronics (ISCAIE)*, pp. 52-56, IEEE, 2016.

25. Guo, X., Dominick, K.C., Minai, A.A., Li, H., Erickson, C.A., Lu, L.J., Diagnosing Autism Spectrum Disorder from Brain Resting-State Functional Connectivity Patterns Using a Deep Neural Network with a Novel Feature Selection Method. *Front. Neurosci.* 11, August, 1–19, 2017.

26. Barik, K., Watanabe, K., Bhattacharya, J., Saha, G., Classification of Autism in Young Children by Phase Angle Clustering in Magnetoencephalogram Signals. In: *2020 National Conference on Communications (NCC)*, pp. 1-6, IEEE, 2020. 2020.

27. Xu, L. *et al.*, Characterizing autism spectrum disorder by deep learning spontaneous brain activity from functional near-infrared spectroscopy. *J. Neurosci. Methods*, 331, 108538, 2020.

28. Haweel, R. *et al.*, A novel framework for grading autism severity using task-based FMRI, In: *2020 IEEE 17th International Symposium on Biomedical Imaging (ISBI)*, pp. 1404-1407, IEEE, 2020.

29. Pavithra, D., Jayanthi, A.N., Nidhya, R., Comparison of Machine Learning Methods for Effective Autism Diagnosis. In: *International Conference on Soft Computing and Signal Processing*, pp. 629-637, Springer, Singapore, 2019.

30. Baadel, S., Thabtah, F., Lu, J., A clustering approach for autistic trait classification. *Inform. Health Soc. Care*, 45, 3, 309–326, 2020.

31. Vaishali, R. and Sasikala, R., A machine learning based approach to classify Autism with optimum behaviour sets. *Int. J. Eng. Technol.*, 7, 4, 18, 2018.

32. Thabtah, F., Abdelhamid, N., Peebles, D., A machine learning autism classification based on logistic regression analysis. *Health Inf. Sci. Syst.*, 7, 1, 12, 2019.

33. Altay, O. and Ulas, M., Prediction of the autism spectrum disorder diagnosis with linear discriminant analysis classifier and K-nearest neighbor in children, in: *2018 6th International Symposium on Digital Forensic and Security (ISDFS)*, IEEE, pp. 1–4, 2018, March.

34. Kosmicki, J.A., Sochat, V., Duda, M., Wall, D.P., Searching for a minimal set of behaviors for autism detection through feature selection-based machine learning. *Transl. Psychiatry*, 5, 2, e514–e514, 2015.

35. Hauck, F. and Kliewer, N., Machine Learning for Autism Diagnostics: Applying Support Vector Classification, in: *Int'l Conf. Heal. Informatics Med. Syst*, pp. 120–123, 2017.

36. Parikh, M.N., Li, H., He, L., Enhancing diagnosis of autism with optimized machine learning models and personal characteristic data. *Front. Comput. Neurosci.*, 13, 9, 2019.

37. Li, B., Sharma, A., Meng, J., Purushwalkam, S., Gowen, E., Applying machine learning to identify autistic adults using imitation: An exploratory study. *PloS One*, 12, 8, e0182652, 2017.

38. Epalle, T.M., Hu, L., Song, Y., Characterising and predicting autism spectrum disorder by performing resting-state functional network community pattern analysis. *Front. Hum. Neurosci.*, *13*, 203, 2019.

39. Küpper, C., Stroth, S., Wolff, N., Hauck, F., Kliewer, N., Schad-Hansjosten, T., Roepke, S., Identifying predictive features of autism spectrum disorders in a clinical sample of adolescents and adults using machine learning. *Sci. Rep.*, *10*, 1, 1–11, 2020.

40. Sharma, M., Improved autistic spectrum disorder estimation using Cfs subset with Greedy Stepwise feature selection technique. *Int. J. Inf. Technol.*, 1–11, 2019.

41. Omar, K.S., Mondal, P., Khan, N.S., Rizvi, M.R.K., Islam, M.N., A machine learning approach to predict autism spectrum disorder, in: *2019 International Conference on Electrical, Computer and Communication Engineering (ECCE)*, IEEE, pp. 1–6, 2019, February.

42. Wall, D.P., Dally, R., Luyster, R., Jung, J.Y., DeLuca, T.F., Use of artificial intelligence to shorten the behavioral diagnosis of autism. *PloS One*, *7*, 8, e43855, 2012.

43. Kanimozhiselvi, C.S. and Pratap, A., Possibilistic LVQ neural network-An application to childhood autism grading. *Neural Netw. World*, *26*, 3, 253, 2016.

44. Nasser, I.M., Al-Shawwa, M.O., Abu-Naser, S.S., Artificial Neural Network for Diagnose Autism Spectrum Disorder. *IJAISR*, ISSN: 2000-002X, 3, 2, 27–32, February – 2019.

45. Thabtah, F. and Peebles, D., A new machine learning model based on induction of rules for autism detection. *Health Inf. J.*, *26*, 1, 264–286, 2020.

46. Demirhan, A., Performance of machine learning methods in determining the autism spectrum disorder cases. *Mugla J. Sci. Technol.*, *4*, 1, 79–84, 2018.

47. Akter, T., Satu, M.S., Khan, M., II, Ali, M.H., Uddin, S., Lio, P., Moni, M.A., "Machine learning-based models for early stage detection of autism spectrum disorders." *IEEE Access*, *7*, 166509–166527, 2019.

48. Erkan, U. and Thanh, D.N., Autism Spectrum Disorder Detection with Machine Learning Methods. *Curr. Psychiatry Res. Rev. Curr. Psychiatry Rev.*, 15, 4, 297–308, 2019.

49. Sumi, S., Chandra, J., Saravanan, N., Empirical Evaluation of Data Mining Classification Methods for Autistic Children. *Int. J. Trend Res. Dev. (IJTRD)*, 7–10, ISSN: 2394-9333, 2016.

50. Sherkatghanad, Z., Akhondzadeh, M., Salari, S., Zomorodi-Moghadam, M., Abdar, M., Acharya, U.R., Salari, V., Automated detection of autism spectrum disorder using a convolutional neural network. *Front. Neurosci.*, 14, 13, 1325, 2019.

51. Sadiq, S., Castellanos, M., Moffitt, J., Shyu, M.L., Perry, L., Messinger, D., Deep Learning based Multimedia Data Mining for Autism Spectrum

Disorder (ASD) Diagnosis, in: *2019 International Conference on Data Mining Workshops (ICDMW)*, IEEE, pp. 847–854, 2019, November.

52. Casebeer, J., Sarker, H., Dhuliawala, M., Fay, N., Pietrowicz, M., Das, A., "Verbal Protest Recognition in Children with Autism." in: *2018 IEEE International Conference on Acoustics, Speech and Signal Processing (ICASSP)*, IEEE, pp. 301–305, 2018, April.

53. Rathore, A., Palande, S., Anderson, J.S., Zielinski, B.A., Fletcher, P.T., Wang, B., Autism Classification Using Topological Features and Deep Learning: A Cautionary Tale, in: *International Conference on Medical Image Computing and Computer-Assisted Intervention*, Springer, Cham., pp. 736–744, 2019, October.

54. Zhang, Y., Chen, Y., Hu, T., PANDA: Prioritization of autism-genes using network-based deep-learning approach. *Genet. Epidemiol.*, *44*, 4, 382–394, 2020.

55. Raj, S. and Masood, S., Analysis and Detection of Autism Spectrum Disorder Using Machine Learning Techniques. *Proc. Comput. Sci.*, *167*, 994–1004, 2020.

56. Di Nuovo, A., Conti, D., Trubia, G., Buono, S., Di Nuovo, S., Deep learning systems for estimating visual attention in robot-assisted therapy of children with autism and intellectual disability. *Robotics*, 7, 2, 25, 2018.

57. Niu, K., Guo, J., Pan, Y., Gao, X., Peng, X., Li, N., Li, H., Multichannel deep attention neural networks for the classification of autism spectrum disorder using neuroimaging and personal characteristic data. *Complexity*, 2020, 1357853, 9, 2020.

58. Eslami, T. and Saeed, F., Auto-ASD-network: a technique based on deep learning and support vector machines for diagnosing autism spectrum disorder using fMRI data, in: *Proceedings of the 10th ACM International Conference on Bioinformatics, Computational Biology and Health Informatics*, pp. 646–651, 2019, September.

59. Tao, Y. and Shyu, M.L., SP-ASDNet: CNN-LSTM based ASD classification model using observer scanpaths, in: *2019 IEEE International Conference on Multimedia & Expo Workshops (ICMEW)*, IEEE, pp. 641–646, 2019, July.

60. Rad, N.M. and Furlanello, C., Applying deep learning to stereotypical motor movement detection in autism spectrum disorders. *2016 IEEE 16th International Conference on Data Mining Workshops (ICDMW)*, IEEE, 2016.

61. Shahamiri, S.R. and Thabtah, F., Autism AI: a New Autism Screening System Based on Artificial Intelligence. *Cognit. Comput.*, 12, 4, 766–777, 2020.

62. Sadouk, L., Gadi, T., Essoufi, E.H., A novel deep learning approach for recognizing stereotypical motor movements within and across subjects on the autism spectrum disorder. *Comput. Intell. Neurosci.*, 2018.

63. Misman, M.F. *et al.*, Classification of Adults with Autism Spectrum Disorder using Deep Neural Network, *2019 1st International Conference on Artificial Intelligence and Data Sciences (AiDAS)*, IEEE, 2019.

64. Bleuler, E., *Dementia Praecox or the Group of Schizophrenias*, translated by J. Zinkin. International Universities Press, New York, 1950.

65. Robins, D.L., Fein, D., Barton, M., Modified checklist for autism in toddlers, revised, with follow-up (M-CHAT-R/F) TM. LineageN, 2009.

66. Krug, D.A., Arick, J.R., Almond, P.J., ASIEP: Autism Screening Instrument for Educational Planning. Pro-ed, 1980.

67. Gray, K.M., Tonge,B.J., Screening for autism in infants and preschool children with developmental delay. *Australian and New Zealand Journal of Psychiatry*, 39, 5, 378–386, 2005.

11

Drug Target Module Mining Using Biological Multifunctional Score-Based Coclustering

R. Gowri[1]* and R. Rathipriya[2]

[1]Deparment of Computer Science, Sona College of Arts and Science, Salem, Tamilnadu, India
[2]Deparment of Computer Science, Periyar University, Salem, Tamilnadu, India

Abstract

The novel drug discovery for most of the complex diseases is based on the drug target proteins. In many cases, the pathogen proteins may learn to overplay on the target proteins, and the targeted therapy may fail. For this issue, the targeted therapy can be developed based on the drug target modules. In this chapter, a multifunctional score based coclustering approach CoClustering with MapReduce MR-CoC$_{multi}$ is introduced for drug target module mining with five novel biological scores namely hydrophobic residues density, sequence length, polar residues density, amino acid density, molecular weight scores. These scores are also proposed for this purpose. The results evident that, the MR-CoC$_{multi}$ outperforms the existing approach. Based on the biological functionality and drug target proteins in the results the drug target modules are suggested.

Keywords: Drug target, protein interaction network, co-clustering, functional coherence, hydrophobic, targeted therapy, map-reduce, functional module

11.1 Introduction

The drugs for treating some of the lethal diseases, like cancer, leprosy, corona, and so on, are still undiscovered. The study of such a deadly pathogens' interactions with host proteins helps to analyze their severity, nature,

Corresponding author: gowrics15@periyaruniversity.ac.in

R. Nidhya, Manish Kumar and S. Balamurugan (eds.) Tele-Healthcare: Applications of Artificial Intelligence and Soft Computing Techniques, (249–284) © 2022 Scrivener Publishing LLC

and characteristics obviously. This kind of analysis is required for the disease diagnosis, drug discovery, and therapy development. Currently, the targeted therapy, a rational drug design emerged for cancer. They are customized based on the potential target proteins. There are some limitations seen in this kind of therapy: i) target proteins itself get mutated, leading to failure of the therapy; ii) pathogens will choose a different way to achieve cell multiplication; iii) the pathogens causing these diseases are multitarget resistant. These limitations are because of the therapy depending on single target proteins. For effective targeted therapy, the drug target module (DTM) can be chosen instead, which consist of many target proteins.

The DTM is a functional module, a set of proteins densely connected with each other and possess a specific functionality, and most of the participants in the module are potential drug targets. There is no computational method for finding the DTMs and manually finding DTM is difficult for the biologist, so a computational approach is required to mine dense modules in Protein Interaction Network (PIN). Besides, the biological characteristics of the modules have to be considered for yielding drug target-based modules. In this paper, a computational approach MR-CoC$_{multi}$, which is an extended version of MR-CoC with five novel biological score measures for mining the drug target-based modules, is proposed. The MR-CoC [1, 2] is proposed to mine functional modules based on density score. This approach proved that they overcome the issues of existing approaches.

Further the biological measures are proposed to mine biologically significant modules. The functional modules are significant in various purposes, like disease diagnoses, so on. For this purpose, the drug target-based characteristics are proposed in this chapter. These measures are used to quantify the biological significance of the proteins. This approach is attempted on the general homo-sapiens PIN. The resultant modules are tested for the presence of the drug target participants and their biological significances for suggesting the new DTM. This chapter further discusses the related works, the materials and methods, the proposed approach, experimental analysis, and finally summary of this research.

11.2   Literature Study

Because there is no trace of computational approach for DTM mining in the literature, the proposed approach is studied based on their computational characteristics, i.e., the coclustering performance. The previous studies [1, 2] have proven that score-based CoClustering with MapReduce (MR-CoC) outperformed the existing functional module mining approaches and

Table 11.1 Biological properties of drug targets as per literature.

Related works	Sequence length	Amino acid composition	Hydrophobicity	Polarity	Network topology	Iso-electric point	Keywords	GO terms	Protein domain	Membrane location	PEST motif	Low-complexity regions	Molecular weight	EC number	Glycosylation	Phosphorylation
Bull & Doig, (2015)	✓	✓	✓	✓	✓	✓	×	×	×	✓	✓	✓	✓	✓	✓	✓
Bakheet & J.Doig (2009)	✓	✓	✓	✓	✓	×	×	×	×	✓	✓	✓	✓	✓	✓	✓
Nguyen & Ho, (2012)	✓	×	×	×	✓	×	✓	✓	✓	×	×	×	×	×	×	×
Kim, Jo, Han, Park, & Lee (2017)	✓	×	✓	✓	×	×	×	✓	×	✓	✓	×	×	×	×	×
Chordia, Lakhawat, & Kumar, (2017)	✓	×	✓	×	×	×	×	×	×	✓	✓	×	✓	×	✓	×

(Continued)

Table 11.1 Biological properties of drug targets as per literature. (*Continued*)

Related works	Sequence length	Amino acid composition	Hydrophobicity	Polarity	Network topology	Iso-electric point	Keywords	GO terms	Protein domain	Membrane location	PEST motif	Lowcomplexity regions	Molecular weight	EC number	Glycosylation	Phophorylation
Bakheet & Doig, (2010)	✓	✓	✓	✓	✓	✗	✗	✗	✗	✓	✓	✓	✓	✓	✓	✓
Wanga, Liu, Tang, & Xie (2014)	✓	✓	✓	✓	✗	✓	✓	✓	✓	✓	✓	✓	✓	✓	✓	✓
Gashaw, Ellinghaus, Sommer, & Asadullah, (2011)	✗	✗	✗	✗	✗	✗	✓	✓	✗	✓	✗	✗	✓	✗	✓	✓
Feng, Wang, & Wang, (2017)	✗	✗	✓	✓	✓	✗	✗	✗	✗	✗	✗	✗	✗	✗	✗	✗

coclustering approaches. In that study, the authors have reviewed various approaches like xMotif [3], BiMax [4], BicBin [5], BicSim [6], BMF [7], BiBit [8], BBK [9], BitTable [10], BiBinCons & BiBinAlter [11] ParBiBit [12], and so on. The various limitations of functional module mining identified by these authors are missing the overlapped coclusters & quality coclusters, scalability issue, more time consumption and ignorance of functional characteristics of modules. The previous approach has satisfied all the issues except the usage of functional properties. This chapter is focuses on the biological properties of the functional modules. The biological properties of the drug targets are studied for proposing novel biological measures.

Further, the nature of drug targets are quantified using the biological measures proposed. These properties are selected based on the nature of drug target proteins suggested by various biologists and researchers over time. These properties are classified as simple sequence properties, amino acid composition properties, expression levels, posttranslational properties, structural properties, inter-protein relationships, and so on. Table 11.1 shows the study undertaken for the selection of the biological properties of the proteins. Properties like sequence length, eight amino acid composition, hydrophobicity, network topology, polarity, and molecular weight were chosen for this research work based on their significance highlighted in the literature.

11.3   Materials and Methods

This section discusses the basic terminologies, and existing methods used in this research. The terminologies used in this research are categorized under biological terminologies and technical terminologies.

11.3.1   Biological Terminologies

The biological terminologies represent various concepts that are related to biologically in this research. As this research deals with the bioinformatics concept, various terminologies related to biology are discussed in this subsection for the better understanding of this research. They are protein, PINs, protein modules, functional modules, protein complexes, and so on.

- **Protein:** The proteins are the linear chain of 22 amino acids, which called a sequence of amino acids. They are one-dimensional data, i.e., a lengthy string of alphabet [13–15], as in Figure 11.1. They are the transcripts of the gene or part of a gene. It is used to represent the functionality of the biological systems. They are responsible for various physical and chemical activities in the cell. The central dogma shows the pathway of the protein clearly, as in Figure 11.1.

- **Molecular Networks:** The molecular networks are the network between the various biological products like genes, RNA, proteins, etc. they are used to represent the relation/connectivity and communication between these products. They are formed based on the chemical reactions in the cell [13–15].

- **PIN:** They are the molecular networks formed by the proteins. They are used to highlight the interactions of various proteins in the different parts of the cell [13–15, 38]. These networks are used to transfer signals and commands to various portions of the system. Figure 11.2 displays the sample PIN of 100 random proteins, which is generated using STRING [34, 35].

- **Protein Modules:** The protein modules are the group of proteins that are responsible for a particular function of the cell. It is a part of a PIN that is connected densely with one another than with the other proteins in the network [15].

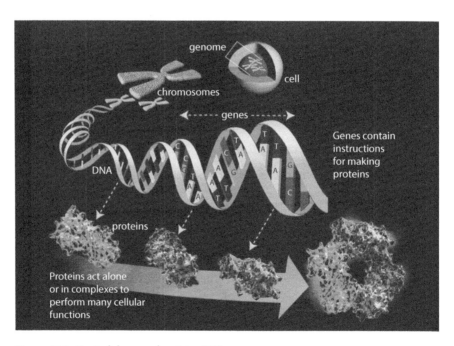

Figure 11.1 Central dogma of proteins [16].

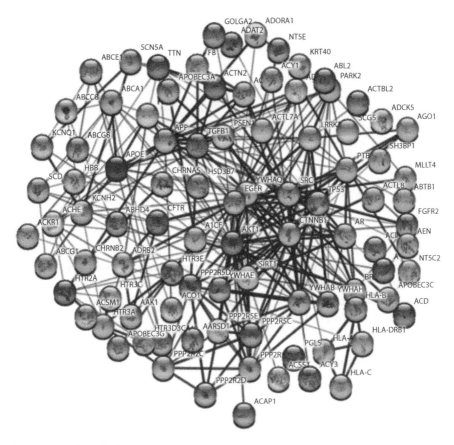

Figure 11.2 Sample PIN.

They are the highly cohesive sections of the PIN. Figure 11.3 highlights the sample protein modules.

- **Protein Complex vs. Functional Modules:** Both protein complex [36] and functional modules are protein modules. The protein modules are static, i.e., they are seen in the same place all the time. However, the functional modules are dynamic, i.e., they are not seen in the same place all the time; they can be formed anywhere anytime [14, 15]. The functional modules formations are due to protein folding, pathogen infections, protein abnormalities, and so on. So, the functional modules can be used to predict the presence of pathogen infections, disease, abnormalities, and so on, they used for drug discovery, target identification,

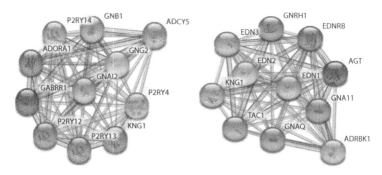

Figure 11.3 Sample protein modules.

treatment suggestions, treatment discovery, and so on, for various complex diseases [15].

- **Drug Targets:** The drug targets are potential proteins that are responsible for transporting the drug to infected parts, boost the efficacy of the drug, bind with the drug for effective treatment [17].

11.3.2   Functional Coherence

It is a measure of the protein module to evaluate the consistency of each functional annotation within the protein module [18]. The functional annotations are the biological functional descriptors associated with each protein. It represents their roles in the biological system under various aspects. These functional annotations for each protein module are measured to project their characteristics. The commonality of these functional annotations is measured using the functional coherence measure (FC). It is the ratio between the number of proteins that possesses a functional annotation and the proteins' count in the protein module.

$$FC_j\left(PM_i\right) = \frac{\left|p_{ij} \in PM_i\right|}{\left|p_i\right|} \tag{11.1}$$

The functional coherence (FC) of the jth annotation in the ith Protein Module (PM) is given in equation (11.1). The "p_{ij}" represents the proteins possessing jth annotation in the ith module, "p_i" is the proteins in the ith module. The value of FC_j lies between "1" and "0," where "1" represents all the proteins in the module has the jth annotation. Based on this FC value, the functionality of the protein module is described. This measure is used in this research to determine the functionalities of the resultant protein modules.

11.3.3   Biological Significances

The biological significances of the proteins are represented using the functional annotations. The functional annotations are the de-facto standard for describing the functional aspects of molecular products like proteins [19, 20]. These significances are categorized mainly under three types, they are as follows:

- *Molecular function:* They are activities, like binding, catalysis, and so on, that occur at the molecular level. They are occurred by single bioproduct (protein) or group of bioproducts (protein complex) that depends on their location and environmental factors. The Molecular functional annotations represent only the bioproduct activity and not the bioproduct combination responsible for this activity [21, 22].
- *Biological Process:* It represents the fundamental biological processes of the bioproducts at the cellular level, such as metabolic activity, transportation, and so on. They are the combination of one or more molecular functions to execute a biological activity in the cell. They are performed by one or more bioproducts [21, 22].
- *Cell Component:* It represents the relative location or cellular compartments of the bioproduct when they perform any molecular functions. They are typically determined based on various aspects like relative cellular structures, cellular compartments, and stable macromolecular complexes they are located [21, 22].

11.3.4   Existing Approach: MR-CoC

Authors Gowri and Rathipriya (2020) have proposed Score-based Coclustering with MapReduce (MR-CoC) for functional module mining in PIN. The overview of this approach is shown in Figure 11.4. This approach uses the density of interactions in the PIN as a measure to find protein modules in PIN. The pseudocode of this approach is given in

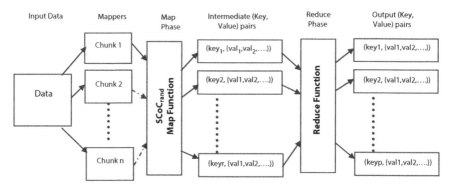

Figure 11.4 Overview of the MR-CoC model.

algorithm 11.1. This approach can be further referred from the previous research work [2].

Algorithm 11.1 MR-CoC

Input : Binary Data Matrix (D)
Output : coclusters(M = {C_1, C_2...C_{ns}})
Step 1: Dividing the given data into input chunks
Step 2: For each input chunk the mapper function will be invoked
   # Map Phase
Step 3: For each Input Chunk i
   a. Apply SCoC$_{rand}$ approach and return intermediate KV pairs {cocluster, count}
   # Reduce Phase
Step 4: For each key generate output KV pair {cocluster_size, cocluster}
   # After MR phases
Step 5: Evaluate and visualize the obtained coclusters.

11.4 Proposed Approach: MR-CoC$_{multi}$

In this section, the novel biological scores and multifunctional MR-CoC approach are proposed for DTM mining in PIN. The multifunctionality of this approach represents the multiobjective, i.e., usage of more than one score measure that are proposed in this chapter. This section further discusses the Biological measures and MR-CoC$_{multi}$ in detail.

11.4.1   Biological Score Measures for DTM

The DTMs are densely connected proteins with potential drug targets and their characteristics. The significant facts about drug targets are: a) used to bind with the drug [23]; b) used to boost the efficacy of the drug [23]; c) used to transport the drug to the required parts of the biological system [24–26]; d) present in the membrane regions [26]; e) form of enzymes, receptors, transporters, ion-binding channels, etc. [24, 27]; f) involved more in operational genes, oxidation and reduction of cell respiration, and enzyme catalytic activities [28]; g) some common properties of drug target proteins are cellular activity, localization, regulation, signaling, and differentiation [28].

In this subsection, the five novel biological density scores are proposed for DTMs. From the literature five biological properties are chosen. They are hydrophobicity, sequence length, polarity, eight amino acid composition, and molecular weight. The proposed biological measures are hydrophobic residues density score (S_h), sequence length score (S_{len}), polar residues density score (S_p), amino acid density score (S_{aa}), molecular weight score (S_m). Table 11.2 describes these measures with their mathematical representations and necessities in detail.

11.4.2   Multifunctional Score-Based Co-Clustering Approach

Multifunctional Score-based Co-Clustering (MR-CoC) approach was developed in three stages to overcome the existing issues in the coclustering approaches [2, 29]. The proposed MR-CoCmulti approach involves various steps, as given in algorithm. It is the MR-CoC approach enhanced with multi-SCoC function. Algorithm 3 shows the multi-SCoC function, which is an improved version of SCoC [1]. It is proposed to match with the multiscore functionality. The multifunctional score is a score vector containing the flags representing the satisfaction of the score values. The condition of each score signifies the biological quality of the drug targets. It is evaluated using the equation (11.7). These measures quantify the biological quality of the protein modules. The threshold values for each measure are fixed based on the literature study. They are useful in finding the biologically significant modules, which are used as a multifunctional measure in MR-CoC.

The MR-CoC$_{multi}$ approach is applied to extract the dense coclusters (subnetworks), i.e., the functionally dense protein modules from this PIN. The protein interaction pairs are taken as input; fix the number of seeds and seed size on the trial and error basis; generate the adjacency matrix for

Table 11.2 Mathematical representations of proposed biological score measures.

Biological score measures	Mathematical representation	Notations	Necessity
Hydrophobic residues density: the average of the proportions of hydrophobic residues present in the proteins of the module.	$$S_h = \frac{1}{n_p} \sum_{i=1}^{n_p} \left(\frac{\|p_i\|_h}{n_a(p_i)} \right) \quad (11.2)$$	$n_p \rightarrow$ number of proteins in the module, $\frac{\|p_i\|_h}{n_{ai}} \rightarrow$ proportion of the hydrophobic residues of p_i, $\|P_i\|_h \rightarrow$ norm of hydrophobic residues p_i, $n_a(p_i) \rightarrow$ number of amino acid in p_i	The drug targets are hydrophobic [28]. Most of the drug targets are hydrophobic pockets [30]. The hydrophobic interactors are the basis for most of the phenomena of the biological system. They are activators, initiators, and inducers for various phenomena. The presence of hydrophobic proteins in the cell membrane regions helps the drugs to bind with them easily.

(Continued)

Table 11.2 Mathematical representations of proposed biological score measures.

Biological score measures	Mathematical representation	Notations	Necessity
Sequence length score: The average sequence length of the proteins in the protein module.	$S_{len} = \dfrac{1}{n_p}\displaystyle\sum_{i=1}^{n_p}\left(len(p_i)\right)$ (11.3)	$n_p \rightarrow$ number of proteins in the module, $len(p_i) \rightarrow$ sequence length of p_i	The target proteins are lengthy in nature [26]. The drug target proteins will have more than 550 amino acids [26]. The lengthier sequence increases the number of positive proteins.
Polar residues density: The density of the polar residues in each protein of the given module.	$S_p = \dfrac{1}{n_p}\displaystyle\sum_{i=1}^{n_p}\left(\dfrac{\|p_i\|_p}{n_a(p_i)}\right)$ (11.4)	$n_p \rightarrow$ number of proteins in the module, $\dfrac{\|p_i\|_p}{n_{ai}} \rightarrow$ proportion of the polar residues of p_i, $\|p_i\|_p \rightarrow$ norm of polar residues p_i, $n_a(p_i) \rightarrow$ number of amino acid in p_i	The drug targets are less polar [26]. It is a simple sequence property [26]. It is suggested by most of the researchers and biologists.

(Continued)

Table 11.2 Mathematical representations of proposed biological score measures.

Biological score measures	Mathematical representation	Notations	Necessity
Amino acid density: The average count of eight significant amino acids in the module.	$$S_{aa} = \frac{1}{n_p} \sum_{i=1}^{n_p} \left(\frac{cnt_{aa}(p_i)}{n_a(p_i)} \right) \quad (11.5)$$	$n_p \rightarrow$ number of proteins in the module, $cnt_{aa}(p_i) \rightarrow$ count of 8 amino acids in p_i, $n_a(p_i) \rightarrow$ number of amino acid in p_i	These are essential amino acids that are indispensable to the body and for various activities. The drug targets are rich in these amino acids. They are L, I, K, T, M, F, V and W [31].
Molecular Weight Score: the average molecular weight of the proteins in the protein module	$$S_m = \frac{1}{n_p} \sum_{i=1}^{n_p} \left(mwt(p_i) \right) \quad (11.6)$$	$n_p \rightarrow$ number of proteins in the module, $mwt(p_i) \rightarrow$ molecular weight of p_i,	The drug targets are small-molecular weight compounds. The enzymes, receptors, transcription factors, ion channels, transport proteins, and so forth are small molecular weight chemical compounds [17].

each; for each seed perform the mapreduce function to find the maximal cocluster in that seed. Here the maximal cocluster represents biologically enriched coclusters.

$$mulscr = \begin{cases} \begin{cases} 1, & if\ S_h > 0.6 \\ 0, & otherwise \end{cases} \\ \begin{cases} 1, & if\ S_{len} > 550 \\ 0, & otherwise \end{cases} \\ \begin{cases} 1, & if\ S_{sp} > 0.56 \\ 0, & otherwise \end{cases} \\ \begin{cases} 1, & if\ S_{aa} > 5.91 \\ 0, & otherwise \end{cases} \\ \begin{cases} 1, & if\ S_m > 900 \\ 0, & otherwise \end{cases} \end{cases} \tag{11.7}$$

Algorithm 11.2: MR-CoC$_{Multi}$

Input: Protein Interactions

Output : coclusters ($M = \{C_1, C_2...C_{ns}\}$)
Step 1: Fix the number of seeds (n_s) to be generated and size of the seed (len_s)
Step 2: Generate n_s seeds of size len_s
Step 3: Generate the Adjacency Matrix on PIN
        # **Map Phase**
Step 4: For each seed s_i
   a. Apply multi-SCoC approach and return intermediate KV pairs {cocluster, {count, functional_score vector}}*
        # **Reduce Phase**
Step 5: For each key generate output KV pair {cocluster_size, {cocluster, functional_score vector}}
        # **After MR phases**
Step 6: Evaluate and visualize the obtained coclusters.

Algorithm 11.3: multi-SCoC

Input: Seed Vector
Output : cocluster, multiscore
Step 1: Evaluate the multiscore of C(cocluster)using eq (11.7).
Step 2: If any three scores satisfy their threshold-conditions then
      a. Evaluate row multiscore and column multiscore of C
      b. Remove either row or column with low multiscore from C
      c. Evaluate the multiscore of C using eq (11.7).
Step 3: Return C and multiscore

11.5   Experimental Analysis

The MR-CoC$_{multi}$ approach experimented in Matlab environment. The MapReduce (MR) framework in Matlab is adapted to implement this approach. The default MR setup has been chosen. This experiment is conducted in a standalone machine with I7 processor and 8 GB RAM, other experimental as in Table 11.3. The data sets used in this research work are as follows:

- **PIN Data Set:** The PIN data have a high set of interactions that refer to the edge of two proteins. In this research, the general Homo Sapiens PIN is chosen from STRING [34, 35]

Table 11.3 Experimental setup: MR-CoC and MR-CoC$_{multi}$.

Environmental aspects	Description
Environment	Matlab 2016b (Map Reduce Model)
Workers	10 (default)
Data Set	Homo Sapiens PPI
Interaction Count	85,48,003
Proteins Count	19, 427
Seed vector length	50 proteins
Minimum size of Protein Module	3,4,5 proteins

database, which consists of 19,427 proteins and 85,48,003 interactions.

- **Drug Target Data Set:** The drug target proteins used for analyzing the characteristics of protein modules, by verifying the presence of drug target proteins in it. The standard therapeutic targets are taken from the Therapeutic Target Database (TTD) [32].

11.5.1   Experimental Results

The proposed MR-CoC$_{multi}$ approach is experimented in this section and applied to the Homo sapiens data set. Its results are compared with the MR-CoC approach, as in Tables 11.4 to 11.6. It was tested with in different seed setups and different minimum subnetwork sizes. It highlights the number of cliques (complete subgraph) and noncliques (dense subgraphs) extracted using MR-CoC and MR-CoC$_{multi}$. Figure 11.5 shows the computational time spent under different experimental setups. From these results, it is clear that the number of cliques extracted by MR-CoC$_{multi}$ is less than the MR-CoC. The consideration of the functional measures signifies the functional density than the physical network density. It extracts functionally dense protein modules, which is justified through their biological significances. Similarly, the usage of the multifunctional score increases the computational time of MR-CoC$_{multi}$ than the MR-CoC approach which is

Table 11.4 Experimental results of MR-CoC and MR-CoC$_{Multi}$ (module size =3).

Number of seeds (million)	Cliques		Noncliques	
	MR-CoC	MR-CoC$_{multi}$	MR-CoC	MR-CoC$_{multi}$
1	2,910	2,871	3,181	6,712
5	2,174	3,119	4,522	7,273
10	4,372	5,129	7,188	8,177
50	5,917	6,567	8,620	9,978
100	8,539	9,113	11,861	12,988
500	6,433	12,789	10,865	13,823
1000	18,862	19,011	37,297	32,911

Table 11.5 Experimental results of MR-CoC and MR-CoC$_{Multi}$ (module size =4).

Number of seeds (million)	Cliques		Noncliques	
	MR-CoC	MR-CoC$_{multi}$	MR-CoC	MR-CoC$_{multi}$
1	821	589	2,766	3,833
5	1,139	883	3,178	4,193
10	2,897	1,983	2,190	4,291
50	3,200	2,199	4,822	5,399
100	3,176	2,887	8,821	9,277
500	5,192	3,022	6,975	10,812
1000	11,862	6,199	19,021	11,078

Table 11.6 Experimental results of MR-CoC and MR-CoC$_{Multi}$ (module size = 5).

Number of seeds (million)	Cliques		Noncliques	
	MR-CoC	MR-CoC$_{multi}$	MR-CoC	MR-CoC$_{multi}$
1	683	417	2,194	3,411
5	812	522	3,178	3,920
10	2,381	1,098	2,190	3,811
50	1,782	1,165	4,822	5,192
100	2,910	1,996	8,821	9,392
500	4,987	2,772	6,975	10,992
1000	10,192	5,988	19,021	25,728

seen clearly in Figure 11.5. The biological significances of these protein modules are discussed further in this section.

The biological process (BP)-, molecular function (MF)-, and cell component (CC)-based significances of the MR-CoC$_{multi}$ results are obtained

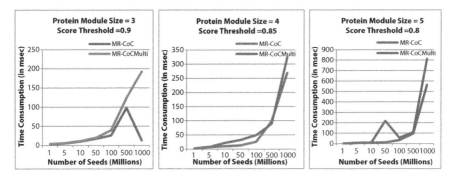

Figure 11.5 Computational time spent by MR-CoC and MR-CoC$_{multi}$.

from the STRING database. Some of the modules are taken randomly from the results. The significances of the results are in Tables 11.7 to 11.9. These results are tabulated based on different combinations of significances are as follows:

- Presence of two drug target proteins (Table 11.7)
- Presence of receptors in the membrane region (Table 11.8)
- Presence of transporters in the membrane region (Table 11.9)

As discussed earlier in this section, the drug targets are involved in the binding, transporting, receptor activities, and so forth, and they are located in the cell membrane regions. Initially, these resultant modules are tested for the occurrence of drug target proteins in them. These potential target proteins are taken from the therapeutic target database (TTD).

Tables 11.7 to 11.9 show the overall biological significances of 13 sample protein modules in the MR-CoC$_{multi}$ results. In these tables, the first column lists the participants and network structure of protein module, followed by the significant annotations under BP, MF, and CC with highest functional coherences (FC) in that protein module. The functional coherence of an annotation represents the percentage of participants possess that annotation in common. These modules are uniquely named in the format, FM#. Usage of functional measures increased the functional coherence of the proteins in each module, which is better than the MR-CoC approach. It is clearly evidenced from these results.

Table 11.7 Biological functionalities of functional modules with two drug target participants.

DTM	Biological significance		FC
	FM21		
	BP	**Receptor Signaling**	1
		Responding and Regulating Activity: responding to nitrogen compound, endogenous stimulus, oxygen-containing compound, and organic substance regulation of signaling	0.7
	MF	**Protein Binding**	0.7
		Regulator and receptor activity	0.4
	CC	**Membrane, plasma membrane**	0.9
		Plasma membrane bounded cell projection part	0.7
ADRBK1, **CHRM3, EDNRB**, GNAQ, GNB5, GNG7, GRM1, GRM5, OXT, PLCB1, TACR1	*Remarks: This module contains receptors in the membrane region with two potential drug targets.* *These proteins are acts as transducers, which will be seen in sense organs like eye, ear, skin, etc.*		

(Continued)

Table 11.7 Biological functionalities of functional modules with two drug target participants. (*Continued*)

DTM	Biological significance		FC
	FM8		
	BP	**Regulating, Responding and Receptor Activity:** regulating cell proliferation and cellular process; response to chemical; cell surface receptor signaling	1
		Regulation and Signaling Activity: tyrosine kinase signaling pathway, positive regulation of cell, subcellular component movement, cell migration	0.9
	MF	**Protein Binding**	1
		Binding Activity: ion, signaling receptor, and cytokine receptor binding	0.7
	Remarks: *All proteins in this module possess protein binding activity at molecular level and receptor, responding and regulating activity at biological level. Shows combination of DT characteristics with 2 drug target proteins FLT1 and FLT4 The proteins in this module are glycoproteins and possess repeating sequence motifs and di-sulphide bonds which are responsible for protein folding.*		

FIGF, **FLT1**, **FLT4**, GRB2, ITGB1, KDR, NRP2, PLCG1, SHC1, VEGFA, VEGFC

(*Continued*)

Table 11.7 Biological functionalities of functional modules with two drug target participants. (*Continued*)

DTM	Biological significance			FC
	FM9			
	BP	**Transporting, Responding, and Regulating Activity:** Localization, response to stimulus, ion transport		1
		Transporting Activity: ion transmembrane and sodium ion transport; regulation of body fluid levels		0.8
	MF	**Catalytic and Transferase Activity:** molecular function regulator		0.5
		Binding and Regulation Activity: ion channel regulation, ATP binding		0.4
	CC	**Plasma membrane**		0.2
		Bicellular tight junction		0.1

NEDD4L, **AF1**, SCNN1A, **CNN1B,** CNN1D, CNN1G, SGK1, TSC22D3, NK1, WNK3, WNK4

Remarks: *This module has transporting, regulating and responding natured proteins.*
This module possesses alternative splicing mechanism with phosphoproteins [33, 39].

(*Continued*)

Table 11.7 Biological functionalities of functional modules with two drug target participants. (*Continued*)

DTM	Biological significance		FC
	FM23		
F2, F2R, F5, FGA, FGB, FGG, GP1BA, PROC, SERPINC1, SERPIND1, THBD	BP	**Regulating the cellular processes:** blood coagulation,	0.9
		Regulating, Transporting and Responding Activity: regulating the cellular protein metabolic process, and multicellular organismal process, response to chemical	0.7
	MF	**Binding Activity:** metal ion binding	0.7
		Signaling receptor binding	0.4
	CC	**Cytoplasm**	1
		Regulating the cellular processes: blood coagulation,	0.9
	Remarks: It has 2 drug targets and regulating and responding characteristic. It is responsible for blood coagulation mechanism, [37,38] enriched with glycoprotein and signal polymorphism as well. So this module can be used to treat inflammatory syndromes.		

(*Continued*)

Table 11.7 Biological functionalities of functional modules with two drug target participants. (*Continued*)

DTM	Biological significance		FC
	FM24		
	BP	**Signaling and Receptor Activity:** regulating cell surface receptor and immune response	1
		Localization, Responding and Regulation Activity: response to stress, immune, to stimulus regulating of response, cell activation and immune system process	0.8
	MF	**Binding Activity:** protein-complex binding	1
		Receptor Activity: transmembrane signaling receptor activity	0.6
	CC	**Plasma membrane**	1
		Cell surface	0.7
CLEC4E, FCAR, **FCER1A, FCER1G,** FCGR2B, FCGR3A, GP6, ITGB2, LYN, PLCG2, SYK	***Remarks:*** *It has signaling receptors in plasma membrane region with two drug target proteins.* *It is responsible for protein folding which possess sequence motifs, disulphide bonds and transmembrane helix. They used to treat tuberculosis.*		

Table 11.8 Biological functionalities of functional modules with receptors in membrane region.

DTM	Biological significance		FC
	FM2		
ADCY5, **ADORA1**, GABBR1, GNAI2, GNB1, GNG2, KNG1, P2RY12, P2RY13, P2RY14, P2RY4	**BP**	**Receptor and Signaling Activity:** regulation of biological quality	1
		Receptor Activity: G protein-coupled signaling pathway	0.8
	MF	**Receptor Activity:** G protein-coupled	0.5
		Binding Activity: carbohydrate derivative binding	0.4
	CC	**Plasma Membrane**	1
		integral component of membrane	0.7

Remarks: *It has receptor and signaling proteins in the membrane region with one drug target protein. They possess transducer character, which converts the external stimuli into biological signals. They are seen in the sense organs*

(*Continued*)

Table 11.8 Biological functionalities of functional modules with receptors in membrane region. (*Continued*)

DTM	Biological significance		FC
	FM7		
	BP	**Receptor and Responding Activity:** G protein-coupled; responding to organo-nitrogen compound, oxygen-containing compound and aromatic compound	1
		Receptor and Regulating Activity: G protein-coupled; regulating the biological quality	0.8
	MF	**Binding Activity:** drug, cation, and organic cyclic compound binding	0.7
		Binding and Cyclase Activity: adenylate, and guanylate cyclase activity; ATP and metal ion binding	0.6
ADCY1, ADCY2, ADCY4, ADCY5, ADCY7, ADCY8, ADCY9, CALY, CRHR1, **DRD1**, NPS	**CC**	**Plasma Membrane**	0.9

Remarks: It has regulating receptor proteins in membrane region. They possess gap junction and signaling pathways useful for the drug discovery. They has ovarian steroidogenesis pathway in common. These proteins are glycol proteins with transmembrane helix which are useful in protein folding and possess drug target characteristic.

(*Continued*)

Table 11.8 Biological functionalities of functional modules with receptors in membrane region. (*Continued*)

DTM	Biological significance		FC
	FM15		
GRB14, IGF1, IGF1R, INS, **INSR,** INSRR, IRS1, IRS2, PTPN1, PTPN2, SHC1	**BP**	**Receptor Activity:** regulating of cellular process, primary metabolic process, and multicellular organismal process	0.9
		Receptor and Regulating Activity: transmembrane receptor protein, regulation of signal transduction	0.8
	MF	**Binding Activity:** protein and signaling receptor binding	1
		Receptor and Binding Activity: enzyme, catalytic and protein-containing complex insulin receptor binding	0.8
	CC	**Membrane, plasma membrane**	1
		protein-containing complex	0.6
	Remarks: They possess *Longevity regulating pathway - multiple species, AMPK signaling pathway, Insulin signaling pathway, FoxO signaling pathway in common. These proteins are phophoproteins used for binding drug effectively. This module also possess drug target characteristic*		

(Continued)

Table 11.8 Biological functionalities of functional modules with receptors in membrane region. (*Continued*)

DTM	Biological significance			FC
	FM20			
	BP	**Receptor Activity:** G protein-coupled, multicellular organismal process		1
		Response to external stimulus, regulation of biological quality, regulation of response to stimulus, response to chemical		0.9
	MF	**Receptor Binding**		1
		Receptor Activity: G protein-coupled, molecular function regulator, hormone activity		0.5
	CC	**Extracellular space**		0.6
		Plasma membrane		0.4
ADRBK1, AGT, EDN1, EDN2, EDN3, **EDNRB**, GNA1, GNAQ, GNRH1, KNG1, TAC1	**Remarks:** *This module has receptor binding activity. It possesses disease mutation [40] in common, which are responsible for mutated diseases.*			

Table 11.9 Biological functionalities of functional modules with transporters in membrane region.

DTM	Biological significance		FC
F10, F1, F2, **F8**, F9, LMAN1, MCFD2, PLG, PROC, SERPINC1, VWF	**FM5**		
	BP	**Transport Activity:** blood coagulation, and vesicle-mediated transport	0.9
		Transport Activity: Golgi vesicle-mediated transport	0.8
	MF	**Binding Activity:** metal ion, and calcium ion binding	1
		Binding Activity: ion binding	0.8
	CC	**Extracellular Region Part, Membrane**	0.9
		Membrane-Bounded Organelle	0.8
	Remarks: It has Complement and coagulation cascade proteins, which is used in treating blood clots. It has other drug target characteristics as signaling, disease mutation, Disulphide bond and polymorphism in common.		

(*Continued*)

Table 11.9 Biological functionalities of functional modules with transporters in membrane region. (*Continued*)

DTM	Biological significance		FC
	FM9		
	BP	**Transport and Response Activity:** ion transport, localization, response to stimulus	1
		Transport and Response Activity: ion transmembrane, and sodium ion transport; regulating the body fluid levels and chemical homeostasis	0.8
	MF	**Catalytic Activity:** transferase activity, molecular function regulator,	0.5
		Regulating and Binding Activity: ion channel regulatin, ATP binding	0.4
		Plasma membrane	0.2
 NEDD4L, **RAF1**, SCNN1A, **SCNN1B**, SCNN1D, SCNN1G, SGK1, TSC22D3, WNK1, WNK3, WNK4	CC	**Bicellular Tight Junction**	0.1
	Remarks: *It is enriched with phospho-proteins which are used for drug target activation*		

(Continued)

Table 11.9 Biological functionalities of functional modules with transporters in membrane region. (*Continued*)

DTM	Biological significance		FC
	FM14		
	BP	**Responding to chemical**	1
		transport and response Activity: responding to drug, organic substance, nitrogen compound, and stress	0.7
	MF	**Transporter Activity:** carboxylic acid, amino acid, and secondary active transmembrane transportation	0.5
		Transporter Activity: drug, cation, and L-amino acid transmembrane transportation	0.4
	CC	**Plasma membrane**	0.8
		Integral Component of Plasma Membrane	0.6
ATF4, BSG, CD44, GCLM, KYNU, NFE2L2, SLC1A2, SLC1A5, SLC1A7, SLC3A2, **SLC7A1**	**Remarks:** *Most of the proteins are in cell membrane region which are used for cell membrane synthesis that are used as anti-fungal drug targets.*		

11.6   Discussion

The DTMs are set of proteins, which contain potential drug targets, as well as the characteristics of drug targets. A computational method for DTMs prediction is demonstrated in this chapter. So far, the drug target prediction, drug target interaction predictions only concentrated. This kind of modules is used for the development of targeted therapies. These customized therapies are dependent on drug targets. Most of the complex diseases are treated with such therapies. But in some cases, the pathogens are multitarget resistant and overplays on the target proteins. For such situations, the targeted therapy can be developed based on DTM.

From the results, the DTMs are suggested. The characteristics of drug targets are analyzed from the biological significances of the results. The nature of drug targets is in different forms. They are the combination of receptors, enzymes, transporters, binding proteins, and so on, as discussed earlier. The drug target characteristic of resultant DTMs are discussed in these tables under the remarks part. Sample modules are chosen randomly from the results; among them the following modules possess drug target characteristics. The DTM 21, 8, 9, 23, 24 are possessing two drug target proteins. DTM 2, 7, 15, 20 are having receptor proteins in the membrane region with high functional coherence. Similarly DTM 5, 9, 14 are having transporters in membrane region. The other module-specific drug target characteristics are represented in the remarks part. These modules are highly enriched with drug target characteristics.

11.7   Conclusion

This chapter attempted on the DTM mining in PIN. The multifunctional MR-CoC is proposed for this purpose five novel biological scores namely hydrophobic residues density, sequence length, polar residues density, amino acid density, molecular weight scores also proposed. This approach is attempted on Homo-sapiens PIN. The results evidenced the proposed approach can extract functionally dense DTMs than the existing approach. From the results, new DTMs also suggested for further processing. In the future, disease-specific biological measures can be adopted and the patient-specific PIN can be used for patient-specific analysis.

Acknowledgment

The first author acknowledges the UGC for the financial support to her research under the UGC NET JRF (Student Id: 3384/(OBC)(NET JULY-2016)) Scheme.

References

1. Gowri, R. and Rathipriya, R., Score-based Co-Clustering for Binary Data,". *Int. J. Comput. Intell. Inf.*, 7, 2, 105–111, 2017.
2. Gowri, R. and Rathipriya, R., Functional Module Mining in Protein Interaction Networks using Co-Clustering,", in: *Intelligent IoT Systems for Big Data Analysis: Concepts, Applications, Challenges, and Future Scope*, Apple Academic Press (in printing), US & Canada, 2020.
3. Murali, T. and Kasif, S., Extracting Conserved Gene Expression Motifs from Gene Expression Data,. *Pac. Symp. Biocomput.*, 8, 77–88, 2003.
4. Prelic, A., Bleuler, S., Zimmermann, P., Wille, A., BuÈhlmann, P., Gruissem, W., "A Systematic Comparison and Evaluation of Biclustering Methods for Gene Expression Data,. *Bioinformatics*, 22, 9, 1122–1129, 2006.
5. Uitert, M.V., Meuleman, W., Wessels, L., "Biclustering Sparse Binary Genomic Data, *J. Comput. Biol.*, 15, 10, 1329–1345, 2008.
6. Noureen, N. and Qadir, M.A., BiSim: A Simple and Efficient Biclustering Algorithm, in: *International Conference of Soft Computing and Pattern Recognition*, 2009.
7. Zhang, Z.-Y., Li, T., Ding, C., Ren, X.-W., Zhang, X.-S., Binary matrix factorization for analyzing gene expression data. *Data Min. Knowl. Discovery*, 20, 28–52, 2010.
8. RodrõÂguez-Baena, D., PeÂrez-Pulid, A., Ruiz, J.A., "A Biclustering Algorithm for Extracting Bit-Patterns from Binary Datasets,". *Bioinformatics*, 27, 19, 2738–2745, 2011.
9. Voggenreiter, O. and Bleuler, S., Exact biclustering algorithm for the analysis of large gene expression data sets,. *BMC Bioinf.*, 13, 1–2, 2012.
10. Király, A., Gyenesei, A., Abonyi, J., Bit-Table Based Biclustering and Frequent Closed Itemset Mining in High-Dimensional Binary Data,. *ScientificWorldJournal*, 2014, 1–7, 2014.
11. Saber, H. and Elloumi, M., Efficiently Mining Gene Expression Data via Novel Binary Biclustering Algorithms,. *J. Proteomics Bioinform.*, S9, 1–7, 2015.
12. GonzaÂlez-Dominguez, J. and Exposito, R.R., ParBiBit: Parallel tool for binary biclustering on modern distributed-memory systems, *PloS One*, 13(4), 2018.

13. Enright, A.J., Ouzounis, C.A., Pereira-Leal, J.B., Detection of Functional modules from protein Interaction Networks,. *PROTEINS: Structure, Function, Bioinf.*, 54, 49–57, 2004.

14. US Department of Health and Human Services, *Structures of Life*, National Institute of Health, National Institute of General Medical Services, 2007.

15. Spirin, V. and Mirny, L.A., Protein Complexes and Functional Modules in the Molecular Networks,. *PNAS*, 100, 21, 12123–12128, 2013.

16. Wang, R., *Central Dogma of Molecular Biology,*, Wiley, USA, 2015, [Online]. Available: http://fourier.eng.hmc.edu/bioinformatics/intro/node8.html.

17. Gashaw, I., Ellinghaus, P., Sommer, A., Asadullah, K., What makes a good drug target?. *Drug Discovery Today.- Elsevier*, 16, 1037–1043, 2011.

18. Bastos, H.P., Sousa, L., Clarke, L.A., Couto, F.M., Functional coherence metrics in protein Families. *J. Biomed.l Semantics*, 7, 41, 1–11, 2016.

19. Chagoyen, M. and Pazos, F., Quantifying the biological significance of gene ontology biological processes—implications for the analysis of systems-wide data. *Bioinformatics*, 26, 3, 371–384, 2010.

20. d. Plessis, L., Skunca, N., Dessimoz, C., The what, where, how and why of gene ontologyça primer for bioinformaticians,. *Brief Bioinform.*, 12, 6, 723 – 735, 2011.

21. Bult, C., Blake, J., Smith, C., Kadin, J., Richardson, J., Mouse Genome Database Goup, "Mouse Genome Database (MGD). *Nucleic Acids Res.*, D801– D806, 47, 2019.

22. Sussman, J.L. and Prilusky, J., As life is more than 2D, Proteopedia helps to bridge the gap between 3D structure & function of biomacromolecules. February 2019. [Online]. Available: www.proteopedia.org.

23. Imming, P., Sinning, C., Meyer, A., Drugs, their targets and the nature. *Nat. Rev. Drug Discovery*, 5, 821–834, 2007.

24. Chordia, N., Lakhawat, K., Kumar, A., "Identification of Drug Target Properties and its validation on Helicobacter pylori". *Can. J. Biotech.*, 9, 44–49, 2017.

25. Bull, S.C. and Doig, A.J., Properties of Protein Drug Target Classes. *PloS One*, 10, 3, 1–44, 2015.

26. Bakheet, T.M. and Doig, A.J., Properties and identification of human protein drug target. *Bioinformatics*, 25, 4, 451–457, 2009.

27. Feng, Y., Wang, Q., Wang, T., "Drug Target Protein-Protein Interaction Networks: A Systematic Perspective. *BioMed. Res. Int.*, 2017, 1–13, 2017.

28. Kim, B., Jo, J., Han, J., Park, C., Lee, H., "In silico re-identification of properties of drug target proteins. *BMC Bioinf.*, 18, 7, 35–44, 2017.

29. Gowri, R. and Rathipriya, R., "Cohesive Sub-Network Mining in Protein Iteraction Network using Score based Co-clustering with MapReduce Model, in: *Advances in BigData and Cloud Computing*, pp. 227–236, 2018.

30. Hussein, H.A., Borrel, A., Geneix, C., Petitjean, M., Regad, L., Camproux, A.-C., "PockDrug-Server: a new web server for predicting pocket druggability on holo and apo proteins. *Nucleic Acids Res.*, 43, w436–w442, 2015.

31. Vladimir Masenko, *Amino Acids Guide*, Russia, 2007, [Online]. Available: https://aminoacidsguide.com/.

32. Zheng, C.J., Han, L.Y., Yap, C.W., JI, Z.L., Cao, Z.W., Chen, Y.Z., Therapeutic Targets: Progress of Their Exploration and Investigation of their Characteristics. *Pharmacol. Rev.*, 58, 2, 259–279, 2006.

33. Ji, Y., Mishra, R.K., Davuluri, R.V., In Silico analysis of alternative splicing on drug-target gene interactions. *Sci. Rep.*, no. 134, 1–13, 2020.

34. Franceschini, A., Szklarczyk, D., Frankild, S., Kuhn, M., Simonovic, M., Roth, A., Lin, J., Minguez, P., Bork, P., Mering, C. v., Jensen, L., STRING v9.1: protein-protein interaction networks, with increased coverage and integration. *Nucleic Acid Res.*, 808–815, 2013.

35. Szklarczyk, D., Gable, A., Lyon, D., Junge, A., Wyder, S., Huerta-Cepas, J., Simonovic, M., Doncheva, N., Morris, J., Bork, P., Jensen, L., Mering, C. v., STRING v11: protein-protein association networks with increased coverage, supporting functional discovery in genome-wide experimental datasets,. *Nucleic Acid Res.*, 47, D1, 607–613, 2019.

36. Giurgiu, M., Reinhard, J., Brauner, B., Dunger-Kaltenbach, I., Fobo, G., Frishman, G., Montrone, C., Ruepp, A., CORUM: A Comprehensive Resource of Mammalian Protein Complexes. *Nucleic Acid Res.-2019*, Vol: 47, D1, D559-D 563, 2018.

37. Panteleev, M.A., Andreeva, A.A., Lobanov, A., II, Drug Target Selection in Blood Coagulation: What can we get from Computationsl systems Biology Models?. *Curr. Pharm. Des.*, 26, 18, 2109–2115, 2020.

38. Jennewein, C., Paulus, P., Zacharowski, K., "Linking inflammation and coagulation: novel drug targets to treat organ ischemia. *Curr. Opin. Anesthesiol.*, 24, 4, 375–380, 2011.

39. Pierobon, M., Petricoin 3rd, E.F., Wulfkuhle, J.D., "Phosphoprotein-based Drug Target Activation mapping for Precision Oncology: A view to the Future. *Expert Rev. Preoteomics*, 24, 4, 15, 11, 851–853, 2018.

40. N. c. Institute, *Disease-Causing Mutation*, National Cancer Institute, USA, 2019, [Online]. Available: www.cancer.gov.

12

The Ascendant Role of Machine Learning Algorithms in the Prediction of Breast Cancer and Treatment Using Telehealth

Jothi K.R.[1]*, Oswalt Manoj S.[2], Ananya Singhal[1] and Suruchi Parashar[1]

[1]School of Computer Science and Engineering, Vellore Institute of Technology, Vellore, India
[2]Sri Krishna College of Engineering and Technology, Coimbatore, India

Abstract

Telehealth has become a necessary technology in this pandemic situation. Treatment can be taken from the patient's premises through the connectivity of various devices like computers and mobile devices. This helps us to access the healthcare services remotely and thereby manage the health. So the importance of data science, cloud computing in association with Internet of Things (IoT) and telehealth has drawn more interest in the research community, industry sectors and also among public. Towards monitoring the healthcare conditions of an individual either in the hospital premises or in the remote environment, the support from the Internet of Things (IoT) devices along with the sensors is required. This chapter focuses on the techniques to predict the malignant in breast cancer and provide the healthcare services to the cancer survivor remotely through tele-healthcare. The analysis can happen in a faster way through which we could get some expert interferences and also better recommendations toward treatment and health. We can also get an ambient assisted living through the integrated technologies. The data set has been taken from UCI repository and also from kaggle repository. Through the machine learning classification methods like logistic regression, K-nearest neighbor, support vector machines, Kernel support vector machine (K-SVM), decision tree algorithm, and random forest classification it is possible to find whether the cancer is benign or malignant. The implementation is done using python. Initially, the data exploration is done followed by the preprocessing of the data and then the feature scaling and model selection and evaluation

*Corresponding author: jothi.kr@vit.ac.in

R. Nidhya, Manish Kumar and S. Balamurugan (eds.) Tele-Healthcare: Applications of Artificial Intelligence and Soft Computing Techniques, (285–316) © 2022 Scrivener Publishing LLC

is done. It is observed that all our models show an accuracy of 93% and above except the decision tree algorithm. The highest accuracy is displayed by K-SVM, i.e., 97.3%. We have also used the confusion matrix for predicting the count of predicted classes that has ended by being classified as wrong with respect to the true class. However, after the prediction, the patient can be given remote treatment based on the severity of the cancer.

Keywords: SVM, K-SVM, breast cancer, telehealth

12.1   Introduction

In women, breast cancer is one of the most common cancer among the ones that are prevalent and represents about 25% of all the cases. In 2015, 2.1 million people were diagnosed with the same. The cause of the disease is the uncontrolled mitotic division of cells in the breast tissue, which occur continuously and is present as palpable breast swelling. This can be diagnosed by doctors via physical examination and can be detected in X-rays. Diagnosis of the breast cancer in an early phase increases the survival rate of the patients. The key difficulty while detecting the tumor is the classification or the segregation of breast tumor into malignant (cancerous) and benign (noncancerous). When the tumor cells infiltrate into nearby tissues and spread in different parts of the body, they can be deemed as malignant (cancerous). While in the case of benign (noncancerous) tumor, the tumor cells are located in the breast tissue and do not infiltrate into the adjacent tissues. However, a benign tumor can enlarge in size and can press nearby blood vessels and nerves and can cause serious aftereffects. The early diagnosis and prediction of breast cancer [1] helps in early clinical treatment and thus increases the survival rate significantly.

Classification and data mining methods are two such methods, which prove to be an effective way to classify data, specifically in the medical field, where the results generated by these methods form the basis of further analysis and decisions. Furthermore, a precise and an early classification of the tumors can help the patients avert unnecessary treatments and payments. Using the data set obtained from the diagnosis, we can apply multiple machine learning models to compare and analyze which one is giving highest accuracy of prediction. The data set used here is the one generated by Dr. William H. Wolberg, a physician at the University of Wisconsin Hospital at Wisconsin, USA has created a breast cancer data set using several digitalized images of breast tumor cells obtained after the fine needle aspiration cytology (FNAC) of breast masses. The images obtained enables us to understand the various features of tumor cell nuclei, which in turn helps us to classify the breast masses as malignant or benign [8].

12.1.1   Objective

The two objectives of this work are as follows:

- To study and observe the parameters of cells in the breast mass which help in classifying it as benign or malignant.
- To observe the general trends occurring in the data set that may help us in analyzing which model yields the highest accuracy and is most suitable for prediction.

The final target is to divide/classify the breast cancer as benign or malignant by applying various machine learning techniques that will fit the function accurately and will help us classify the new input.

12.1.2   Description and Goals

In this work, we made use of the UCI machine learning repository for the data set, which contains 569 observations and 32 varied parameters for each of it. The column named "diagnosis" is our dependent variable, stating whether the cancer is M, as in, malignant or B, as in, benign. We have used pandas' visualization, which is built on top of matplotlib library, to find the data distribution of the various parameters. We then convert all the categorical data into numerical data wherein Malignant is replaced with 1 and Benign is replaced with 0. Following this, we divide the data into two parts—training data and testing data. The training data set has a known output and the model learns through these data, so that it can be generalized for the other data. The testing data set is basically used to check our model's prediction and accuracy obtained from it.

Since the data set includes features that varies highly in terms of magnitude, unit, and range, the machine learning algorithms [10, 16] use the measure—Euclidean distance—to bring all the features to the same level of magnitudes by scaling. This process is known as feature scaling. After these steps, we select the classification algorithm to be used. We aim to obtain the accuracy of the following algorithms to find the best suitable one. The algorithms are as follows: K-nearest neighbor (kNN) algorithm, Kernel support vector machine (K-SVM) algorithm, random forest classification algorithm, decision tree algorithm, SVM algorithm and logistic regression algorithm. The software used for the work is Google Colab and the language used is Python 3. Various libraries like Pandas (Data manipulation and analysis), Numpy (Fundamental scientific computing), Matplotlib (Plotting and visualization), Seaborn (Statistical data visualization), and Scikit-Learn (Machine Learning and Data Mining) are used in this work. We have four milestones. They are as follows:

12.1.2.1   Data Exploration

The examination of data set is done by using head() method and the dimension matrix of data set using shape. Finding if any missing data or outliers are present in the data set with the help of info(), Compact examination of data types of the attributes through dtypes and visualizing the count of malignant and benign values in diagnosis attribute.

12.1.2.2   Data Pre-Processing

Replacement of categorical value to numerical value to avoid matching of the input with keywords, visualization of all attribute with respect to diagnosis through histogram, making a hue scale based on diagnosis, plot a correlation matrix, taking all attributes into consideration, setting the independent (X) and dependent (Y) variables and splitting of data set into training set and test set.

12.1.2.3   Feature Scaling

Bringing of all attribute values to same level of magnitude for easy working of classification algorithms.

12.1.2.4   Model Selection and Evaluation

Accuracy is calculated between actual data and predicted data; confusion matrix is referred for the proof of accuracy as the higher sum of data actually correct and predicted correct and actually wrong and predicted wrong, accuracy is higher. The accuracy is calculated from logical regression; an ML predictive analysis algorithm that is used for classification problems that work on discrete data sets, based on concept of probability. The accuracy was calculated from kNN algorithm, which supports unsupervised learning and discrete data set, which is the key idea of similarity (parameters like, distance or closeness). The accuracy was calculated from SVM algorithm, a supervised ML algorithm that plots each data item with value of each attribute being the value of coordinate. The accuracy was calculated from K-SVM, SVM algorithm makes use of kernel defined in a set of mathematical functions that assist in taking data items as input and convert them into the desired form. The data items are graphs, text, images, sequence data, and also vectors. The accuracy calculated from decision tree algorithm, a supervised learning algorithm that creates training model, which can be used for prediction of class or value of target variable by learning decision rules resulting in a decision tree from training data. The accuracy calculated from random decision tree algorithm, a supervised learning algorithm where decision trees is created on data trained, predicts each of them and selects the best solution by means of voting.

12.2 Literature Review

Specialists realize that breast malignancy happens when some breast cells start to develop anomalously. These cells partition more quickly than sound cells do and keep on gathering, framing a bump or mass. Cells may spread (metastasize) through breast to lymph hubs or to different pieces of a woman's body. Breast malignant growth frequently starts with cells in the milk-delivering conduits (intrusive ductal carcinoma). Breast cancer may likewise start in the glandular tissue called lobules (obtrusive lobular carcinoma) or in different cells or tissue inside the breast.

Specialists have recognized that hormonal, way of life, and natural factors [2] may expand your danger of breast malignancy. However, it is not satisfactory why a few people who have no danger factors, create cancer, yet others with hazard factors, never do.

All things considered, breast cancer is brought about by a perplexing communication of hereditary cosmetics and your current circumstance. Specialists gauge that around 5% to 10% of breast cancer are connected to quality changes that went through ages of a family. Various acquired changed qualities that can improve the probability of breast cancer have been recognized. The most notable are breast malignant growth quality 1 (BRCA1) and breast cancer quality 2 (BRCA2), the two of which altogether increment the danger of both breast and ovarian malignant growth. On the off chance that you have a solid family background of breast malignancy or different diseases, your primary care physician may prescribe a blood test to help distinguish explicit transformations in BRCA or different qualities that are being gone through your family. Table 12.1 represents the literature review of the methods, parameters and model used. Think about approaching your primary care physician for a reference to a hereditary guide, who can survey your family well-being history. A hereditary

Table 12.1 Literature review of the methods, parameters, and model used.

S. no.	Method used	Advantages	Parameters used	Model used	Results and issues
1	Thrombotic biomarkers are used to predict malignant with early stage breast cancer [1]	The biomarkers are one of the unique thresholds for detection.	D-dimer, fibrinogen, prothrombin fragment 1+2	Cox regression multivariate analysis and used for generating a risk assessment model.	The plasma role of the most important prothrombin fragment in the breast has been discussed. Cancer patients to provide rationale for the new beneficial plans.
2	Natural language processing facilitates breast cancer research [2]	NLP studies how with the help of different data sets new data can be formed and analyzed.	Cancer genes and its variants	SVM, CNN (Convolution Neural Network), Naïve Bayes	NLP-based search engine provides a list of articles for an alternate and help researchers in alternate interpretations, verifying associations, and genomic analysis. It estimates of developing cancer for each vulnerability gene.

(Continued)

Table 12.1 Literature review of the methods, parameters, and model used. (*Continued*)

S. no.	Method used	Advantages	Parameters used	Model used	Results and issues
3	Natural language processing is used to make a malignant breast cancer cohort from linked cancer registry. It also is built using electronic medical records data [3]	The replica can be used to make effective medicine in the precise treatment.	Database of female patients treated at Stanford Healthcare with an incident breast cancer diagnosis from 2000 to 2014	Semisupervised ML, logistic regression	Model combined with EMR and CCR data helped physicians to accurately label breast cancer patient as recurrent metastatic or not.
4	NLP to detect the timeline of metastatic recurrence of malignant in breast [4]	If we once know the time of cell contusion, we can easily declare its stage	OncoSHARE database	Neural Network Model	Model helps in identifying and predicting the timing of distant metastatic recurrence from EMR and understand cancer survival outcome.

(Continued)

Table 12.1 Literature review of the methods, parameters, and model used. (*Continued*)

S. no.	Method used	Advantages	Parameters used	Model used	Results and issues
5	Breast cancer diagnosis using feature ensemble learning based on stacked sparse autoencoders and softmax regression [5]	Softmax Regression has been proven as the most precise Technique of statistical measures	data sets from the UCI machine learning repository	Ensemble Learning – Sparse Autoencoders and Softmax Regression (SSAE-SM) model and performance metrics like accuracy etc.	Proves that automated diagnosis system helped in early detection. Diagnosis of breast cancer in beginning state to improve the survival rate.
6	A frame semantic overview of NLP-based information extraction for cancer-related EHR note [6]	Electronic health record templates provide easy data collection	EHR of cancer patients.	NLP technique based on linguistic theory of frame semantics.	Model helped in extracting important cancer related information from unstructured EHR notes. The notes served as a useful resource for future biomedical researchers.

(*Continued*)

Table 12.1 Literature review of the methods, parameters, and model used. (*Continued*)

S. no.	Method used	Advantages	Parameters used	Model used	Results and issues
7	Prediction of malignant and benign breast cancer: a data mining approach in healthcare [7]	Data mining algorithms have different approaches Of problem solving	UCI repository	Ada Boost M1, Decision Table, J-Rip, J48, Lazy IBK, Lazy K-star, Logistics Regression, Naïve Bayes, Random Forest and Random Tree	This work focuses on different classification techniques implementation for data mining in predicting malignant and benign breast cancer.
8	Prediction of benign and malignant breast cancer using data mining techniques [8]	Popularity of Naïve Bayes Algorithm with rows of different parameters	683 benign and malignant breast cancer cases	popular data mining algorithms (Naïve Bayes, RBF Network, J48) to develop the prediction models using a large data set	RBF Network came out to be the second with 96.77% accuracy; J48 came out third with 93.41% accuracy.

(Continued)

Table 12.1 Literature review of the methods, parameters, and model used. (*Continued*)

S. no.	Method used	Advantages	Parameters used	Model used	Results and issues
9	Using natural language processing and machine learning to identify breast cancer local recurrence [9]	SVM gives best results in feature scales leaving no nulls.	Electronic Health Records (EHR)	SVM	NLP through Metamap concept provides an automated way to identify local recurrences in breast cancer patients.
10	Breast cancer detection using machine learning algorithms [10]	The learning of prediction sets is easier in ML algorithms	Wisconsin Diagnosis Breast Cancer data set	Random Forest, kNN and Naïve Bayes.	The model helps in early diagnosis and prognosis of breast cancer type with an accuracy of >94% by classifying them as benign or malignant.

(*Continued*)

Table 12.1 Literature review of the methods, parameters, and model used. (*Continued*)

S. no.	Method used	Advantages	Parameters used	Model used	Results and issues
11	Deep learning model based breast cancer histopathological image classification [11]	Image processing mixed with CNN gives the benefit of training data set.	2D and 3D Histopathology images of breast cancer patients	Deep CNN-BiCNN	Model achieves an automated classification of breast cancer. BiCNN has data augmentation and transfer learning manner for overcoming overfitting problem.
12	Deep learning analytics for diagnostic support of breast cancer disease management [12]	ANN is faster and more efficient and old data mining that is more clinicallyreal than the traditional BI-RADS scores.	Clinical data, mammographic reports and breast biopsy reports	BN, ANN, Support Vector Machine	The output is a probability measure of biopsy recommendation It enhances engagement between the patient and clinician in making decision.

(*Continued*)

Table 12.1 Literature review of the methods, parameters, and model used. (*Continued*)

S. no.	Method used	Advantages	Parameters used	Model used	Results and issues
13	Diagnosing assessment of DL algorithms to detect lymph node malignant in breast cancer [13]	H&E stained Tissue contains genomic information which directly tells the tumor cell growth.	Tissue section of lymph nodes	Deep learning algorithms	Automated deep learning algorithms is applied on images of H&E stained tissue section of lymph node of women with breast cancer to detect metastasis which improved diagnostic accuracy and efficiency.
14	Text mining, pattern clustering for relation extraction of malignant in genes [14]	Text mining gives the word characteristics and specifics for pattern judgment, which is the easiest.	Sentence Mining with minimum of 10 words per sentence	Text mining techniques, Simple clustering and K-means clustering	The model is able to extract the information which help in medical relations of cancer genes.

(Continued)

Table 12.1 Literature review of the methods, parameters, and model used. (*Continued*)

S. no.	Method used	Advantages	Parameters used	Model used	Results and issues
15	Extraction of biomedical information related to breast cancer using text mining [15]	Text mining gives the word characteristics and specifics.	300,000 biomedical articles	Conditional Random Fields (CRFs), entity recognition tool ABNER	The model helps in extracting biomedical entities and their relationships which are then written in the original data set as annotated breast cancer corpus. This can prove helpful in further research and development of medical text mining.
16	Using ML algorithms for breast cancer risk prediction and diagnosis [16]	Support Vector machine is the precise form of Algorithm result.	WEKA data mining	SVM, Decision Tree C4.5, Naive Bayes and kNN	Overall results show that SVM results 97.13% with lowest error rate, which is the highest precision.

(*Continued*)

Table 12.1 Literature review of the methods, parameters, and model used. (*Continued*)

S. no.	Method used	Advantages	Parameters used	Model used	Results and issues
17	DL for magnification independent breast cancer histopathology image classification [17]	All tissues and staining reports are in one place.	Histopathology Image	Histopathology Image Classification using CNNs	The implementation has power to directly benefit from extra training data set, and such data could be captured with same or different levels than previous data.
18	Automatically predict the tumor in breast cancer with the dimension in fractions [18]	Fractal Dimension gives accuracy on magnified levels.	F1 score	SVM	The results show great promise in the use of fractal dimension to predict & analyze tumor malignancy.
19	Breast cancer staging using NLP [19]	Normal report can be sent to automatic machines for digital records for efficiency.	Breast cancer pathology reports	Sentence Segmentation	Model developed an automated system for analyzing lab reports which help in finding the stage of cancer in patients according to TNM classification.

(Continued)

Table 12.1 Literature review of the methods, parameters, and model used. (*Continued*)

S. no.	Method used	Advantages	Parameters used	Model used	Results and issues
20	CEA, AFP, CA125, CA153, and CA199 in metastatic pleural effusions analyze the reason [20]	Staining and biomarkers give the accurate timing of cell infusion	five tumor biomarkers have been used in the study	Kruskal-Wallis or Mann-Whitney U tests	The results depicted that the two tumor markers may increase the efficiency and cure for effusions of primaries.
21	Sentence-based analysis of Breast Cancer Radiology [21]	Machine learning training model is generated for the Text mining.	Radiology reports	Decision tree (DT), SVM, probabilistic naïve Bayes (NB), and kNN	A pipeline model for automatic sentence classification is made for efficient results.
22	Potential of MR to analyze tumor grading of breast cancer [22]	Mammography gives the invasive prospective of tumor cells which are the most precise in handling genomic markers.	Lymph node metastasis and tumor grading	mammography and ultrasound, MR mammography (MRM)	Detailed dynamic and morphological MRM descriptors with tumor grading applying Univariate and multivariate approach gives the exact marker information of the tumor cell.

(*Continued*)

Table 12.1 Literature review of the methods, parameters, and model used. (*Continued*)

S. no.	Method used	Advantages	Parameters used	Model used	Results and issues
23	Diffusion weighted magnetic resonance imaging is used to determine locally advanced breast cancer undergoing chemotherapy [23]	Correlation has been proved as the best statistical measure	using single- shot spin-echo echoplanar imaging	Spearman's rho correlation test	ADC increase seen in the NACT does not correlate with tumor volume changes.
24	Predicting breast cancer survivability using data mining techniques [24]	Data is organized using SOM radial basis which is the best parameter to understand the tumor cause.	Wisconsin breast cancer data (WBCD) and Shiraz Namazi Hospital breast cancer data (NHBCD)	Self-organizing map (SOM), radial basis function network (RBF), general regression neural network (GRNN) and probabilistic neural network (PNN)	The model helped in knowing the % of disease development in breast cancer patients and hence help in predicting the survivability of those patients.

(*Continued*)

Table 12.1 Literature review of the methods, parameters, and model used. (*Continued*)

S. no.	Method used	Advantages	Parameters used	Model used	Results and issues
25	Predicting survival and early clinical response to primary chemotherapy for patients with locally advanced breast cancer using DCE-MRI [25]	The response to the primary chemotherapy was good.	Estrogen receptor (ER) and progesterone receptor (PgR)	Locally Advanced Breast Cancer Using DCE-MRI	It is obvious that the response of primary breast cancer to NAC is helpful for prognosis and it can be used as an in vivo assessment of chemo sensitivity.
26	Prediction model building and feature selection with support vector machines in breast cancer diagnosis [26]	Classifier is slightly better than that of LDA in the negative hit ratio	{HSV-1, HHV-8} or {HSV-1, HHV-8, CMV}	SVM	The classificatory accuracy of the SVM-based classifier is slightly better than that of LDA in the negative, positive and overall hit ratio.

(*Continued*)

Table 12.1 Literature review of the methods, parameters, and model used. (*Continued*)

S. no.	Method used	Advantages	Parameters used	Model used	Results and issues
27	Prediction of BRCA1 status in patients with breast cancer using estrogen receptor and basal phenotype [27]	BRCA2 mutations were also of bigger overall range as a statement	BRCA1 mutations were of higher grade	Estrogen Receptor and Basal Phenotype	Breast cancers due to BRCA2 mutations show higher grades and less tubule formation but were not significantly different from controls with respect to mitoses, pleomorphism, steroid receptor expression, or mutation in TP53.
28	Analysis and prediction of prognosis of estrogen receptor-positive breast cancer with combination of selected estrogen-regulated genes [28]	ERG Images are the precise use of ERG receptors	ERGs, histone deacetylase 6 (HDAC6)	means of real-time reverse transcription-PCR in 14 ER-positive human breast cancer tissues	Assessment of the expression levels of these ERGs will contribute to the clinically useful stratification of ER-positive breast cancer patients.

(*Continued*)

Table 12.1 Literature review of the methods, parameters, and model used. (*Continued*)

S. no.	Method used	Advantages	Parameters used	Model used	Results and issues
29	Neoadjuvant chemotherapy of locally advanced breast cancer: predicting response MR spectroscopy [29]	Chemotherapy of cancer cells provide treatment measures records.	Primary systemic therapy (PST)	MR Spectroscopy	The model helps in predicting whether the chosen drug will be effective for the treatment in the case of a particular individual.
30	Predicting breast cancer survivability: a comparison of three data mining methods [30]	ANN is used for providing variations in training data sets. This provides precise sets.	prognostic factors	ANN, decision trees & logistic regression	The ANN model came out with 91.2% accuracy and the logistic regression models came out to be the worst of the three with 89.2% accuracy.

instructor can likewise examine the advantages, dangers, and restrictions of hereditary testing to help you with shared dynamic.

12.3   Architecture Design and Implementation

The architecture design is given below in Figure 12.1, which comprises of the following steps: Initially the data set is loaded and the Data Exploration process takes place. This process is done to understand the attributes to be used. The next step is Data Preprocessing which involves the conversion of the data in to a proper format. The next step is feature scaling which brings all the values within the same range, and the last step is model selection and evaluation. This gives the proper model.

Phase 1: Data Exploration

Load the data set in the Google Colab so that the data set can be read and displayed. To do so, the content of the drive has to be mounted and Pandas

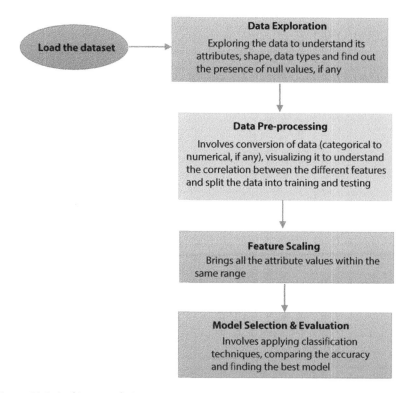

Figure 12.1 Architecture design.

```
from google.colab import drive
drive.mount('/content/drive')

import pandas as pd
df = pd.read_csv('/content/drive/My Drive/Colab Notebooks/data.csv')
df
```

Figure 12.2 Commands to load the data set.

library should be imported to read and display the data set. Figure 12.2 represents the commands to load the data set. The functions used are as follows:

Install pandas profiling so that if required later, it can be used to generate a profiling report that will help us understand the relations between the different variables. The installation is done at the start so that after the process is complete and the kernel is restarted, we do not have to run a lot of functions again since the start. After doing so, import the required libraries and packages that help in plotting and visualizing the data. After importing the libraries, display information about the data set like the number of columns, its data types, and so on. Also, check if there are any null values present in the data set which might hamper the accuracy of it. This can be done using functions like: df.head() which displays the first 5 rows of the data set, df.columns that displays the names of the columns, df.shape() which displays the number of rows and columns, df.info() that displays columns and their data types, df.dtypes, which displays columns and their data types and df.describe() that displays the count, minimum and maximum value, standard deviation, and so on. The info and describe function clearly show that there are no null values present in the data set. Since, "diagnosis" is the column we are trying to predict, we make a plot

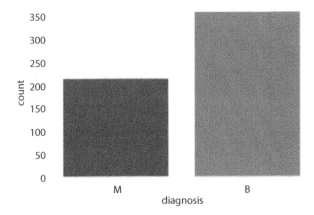

Figure 12.3 Visualizing the count.

to visualize the data of this column only. Figure 12.3 visualizes the count based on the diagnosis. It can be seen that it has two values, i.e., M, as in, malignant or B, as in, benign. It clearly indicates that of the 569 observations/people, 357 of them are marked as B, as in, benign and 212 of them are marked as M, as in, malignant.

After understanding the data, we move on to the next phase.

Phase 2: Data Pre-Processing

In this, first, we start with converting categorical data into numerical data because categorical data are the data that contain label values, for example, F (female) and M (male), T (true), and F (false), etc. Here, "diagnosis," contains categorical/label values—M (malignant) and B (benign). These can be converted to 1 and 0, respectively. The next step is to visualize the entire data set. To do so, we plot histograms, pair plot, and correlation matrix. All these graphs help us understand data better and also the relation between different features that affect the final output. A pair plot is also known as a scatter plot, in which one variable in the same data row is matched with another variable's value. The analysis of the correlation matrix clearly exhibits a strong association between the mean radius and mean perimeter, mean area, and mean perimeter as shown in Figure 12.4.

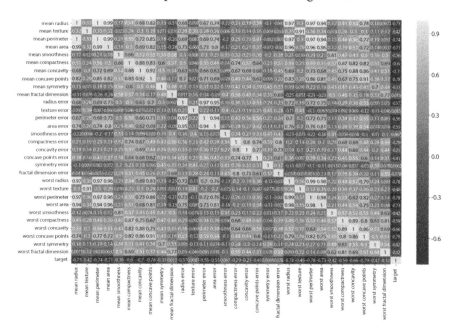

Figure 12.4 Correlation matrix/heat map of correlation between features (with values).

Now that we are done with cleaning, exploring, and preprocessing of the data set, we divide the data set into two parts, i.e., independent variable (X) and dependant variable (Y). These are also known as feature data set and target data set, respectively. In our data set, Y = parameter that we are trying to predict (Output). Here, we are trying to analyse that whether the "diagnosis" is cancerous (malignant) or not (benign). X = These are basically the remaining columns (mean radius, mean texture, mean perimeter, mean area, mean smoothness, etc.), which act as predictors. After this, we create a training and testing data set. Now that the values have been assigned to X and Y, we import the python library that enables us to divide the data set into training and testing data.

Training data are the subset of our data that is used to train our model. Basically, it has a known output, and the model learns through these data in so that it can be generalized for the other data. Testing data are the subset of our data that the model has not seen before. This data set is to test the performance of our model (our model's prediction). To achieve the same, we use the SciKit-Learn library and the train_test_split method. We split our data into 80:20 for training and testing, respectively. Table 12.2 represents the correlation between attributes and the target variable.

Table 12.2 Correlation between attributes and the target variable.

S. no.	Parameters/attributes	Correlation % with the target variable (diagnosis)
1	id	4%
2	diagnosis	100%
3	radius_mean	73%
4	texture_mean	42%
5	perimeter_mean	74%
6	area_mean	71%
7	smoothness_mean	36%
8	compactness_mean	60%
9	concavity_mean	70%
10	concave points_mean	78%

(Continued)

Table 12.2 Correlation between attributes and the target variable. (*Continued*)

S. no.	Parameters/attributes	Correlation % with the target variable (diagnosis)
11	symmetry_mean	33%
12	fractal_dimension_mean	−1%
13	radius_se	57%
14	texture_se	−1%
15	perimeter_se	56%
16	area_se	55%
17	smoothness_se	−7%
18	compactness_se	29%
19	concavity_se	25%
20	concave points_se	41%
21	symmetry_se	−1%
22	fractal_dimension_se	8%
23	radius_worst	78%
24	texture_worst	46%
25	perimeter_worst	78%
26	area_worst	73%
27	smoothness_worst	42%
28	compactness_worst	59%
29	concavity_worst	66%
30	concave points_worst	79%
31	symmetry_worst	42%
32	fractal_dimension_worst	32%

Phase 3: Feature Scaling

Since the data set includes features that vary highly in terms of magnitude, unit, and range, the machine learning algorithms use the measure—Euclidean distance to bring all the features to the same level of magnitudes by scaling. This process is known as feature scaling. This means that we are transforming the feature/independent data so that it fits within a specific scale, like 0 to 100 or 0 to 1.

Phase 4: Model Selection and Evaluation

For our data set, we use classification algorithm of supervised learning since the outcome/target variable—diagnosis has only two values: malignant (1) and benign (0). We have different types of classification algorithms that we use here like kNN algorithm, K-SVM algorithm, random forest classifier algorithm, decision tree algorithm, SVM algorithm, and logistic regression algorithm. To import the methods of classification algorithms, we have used the sklearn library. After this, we predict the test results and check for the accuracy for each model. We then also print the confusion matrix to check for the false positive, false negative, true positive and true negative. It is seen that all our models show an accuracy of 95% and above except decision tree algorithm. The reason for that is that decision tree algorithm is not best suited for huge data sets, instead random forest classifier is preferred to it. Figure 12.5 represents the confusion matrix of kNN, K-SVM, Random forest, Decision tree, SVM and Logistic regression. The reason

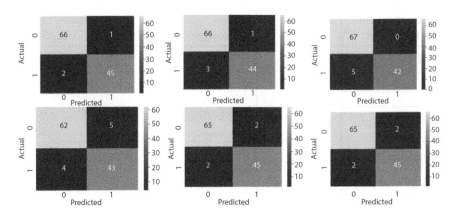

Figure 12.5 (clockwise): Confusion matrix of kNN, K-SVM, random forest, decision tree, SVM, logistic regression.

being that random forest classifiers are multiple single trees each based on a random sample of the training data which outperform single decision trees in terms of accuracy and stability. They can also handle overfitting. The highest accuracy is displayed by K-SVM, i.e., 97.3%. We have used SVM because it is a very versatile and powerful tool, which is capable of performing classification and outlier detection. It is well suited for complex data sets.

12.4   Results and Discussion

According to research, physicians have been able to detect cancer only with 79% accuracy, whereas the accuracy rate greatly increases to around 97% when machine learning models are used. In this work, we have successfully classified a tumor to be malignant versus benign with 97.3% accuracy using the K-SVM. We have taken several digitized cell images of fine needle aspirate (FNA) of a breast mass, and features have been extracted from them to classify tumors as malignant (cancerous) or benign (noncancerous). We computed a number of real valued characteristics for each of these cell nuclei like radius, texture, perimeter, area, smoothness, compactness, concavity, concave points, symmetry, and fractal dimension. Table 12.3 represents the classification techniques along with true and false negative,

Table 12.3 Classification techniques along with true and false negative, positive.

Classification technique	True negative	False positive	True positive	False negative
kNN	67	0	42	5
K-SVM	66	1	45	2
Random Forest	66	1	44	3
Decision Tree	62	5	43	4
SVM	65	2	45	2
Logistic Regression	65	2	45	2

positive. These features are taken as the predictors upon which the output (whether the cell is cancerous or not) is predicted. There can also be seen a strong relation between perimeter and radius alongside concave_points of the breast mass tissue.

The accuracy rate for the classification technique kNN is calculated as 95.61%, K-SVM is calculated as 97.36%, random forest is calculated as 96.49%, decision tree is calculated as 92.10%, SVM is calculated as 96.49% and logistic regression is calculated as 96.49%.

Our analysis also helped us identify which features help the most in the classification of the tumor. We have used pandas' visualization of the Matplotlib library to construct visualizations for each of these features. Figure 12.6 visualizes the relationship between the highly associated features and Figure 12.7 shows the correlation between the extracted features.

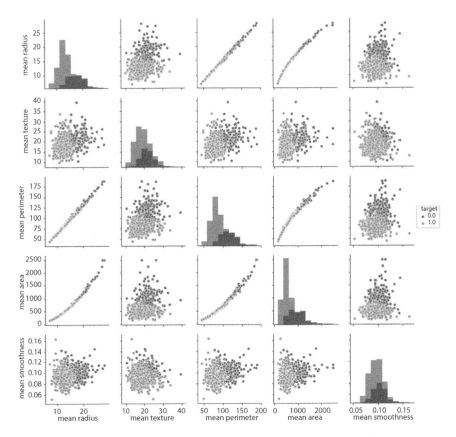

Figure 12.6 Relationship between the highly associated features (orange = benign & blue = malignant).

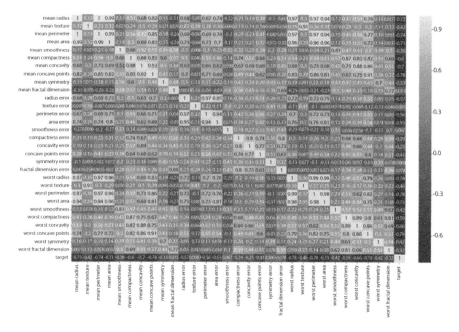

Figure 12.7 Correlation between extracted feature.

12.5   Conclusion

Breast cancer is one of the most common kinds of cancer found in women all over the world. As per the number of cases and related deaths due to it every year, it is considered as a very significant health problem today. Moreover, according to research, physicians have been able to detect cancer only with 79% accuracy, whereas the accuracy rate greatly increases to 91% to 97% when machine learning models are used. Hence, we chose this area as the subject of our project. We have used the machine learning model K-SVM here to extract critical features from complicated data sets that has helped us get a much better prediction accuracy. In our work, we computed a number of real valued characteristics for each of these cell nuclei like radius, texture, perimeter, area, smoothness, compactness, concavity, concave points, and symmetry and fractal dimension. We then calculated the mean value, standard error, and extreme value for each feature that returned a resultant real valued vector. The model we used for the proposed task is K-SVM.

The reason we have used K-SVM is because it has high dimensionality and is also memory efficient since it used only a subset from the training set. Since K-SVM is a binary classification technique, its decision boundary reduces generalization error up to a great extent. We check if our observations are linearly separable in nature, if they are K-SVM fits into it a decision boundary. For the closest points of each class, the largest existing margin is taken to decide the decision boundary. This is popularly called maximum margin hyperplane (MMH). We have used the confusion matrix for predicting the number of predicted classes that ended up being classified wrong with respect to its true class. The accuracy of our model came out to be 97.3%, which is a significant improvement over 79% as predicted by experienced physicians. So based on the prediction of the disease, telehealthcare can be given to the patients by means of the opinion from the physician.

12.6 Future Work

Breast cancer analysis has always been the most concerned yet ignored issue in biomedical and genomic issue culture. The cancer accuracy and precision results have not always been just significant, but also provide the statistics of a world-wide disease. Our work aims to provide more of the future scope parameters, which can be used to treat the cancer tissues well before they start the infusion. The parameters provided can be varied across different cases and vulnerabilities. These parameters are not only limited to precise treatment but also generate a gateway to explore new tumor cells, which are not yet discovered but can be the part of cell infections. The analysis implies that with the integration of data with multiple parameters along with various classification techniques, and feature selection can prove to be an effective tool for analysis and inference in the domain. The future can be simulated and predicted on the basis of machine learning algorithms, which are a huge part of data analysis in this paper. The main aim is not just to provide cure but to predict the cause. The cause can be eliminated before it takes big alterations.

Also, further research can be carried out in the field with respect to unsupervised learning methods as they have not been implemented here to compare on the basis of the accuracy achieved by the models. Apart from this, the focus can also be on how to improve the accuracy and minimize the error rate as much as possible so that its application can be carried out in real-life, thus making the process of detection and diagnosis faster and more accurate.

References

1. Giaccherini, C. *et al.*, Thrombotic biomarkers for risk prediction of malignant disease recurrence in patients with early stage breast cancer. *Haematologica*, 105, 6, 1704–1711, 2020.

2. Hughes, K.S., Zhou, J., Bao, Y., Singh, P., Wang, J., Yin, K., Natural language processing to facilitate breast cancer research and management. *Breast J.*, 26, 1, 92–99, 2020.

3. Ling, A.Y., Kurian, A.W., Caswell-Jin, J.L., Sledge Jr., G.W., Shah, N.H., Tamang, S.R., Using natural language processing to construct a metastatic breast cancer cohort from linked cancer registry and electronic medical records data. *JAMIA Open*, 2, 4, 528–537, 2019.

4. Banerjee, I., Bozkurt, S., Caswell-Jin, J.L., Kurian, A.W., Rubin, D.L., Natural language processing approaches to detect the timeline of metastatic recurrence of breast cancer. *JCO Clin. Cancer Inform.*, 3, 3, 1–12, 2019.

5. Kadam, V.J., Jadhav, S.M., Vijayakumar, K., Breast Cancer diagnosis using feature ensemble learning based on Stacked Sparse Auto encoders and Softmax Regression. *J. Med. Syst.*, 43, 8, 263, 2019.

6. Datta, S., Bernstam, E.V., Roberts, K., A frame semantic overview of NLP-based information extraction for cancer-related EHR notes. *J. Biomed. Inform.*, 100, 103301, 103301, 2019.

7. Kumar, V., Mishra, B.K., Mazzara, M., Thanh, D.N.H., Verma, A., Prediction of malignant & benign Breast Cancer: A Data Mining approach in healthcare applications, Springer, Singapore, pp. 435–442, 2019. arXiv [cs.LG].

8. Chaurasia, V. and Pal, S., Prediction of benign and malignant breast cancer using data mining techniques. *SSRN Electron. J.*, 12, 2, 119–26, 2018.

9. Zeng, Z. *et al.*, Using natural language processing and machine learning to identify breast cancer local recurrence. *BMC Bioinf.*, 19, Suppl 17, 498, 2018.

10. Sharma, S., Aggarwal, A., Choudhury, T., Breast cancer detection using machine learning algorithms, in: *2018 International Conference on Computational Techniques, Electronics and Mechanical Systems (CTEMS)*, 2018.

11. Wei, B., Han, Z., He, X., Yin, Y., Deep learning model based breast cancer histopathological image classification, in: *2017 IEEE 2nd International Conference on Cloud Computing and Big Data Analysis (ICCCBDA)*, 2017.

12. He, T. *et al.*, Deep learning analytics for diagnostic support of breast cancer disease management, in: *2017 IEEE EMBS International Conference on Biomedical & Health Informatics (BHI)*, 2017.

13. Bejnordi, B.E. *et al.*, Diagnostic assessment of deep learning algorithms for detection of lymph node metastases in women with breast cancer. *JAMA*, 318, 22, 2199, 2017.

14. Kawashima, K., Bai, W., Quan, C., Text mining and pattern clustering for relation extraction of breast cancer and related genes, in: *2017 18th IEEE/*

ACIS International Conference on Software Engineering, Artificial Intelligence, Networking and Parallel/Distributed Computing (SNPD), 2017.

15. Gong, L., Yan, R., Liu, Q., Yang, H., Yang, G., Jiang, K., Extraction of biomedical information related to breast cancer using text mining, in: *2016 12th International Conference on Natural Computation, Fuzzy Systems and Knowledge Discovery (ICNC-FSKD)*, 2016.

16. Asri, H., Mousannif, H., Moatassime, H.A., Noel, T., Using machine learning algorithms for breast cancer risk prediction and diagnosis. *Proc. Comput. Sci.*, 83, 1064–1069, 2016.

17. Bayramoglu, N., Kannala, J., Heikkila, J., Deep learning for magnification independent breast cancer histopathology image classification, in: *2016 23rd International Conference on Pattern Recognition (ICPR)*, 2016.

18. Chan, A. and Tuszynski, J.A., Automatic prediction of tumour malignancy in breast cancer with fractal dimension. *R. Soc Open Sci.*, 3, 12, 160558, 2016.

19. Johanna Johnsi Rani, G., Gladis, D., Manipadam, M.T., Ishitha, G., Breast cancer staging using Natural Language Processing, in: *2015 International Conference on Advances in Computing, Communications and Informatics (ICACCI)*, 2015.

20. Wang, X.-F., Wu, Y.-H., Wang, M.-S., Wang, Y.-S., CEA, AFP, CA125, CA153 and CA199 in malignant pleural effusions predict the cause. *Asian Pac. J. Cancer Prev.*, 15, 1, 363–368, 2014.

21. Maghsoodi, A., Sevenster, M., Scholtes, J., Nalbantov, G., Sentence-based classification of free-text breast cancer radiology reports, in: *2012 25th IEEE International Symposium on Computer-Based Medical Systems (CBMS)*, 2012.

22. Dietzel, M. *et al.*, Potential of MR mammography to predict tumor grading of invasive breast cancer. *Rofo*, 183, 9, 826–833, 2011.

23. Nilsen, L., Fangberget, A., Geier, O., Olsen, D.R., Seierstad, T., Diffusion-weighted magnetic resonance imaging for pretreatment prediction and monitoring of treatment response of patients with locally advanced breast cancer undergoing neoadjuvant chemotherapy. *Acta Oncol.*, 49, 3, 354–360, 2010.

24. Sarvestani, A.S., Safavi, A.A., Parandeh, N.M., Salehi, M., Predicting breast cancer survivability using data mining techniques, in: *2010 2nd International Conference on Software Technology and Engineering*, 2010.

25. Johansen, R. *et al.*, Predicting survival and early clinical response to primary chemotherapy for patients with locally advanced breast cancer using DCE-MRI. *J. Magn. Reson. Imaging*, 29, 6, 1300–1307, 2009.

26. Huang, C.-L., Liao, H.-C., Chen, M.-C., Prediction model building and feature selection with support vector machines in breast cancer diagnosis. *Expert Syst. Appl.*, 34, 1, 578–587, 2008.

27. Lakhani, S.R. *et al.*, Prediction of BRCA1 status in patients with breast cancer using estrogen receptor and basal phenotype. *Clin. Cancer Res.*, 11, 14, 5175–5180, 2005.

28. Yoshida, N. *et al.*, Prediction of prognosis of estrogen receptor-positive breast cancer with combination of selected estrogen-regulated genes. *Cancer Sci.*, 95, 6, 496–502, 2004.

29. Meisamy, S. *et al.*, Neoadjuvant chemotherapy of locally advanced breast cancer: predicting response with in vivo (1)H MR spectroscopy–a pilot study at 4 T. *Radiology*, 233, 2, 424–431, 2004.

30. Delen, D., Walker, G., Kadam, A., Predicting breast cancer survivability: a comparison of three data mining methods. *Artif. Intell. Med.*, 34, 2, 113–127, 2005.

13

Remote Patient Monitoring: Data Sharing and Prediction Using Machine Learning

Mohammed Hameed Alhameed[1], S. Shanthi[2], Uma Perumal[1*]
and Fathe Jeribi[3]

[1]*College of Computer Science and Information Technology, Department of Computer Science, Jazan University, Jazan, Saudi Arabia*
[2]*Malla Reddy College of Engineering and Technology, Telangana, India*
[3]*College of Computer Science and Information Technology, Department of Information Technology and Security, Jazan University, Jazan, Saudi Arabia*

Abstract

Healthcare is a field that is developing with the exponential increase in technology and services. Disruptive technology has opened up great possibilities in remote patient monitoring. Artificial intelligence–based remote patient monitoring adopting wearable technology and a variety of health monitoring gadgets play a significant role in digitally connecting patients from home to healthcare experts.

The versatility and the utilization of the latest technologies enable "patient monitoring, healthcare information technology, intelligent assistance diagnosis, and information analysis collaboration treatment" by identifying at risk patients. Patient access to health records and resources via web and mobile backed with cloud-based data collection, monitoring, and analytics capabilities reduce recurrent hospital visits and raise alert messages in case of any abnormalities.

Machine learning algorithms search through an enormous amount of health-related data, analyze it, and predict outcomes for individual patients using unique client identifier and support clinical decision making. The importance of security and privacy challenge-related issues is the main concern in the transfer medical and the logging of data transactions; to overcome this issue, we propose a block diagram that protects and denies illegal access. Several sick people suffer because of a lack of not getting proper assistance and apt solution on time for their problem.

The proposed system recommends an instantaneous solution and provides proper assistance during an emergency, by predicting its seriousness using modern

Corresponding author: prmluma@gmail.com; uperumal@jazanu.edu.sa

R. Nidhya, Manish Kumar and S. Balamurugan (eds.) Tele-Healthcare: Applications of Artificial Intelligence and Soft Computing Techniques, (317–338) © 2022 Scrivener Publishing LLC

algorithms. Using various "supervised and unsupervised machine learning algorithms" the data set is trained and analyzed to predict the disease for a particular patient or the patient's health. The data stored in the database are tested by the k-nearest neighbor classifier and linear regression. The accurate classification is made by the classifier which hardly needs manual rechecking. Hence, the system proposed by the authors has scalability that deals with the online prediction and facilitates patient care remotely.

Keywords: Healthcare, remote patient monitoring, artificial intelligence, wearable devices and machine learning

13.1   Introduction

Health can be defined as "a state of physical, mental, and social well-being and not merely the absence of disease or infirmity" [1]. Encouraging healthy lifestyles, such as a properly balanced diet, exercising, controlling weight gain, are the factors to maintain and enhance good health and longevity. Sometimes health can deteriorate because of unforeseen reasons like accidents, sudden fatal disease, and the effects of age problems. Therefore, it is a fundamental necessity that healthcare facilities are needed to restore health. Healthcare can include in a professional medical setting, under hospital care, clinic visits to medical providers, nursing care plan, and medication. For decades, patients were always dependent on their doctor for the management of their health conditions.

A health system is generally referred to as a healthcare system or healthcare system established to deliver healthcare facilities to the people who need medical services. As per the World Health Organization (WHO), a well-working medical service system requires assets, resources, a financing mechanism, well-prepared, adequate specialists, and reliable information on which to base decisions and procedures and deliver quality medicines [2]. The reasons that decide health status incorporate factors like living and working in hygienic conditions, general socioeconomic and environmental conditions, and admittance to better medical care facilities and administrative services [3]."

13.1.1   Patient Monitoring in Healthcare System

Patient monitoring means extreme vital signs, continuous observations and recording measurements of the patient on one or more medical parameters, physiological function, and, to guide management decisions, and recommend therapeutic interventions, and review of interventions at regular intervals.

The most essential feature of a patient monitoring system (PMS) alerts the medical staff about potentially life-threatening occurrences; many also provide physiologic data used to control and monitor directly connected life-support devices [4, 5].

The current PMS with regard to their level of technology (Figure 13.1).

Monitors are used to capturing immense data efficiently and display the continuous follow-up measurements of patient parameters, such as cardiac index, respiratory rate, blood pressure; blood-oxygen saturation (SpO_2), blood-glucose, body temperature, and many other relevant parameters has become a common attribute for the care of extremely critically ill patients. The most significant accomplishment of the captured data is sent to the centralized monitor for effective and immediate decision-making process [5, 6] and judge on whether there is improvement, deterioration, or absence of change and review of the care plan.

The bedside monitors, conventional oscilloscopes, and analog-computer technology for decoding the signal used to take a huge amount of time [7, 8]. As information technology has enhanced, it is a time of unparalleled change in the monitoring systems. Innovative database storage functionality, report-generation, some decision-making capabilities, alarming and alerting features equipped with some specialized communication interface, scalability, and flexibility of the signal interpretation [6] are popular computer-based patient monitors. Therefore, the aim of the PMS is to give an early warning signal about the patient's health condition.

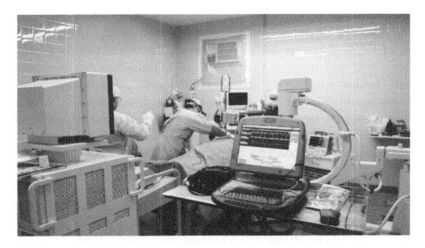

Figure 13.1 Example of patient monitoring system from https://atltechnology.com/blog/components-of-patient-monitoring-systems/

As COVID-19 pandemic has halted many aspects of our day-to-day life activities and has created a paradigm shift to adopt "remote patient monitoring systems." The biggest challenges in the world today are the healthcare system that struggles to care for COVID-19 patients. The evolution of Mobile, Internet, and sensor technology are the main driving forces for the developments in the field of information technology, which paved the way major aspects of remote patient monitoring (RPM) systems. Home-care monitoring assists faster, reliable, more effective coordination and cost-saving rehabilitation [9] and mobilization of patients. Remote patient monitoring is a paradigm shift toward an advanced e-health ecosystem.

The terminologies, such as RPM, telemedicine, telehealth, and mobile health, mean monitoring of patient's health condition outside of the hospital environment using innovative information technology resources. A digital health monitoring device that could reduce the number of times they had to physically visit a doctor or hospital it is like a boon for the patient during the current crisis. These patient monitors to aid in decreasing the number of hospital readmissions, transform health, and improve the quality of life by maintaining constant communication between patient and physician. This efficiently helps to combat challenges a patient faces in his or her life. Remote patient monitoring offers very comprehensive care to assist chronic disease management, and with utmost importance for self-management support [8, 9]. The modern digital technology and telecommunications infrastructure enable monitoring patients remotely. According to "Healthcare Information and Management Systems Society," Inc. (HIMSS), the universal advisor and thought leader behind the transformation of the health ecosystem utilizing the resources of information and technology. They predict that there will be a steady [10] raise in the ratio of RPM. It is expected that there will be more than four million patients who will monitor their health conditions remotely by 2020. A health checker system [11] proposed utilizes the advanced concepts of wireless sensor network (WSN) and embedded technologies. Wearable technologies have become a standard part of life for patients. The latest wearable sensors tools track [12, 13] metrics such as oxygen saturation, blood pressure, heart rate, and sleep patterns. The data is sent from medical devices to the online platform. To record the readings initially higher and lower boundaries are set up by the physicians for "vital metrics" such as "blood pressure", [14] "blood glucose", "body temperature", "oxygen saturation", and "pulse." The patient is monitored, that process is depicted in (Figure 13.2), and for irregularities in those metrics each time a vitals reading is recorded through the gadgets and connects with patient fitness facts or electronic medical records. Whenever, a vital metrics crosses [15, 17] a

Figure 13.2 RPM process.

threshold range (higher or lower boundary) and fluctuate or deviate from the set variety, an immediate alert is notified in the central system, and it sends out a swift SMS to the health practitioner, informing him/her that the threshold value has been breached [16]."

The rest of the chapter is organized as follows: section 13.2 describes the literature survey while section 13.3 describes the problem statement. Section 13.4 describes various machine learning algorithms and cloud computing architecture, proposed system and algorithms are described in section 13.5, section 13.6 summarizes the results of the proposed algorithms, section 13.7 describes the privacy and security challenges and Section 13.8 concludes the findings and discusses future enhancement.

13.2   Literature Survey

The "supervised machine learning algorithms primarily deal with a classification, such as random forest (RF), Linear Classifiers, Naïve Bayes Classifier, Logistic Regression, Quadratic Classifiers, K-Means Clustering, Boosting, Neural networks, Decision Tree, Support Vector Machine, and Bayesian Networks" [18].

The authors have discussed the k-nearest neighbor (KNN) algorithm for classification and regression. A novel algorithm for the danger of diabetes mellitus was proposed in the paper [19]. Using classification algorithms type 2 diabetes diseases and hypertension was predicted. The system objective is to examine and predict the recorded patient's BP and glucose readings. In case of any abnormality detected the person is notified [20, 21]. To predict the diabetic disorder decision tree classifiers, KNN, logistic regression (LR), and support vector machines (SVMs), techniques are used. The authors [14, 22] compare and choose the best performance of these models [14, 22] for predicting diabetic disease.

The author in their paper discussed the proposed model of readmissions and risk prediction. The medical data set was collected from different hospitals, and the result was 3.8% accurate [19]. A patients' monitoring platform was proposed by [23] where the sensors are "implanted in patients' bodies to get vital data." After the proper acquisition, processing, storage tasks the results were accurate, but scalability was the main concern.

The work of Tr *et al.* [24] proposes wireless sensor networks and using the latest gadgets, such as wearable devices to gather and monitor patient's data. The author proposes RPM work on cloud computing in Mueller and Pantos [25], a framework design that provides a faster, secure platform from unauthorized access and ubiquitous services at a lower cost solving the issues related to the healthcare sector.

The authors in their paper discussed the architecture for monitoring patients with diabetic disorder using algorithms J48 and RF for data classification [26], data accumulated by the sensors are transmitted through Smartphones to the cloud database storage and to determine the patient's level of risk [27].

13.3 Problem Statement

Remote patient monitoring is an innovative technology to monitor patients outside of the hospital settings. Patients suffering from diabetics need continuous and constant monitoring of their health. Remote patient monitoring helps in recording and sending the patient data from various sensors to the cloud server. The practitioners can view and assess the data and provide feedback to the patients. Using machine learning algorithms, we predict the patient data available in the cloud database depending on the emergency the doctors are swiftly alerted about the patient's condition and their timely intervention. In this paper two "machine learning algorithms," KNN and LR are used for accurate prediction. The data which is transmitted from the sensors to the cloud server is taken and analyzed on those two machine learning algorithms with proper training and testing data. We also compare the performance measures and provide the prediction. We also suggest overcoming the issues of data security, privacy, and scalability.

13.4 Machine Learning

13.4.1 Introduction

Normally, a person uses his or her brain to grasp and analyze the information from surroundings and accordingly takes proper decisions. On the

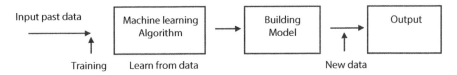

Figure 13.3 Block diagram of the machine learning algorithm.

other hand, machines are not expected to be intelligent which means a machine cannot analyze and make decisions abruptly. The era of "Artificial Intelligence (AI) a branch of computer science" has evolved and completely changed this concept and it is possible for machines to think drastically as the same level of intelligence as humans. Machines are designed with the capacities to accumulate data via sensors identical to the human senses and afterward measure the assembled data by using computational intelligence tools and machine learning techniques [28] to forecast and for the decision-making process.

Without human intervention, the machine learning system learns and improves from the experience and focuses on the development of programs that can analyze the data. The key idea (Figure 13.3) is to make predictions on huge amounts of data by using algorithms and inductively can solve problems by machines, i.e. using computers.

A supervised machine learning algorithm generates a function or a model to predict the label of data based on their features which the humans have provided, maps inputs to desired outputs.

The classification algorithms are either "Binary Classifier" or "Multiclass Classifier." The purpose of this algorithm is used to classify the discrete values, such as male or female, and so on. For instance, a computer program is trained on the training data set. The correlations between "dependent and independent variables" can be found using Regression. It can be either linear or nonlinear [29, 30]. The prediction for example is of house prices, salary, age, weather forecasting, and so on.

The Process of Supervised Machine Learning

The following flowchart (Figure 13.4) illustrates the general process of supervised machine learning.

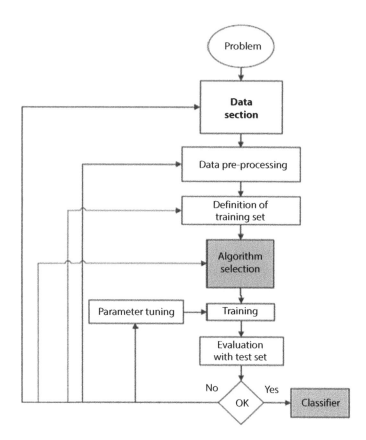

Figure 13.4 Flowchart of supervised machine learning process.

13.4.2   Cloud Computing

Cloud computing technology can greatly improve the level of healthcare services. In RPM, one of the important aspects is to securely transfer patient's real-time data to the healthcare system for assessment and recommendations. Cloud computing applications and architecture can handle huge amounts of data that are shared among patients and physicians all around the globe. The architecture is mainly based on client/server that consists of computing resources such as "(networks, servers, storage, applications, and services)." "Multiprocessor, virtualization technology, network-based distributed data storage, and networking, the use of remote servers hosted on the Internet" can collect, store, and manage data efficiently. Cloud computing refers to both the applications delivered as services over the "Internet and hardware and software in data centers that provide services" [23, 39].

Benefits of cloud computing in healthcare

- Mobility of records: a patient medical record system is required in an emergency at multiple places, i.e., by two or more health institutions. Implementation of cloud technologies can be easily adapted and simultaneously data can be shared.
- Speed: swift and accurate and reliable access to all the important information is feasible by using cloud-based technologies and services [31].
- Security and privacy: storage of encrypted medical records in the cloud and backup secure data. Permission-based secured login ensures data security [31].
- Privacy and data security issues: The data in the cloud storage primarily contain details regarding the sick persons, personal, and vital information. To prevent access to the malicious users' records need to be properly safeguarded. The healthcare organizations implementing Cloud Technologies have major concerns associated with data privacy, "data jurisdiction," "security," and "compliance" [27].

13.4.3   Design and Architecture

One of the advantages offered by cloud computing is an efficient exchange and sharing of medical data in a timely and effective manner. It has additionally relieved healthcare facilitators of the rigor concerned to control and manage infrastructure and furthermore provides them with abundant opportunity to get acquainted themselves with information technology service providers [31]. Adopting disruptive technology and a variety of health monitoring gadgets, patients are connected and monitored from home or remote location to the healthcare experts (Figure 13.5). The collected patient's vital data, the client is transferred as a unique client identifier through the Internet to the cloud server, to intelligently analyze and predict patient's health status and clinical decision making and recommendations. The cloud is equipped with an algorithm computation module. The new data received from the patient is processed with the computation module and then compares the calculated result with the existing result. If the results are out of boundaries then immediately the physician is alerted about the abnormality and a communication is established with the patient.

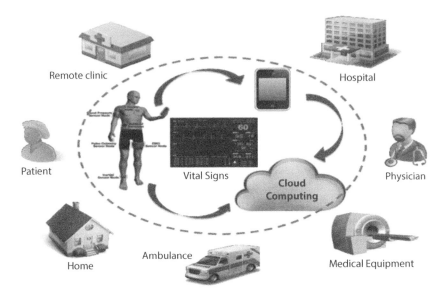

Figure 13.5 Illustrates the general description of cloud design from: https://www.researchgate.net/figure Telemedicine-based-on-Mobile-Cloud-Medical-Monitoring_fig1_261349788

The medical report can be viewed using electronic gadgets by the patient or physician anytime anywhere in the world. It allows flexible scaling.

13.5   Proposed System

Real-time data generally consists of noises, missing values, which is improper for direct access for machine learning models. Using such irrelevant and unpredictable "data knowledge discovery" during the training phase, it is further complicated and predicts inaccurate results so it is compulsory to clean it and put it in a formatted and organized way. There are some techniques to handle specifically the missing data that would be most appropriate for the Machine Learning Algorithms [32].

Data preprocessing techniques can be classified as data cleaning, data transformation, and feature selection. "Data cleaning and transformation are used to remove outliers and standardize the data so that they take a form that can be easily used to create a model." The result of data preprocessing is a new feature set to enhance the classification performance. The fact is that the "dimensionality" of the data allows classification algorithms to operate more effectively. The accuracy or precision of the classification result is compact, easily "interpreted" representation of the target concept [33].

Python "scikit-learn" library is utilized to build and predict in machine learning. It provides necessary tools for performing tasks as "evaluating models, tuning parameters, and preprocessing" data. An open-source Scikit-learn manages its operations with the same ecosystem and code [34, 35].

Proposed Methodology

The new proposed study follows the supervised machine learning techniques (MLTs) to predict Diabetes Mellitus (DM) at an early stage to save human life. Systematic surveys on diabetic patient's medical data characteristics are considered. "Machine learning algorithms" are used to predict and diagnosis the complications involved in healthcare management. Before model construction, the feature set is meticulously calculated and filter methods are filtered out. The proposed system predicts the abnormalities using KNN Classifier and Linear Regression algorithms.

K-nearest neighbor

The most prominent machine learning algorithm based on supervised learning techniques is KNN algorithm. The algorithm training phase mainly focuses on the training samples by storing the "feature vectors and class labels." In the classification phase, the constant K is user-defined. The Unlabelled vector ("a query or test point") focuses on classifying the label by assigning the K training samples makes to the nearest query point. In KNN algorithm to take "vote" the K factor is used as the number of nearest neighbors. For the sample object, different values for the "K" are selected to generate different classification results. For the better and accurate "performance evaluation TP, FP, TN, and FN as true positive (the number of instances correctly predicted as required), false positive (the number of instances incorrectly predicted as required), true negative (the number of instances correctly predicted as not required) and false negative (the number of instances incorrectly predicted as not required). Four measurements: accuracy, precision, recall, and F1-score are applied for better accuracy and prediction."

Linear Regression

The simplest machine learning algorithm is linear regression which comes under the "Supervised Learning technique for solving regression problems." The objective is to predict the "continuous dependent variable with the help of an independent variable." The principle objective is to locate the best fit line that can precisely anticipate the output for the continuous dependent variable. The regression method is more efficient in forecasting and predicting the cause and effect relationship between variables.

This system provides a platform for remote monitoring and supervising patients. The stages of the process are data collection from monitoring devices, storage of data in the cloud, analysis of the stored data using machine learning algorithms, and prediction for abnormalities of the health condition. "The input value is the attribute value of the patient, $X = (x_1, x_2, \cdots, x_n)$ which includes the patient's personal information" such as age, gender, if female pregnant or not, BP, height, weight, living habits (smoking or not), marital status, heart disease, temperature and the prevalence of symptoms, and so on.

The proposed system is separated into training and testing parts. 70% of data are considered for training and 30% of data are considered for testing purposes. The data from the wearable devices are sent through a Smartphone via networks to cloud storage. Sometimes due to human or network error, inconsistent data may be sent to the database then the learning algorithm should prompt with an error message and no attempt will be made to find a function that exactly matches the training examples. The importance of the factors is calculated based on the available trained data set. All attributes values are numeric; "for every 3 hours an oral glucose tolerance test, diastolic blood pressure, triceps skin fold thickness, 3-hour serum insulin, body mass index, diabetes pedigree function, age (years), number of times pregnant and class variable." The accumulated data from the cloud will be retrieved; processed and analyzed using KNN and linear regression techniques to determine the analysis result. In the final step, we get some results based on which we can predict the risk of diabetes patients. If the predicted result is normal, positive feedback is sent to the user and physicians. If any abnormality is detected an alert message will be immediately sent to the patient. Also, the alert message will be forwarded to the physicians for medication and decision-making. A comprehensive report from the electronic medical record system is made available to the doctor that enables them to track the present location of the patient. In case of serious emergency by sending an ambulance the practitioners expedite their process to move the sick person quickly to the hospital. A team of doctors will be recommended for patient treatment. The block diagram of the entire setup is depicted in (Figure 13.6). This way, the patient gets timely help and appropriate solutions for their problem. Therefore, accurate classification is made by the classifier which hardly needs manual

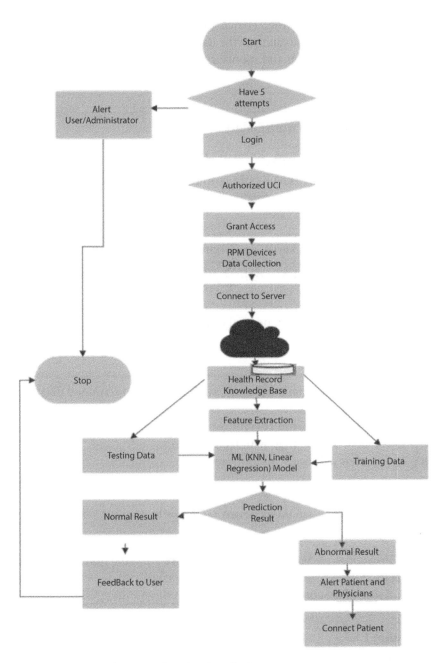

Figure 13.6 Proposed system of RPM and prediction.

intervention and rechecking. Hence the proposed system emulates the decision-making ability to analyze the data and has scalability, which manages the online prediction and monitoring the patient remotely.

Algorithm 13.1:

Input: User record {I to n attributes}
Output: Projected value
Step 1: T = (Ti,j) data matrix
Step 2: Tk = (tk1,tk2...tkn) Read t {1 to n} from current record.
Step 3: Tij^ predict the current value
Step 4: Tik k#j attributes value
Step 5: tij^ = $a_0 + a_1 t_{i1} + a_2 t_{i2} + ...$
Step 6: a_k = $Cov(A_i,A_j) / Var(A_i)$ A denotes attributes a_k coefficients
Step 7: a = $\sum_k (tki - \hat{A}i)(tkj - \hat{A}j) / \sum_k (tki - \hat{A}i)$ Predict the value

tij = actual value
tij^ = predicted value classify normal or abnormal

Algorithm 13.2:

Input: User record {1 to n attributes}, average score from trained database.
Output: Projected value
Step 1: Read I {1 to n} from current record.
Step 2: For each sample map with train features.
Step 3: Calculate average score of train DB

$$AvgTScore = \sum_{k=0}^{n}(Sc)$$

Step 4: PreScore = *(CScore +AvgTScore) CScore a scoring function in terms of correlation*
Step 5: Return PreScore

Algorithm 13.3:

Step 1: Select K.value
Step 2: Search for the K observations in the training data
Step 3: Predicted response value from the K nearest neighbors the training set

Data Set: D = f(xi, ci) , for i = 1 to m} , where xi = $(v^i_1, v^i_2, ..., v^i_n)$ is an observation that belongs to class c_i

Input: x = (v1, v2, ..., vn) data to be classified
Result: class to which x belongs
range← Ø;
for yi in D **do**
    di ← d(yi, x);
    range ← range Ú {di};
end

Sort range = {di, for i = 1 to m} in descending order;
Get the first K cases closer to x, D^K_x;
class ← most frequent class in D^K_x

Evaluation Metric

Imbalanced data sets are evaluated using F-Score, because of the dominating effect of the majority class. F-Score considers both the precision and the recall of the test to compute the score.
"Accuracy = (TP + TN)/(TP + FP + TN + FN)
Precision = TP/(TP + FP)
Recall = TP/(TP + FN)
F1-Score = (2 X Precision X Recall) / (Precision + Recall)"

13.6   Results and Discussions

The machine learning algorithm's efficiency and effectiveness can be evaluated based on some of the feature and feature importance which is carefully measured as shown in Figure 13.7. We performed an extensive study of two algorithms and carried out with the experimental analysis of different patient's real-time data; depicted in Figure 13.8 which shows the result of the average performance for 250 instances and measures the accuracy using classification algorithms like KNN and Linear regression. All the experiments were examined on Intel Pentium Processor. The algorithms were implemented using Python "Scikit-learn" which is a very efficient tool for data predictive analysis. The data set is meticulously analyzed and predicted for any abnormal input data detection. Accuracy "is the ratio of the number of accurate predictions to the total number of the given input samples" shown in (Figure 13.9). Several major factors affect the accuracy of algorithms. If any value is found inappropriate in the data set, an alert message is sent to the user and immediately seeks the doctor's intervention. To get increased accuracy, K and mean values should be low. Also, the nature of the data set is more reliable with the algorithm which makes the accuracy higher (Figure 13.10).

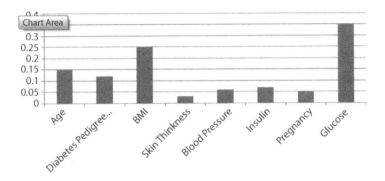

Figure 13.7 Important features of patient's data.

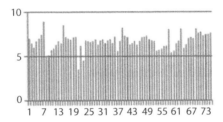

Figure 13.8 Prediction based on the diabetes data.

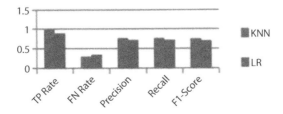

Figure 13.9 Performance results of TP, FN, precision, recall, and F1 score.

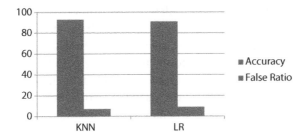

Figure 13.10 Performance analysis of algorithms.

13.7   Privacy and Security Challenges

When the vital signs are uploaded in cloud computing it also contains personal, private, and confidential information about a person. Cloud computing has high levels of electronic patient data over the Internet and in the cloud, which can be used to remotely monitor and treat patients [36, 37]. Patient's health condition status and medical records should be properly protected to prevent unauthorized, misuse of information, disclosure, interference, and modification or destruction. "Global concerns related to data jurisdiction, the privacy of data, security, and compliance are having a huge impact on the adoption of these cloud technologies while healthcare organizations" are in imminent need to provide a trustworthy cloud computing environment [38]. Regardless of its advantages, there are several security and protection challenges that immediately need attention for the realization of its competent full-scale deployment in the cloud. As it is obvious that security is the main concern to overcome all the limitations associated with cloud technologies. The proposed method adopts the collocation and hybrid cloud infrastructure model as it has many advantages like flexibility, greater scale, confidentiality, integrity, availability, trust, and privacy.

- Confidentiality: electronic medical records is not permitted or disclosed to unauthorized persons or processes.
- Integrity: ensures that electronic medical records have not been altered or destroyed by hackers.
- Availability: electronic medical records are easily accessible for authorized personnel only.
- Trust management: strictly follows the security policies that the access will not be provided to unauthorized parties and data should be protected from malicious users.

- Privacy: this system provides an environment where patient's records are stored and can be accessed from anywhere. Each patient is given a unique client identifier (UCI) number to provide access to the cloud storage. The patient should use the number to login and get connected to the cloud storage. The details of the patients will be stored with UCI in the database. Whenever patients visit the hospital for treatment, their stored medical data can be directly fetched from the database by using their identification number. This ensures data confidentiality and identity privacy with high efficiency.

13.8 Conclusions and Future Enhancement

The versatility and the utilization of the latest technology tools play a vital role in RPM systems. Patients can access medical health records via web and mobile backed by cloud-based data collection; monitoring and analytics capabilities reduce recurrent hospital visits and raise alert messages in case of any abnormalities. Machine learning algorithms search through an enormous amount of health-related data, analyze it and predict outcomes for individual patients based on their unique client identifier and support the clinical decision-making process.

The database server in the cloud is secured by the authentication and verification process. The real-time patient data stored in the database is rigorously tested by the KNN classifier and linear regression. The result inference shows that the best accurate classification is made by the classifier which makes the remote monitoring more efficient and successful. Therefore, the health system all over the world should invest in new technology for the betterment of the people and society. Eventually, the death rate can be reduced due to timely help and early detection and diagnosis. The entire health system gets streamlined and even the patients in the isolated regions can be assured about the medical treatment diligently.

However, patient records grow exponentially with time; our focus on future research directions is to further enhance our study on broader aspects and improving the work on Big Data by incorporating other "Machine Learning algorithms, such as J48, Decision Tree, and Random Forest." We also aim at other diseases for gauging their effectiveness in producing accurate results.

References

1. Constitution of the World Health Organization. Geneva. *World Health Organ,* 1948. (http://apps.who.int/gb/bd/PDF/bd47/EN/constitution-en. pdf, accessed 7 May 2009).
2. Closing the gap in a generation: Health equity through action on the social determinants of health. World Health Organization, Geneva, 2008.
3. Health Topics: Health Systems. World Health Organization, Retrieved 2013-11-24. www.who.int.
4. Das, P., Deka, R., Sengyung, S., Nath, B.Kr., Bordoloi, H., A Review Paper On Patient Monitoring System. *J. Appl. Fundam. Sci. JAFS,* 1, 1, 2, 264–267, November 2015.
5. Sanders, T.H., Devergnas, A., Wichmann, T., Clements, M.A., A Telehealth System for Parkinson's Disease Remote Monitoring. The PERFORM approach, in: *Proceedings of the Annual International Conference on Medical Bio Science,* 2013.
6. Mirkovic, J., Bryhni, H., Ruland, C.M., A framework for the development of ubiquitous patient support systems, in: *2012 6th International Conference on Pervasive Computing Technologies for Healthcare (PervasiveHealth) and Workshops,* pp. 81–88, 2012.
7. Tamura, T. *et al.,* Assessment of participant compliance with a Web-based home healthcare system for promoting specific health checkups. *Biocybern. Biomed. Eng.,* 34, 1, 63–69, 2014.
8. Varady, P., Benyo, Z., Benyo, B., An Open Architecture Patient Monitoring System Using Standard Technologies, *IEEE Transactions on Information Technology in Biomedicine,* 6, 1, March 2002.
9. Mosenia, A., Sur-Kolay, S., Raghunathan, A., Jha, N., Wearable Medical Sensor-based System Design. *IEEE Transac. MultiScale.,* 3, 2, 124–138, 2017 May 20.
10. Kakde, S. *et al.,* Implementation of healthcare monitoring system using raspberry pi. *IEEE ICCSP 2015 Conference,* 2, 1083–1086, 2015.
11. MC10. BioStamp nPoint: Wearable healthcare technology & devices. [Online] Available from: https://www.mc10inc.com.
12. Hayeri A. 922-P: Diabits—an AI-powered smartphone application for blood glucose monitoring and Predictions. *Diabetes Journal,* 2019.
13. Appelboom, G., Camacho, E., Abraham, M.E. *et al.,* Smart wearable body sensors for patient self-assessed and monitoring, *Arch. Public Health,* 72, 1, 28, 2014. https://doi.org/10.1186/2049-3258-72-28.
14. Indoria, P. and Rathore, Y.K., A survey: Detection and Prediction of diabetics using machine learning techniques. *IJERT,* 07, 03, 2018.
15. Bayasi, N., Revolution of Glucose Monitoring Methods and Systems: A Survey. *IEEE,* © 92–93, 2013.

16. Abdullah, Dr., An Expert System of Determining Diabetes Treatment Based on Cloud Computing Platforms. *(IJCSIT) Int. J. Comput. Sci. Informat. Technol.*, 2, 5, 1982–1987, 2011.

17. Srivastava, A.K., Analysis of diabetic dataset and developing prediction model by using HIVE and R. *Indian J. Sci. Technol.*, 9, 47, 1–5, 2016.

18. Taiwo, O.A. and Zhang, Y., Types of Machine Learning Algorithms, New Advances in Machine Learning. InTech, University of Portsmouth United Kingdom, pp. 3–31, 2010.

19. Zheng, B., Zhang, J., Yoon, S.W., Lam, S.S., Khasawneh, M., Poranki, S., Predictive modeling of hospital readmissions using metaheuristics and data mining. *Expert Syst. Appl.*, 42, 20, 7110–7120, 2015.

20. Avila-Garcia, M.S., Trefethen, A.E., Brady M., Gleeson, F., Goodman, D., Lowering the Barriers to Cancer Imaging. *eScience, 2008. eScience '08. IEEE Fourth International Conference on*, pp. 63–70, 7–12 Dec. 2008.

21. Sowjanya, K., MobDBTest: A machine learning based system for predicting diabetes risk using mobile devices. *IEEE International Advance Computing Conference (IACC)*, 2015.

22. Uddin, S., Khan, A., Hossain, M.E., Moni, M.A., Comparing different supervised machine learning algorithms for disease prediction, *BMC Med. Inform. Decis. Mak.*, 19, 281, 2019. https://doi.org/10.1186/s12911-019-1004-8

23. The NIST Definition of Cloud Computing, in: *Recommendations of the National Institute of Standards and Technology*, vol. 2, pp. 800–145, Special Pub, USA, 2011, available at csrc.nist.gov/publications/nistpubs/800-145/SP800-145.pdf.

24. Tr, S., As, M., Mh, A., An ad hoc wireless sensor network for telemedicine applications. *Arab. J. Sci. Eng.*, 32, 131–143, 2007.

25. Mueller, C. and Pantos, G., In the Cloud: Healthcare Delivery in the Digital Age. *Benefits Mag.*, 49, 34–36, July, 2012.

26. Vujin, V. and Milenkovic, M.J., Implementation of Cloud Computing in the Healthcare System. *Metalurgia Int.*, XVII, 9, 161–165, 2012.

27. Bowen, J.A., Cloud Computing: Issues in Data Privacy/Security and Commercial Considerations. *Comput. Internet Law* 28, 8, 1–8, 2011.

28. Kavakiotis, I., Tsave, O., Salifoglou, A., *Machine Learning and Data Mining Methods in Diabetics Research*, Elsevier, Jan 8, 2017.

29. Taiwo, O.A., Types of Machine Learning Algorithms, in: *New Advances in Machine Learning*, Y. Zhang (Ed.), pp. 3–31, InTech, University of Portsmouth, United Kingdom, 2010.

30. Kotsiantis, S.B., Supervised Machine Learning: A Review of Classification Techniques. *Informatica*, 31, 249–268, 2007.

31. Rao, S., Rao, N., Kumari, K., Cloud Computing: An overview. *J. Theor. Appl. Inf. Technol.*, 9, l, 71–76, 2009.

32. Lakshminarayan, K., Harp, S., Samad, T., Imputation of Missing Data in Industrial Databases. *Appl. Intell.*, 11, 259–275, 1999.

33. Kotsiantis, S.B., Kanellopoulos, D., Pintelas, P.E., Data Preprocessing for Supervised Leaning, in: *World Academy of Science, Engineering and Technology*, vol. 1, pp. 856–861, 2007.

34. Liu, Y.(Hayden), Python Machine Learning by Example: The Easiest Way to Get into Machine Learning, Book Packt Publishing, 254 pages, May 31, 2017.

35. Haenel, V., Gouillart, E., Varoquaux, G., Python Scientific Lecture Notes, Release 2013.2 beta (euroscipy 2013).

36. Zou, Q., Qu, K., Luo, Y., Yin, D., Ju, Y., Tang, H., Predicting Diabetes Mellitus with Machine Learning Techniques. *Front. Genet.*, 9, 515, 2018.

37. Nkosi, M. and Mekuria, F., Cloud computing for enhanced mobile health applications, in: *2nd International Conference on Cloud Computing Technology and Science (CloudCom)*, Indianapolis, IEEE, USA, NY, 2010.

38. Haufe, K., Dzombeta, S., Brandis, K., Proposal for a security management in cloud computing for healthcare. *Sci. World J.*, 2014, 146970, 2014 Feb 19.

39. Mell, P. and Grance, T., The NIST Definition of Cloud Computing. *Communications of the ACM*, 53, 50, 2010.

14

Investigations on Machine Learning Models to Envisage Coronavirus in Patients

R. Sabitha¹*, J. Shanthini², R.M. Bhavadharini³ and S. Karthik⁴

¹Department of Computer Science and Engineering, Karunya Institute of Technology and Sciences, Coimbatore, India
²Department of Computer Science and Engineering, Dr. NGP Institute of Technology, Coimbatore, India
³Department of Computer Science and Engineering, Easwari Engineering College, Chennai, India
⁴Department of Computer Science and Engineering, SNS College of Technology, Coimbatore, Tamil Nadu,, India

Abstract

The outbreak of the novel coronavirus pandemic (COVID-19) caused severe threats to humankind across the globe. The COVID-19 virus fits to the large family of virus that stimulate illness that may range from common flu to severe diseases like Middle East respiratory syndrome (MERS-CoV) and severe acute respiratory syndrome (SARS-CoV). Hence, the virus affects the mankind variably ranging from mild to moderate and sometimes very severe leading to mortality. The virus is contagious, and necessary prevention and protection mechanism protocols have been strictly adhered by the public to prevent the community spread which has not succeeded. Researchers have investigated that the spread of the severity of spread could be achieved through herd immunity. This pandemic outbreak has affected the globe to a great extent; hence, effective mechanisms are under investigation to diagnose the disease at the initial stages to prevent spread.

Machine learning (ML), a subset of artificial intelligence (AI), provides models that have the ability to inevitably learn and evolve over experience. The ML algorithms are used in diverse applications, its contribution to medical management

*Corresponding author: sabitha@karunya.edu

R. Nidhya, Manish Kumar and S. Balamurugan (eds.) Tele-Healthcare: Applications of Artificial Intelligence and Soft Computing Techniques, (339–358) © 2022 Scrivener Publishing LLC

especially in preventive medicines, medicinal chemistry, imaging, and genetic medicines are inevitable. The sovereign intelligence and capability of ML algorithms make it manifest to use it in the COVID-19–based research. This chapter focusses on usage of ML algorithms to detect the severity of COVID-19 virus in human kind. The model investigates on predicting the severity of risk, risk of infection, and who is at risk of developing a severe case.

The ML algorithms described in this chapter aims at identifying the presence of the disease in a patient. This work analyzes the foreseen of the diseased people from people with minor indications built on 111 impute relating to medical and the clinical examination facts. The diagnostic knowledge entailed attributes, such as age group, gender, body temperature, respiratory proportion, heart rate, and BP. The blood/urine examination data contain information related to various categories of blood examination values and urine examination values. Numerous ML models, such as Naive Bayes, SVM, artificial neural network, k-nearest neighbor (kNN), convolutional neural network (CNN), logistic regression, and decision tree were used in prediction and severity analysis. The experimentation may investigate the effectiveness of the above algorithms for detecting the patients infected with the virus as well as the severity level. Further, this research could be enhanced to provide treatment recommendations in the future.

Keywords: Machine learning, tele-health, SVM, Naive Bayes, neural networks, COVID, k-NN, CNN

14.1   Introduction

Machine learning (ML), a subset of artificial intelligence (AI), provides models that have the ability to inevitably learn and evolve over experience. The ML models has been employed and proved to be powerful in diversified fields. Hence, application of ML becomes essential in COVID-19–based research [1].

Coronavirus (COVID-19) is a virus infection, named severe acute respiratory syndrome-corona virus-2 (SARS-CoV-2), appeared in Wuhan toward the end of 2019 [1, 2]. Because of the pandemic outbreak, COVID-19 has emerged as a deadly disease that threatened human lives and instigated upsetting economic distress that arose since that time. The typical outburst of the novel coronavirus pandemic (COVID-19) instigated severe threats to the human kind across the globe. COVID-19 belongs to a large family of virus that stimulate illness that may range from common flu to severe diseases like Middle East respiratory syndrome (MERS-CoV) and severe acute respiratory syndrome (SARS-CoV). Hence, the virus affects the mankind variably ranging from mild to moderate and sometimes very severe leading to mortality. It is a new strain, which has not been formerly found affecting mankind. The virus is contagious and necessary prevention and protection mechanism protocols have been strictly adhered by the public to prevent the community spread, which has not succeeded. Researchers have investigated that the spread of the severity of spread could be achieved through herd immunity [2, 3]. Around 321 vaccine candidates are in development stage as of October 2020; however, no candidate has accomplished clinical trials to prove its safety and efficacy. This pandemic outbreak has affected the globe to a great extent; hence, effective mechanisms are under investigation to diagnose the disease at the initial stages to prevent spread. Significant volumes of researches have been initiated to analyze and drive deep into finding effective solutions in terms of medical advancements and also with providing decision support/ ML solutions. The ML algorithms have been extensively used in detect the presence of virus from radiology images. Many algorithms are available in literature that have been effective in disease prediction. The main aim of this chapter deals with identifying the severeness of the disease in a patient.

Objective of the Research:

- o Identifying the severity of the disease in a patient
- o Investigate the effectiveness of various algorithms in literature for detecting the patients infected with the virus, as well as the severity level.

14.2   Categories of ML Algorithms in Healthcare

Varieties of ML algorithm are applied in various healthcare applications represented in Figure 14.1. To list a few—support vector machines (SVM), neural networks (NN), random forest (RF), decision tree (DT), and Naïve Bayes (NB). The graph represented in Figure 14.2 showcases the applicability of various ML algorithms in healthcare. It is identified that the major contributors in medical research have employed SVM and NN, the rest algorithms have minimal contribution.

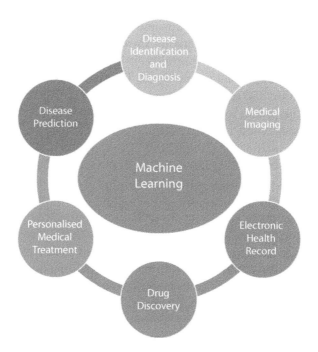

Figure 14.1 Machine learning in medical applications.

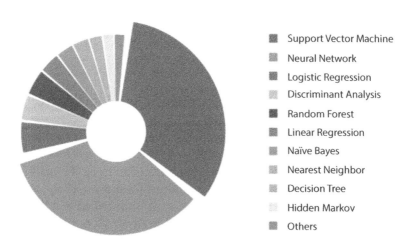

Figure 14.2 Popular ML algorithms in healthcare applications.

14.3   Why ML to Fight COVID-19? Tools and Techniques

Numerous research teams across the globe are contributing to collect data and develop solutions for COVID-19–related diagnosis and treatment. The contribution of research deals in providing few solutions, such as:

- identify severity of disease,
- detect disease in patients,
- advancement in drugs discovery,
- discovering existing drugs,
- prediction of disease,
- comprehend viruses better.

Table 14.1 Methodologies adopted in various applications.

Applicability	Methodology
Identify severity of disease	Predicting the risk of infection Predicting the source of developing a severe case Predicting treatment outcomes
Detect disease in patient	Screening using scans Analysis of radiology reports Employing wearable technology to detect disease AI empowered chatbots for screening and diagnosis
Advancement in drugs discovery & Discovering existing drugs	Forecasting relationships between drugs and proteins Structuring Knowledge graphs
Analyze the source of viruses	Predicting the molecular interaction and folding in virus
Prediction of disease	Employing Social Networks
Analyze the source of viruses	Determining the DNA sequence
Forecast the subsequent pandemic	Employing ML tools and techniques

- analyze the source of viruses, and
- forecast the subsequent pandemic.

Table 14.1 represents the various areas where ML could be applied to fight COVID-19.

Machine Learning is an important means employed to fight against the existing pandemic. This opportunity could be utilized to collect data, identify knowledge, and take meaning action employing the existing skills hence saving many lives—both in the present and in the future [3].

14.4   Highlights of ML Algorithms Under Consideration

As presented in section 14.3, ML has potential applicability not limited to detecting/preventing/analyzing/forecasting. This section presents the overview of various ML algorithms used in this research, such as NB, SVM, artificial neural network (ANN), KNN, CNN, Logistic regression and DT used for prediction and severity analysis.

- ○ **Naïve Bayes**
  Naïve Bayes algorithm is supervised ML algorithm for classification built on Bayes theorem. It is widely used in text classification yet has proven its ability other domains, such as bioinformatics, spam filters, natural language processing, drug testing, and so on. The NB well suits for the input with less or no coordination. Equation 14.1 shows the bayes theorem [4]

$$P\left(\frac{H}{X}\right) = \frac{P\left(\frac{X}{H}\right)P(H)}{P(X)} \tag{14.1}$$

  Consider the H and X are two different events, with P(H) and P(X) as marginal probabilities of those events. P(H/X) is a conditional probability of likelihood of occurrence of event H while event X is true and P(X/H) is vice versa. Now, P(H/X) is a posterior probability of X condition on H. This posterior probability is based on prior probability and information.

The simplicity and speed are the strengths of NB classifier. The zero conditional probability problem and assumption of strong feature independence are major weakness of this algorithm. With the zero conditional probability problem NB classifier lose all the information associated with other probabilities. The assumption of independent features is difficult to implement in real time data.

o **Support Vector Machine**
The SVM [5] is also known as support vector network. It is a supervised learning algorithm based on the statistical learning model. SVM is a nonprobabilistic binary classifier. It is capable of handling both continuous and categorical values. The SVM model uses labeled data to classify them, which makes it fall under supervised learning. However, the unlabeled data can be clustered using support-vector clustering algorithm, created by HavaSiegelmann and Vladimir Vapnik. The SVM has flavors [6], such as linear SVM, nonlinear SVM and Lagrangian SVM. If a data domain can be divided linearly, it is a linear SVM with linear, Equation 14.2

$$y = wx' + \gamma. \tag{14.2}$$

If a data domain cannot be divided linearly and transforms to a feature space in which data domain can be classified in unique classes, then it is called as nonlinear SVM and follows nonlinear, Equation 14.3

$$y = w\phi(x') + \gamma \tag{14.3}$$

The Lagrangian SVM is realized using matrix multiplication and matrix expansion

o **Artificial Neural Network**
Artificial Neural Network [7] is a data-driven model used for nonlinear system. It is capable of capturing complex nonlinear behaviors in input, in specific Feed-Forward multilayer perceptron is frequently used ANN. Artificial Neural Network consists of multiple nodes, which resembles neurons that are interconnected with each other. These connected nods

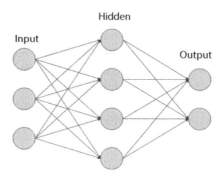

Figure 14.3 Three-layer ANN.

carry weight. Figure 14.3 shows three-layer network. The input layer takes input from the external sources and passes on to the hidden layer or intermediate layer. Each node in the input layer represents a variable in the input source. The input layer will define the conditions upon which the ANN is trained. The nodes in the hidden layers process the input and extract the required features. If we have the linear data and activation function can be placed on input layer, then hidden layer can be eliminated. However, based on the complexity of the problem in hand and the level of accuracy, we need may be three to five hidden layers. Yet, a greater number of neurons may result in overfitting. The output layer presents the end result. The nodes on the output layer represent the types of work ANN is doing. The application of ANN reflects in the number of nodes in the output layer.

- ○ **K-Nearest Neighbor**
  The KNN [8] is the simplest supervised learning algorithm used for both classification and regression problems. However, it works well with nonlinear data and regression problems. The KNN is also known as lazy leaner since when it gets a new data it simply inserts it on the training set, only on the execution, it learns insights of it. The continuous variables use the Euclidean, Manhattan, and Minkowski measures to evaluate the similarity index, whereas categorical variables use Hamming distance, which are given in Equations 14.4, 14.5, 14.6 and 14.7, respectively.

$$\sqrt{\sum_{i=1}^{k}(x_i - y_i)^2} \qquad (14.4)$$

$$\sum_{i-1}^{k} |x_i - y_i| \qquad (14.5)$$

$$\left(\sum_{i=1}^{k} (|x_i - y_i|^q \right)^{1/q} \qquad (14.6)$$

$$D_{H = \sum_{i=i}^{k} |x_i - y_i|} \qquad (14.7)$$

$$x = y \Rightarrow D = 0$$

$$x \neq y \Rightarrow D = 1$$

The KNN is powerful in interpreting the output it is also has simple and ease calculations of K factor compared with other algorithms. The KNN trains itself much faster so it is also called as instance-based learning algorithm. It takes much memory as it stores the entire data set in memory for prediction. When the Euclidean distance is used, it is sensitive to magnitude which makes it inappropriate for large-scale data sets

o **Convolutional Neural Network**
  Convolution neural network is deep learning classification algorithm widely used image classification. Its leaning process in based on chain rule and vector calculation [9]. The CNN has the ability to learn generous layers parallelly with training set. It takes tensors as inputs and passes them through a series layers one after another, namely convolution layer, pooling layer, normalization layer, fully connected layer, loss layer, and so on. The backward error propagation layer is added at last to learn the goodness parameters in CNN. Generally, the end layer is the loss layer used to predict the divergence between the output and the target. There are many functions used to measure the divergence, a simple cost or loss function to calculate the divergence is presented in Equation 14.8.

$$Z = \frac{1}{2} \| t - x^L \|^2 \qquad (14.8)$$

where t is target and x^L is the prediction. A squared l_2 function and cross entropy function are often used in regression and classification problems respectively. The pooling layer makes the summary statistics of the output on certain locations to reduce the output representations and cost. There may be several pooling functions involved, depending on the input and target. The convolution layer takes the features from the input, and the learning parameters are represented as filters. This layer records the relationship between the input point.

- **Logistic Regression**
  The logistic regression [10] is a statistic model uses logistic function for regression problem. It uses the independent variables on input to forecast the dependent variables. The types of logistic regression models include binary logistic regression, multinomial logistic regression, and ordinal logistic regression. In binary logistic regression, there are two categories of dependent variable in, and it has two classes of outcomes. The multinomial models have more than two categories on dependent input and more than two classes as outcome. The outcome L may have two distinct classes: true, false. It uses independent variables of various classes to predict the output. The multinomial linear regression models use log odds ration and iterative maximum likelihood method as fitting function on output. In ordinal model, as the name implies, the independent variable are ranked based on certain sequence.

  o **Decision Tree**
  As the name implies, these algorithms have a tree structure with internal nodes represents attributes of the input data with branches and leaf nodes representing decision rules and outcomes, respectively [11]. These are supervised learning algorithms as the rules are defined. Although used for solving both classification and regression problems, predominantly used in classification problems. It can work on both discrete and continuous variables. The target variable are used to split the tree in to child nodes, the root node may have more than

two bins/classes based on target variable. The input variable decides the degree of purity of the leaf node. The splitting is done till the splitting factor attains the stopping criteria. When the stopping criteria are not optimal, the other way is to allow the tree to grow to its fullest structure and then removing the inappropriate braches, this is called tree pruning. The factors that measure the characteristics of DT are entropy, GINI index, classification error, gain ratio, information gain and towing factor.

14.5   Experimentation and Investigation

The model used to predict the disease is depicted in this section. The model involves various stages as shown in Figure 14.4, the process involves:

1. *Data pre-processing*
The data set used for the study is obtained from Albert Einstein Israelita Hospital located in Saulo Paulo, Brazil. The data set is available in Kaggle for open use. The data set contains details of 5644 patients admitted in the hospital during March 28, 2020, to April 3, 2020. It includes around 111 attributes including blood tests, urine tests, SARS-CoV-2 test, rt-PCR test, influenza A virus's presence to name a few. Among 5644 records, 559 records show the presence of SARS-Cov2 virus infection. The data set has SARS-Cov2 attribute which has string values negative and positive indicating COVID-19 diagnosis cases. The string value "negative" is converted to 0 and "positive" is converted to 1 making it easy for the prediction task.

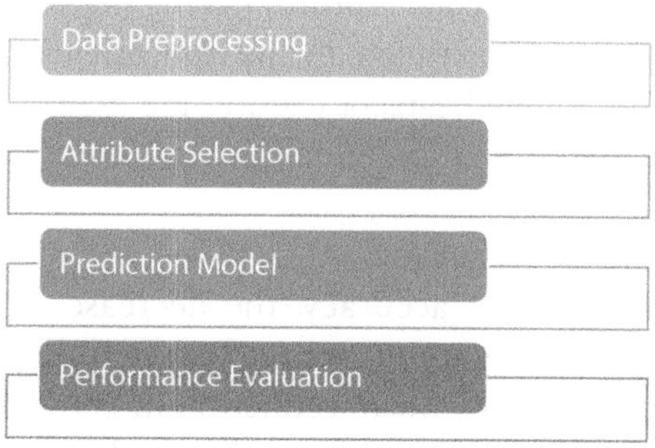

Figure 14.4 Model for prediction.

2. *Attribute Selection*
PCA/LDA
PCA is an unsupervised analysis possibly correlates the attributes into set of values called principal component. In PCA, the n_components values are passed which gives correlated features. PCA is the eigenvector-based multivariate analysis. It is mainly used to reduce the dimensionality of attributes. But it transforms the data set into a new dimensional space without considering the label. Linear Discriminant Analysis (LDA) is used to find a linear combination of features. The LDA explicitly attempts to model the classes of data. In PCA, the principal components separate the classes to some extent; however, in LDA, it takes the different classes [12].

Model-Based Ranking
A classifier is fit to each element and rank the prescient power. This strategy chooses the most dominant features independently and overlooks the prescient power when features consolidated [13].

Univariate Feature Selection
Univariate chooses the best feature by running univariate measurable tests like chi-squared test, F-1 test, and shared data strategies [14].

Recursive Feature Elimination
Recursive feature elimination (RFE) recursively chooses critical subsets of feature dependent on implicit characteristics like coefficients or feature significance of a given estimator. For corresponded feature, it implies that, in general, it computes comparative coefficients. Features having negative coefficients do not contribute that much. In any case, an increasingly intricate situation where heaps of features are managed, this score will help in determination of definitive element [15].

Mean Decrease Accuracy
For mean reduction accuracy, the decrease in precision is measured. Rearranging is a critical element that results in a drop in accuracy. The mean reduction in Gini coefficient is a proportion of how every factor adds to the homogeneity of the nodes in random forest [16].

The highly ranked features which contributes to the prediction and severity analysis has been selected using the various algorithm discussed above are shown in Table 14.2.

3. Applying prediction model

Classification entails assigning the class label to a set of unclassified classes. The set of likely classes used for training is known in advance. The input data, also called the training set, consist of records each having multiple attributes or features (the selected attributes account to 18 features). Every record in the data set is tagged with a class label which represents 0 for negative cases and 1 for positive cases.

The objective of the classification model is to analyze the input data and to develop an accurate description or model for each class using the features present in the data. Various models are used to classify test data for which the class descriptions are not known. Various ML algorithms are analyzed in this research which are trained and tested for its performance. Figure 14.5 showcases the flowchart representing the step-by-step process of the prediction model. The data set that has been preprocessed and reformed in the previous phases is now split into training and testing sets for enhancing the learning process. The existing prediction model are trained using the COVID data set, the trained model is then tested using the test data set and measured for its performance.

4. Performance evaluation

The effectiveness of various prediction models when trained with COVID data set is measured for various parameters such as:

Table 14.2 List of highly ranked attributes.

Platelets	Leukocytes	Basophils
Lymphocytes	Haemoglobin	Monocytes
Eosinophils	Neutrophils	Age
Urea	C reactive Protein	Creatinine
Potassium	Alanine transaminase	Sodium
Prothrombin time	Aspartate transaminase	Albumin

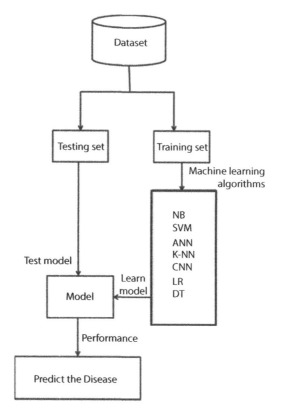

Figure 14.5 Flowchart of prediction model.

- Accuracy—it is the measure of accurately predicted results. It is the ratio of the sum of correctly predicted records to the total number of records.

Accuracy = ((TP+TN)/(TP+TN+FP+FN)) * 100

- Specificity—it measures the proportion of negatives which are correctly identified as such (e.g., the percentage of healthy people who are correctly identified as not having the condition). These two measures are closely related to the concepts of type I and type II errors.

Specificity = TN/(TN + FP)

- Precision—it is calculated based on the retrieval of information at true-positive prediction, false-positive. In healthcare, data precision is calculated as the percentage of positive results returned that are relevant.

Precision = TP/(TP + FP)

- Sensitivity—it measures the proportion of actual positives which are correctly identified as such (e.g., the percentage of sick people who are correctly identified as having the condition).

Sensitivity = TP/(TP + FN)

where TP is true positive; TN, true negative; FP, false positive; FN, false negative.

14.6   Comparative Analysis of the Algorithms

The various prediction models were trained and tested for the COVID data set for the parameters specified in the previous section. The results are elaborated in Table 14.3 and Figure 14.6.

The performance of the model for individual parameters, such as accuracy, specificity, precision, and sensitivity, are shown in separate graphs from Figures 14.7 to 14.10. From the results it is identified that ANN is high in accuracy, specificity and precision, CNN has high value for sensitivity.

Table 14.3 Comparison on various parameters.

Parameter	Model						
	NB	KNN	CNN	ANN	SVM	LR	DT
Accuracy	95.83	96.73	97.02	97.22	97.12	96.73	95.83
Specificity	96.93	97.13	97.15	97.47	97.12	97.13	96.93
Precision	95.83	96.73	97.02	97.32	97.15	96.73	95.83
Sensitivity	95.95	97.3	98.2	97.97	97.97	97.3	95.95

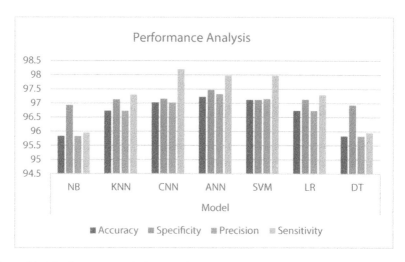

Figure 14.6 Performance analysis on various parameters.

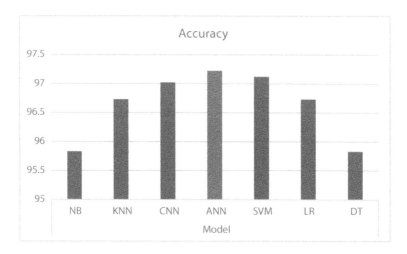

Figure 14.7 Accuracy of various models.

14.7 Scope of Enhancement for Better Investigation

Envisaging COVID-19 virus in humans is perilous for appropriate involvement and inhibition of the spread of the pandemic. Current findings have exposed the usage of clinical test results for diagnosing the virus spread in patients. In this chapter, we have employed prediction models to identify the disease. The ML algorithms described in this chapter aims at identifying the presence of the disease in a patient. This research examined the

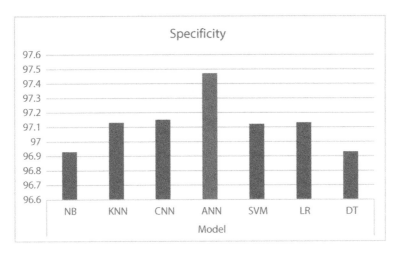

Figure 14.8 Specificity of various models.

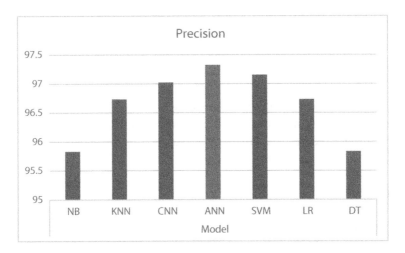

Figure 14.9 Precision of various models.

envisaging of infected persons from those with minor indications built on 111 impute relating to medical and the clinical examination facts. The diagnostic knowledge entailed attributes such as age group, gender, body temperature, respiratory proportion, heart rate, and BP. The clinical examination facts contain information about various categories of values related to blood and urine test. Attribute selection methods are employed where 18 highly ranked attributes were identified, which will majorly be contributing to the prediction process. Various ML algorithms, such as NB, SVM,

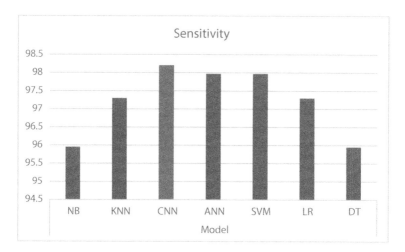

Figure 14.10 Sensitivity of various models.

ANN, KNN, CNN, logistic regression, and DT was used for prediction and severity analyses. The experimentation may investigate the effectiveness of the above algorithms for severeness detection model of the patients with COVID-19. From the results, it was identified that ANN is best when compared with other models in terms of accuracy, specificity, and precision. Further, this research could be enhanced with features that would identify the level of severity in patients and, moreover, could be enhanced to provide treatment recommendations in the future.

References

1. Arnold, D.T., Attwood, M., Barratt, S., Elvers, K., Morley, A., McKernon, J., Oates, A., Donald, C., Noel, A., MacGowan, A. *et al.*, *Blood parameters measured on admission as predictors of outcome for covid-19; a prospective UK cohort study*, 2020, medRxiv URL https://doi.org/10.1101/2020.06.25.20137 935.

2. Banerjee, A., Ray, S., Vorselaars, B., Kitson, J., Mamalakis, M., Weeks, S., Mackenzie, L.S., Use of machine learning and artificial intelligence to predict sars-cov-2 infection from full blood counts in a population. *Int. Immunopharmacol.*, 86, 106705, 2020.

3. Bayat, V., Phelps, S., Ryono, R., Lee, C., Parekh, H., Mewton, J., Sedghi, F., Etminani, P., Holodniy, M., A covid-19 prediction model from standard laboratory tests and vital signs. *SSRN Electronic Journal*, 2020.

4. Han, J., Kamber, M., Pei, J., *Data Mining: Concepts and Techniques*, 3rd Edition, The Morgan Kaufmann Series. Morgan Kaufmann Publishers, 2011.

5. Suthaharan, S., Support Vector Machine, in: *Machine Learning Models and Algorithms for Big Data Classification. Integrated Series in Information Systems*, vol. 36, Springer, Boston, MA, 2016, https://doi.org/10.1007/978-1-4899-7641-3_9.

6. Hearst, M.A., Dumais, S.T., Osuna, E., Platt, J., Scholkopf, B., Support vector machines. *IEEE Intell. Syst. their Appl.*, 13, 4, 18–28, July-Aug. 1998.

7. Walczak, S. and Cerpa, N., Artificial Neural Networks, in: *Encyclopedia of Physical Science and Technology*, Third Edition, pp. 631–645, Academic Press, 2003.

8. Laaksonen, J. and Oja, E., Classification with learning k-nearest neighbors. *Proceedings of International Conference on Neural Networks (ICNN'96)*, Washington, DC, USA, vol. 3, pp. 1480–1483, 1996.

9. Wu, J., *Introduction to convolutional neural networks.* vol. 5, p. 23, National Key Lab for Novel Software Technology, Nanjing University, China, 2017.

10. Wright, R.E., *Logistic regression.* American Psychological Association, APA Dictionary of Psychology, Logistic, 1995.

11. Song, Y.-Y. and Ying, L., Decision tree methods: applications for classification and prediction. *Shanghai Arch. Psychiatry*, 27, 2, 130–5, 2015.

12. Mulatu, D. and Gangarde, R.R., Survey of Data Mining Techniques for Prediction of Breast Cancer Recurrence. *(IJCSIT) Int. J. Comput. Sci. Inf. Technol.*, 8, 6, 599–601, 2017.

13. Tirunagari, S., Poh, N., Abdulrahman, H., Nemmour, N., Windridge, D., titled Breast Cancer Data Analytics With Missing Values: A study on Ethnic, Age and Income Groups, White paper submitted to Quantitative Methods Subject in CORNELL University, 12 Mar 2015.

14. Kibis, E.Y., Büyüktahtakın, PhD., İ. E., Dag, PhD., A., titled Data Analytics Approaches for Breast Cancer Survivability: Comparison of Data Mining Methods. *Proceedings of the 2017 Industrial and Systems Engineering Conference.*

15. Sheoran, Dr. S. K., titled Breast Cancer Classification Using Big Data Approach. *Paripex - Indian J. Res.*, 7, 1, 20–22, January-2018.

16. Verma, D., *Analysis and Prediction of Breast cancer and Diabetes disease data sets using Data mining classification Techniques*, 2017.

15

Healthcare Informatics: Emerging Trends, Challenges, and Analysis of Medical Imaging

G. Karthick[1*] and N.S. Nithya[2]

[1]Department of Electronics and Communication Engineering, Jyothismathi Institute of Technology and Science, Karimnagar, India
[2]Department of Computer Science and Engineering, K.S.R. College of Engineering, Tiruchengode, India

Abstract

Medical data are the information containing multiple observations of the patient. This information helps a physician to understand, diagnose and treat about patient's problem. Descriptive information about the patient is very important to healthcare environment. The type of medical data includes descriptive data, qualitative data to quantitative measurements, recorded signals (ECG, EMG like that) drawings, and photographs. Physicians are the solely responsible person for collecting and interpreting the medical data. Nurses also play an important role for collecting the medical data through continuous observation and recoding of the patient data. Technological devices like laboratory instruments, imaging equipments, monitoring devices in intensive care units, and measurement devices supports recoding and observing the storing the medical data. Whether the medical data are recorded in the format of electronic storage or reported paper, it is very useful for aggregating and analyzing the patient data. Historical data of individual patient are very much important for clinical research. Medical recording is not only an observation or storage but also acts as a communication medium between physicians and other medical people involved in observing and recoding the patient data. Recorded high standard medical data are a preventive measure of serious disorders from people in high-risk future. It also provides a legal record for court in case of any improper treatment by the hospital. However, there will be a lot of issues and challenges in recording and storing this biomedical data. We are in need of separate standard

Corresponding author: karthick.sgs@gmail.com

R. Nidhya, Manish Kumar and S. Balamurugan (eds.) Tele-Healthcare: Applications of Artificial Intelligence and Soft Computing Techniques, (359–382) © 2022 Scrivener Publishing LLC

measurement system for storing and retrieving the medical data for accurate diagnosis. Now, there will be a lot of modern technologies developed for measurement of healthcare informatics. This chapter aims to provide information about current trends, challenges, and issues in healthcare informatics and analyzing the performance of various compression techniques in medical image.

Keywords: Healthcare, intelligent healthcare devices, IoT, cyber threats in healthcare, medical image, image processing, wavelet transform, wavelet compression

15.1   Emerging Trends and Challenges in Healthcare Informatics

15.1.1   Advanced Technologies in Healthcare Informatics

Healthcare informatics is an information system that contains data, communications, and medical care, which are completely changing the healthcare industry today, as most of the medical institutions become reliable with this technology. This technology is also used to improve patient yielding with tools that give remote recording of health issues, and medical equipments are just a practice of mobile tool companies that are operating on applications for interaction between doctors and patients in the current world. The rapid growth of Internet and the fast widen of information through mobile devices have offered new openings in the field of healthcare informatics. The use of mobile devices for patient healthcare is now increased today in the world which requires lot of mobile apps are facilitating patients to easily handle their health, speak with healthcare persons, schedule appointments, and access healthcare information. The smart watch and Fit bit are the most used wearable device in the modern technology, which is used to monitor data, such as heart rate and calories. As the growth of the wearable technology expands, developers are looking for advanced technology for further improvement of monitoring fitness and activity levels of patient healthcare.

Healthcare informatics can produce large amounts of data in different formats, and there is a need for latest techniques and developments in the field of big data analytics, cloud computing, Internet of Things (IoT), image processing, machine learning, and so on. The IoT and machine learning concepts are slowly permeating all the aspects of healthcare system. Intelligence is needed for smart healthcare technologies using IoT. Deep learning (DL) is a subset of machine learning process based on intelligent data learning and methodologies. Deep learning solves problem that were unsolvable with machine learning in the field of healthcare informatics and technology.

Applying DL techniques to IoT with large volume of medical data capable of performing complex predicting modeling and other advanced analytics process for diagnosing diseases in healthcare information system and technology. There is a need of secure privacy to preserve this large volume of medical information, which is very important.

Achieving the best level of security and privacy for data in healthcare system is very important, and it requires suggestions, solutions, demonstrations, and best practices for all forms of security and privacy for healthcare system in the world today. There is a need for latest developments and innovative research results in healthcare informatics and technology. The various emerging trends will be very helpful to the researchers, industrial persons, students, and academic persons in the field of healthcare informatics.

15.1.2   Intelligent Smart Healthcare Devices Using IoT With DL

The IoT and artificial intelligence is going to change the world today. Internet of Things and machine learning concepts in artificial intelligence are slowly permeating all the aspects of our lives. Intelligence is needed for all the devices generated by IoT. There is an interaction between intelligence and IoT. Machine learning concepts make intelligent to devices generated by IoT. Deep learning is a subset of machine learning method based on intelligent data acquiring and techniques. Deep learning solves problems that were unsolvable with machine learning. Deep learning in the medical field supports doctors in analyzing any disease accurately and treat them better, thus resulting in efficient medical decisions. The IoT in the medical field is used to sense, convert, and store data, and DL is used to operate on that data to get absolute information and gain better outcomes. Thus, IoT is called Internet of Medical Things (IoMT) in the healthcare industry. Deep learning merged with IoT in healthcare can be used to help workers in the field of medical field, laboratory persons, and researchers who belong to the healthcare industry. From the evaluation of performance results and large applications, DL has the ability to develop the healthcare in future.

The IoT with DL enhances a regular hospital, turned it into a smart hospital. Deep learning uses the neural networks to improve the computational work and give accurate results. Adding deep neural networks to IoT devices can give about a generation of medical devices able to perform difficult sensing and recognition tasks to identify and detect the disease of the human body accurately. There are lot of advantages behind using IoT with DL in medical field, such as minimization of cost, better and passive treatment, faster disease diagnosis, drugs and equipment management, and errorless data. There will be a lot of challenges and opportunities in the field of healthcare using IoT with DL. Volume of data handled, semisupervised learning, crowd sensing of data, need of advanced model (eliminate the outdated infrastructure), transfer learning, security and privacy issues are the challenges and opportunities in the field of DL with IoT healthcare systems. These challenges and opportunities are very much useful for researchers in this research area. There is a need for upgrading their knowledge and enhancing their technical skills in this research area.

15.1.3   Cyber Security in Healthcare Informatics

Securing the medical data from data breaches is a big challenge in the healthcare industry. The total numbers of breached records and selling of records are increased year by year. Still, a number of healthcare industries are struggling to prevent these issues, and also, efforts for protecting the medical data can be costly and time consuming. Digitalized medical records and continuous increase of telehealth tools have made a risk for easily accessing patient data. The fast growth of the Internet and the fast reach of information through mobile devices have given new inventions that results some healthcare data to be at risk, so it is crucial to be cautious of these dangers. Most of the medical devices are now connected to the Internet, medical place networks, and other medical equipments to give features that enhance healthcare industry and improve the ability of clinicians to treat patients. This will increase the risk of potential cyber security threats and dangerous to security leagues, making an important impact on the safety and effectiveness of the device.

Cyber security is the most significant risk factor for healthcare industry because threats and vulnerabilities cannot be eliminated. To manage the cyber security risk is a very complex one in the heath care environment. If the researchers in the cyber security person incorporate with manufacturers and hospitals of the healthcare industry, then only the healthcare industry will be protected from cyber security risks. A lot of researches have been made to prevent these cyber security risks. Still, there is an accurate and permanent solution needed for this cyber security risk. The research is also in compliance with the Health Insurance Portability and Accountability Act (HIPAA) to make an efficient solution for this cyber security issues in the healthcare industry.

Now Covid-19 has also made number of people working remotely and increasing the use of telehealth tools for virtual care. Cyber security researchers in healthcare industries are now potentially competing with Covid-19 compounding the cyber security risks in healthcare. There is a need to educate and enhance the knowledge of researchers, academician and healthcare industry persons in the area of latest technologies and approaches for handling cyber security threats internally and externally in healthcare informatics.

15.1.4 Trends, Challenges, and Issues in Healthcare IT Analytics

Healthcare data analytics is very important for healthcare industry to make decision in the patient report. Advanced technology has very much changed the entire healthcare industry. Operating a healthcare industry is becoming a complex for improving the operational processes and maintains the hospital management system. Healthcare data analytics is a process that is used to systematically analyze the patient data and supports healthcare professionals to improve the quality of diagnosis, services, and existing methods. Healthcare data analytics method merges the real-time data with historical data for predicting the recent patient problems and develops long-term growth. Healthcare IT analytics is a multistage process. The healthcare analytics analyzes patients' data to discover accurate result and propose treatment accordingly. A lot of innovative ideas, solutions, and treatments have been found by research and development in the area of healthcare analytics.

Artificial intelligence technique analyzes clinical data and produce patient record with highest prediction efficiency. Customized medications and real-time treatment errors can be monitored by AI rigid analytics. Cloud-based technologies play an important role for analyzing the big data involved in the medical field. Analyzing patient data can be enhanced by healthcare IT analytics system based on cloud, which has the greater compatibility with Internet because all healthcare data are Internet-based. Collaborating intelligence with IoT is needed for healthcare analytics to improve the quality of diagnosis. The major factor to combine the intelligence with IoT is health monitoring by using biosensors and wearable devices. There will be a lot of technologies increasingly in the healthcare analytics nowadays. These new innovations and solutions in healthcare analytics are very useful for growing research scholars, academicians, and healthcare industry persons in the field of healthcare.

15.2 Performance Analysis of Medical Image Compression Using Wavelet Functions

Nowadays, the significant challenges are the usage of storage space and bandwidth optimally. To deplete the storage space of images and to transmit the information with minimum bandwidth, image compression plays a prominent role by decreasing the memory size of image and to employ the bandwidth reasonably without diminishing the quality of image. In this paper, the performance analysis of various wavelet basis functions for compression of medical images using wavelet functions, like the Haar, Daubenchies (db), biorthogonal (bior), reverse biorthogonal (rbior), symlets, coiflets (coif), discrete Meyer (dmey), and Fejer Korokin (fk) wavelets, are analyzed with various compression techniques. Here, the performance parameters are analyzed using metrics peak signal to noise ratio (PSNR), mean square error (MSE). The acquired results prove that Haar wavelet basis function with embedded zero-tree wave (EZW) compression technique contribute good PSNR value compared with set partitioning in hierarchical trees (SPIHT), ASWDR, LVL_MMC, GBL_MMC_F compression techniques.

15.2.1 Introduction

Generally, signals will be in time domain but frequency becomes a criterion to process the signals easily. Originally, the images contain more information, which allows more storage space, massive transmission bandwidths, and lasting amount of transmission times. The main aim of image compression is to reduce the size of original image or to decline the storage space by maintaining the quality of the image even after compression. Image compression is generally classified into two types: lossless compression and lossy compression. Lossless compression in images can be reconstructed without changing the intensity values. Lossy compression is used to compress the image and then reconstruct the original image exactly from the compressed image. From this lossy compression, we can bring out the steadiness in compression ratios and image quality.

The discrete wavelet transform has more advantages compared with that of discrete cosine transform. The DWT can perform multiresolution of the signal in spatial domain, as well as frequency domain. The wavelet function uses nonperiodic, nonsmooth, and finite support wavelet basis functions, such as Haar, db, bior, rbior, Symlets wavelets, coif wavelets, dmey, fk wavelets [3]. In this, the performance analysis of different wavelet functions and different sizes of image resolution and compression for a given input image by performing wavelet functions on images and implementing an compression technique is studied. The important aspect of this wavelet functions in compression of images consists of the quality of image by wavelet functions, decompression and calculates the performance in the form of image quality metrics PSNR, MSE, and compression ratios at different decompositions of discrete wavelet transforms [4].

The Figure 15.1 represents the compression of image by different wavelet techniques. In medical images, such as MRI, CT, X-RAY, ultrasonics, are taken as input images. The inputs are given to DWT, where the images get decomposed into high-frequency (HF) and low-frequency (LF) components, and the output of DWT is further given to wavelet basis functions, like Haar, db, bior, rbior, symlets, coif, dmey, Fk wavelets. After that by selecting different compression techniques, like EZW, SPIHT, ASWDR, LVL_MMC, GBL_MMC_F, the compression of image takes place [13]. Then the inverse discrete transform is done and the output of this stage is

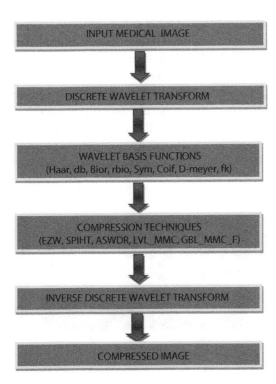

Figure 15.1 Overview for compression of medical image by different wavelet techniques.

the compressed image. Finally, image quality is analyzed between the input image and output image.

15.2.2   Materials and Methods

Here, various types of medical images such as MRI, CT, X-RAY, ULTRASONIC images are collected from various online and offline resources and sample medical input images presents in Figure 15.2. Medical image databases are collected from the following website 1. Medical Image Databases— NCBI—NIH www.ncbi.nlm.nih.gov 2. Datasets-OpenfMRIopenfmri.org 3. sfikas/medical-imaging-datasets: A list of Medical ... - GitHubgithub. com › sfikas › medical-imaging-datasets. Medical images taken for analysis are 168 images (220 MRI images, 40 CT images, 25 X-ray images, and 22 Ultrasonic performance and effectiveness of algorithm are justified over the real images. The results demonstrate the high-compression ratios compared to other techniques [6]. Nedhal Mohammad Al-Shereefi [1] has proposed to develop efficient and effective algorithms for lossy image compression using wavelet techniques. Here, 2d-db wavelet transformation method for the image compression is used which results in 15.03 compression ratio and 43.20 PSNR value for commercial images. The medical images provide 6.85 compression ratio and 32.28 PSNR value [1].

Raid *et al.* [15] presented the use of wavelet-based image compression algorithm EZW. It is a very efficient algorithm for image compression. The sequential encoding may be a general possibility for reducing wavelet converted images because of the details is aimed on higher subbands only. These results give excellent performance to the zero-tree coders. It has been observed that EZW is fast, robust, and economical enough to implement

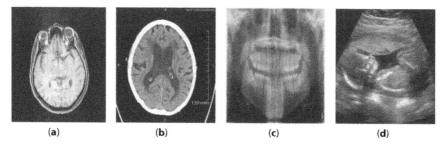

Figure 15.2 Sample input images (a) MRI image, (b) CT image, (c) X-RAY image, (d) ultrasonic image.

it in still and tedious images with certain image compression [15]. Mridul Kumar Mathur [14] has proposed the paper to represent image compression technique. The wavelet transform provides image compression so that it occupies less memory. In this, the data storage capacity and bandwidth are reduced and rate of compression is increased to compress the image. Rasika and Khatke [5] have proposed a paper that contemplates about the digital images that has more memory and storage which takes considerable amount of time to download from Internet. In this, the implementation of wavelet transform and applications are discussed which provide low data storage capacity, band width, and high rate of compression.

15.2.3   Wavelet Basis Functions

Wavelet basis functions are the efficient mathematical tools which are used for the compression of image. According to the scale and resolution of image, these functions are used to analyze and synthesize 1-D, 2-D applications [2]. These are localized in time domain and frequency domain such that they have more advantages compared with that of Fourier transform functions. Wavelet compression methods fabricate higher level of subjective and objective results. Also, wavelet consists of both higher- and lower-frequency functions, which are used to decompose the image. These are analyzed based on wavelet basis functions known as mother wavelets.

Wavelets are then divided into two types denoted as orthogonal wavelets and bior wavelet. Orthogonal wavelets produce nonredundancy representation and symmetry characteristics that produce linear phase. Biorthogonal wavelet produces invertible wavelet transform. The wavelets produce efficient output but computationally more complex as well as expensive.

15.2.3.1   Haar Wavelet

Haar sequence was presented by Alfred Haar in the year 1909, which is used in compression of images effectively. Haar wavelets are the sequence of square-shaped functions, which are grouped together to form a wavelet family or basis. The Haar wavelets are the simple form of wavelets. These functions are recognized as the first known wavelet basis, which are used to compress the images.

Benefits of Haar wavelets are very quick, lower complexity, efficient memory and simple [9]. The Haar wavelet's mother wavelet function $\psi(t)$ is represented as

$$\psi(t)=\begin{cases} 1 & 0\le t\le \dfrac{1}{2} \\ -1 & \dfrac{1}{2}\le t\le 1 \\ 0 & otherwise \end{cases} \tag{15.1}$$

The Haar wavelet function with its scaling function can be expressed as

$$\varphi(x)=\begin{cases} 1, & f\ 0\le x<1 \\ 0, & otherwise \end{cases} \tag{15.2}$$

15.2.3.2   db Wavelet

The db wavelets, based on Ingrid Daubechies, defines a discrete wavelet transform and described by a maximum number of vanishing moments for given support. The db is same with that of Haar wavelet, which is simple and imaginable. The amount of time for db is expanding with the only exception of db10. The greatest PSNR value for decomposition is db25. All other wavelets are then compared as there will not be any variation in the performance. For SPIHT compression model, the result obtained will be the same but the PSNR value is db10, which is meant to be the highest. Considering the obtained results, db10, db25 are recommended to give the good results.

15.2.3.3   bior Wavelet

A bior wavelet is that form of a wavelet in which the associated transform is inverting but it is not required to be orthogonal. Biorthogonal wavelets are symmetric and compact. It gives flexibility for designing bior wavelets than orthogonal wavelets. The symmetry of the filter coefficients will be desirable as it results in linear phase of the transfer function [11]. The amount of time for bior wavelet decomposition and reconstruction will not be linear.

15.2.3.4   rbio Wavelet

The rbio wavelets are derived from the vibration data and are proved using support vector machine classifier. This rbio wavelet was diminishing instant on decomposition for analysis and for the reconstruction of synthesis [12].

15.2.3.5   Symlets Wavelet

Symlet deals with the symmetric property. These are developed gradually from db to achieve integrity in symmetry and simplicity, which will be obtained by reprocessing the function. The amount of time for decomposition and reconstruction of wavelet increases, as we move up. The perfect PSNR for decomposition is obtained and therefore these wavelets are recommended for the compression of images. As we move up further beyond SPIHT, we have Sym10 and Sym25.

15.2.3.6   coif Wavelet

The coif wavelets are the discrete wavelets planed by Ingrid Daubechies, by the appeal of Ronald Coifman, to have scaling functionalities with the disappearing moments. These wavelets are used in many applications. The wavelet function has 2N moments equal to 0 and the scaling function has 2N-1 moments equal to Zero [10]. It has higher levels of computations. In order to increase pixel averaging and differencing these wavelets are used since they show a smoother wavelet and enlarging capacity in many image processing methods. The coif wavelet follows the mirror method.

15.2.3.7   dmey Wavelet

The dmey wavelet is the orthogonal wavelet suggested by Yves Meyer. As in case of the continuous wavelets, they can be applied in adaptive filters, fractal random fields and multifault classification. It is based on symmetric, orthogonal and bior [12]. The dmey wavelets give very good PSNR value. It also has the ability to give better results in the quality of image by compression.

15.2.3.8   fk Wavelet

Fejer-Korovkin wavelet (fk) filter is used for high frequency (HF) component of intra-annual periodicity and a low frequency (LF) component of inter-annual periodicity to extract.FK-MIMO-AR is evaluated by comparing the prediction of MIMO-AR with db wavelet filter. It results in efficiency and coefficient of determination for 15 months ahead that catches forecasting.

15.2.4   Compression Methods

15.2.4.1   *Embedded Zero-Trees of Wavelet Transform*

Embedded zero-trees of wavelet transforms is one of the irreversible method of image compression method. At low bit rate values and high compression ratios many coefficients are generated by a sub band conversion also known as the wavelet transform and the value will be zero or nearest to zero. It takes place because "real world" images contain minimum-frequency information, which is highly correlated. However, the HF information is given highest priority in terms of human view based on the worth of image and form in any high superior coding scheme.

15.2.4.2   *Set Partitioning in Hierarchical Trees*

Set partitioning in hierarchical trees is a powerful wavelet-based image compression method. This is an award-winning method to receive worldwide acclaim and attention from 1995. Many persons, researchers, and users have tested and used SPIHT. It has become the point of reference for state-of-the-art algorithm for image compression. Bit plane sequence method is used for single bit of the image wavelet conversion coefficients in SPIHT codes. So, it has the capability to improve the image properly by coding all the bits of the function [8]. Therefore, the wavelet transform generates the accurate reformation only if their numbers are saved as nonfinite-exact numbers. Practically, it is able to reform the image using rounding after getting original, but is not the systematic method.

15.2.4.3   *Adaptively Scanned Wavelet Difference Reduction*

The adaptively scanned wavelet difference reduction (ASWDR) algorithm of Walker is the most recently used image compression method. The adaptively scanned wavelet determines that this algorithm alters the scanning order which is used to achieve relatively best performance. It is simple deducement of the compression method developed by wavelet difference reduction (WDR). The WDR method manipulates a fixed ordering of the positions of wavelet coefficients, whereas the ASWDR method manipulates a varying order, which has the intention to modify itself to specific image attributes. The ASWDR algorithm has the objective to improve the subjective view aspects of compressed images and raise the decision of intensive measures.

15.2.4.4 Coefficient Thresholding

LVL_MMC: Subband thresholding of coefficients and Huffman Coding
This approach combines several improvements including the quantization of the subband signal samples with low resolution and entropy-coding by means of Huffman coder. As an outcome, the algorithm achieves much better than other methods developed using related techniques.

GBL_MMC_F: Global thresholding of coefficients and fixed encoding
Global thresholding is used to set intensity threshold value such that all pixels having intensity value below the threshold belong to one group and not belongs to the other group. As the boundaries between characters are easily determined in the fixed-length encoding technique, such as ASCII, is used. Fixed length encoding uses the same number of bits for each symbol and k-bit code supports 2k different symbols [7].

15.3 Results and Discussion

The performance analysis of various wavelet basis methods are evaluated based on the following quality measures which reported by Avicibas *et al.* [15], Mrak *et al.* [16], and Eskicioglu *et al.* [17] were taken.

15.3.1 Mean Square Error

The repeatedly used objective to measure the quality of a compressed output image is MSE [18, 19]. If the value of MSE is low, it implies that lesser number of errors are being encountered MSE is defined as:

$$MSE = \frac{1}{m,n}\Sigma(X_{ij} - Y_{ij})\Sigma(X_{ij} - Y_{ij}) \qquad (15.3)$$

15.3.2 Peak Signal to Noise Ratio

Peak signal to noise ratio is used to identify the quality of the image. If the PSNR value is high, the quality of the image will be high [20, 21]. The PSNR is defined as:

$$PSNR = 10\log\frac{255*255}{MSE}dB \qquad (15.4)$$

Here, in this paper, Haar wavelet, db wavelet, bior, rbior, symlets, coif, dmey, Fk wavelets for the medical images are used. Figure 15.3 represents the compression of MRI image using various wavelet basis functions. Table 15.1 represents the performance analysis of wavelet basis functions with different compression techniques and it shows that coif wavelet basis function with EZW compression technique provides necessarily higher PSNR value of 35.26 and lesser MSE value of 13.892 for MRI images. Table 15.2 explicitly shows the performance analysis of wavelet basis functions with different compression techniques, and it shows that Haar wavelet basis function with EZW compression technique provides higher PSNR value of 35.99 and lesser MSE value of 17.197 for CT images. Table 15.3 determines the performance

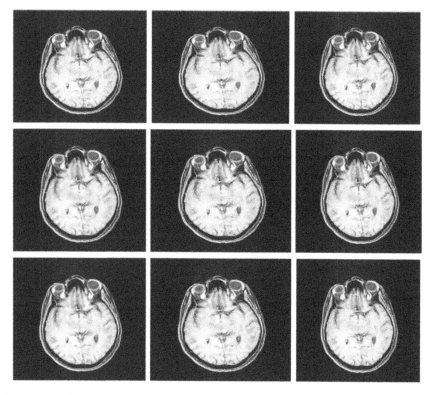

Figure 15.3 Compression of MRI image using various wavelet basis functions. (Original image (1st row left), compressed images of Haar, db, bior, rbior, Symlets, coif, dmey, Fk wavelets are placed in the 1st row middle, 1st row right, 2nd row left, 2nd row middle, 2nd row right, 3rd row left, 3rd row middle, 3rd row right respectively).

Table 15.1 Performance analysis of MRI image compression using wavelet basis functions.

Wavelet functions	EZW		SPIHT		ASWDR		LVL_MMC		GBL_MMC_F	
	MSE	PSNR	MSE	PSNR	MSE	PSNR	MSE	PSNR	MSE	PSNR
Haar	14.634	34.6	67.932	29.984	19.18	33.788	281.62	22.526	215.18	25.084
db	14.054	35.226	60.83	30.792	17.344	34.372	233.16	23.506	212.2	26.11
bior	14.794	35.032	62.826	30.63	17.966	34.322	208.7	24.334	190.41	27.224
rbio	14.192	35.12	56.764	30.874	16.89	34.564	239.47	24.27	265.56	25.988
Symlets	13.996	35.2	59.34	30.864	16.906	34.466	178.24	25.662	225.07	26.78
coif	13.892	35.26	59.206	30.862	16.898	34.386	164.08	24.55	218.79	24.858
dmey	14.358	35.118	62.268	30.72	17.33	34.282	196.31	24.01	229.32	26.714
fk	13.936	35.106	61.992	30.418	17.638	34.078	193	23.922	171.74	25.044

Table 15.2 Performance analysis of CT image compression using wavelet basis functions.

Wavelet functions	EZW		SPIHT		ASWDR		LVL_MMC		GBL_MMC_F	
	MSE	PSNR	MSE	PSNR	MSE	PSNR	MSE	PSNR	MSE	PSNR
Haar	17.197	35.99	28.24	32.573	22.91	34.67	253.61	26.07	132.29	27.04
db	53.61	35.67	45.96	32.15	28.78	34.623	197.24	26.913	96.7	28.47
bior	80.513	32.33	73.106	34.683	38.216	33.006	111.16	28.64	83.96	29.04
rbio	34.033	33.633	68.13	30.95	36.96	33.14	191.15	26.17	87.69	25.436
Symlets	32.16	33.906	69.38	31.276	36	33.296	248.86	27.62	81.63	25.96
coif	53.62	32.276	71.03	31.21	36.886	33.183	164.05	26.95	99.17	28.835
dmey	35.5	33.476	76.87	30.57	39.626	32.903	150.18	27.226	114	27.79
fk	32.97	33.79	72.3	30.79	37.193	33.12	169.88	27.16	108.26	28.343

Table 15.3 Performance analysis of X-RAY image compression using wavelet basis functions.

Wavelet functions	EZW		SPIHT		ASWDR		LVL_MMC		GBL_MMC_F	
	MSE	PSNR	MSE	PSNR	MSE	PSNR	MSE	PSNR	MSE	PSNR
Haar	47.136	31.24	102.81	28.45	51.458	31.038	74.666	29.544	90.19	29.504
db	30.036	33.406	70.568	30.11	33.442	32.928	31.996	33.358	45.566	31.74
bior	30.534	33.322	73.898	29.896	34.006	32.838	30.77	33.324	40.302	32.216
rbio	30.718	33.296	67.028	30.238	32.598	33.004	39.626	32.568	54.334	33.168
Symlets	29.586	33.464	69.598	30.182	32.742	33.028	32.502	33.258	44.152	31.818
coif	28.232	33.656	67.864	30.304	31.004	33.256	30.256	33.61	42.528	32.01
dmey	28.776	33.58	70.504	30.122	32.102	33.11	28.278	33.956	45.628	31.712
fk	42.474	33.872	94.2	28.776	46.502	31.478	66.096	30.064	75.678	29.434

Table 15.4 Performance analysis of ULTRASONIC image compression using wavelet basis functions.

Wavelet functions	EZW		SPIHT		ASWDR		LVL_MMC		GBL_MMC_F	
	MSE	PSNR	MSE	PSNR	MSE	PSNR	MSE	PSNR	MSE	PSNR
Haar	60.23	30.33	75.93	29.33	65.04	30	94.54	28.37	122.2	27.26
db	38.84	32.24	50.2	31.12	42.52	31.85	39.43	32.17	62.59	30.17
bior	40.33	32.07	53.11	30.88	44.83	31.61	38.05	32.33	55.37	30.7
rbio	39.63	32.15	48.34	31.29	42.02	31.9	49.18	31.21	74.51	29.41
Symlets	38.61	32.31	49.07	31.22	41.53	31.95	39.76	32.14	58.83	30.43
coif	35.27	32.66	46.02	31.5	38.5	32.28	34.65	32.73	57.35	30.55
dmey	35.96	32.57	48.41	31.28	40.77	32.03	34.19	32.79	56.11	30.64
fk	54.54	30.76	68	29.81	58.71	30.44	74.37	29.13	98.52	28.2

analysis of wavelet basis functions with different compression techniques and it shows that dmey wavelet basis function with LVL_MMC compression technique provides higher PSNR value of 33.956 and dmey wavelet basis function with EZW compression technique lesser MSE value of 28.232 for X-RAY images. Table 15.4 depicts the performance analysis of wavelet basis functions with different compression techniques, and it shows that dmey wavelet basis function with LVL_MMC compression technique provides higher PSNR value of 32.79 and lesser MSE value of 34.19 for ULTRASONIC images.

A plot of PSNR and MSE for medical images, such as MRI, CT, X-RAY, ULTRASONIC images, are shown in the below figures (Figures 15.4–15.11). The figures show that the Haar wavelet basis function with EZW compression technique gives the higher PSNR value and less MSE value. Therefore, it is evident that the performance of discrete wavelet basis functions provides higher PSNR value compared with other compression techniques.

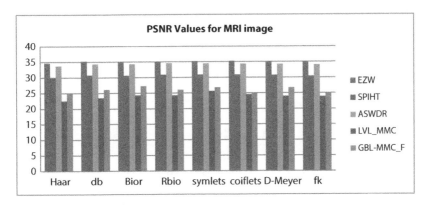

Figure 15.4 Comparison graph of PSNR at different wavelets for MRI image.

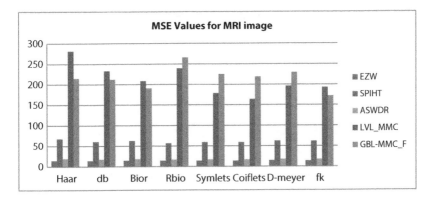

Figure 15.5 Comparison graph of MSE of different wavelets for MRI image.

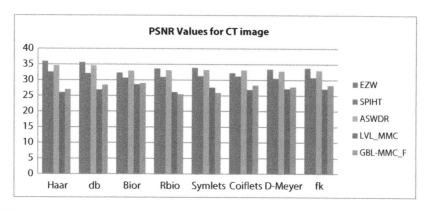

Figure 15.6 Comparison graph of PSNR at different wavelets for CT image.

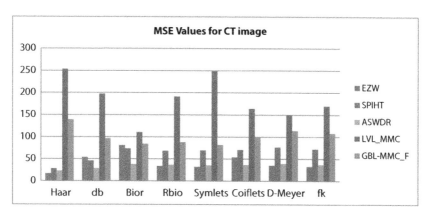

Figure 15.7 Comparison graph of MSE of different wavelets for CT image.

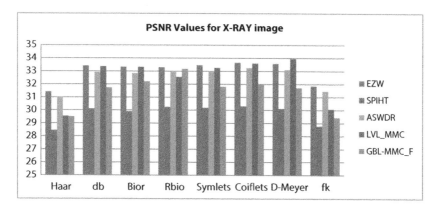

Figure 15.8 Comparison graph of PSNR at different wavelets for X-RAY image.

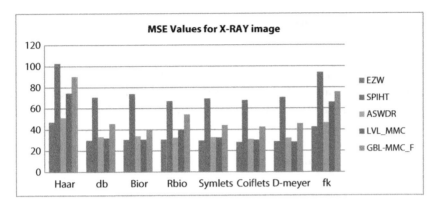

Figure 15.9 Comparison graph of MSE of different wavelets for X-RAY image.

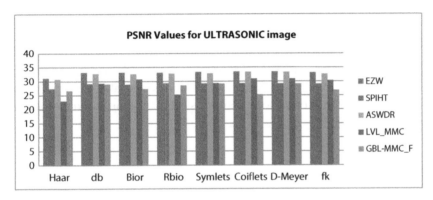

Figure 15.10 Comparison graph of PSNR of different wavelets for ULTRASONIC image.

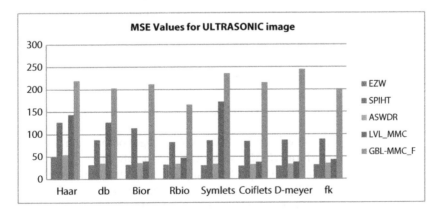

Figure 15.11 Comparison graph of MSE of different wavelets for ULTRASONIC image.

15.4   Conclusion

In image compression, different wavelet basis functions are used which provides high compression ratios and also helps in enhancing the quality of image without degradation. In this paper, we have increased quality of the image using wavelet functions of the images, which is being carried out in different types of medical images and is compared using quality measures such as MSE, PSNR. From the result, it is evident that the compression technique using wavelets provide good performance compared to other techniques. So, by analyzing all the wavelets (Haar, db, bior, rbior, Symlets, coif, dmey, fk) and compression techniques (EZW, SPIHT, ASWDR, LVL_MMC, GBL_MMC_F) into consideration. Therefore, Haar wavelet basis function with EZW compression technique deliberately provides high quality of images.

15.4.1   Summary

This chapter has provided the information about the emerging trends, challenges and issues in healthcare informatics and also performed the comparative analysis of various compression techniques used in medical image processing.

References

1. Al-Shereefi, N.M., Image compression using wavelet transform. *JUBPAS*, 21, 4, 110–119, 2013.
2. Gric, S., Kers, K., Gric, M., Image compression using wavelets. *Proceedings of IEEE International Symposium on Industrial Electronics*, 2002.
3. Averbuch, A., Lazar, D., Israeli, M., Image compression using wavelet transform and multiresolution decomposition. *IEEE Trans. Image Process.*, 5, 1, 4–15, 1996.
4. Mathur, M.K., Image compression using wavelet transform. *Imp. J. Interdiscip. Res. (IJIR)*, 2, 9, 82–84, 2016.
5. Khatke, R.N., Image compression using wavelet transform. *Imp. J. Interdiscip. Res. (IJIR)*, 2, 9, 82–84, 2016.
6. Mozammel, M., Chowdhury, H., Khatun, A., Image compression using discrete wavelet transform. *IJCSI*, 9, 4, No 1, 327–330, July 2012.
7. Manigandan, M.D. and Deepa, S., Comprehensive study on the effect of Entropy Encoding Algorithms on Medical Image Compression. *Int. Res. J. Eng. Technol. (IRJET)*, 05, 04, 3460–3468, April 2018.

8. Singh, P. and Singh, P., A Modified SPIHT Algorithm Using Coefficients Thresholding Method for Lossy Image Compression. *Int. J. Adv. Res. Comput. Sci. Software Eng.*, 3, 6, 1400–1406, June 2013.

9. Porwik, P. and Lisowska, A., The Haar–Wavelet Transform in Digital Image Processing: Its Status and Achievements. *Mach. Graph. Vis.*, 13, 1/2, 79–98, 2004.

10. Daubechies, I., Orthonormal Bases of Compactly Supported Wavelets. *Commun. Pure Appl. Math.*, 41, 906–966, 1988.

11. Jiang, B., Yang, A., Wang, C., Hou, Z., Implementation of Bi-orthogonal Wavelet Transform Using Discrete Cosine Sequency Filter. *Int. J. Signal Processing, Image Process. Pattern Recognition*, 6, 4, 179–190, 2013.

12. Saini, N. and Sethy, P., Performance Based Analysis of Wavelets Family for Image Compression-A Practical Approach. *Int. J. Comput. Appl.*, 129, 9, 17–23, 2015.

13. Kaur, H., Kaur, R., Kumar, N., Review of Various Techniques for Medical Image Compression. *Int. J. Comput. Appl.*, 123, 4, 23–29, August 2015.

14. Goyal, R. and Jaura, J., A Review of Various Image Compression Techniques. *Int. J. Adv. Res. Comput. Sci. Software Eng.*, 4, 7, 1–6, July 2014.

15. Raid, A.M., Khedr, W.M., El-dosuky, M.A., Ahmed, W., Image Compression Using Embedded Zerotree Wavelet. *SIPIJ*, 5, 6, 33–39, December 2014.

16. Aggarwal, P. and Rani, B., Performance Comparison of Image Compression Using Wavelets. *Int. J. Comput. Sci. Commun.*, 1, 2, 97–100, 2010.

17. Vijayvargiya, G., Silakari, Dr. S., Pandey, Dr. R., A Survey Various Techniques of Image Compression. *IJCSIS*, 11, 10, 51–55, October 2013.

18. Kaur, S., Sahib, S.G.G., Sahib, F., A Review Various Wavelet Based Image Compression Techniques. *IJSR – Int. J. Sci. Res.*, 2, 5, 1–4, May 2013.

19. Avicibas, I., Sankur, B., Sayood, K., Statistical Evaluation of Image Quality Measures. *J. Electron. Imaging*, 11, 206–223, 2002.

20. Mrak., M., Grgic, S., Grgic, M., Picture Quality Measures in Image Compression Systems. *EUROCON*, Ljuijana, Slovenia, 2003.

21. Eskicioglu, A.M. and Fisher, P.S., Image Quality Measures and their Performance. *IEEE Trans. Commun.*, 43, 2959–2965, 1995.

Index

Also of Interest

Check out these published and forthcoming titles in the "Artificial Intelligence and Soft Computing for Industrial Transformation" series from Scrivener Publishing

Advances in Artificial Intelligence and Computational Methods for Transportation Safety
Edited by Naga Pasupuleti, Naveen Chilamkurti, B. Balamurugan, T. Poongodi
Forthcoming 2022. ISBN 978-1-119-76170-9

The New Advanced Society
Artificial Intelligence and Industrial Internet of Things Paradigm
Edited by Sandeep Kumar Panda, Ramesh Kumar Mohapatra, Subhrakanta Panda and S. Balamurugan
Forthcoming 2022. ISBN 978-1-119-82447-3

Digitization of Healthcare Data using Blockchain
Edited by T. Poongodi, D. Sumathi, B. Balamurugan and K. S. Savita
Published 2022. ISBN 978-1-119-79185-0

Tele-Healthcare
Applications of Artificial Intelligence and Soft Computing Techniques
Edited by R. Nidhya, Manish Kumar and S. Balamurugan
Published 2020. ISBN 978-1-119-84176-0

Impact of Artificial Intelligence on Organizational Transformation
Edited by S. Balamurugan, Sonal Pathak, Anupriya Jain, Sachin Gupta, and Sachin Sharma and Sonia Duggal
Published 2022. ISBN 978-1-119-71017-2

Artificial Intelligence for Renewable Energy Systems
Edited by Ajay Kumar Vyas, S. Balamurugan, Kamal Kant Hiran Harsh S. Dhiman
Published 2022. ISBN 978-1-119-76169-3

Artificial Intelligence Techniques for Wireless Communication and Networking
Edited by Kanthavel R., K. Ananthajothi, S. Balamurugan and R. Karthik Ganesh
Published 2022. ISBN 978-1-119-82127-4

Advanced Healthcare Systems
Empowering Physicians with IoT-Enabled Technologies
Edited by Rohit Tanwar, S. Balamurugan, R. K. Saini, Vishal Bharti and Premkumar Chithaluru
Published 2022. ISBN 978-1-119-76886-9

Smart Systems for Industrial Applications
Edited by C. Venkatesh, N. Rengarajan, P. Ponmurugan and S. Balamurugan
Published 2022. ISBN 978-1-119-76200-3

Intelligent Renewable Energy Systems
Edited by Neeraj Priyadarshi, Akash Kumar Bhoi, Sanjeevikumar Padmanabam, S. Balamurugan, and Jens Bo Holm-Nielson
Published 2022. ISBN 978-1-119-78627-6

Human Technology Communication
Internet of Robotic Things and Ubiquitous Computing
Edited by R. Anandan, G. Suseendran, S. Balamurugan, Ashish Mishra and D. Balaganesh
Published 2021. ISBN 978-1-119-75059-8

Nature-Inspired Algorithms Applications
Edited by S. Balamurugan, Anupriya Jain, Sachin Sharma, Dinesh Goyal, Sonia Duggal and Seema Sharma
Published 2021. ISBN 978-1-119-68174-8

Computation in Bioinformatics
Multidisciplinary Applications
Edited by S. Balamurugan, Anand Krishnan, Dinesh Goyal, Balakumar Chandrasekaran and Boomi Pandi
Published 2021. ISBN 978-1-119-65471-1

Fuzzy Intelligent Systems
Methodologies, Techniques, and Applications
Edited by E. Chandrasekaran, R. Anandan, G. Suseendran, S. Balamurugan
and Hanaa Hachimi
Published 2021. ISBN 978-1-119-76045-0

Biomedical Data Mining for Information Retrieval
Methodologies, Techniques and Applications
Edited by Sujata Dash, Subhendu Kumar Pani, S. Balamurugan and Ajith
Abraham
Published 2021. ISBN 978-1-119-71124-7

Design and Analysis of Security Protocols for Communication
Edited by Dinesh Goyal, S. Balamurugan, Sheng-Lung Peng and O.P.
Verma
Published 2020. ISBN 978-1-119-55564-3

www.scrivenerpublishing.com

Printed and bound by CPI Group (UK) Ltd, Croydon, CR0 4YY

27/10/2024

14580132-0004